Studies of Organized Crime

Volume 15

Series Editor

Dina Siegel, Willem Pompe Institute, Utrecht University, Utrecht, The Netherlands

This series will publish theoretically significant books in two primary areas. One is the political economy of organized crime and criminality whether at the transnational, national, regional or local levels (focus on financial crime, political corruption, environmental crime, and the expropriation of resources from developing nations). The other is human rights violations particularly in Third World countries. Manuscripts that cover either historical or contemporary issues of the above, utilizing qualitative methodologies, are equally welcome. In addition, we are particularly interested in publishing the work of sophisticated junior scholars.

More information about this series at http://www.springer.com/series/6564

Daan P. van Uhm

The Illegal Wildlife Trade

Inside the World of Poachers, Smugglers and Traders

Springer

Daan P. van Uhm
Willem Pompe Institute
Utrecht University
Utrecht
The Netherlands

ISSN 1571-5493
Studies of Organized Crime
ISBN 978-3-319-42128-5 ISBN 978-3-319-42129-2 (eBook)
DOI 10.1007/978-3-319-42129-2

Library of Congress Control Number: 2016946943

Printed on acid-free paper

This Springer imprint is published by Springer Nature
The registered company is Springer International Publishing AG Switzerland

Foreword

The academic study of global trafficking in humans is as necessary as it is in non-humans. In the last 50 years libraries full of books and articles have been written about human trafficking and smuggling. However, there are a very limited number of publications on illegal activities with regard to animals and animal products. There is, however, no reason for criminologists to continue to exclude these issues from their studies and to leave them only for biologists, zoologists or environmental lawyers. Especially for cultural criminology this new area can be important, if we take seriously the ambition and call of the leading cultural criminologists to discover new fields of understudies using original innovative research methods.

In this book, Daan P. van Uhm has readily accepted this challenge by combining and exploring two criminological issues: the transnational crime of the illegal trade in wildlife and the 'green' perspective of cultural criminology.

The interrelationship between the upper- and underworld, the flourishing activities of organized crime groups, which extensively use advanced technology and make huge profits from the wildlife trade, on the one hand, and the dependence of local communities and corrupt officials on the illicit activities of hunters, fishermen and poachers in order to be able to survive in difficult economic conditions, on the other hand, manifest the complex nature of this phenomenon. It becomes clear from the present analysis that the reality is not black and white, 'bad' or 'good'; there are too many actors involved in the illicit trade chain with various motives, expectations and aspirations. When a poor fisherman in a remote village on the shores of the Caspian Sea describes his poaching activities as an act of survival and remembers with nostalgic sentiments the 'good old Soviet times' when he was considered a hero of the socialist economy and the pride of society, his story could provide a much deeper and complex explanation for the nature of this kind of crime than the prevailing stereotypes of blood-thirsty, merciless criminals. The same is true for the non-negotiable, almost sacred belief of a Chinese patient in the powers of traditional medicine, a belief which is transmitted from generation to generation, and which is often illustrated with 'examples of success'. Who are we then, the Westerners, to dare to challenge these rich and very long traditions by introducing unacceptable regulations? These are precisely aspects which cultural criminology adds to the study of organized crime's activities and which challenge the existing explanations and logic.

Some of the issues discussed in this book can be generalized for other illicit activities, for example the trafficking in drugs, works of art, arms or tobacco. The modus operandi, the variety of roles both within and outside the criminal networks, the facilitative functions of legal actors, etc. are usually discussed in the rich body of literature on organized crime in general, and on illicit markets in particular. Little is known, however, when it comes to the illicit wildlife trade and wildlife markets in particular. van Uhm focuses on three specific case studies on three different continents and shows, in a masterly fashion, not only common patterns of trafficking, but also the unique sociocultural conditions and settings in which the wildlife trade is developed. The combined qualitative and quantitative methods of the research and especially his ethnographic fieldwork allow him to dig deeper under the statistics and to look for multiple aspects in order to explain this phenomenon.

The second *leidmotief* of this book is green criminology, a new area of study, which has recently conquered the hearts and minds of many critical and cultural criminologists, with its focus on environmental harm, the danger of ecocide, insatiable (Western) consumerism, and the victimization of poor local communities in various parts of the world. The contribution of van Uhm's work here is mainly in reconsidering the meaning of luxury, from caviar to traditional medicine, and its socially constructed and manipulated value, which leads at the end to disastrous consequences for nature and wildlife.

van Uhm rejects the anthropocentric approach and chooses the ecocentric approach, which doubts the artificial distinction between humans and non-humans, emphasizing the growing concern about the reduction in biodiversity due to human activities. In this regard, the worldwide illicit trade in wildlife is one of the most extreme examples of human evils and a very serious form of crime.

This book is a good example of how an excellent ethnographic study, combined with multidisciplinary theoretical explanations, contribute not only to social science research, but also to the efforts of many concerned academic researchers to make the public at large aware of the growing risks and dangers of globalization, and to urge policy-makers to think creatively so that possible solutions can be found.

Dina Siegel
Utrecht University, The Netherlands

Acknowledgements

Since ancient times wildlife has fascinated, inspired, impressed and frightened people all over the world. During this research I came to understand how symbolic, functional and social meanings of wildlife influence the black market in both Western and oriental cultures and civilizations. By uncovering the world of poachers, smugglers and traders, the illegal wildlife trade has gained a face. It turned out to be a lucrative and organized business driven by inequalities, corruption and a desire for unique and rare species with disastrous global consequences. Fortunately, humans have become more aware of the declining animal populations and their loss for future generations. Hopefully, the insights in this book will provide assistance in safeguarding the future of wildlife with which we share our planet.

Writing this book would not have been possible without the support, participation and effort of numerous people. I am indebted to many informants who told me their stories and shared their secrets with me. They opened the doors of their houses, provided me with guidance and advice and introduced me to the fascinating business of wildlife. Their stories, visions and hospitality during my fieldwork in Azerbaijan, China, Kazakhstan, Morocco and Russia will be preserved in my memory. I am gratefully thankful to them for all their help and unique experiences.

My foremost gratitude goes to Dina Siegel who convincingly supported me through the entire research. I will never forget her unexpected invitation to write my dissertation under her supervision, and I would have done it all again; it is amazing how one moment can change one's life. She always stood by me, shared her knowledge, understandings and perspectives and convinced me to carry out ethnographic research abroad. Not only she was very inspiring and encouraged my intellectual freedom, but she has also become a great research partner.

I would also like to thank all my other colleagues at the Willem Pompe Institute and especially Tim Boekhout van Solinge for all our conversations on environmental global issues that substantially inspired me during my research. Following his lectures that stressed the importance of studying green crimes already persuaded me to focus on wildlife crimes during my bachelor's courses in criminology. I am also grateful to Damián Zaitch whose constructive suggestions to improve this book were of great value, Brenda Oude Breuil who shared her fieldwork experiences, John Vervaele who kept me informed of news on wildlife trafficking and Constantijn Kelk for the intellectual discussions about the role of animals in current society. Furthermore, I thank my paranymphs Veronika Nagy and Elina Kurtovic for their special assistance and support.

I am grateful to the support of David van Gennep, Eline Lauret and Raquel García (AAP Sanctuary for exotic animals) and Gernant Magnin and Christiaan van der Hoeven (WWF). Furthermore, I thank all (former) Ph.D. candidates for the good times: Roos de Wildt, Rosa Koenraadt, Joep Rottier, Sjaak Zhang, Mark Hornman, Elena Krsmanović, Stephanie Rap, Lianne Kleijer-Kool, Paula Gil Larruscahim, Hanneke Mol, Kristien Hepping, Jessica de Jong, Byron Villagómez, Julia Rushchenko and intern Grethe Pettersen.

Finally, I would like to acknowledge my friends and family who have remained close to me in my life. And of course I want to express my immeasurable thanks to my girlfriend Harma for being at my side and supportive in my work. Last but not least, my son Atilla who has made my life indescribably more colourful and meaningful than ever before.

Utrecht, The Netherlands
March 2016

Contents

About the Author

Dr. Daan P. van Uhm is Assistant Professor at the Willem Pompe Institute for Criminal Law and Criminology at the Utrecht University, the Netherlands. He conducted research on various forms of environmental crime, such as transnational illegal wildlife trafficking, deforestation and timber trade in Southeast Asia and the illegal trade in dogs in Europe, and assisted in several lawsuits. During 2012–2015, Daan van Uhm worked as a Ph.D. candidate at the Willem Pompe Institute and he obtained his Ph.D. in criminology at Utrecht University in 2016. van Uhm primarily focuses on research in the context of green crimes and harms.

List of Abbreviations

BCE	Before Common Era
BEIC	British East India Company
BSE	Bovine Spongiform Encephalopathy
CBD	Convention on Biological Diversity
CE	Common Era
CIA	Central Intelligence Agency
CITES	Convention on International Trade in Endangered Species of Wild Fauna and Flora
DEFRA	Department for Environment, Food and Rural Affairs
EC	European Commission
ECOSOC	Economic and Social Council United Nations
EFSA	European Food Safety Authority
EIA	Environmental Investigation Agency
EU	European Union
EUROPOL	European Union's law enforcement agency
EU-TWIX	European Union Trade in Wildlife Information eXchange database
FAO	Food and Agriculture Organization of the United Nations
FBI	Federal Bureau of Investigation
FWS	Fish and Wildlife Service
IFAW	International Fund for Animal Welfare
INTERPOL	International Criminal Police Commission
IUCN	International Union for the Conservation of Nature
KGB	Komitet Gosoedarstvennoj Bezopasnosti (Committee for State Security)
LEMIS	Law Enforcement Management Information System
NGO	Non-Governmental Organization
RSPCA	Royal Society for the Prevention of Cruelty to Animals
SARS	Severe Acute Respiratory Syndrome
TCM	Traditional Chinese Medicine
TRAFFIC	The wildlife trade monitoring network

UNEP	United Nations Environment Programme
UNODC	United Nations Office on Drugs and Crime
USSR	Union of Soviet Socialist Republics
VOC	Vereenigde Oostindische Compagnie (Dutch East India Company)
WCMC	World Conservation Monitoring Centre
WCS	Wildlife Conservation Society
WHO	World Health Organization
WIC	West-Indische Compagnie (Dutch West India Company)
WSPA	World Society for the Protection of Animals
WWF	World Wide Fund for Nature

List of Figures

List of Tables

List of Maps

List of Illustrations

Introduction

Today everyone is aware of the worldwide destruction of the environment. The mass species extinction, global deforestation, oil dumping and global warming have become much-discussed environmental topics in the twenty-first century. The impact of the excessive hunting of iconic species, such as the tiger, elephant and rhinoceros, is broadly highlighted by global concerns from the international community. This is illustrated by the poaching levels of rhinoceros in South Africa that increased by 9,000 %; from 13 animals recorded in 2007 to 1,215 in 2014. If this alarming trend continues, the species will disappear within a couple of years from our planet. It is not unthinkable that future generations can only admire these species locked in zoos, or worse, from pictures in a book, as has happened with the Dodo. In order to point out that something must be done to prevent this ecological crisis caused by human activities, world leaders stress the need to take action and large demonstrations around the world are being organized by environmental organizations and joined by citizens at large. Not only is the world shocked by the rapid disappearance of species, but the actors behind these environmental crimes would consist of violent gangs and highly organized criminal groups, which can threaten national and international security.

Although biologists, ecologists and environmentalists have paid attention to the trade in wildlife for some time, the efforts by criminologists to study these crimes have been rather limited. The few criminological studies that have focussed on the wildlife trade have been mainly based on desk research or interviews with enforcement officials, non-governmental organizations (NGOs) and experts, while quantitative research that is currently available focuses on specific animal species instead of providing a global overview of the situation. This exploratory research consists of an important scientific addition in terms of qualitative and quantitative data. Wildlife seizures over a 10-year period in the European Union (EU) were statistically analyzed for the first time and, moreover, people actually involved in the illegal trade in wildlife were interviewed to provide an insight into the illegal wildlife trade. This study aims to contribute to criminological research in terms of understanding and describing the nature of the illegal wildlife trade.

To understand the illegal trade I travelled to important source countries of illegal wildlife, such as Russia, Morocco and China, to conduct fieldwork and to talk to those involved about their illegal wildlife business. While I was warned that it would be difficult to speak to the actors who are directly involved in the illegal wildlife trade, interviewees were surprisingly talkative about their business. Not only small-scale retailers but also big players have provided, sometimes extremely detailed, information about their illegal activities making it possible to get a clear picture of the entire process. In this book I follow the route of the illegal wildlife trade from the poor poaching areas to the rich business districts as it passes through countless hands and places, and is transformed from animals or eggs into desirable items in the West. I will discuss the illegal wildlife trade from a historical, sociological, ecological and criminological perspective to understand the current situation and to sketch the expectations in the near future.

In Chap. 1, I elaborate on the global history of the wildlife trade, from the ancient Egyptians to modernity, in order to understand the social context of the trade. What kinds of wildlife have been traded in the past and for whom was the trade intended? What was the functional or symbolic value of the trade and what can we learn from history to understand the present situation of the wildlife trade? It turns out that a wide variety of live animals and products thereof have been traded for functional, symbolic or entertainment purposes. From ostrich eggs for the treatment of fractured skulls, live monkeys as ladies' pets to caviar as a delicacy for the upper classes. However, the impact of the diverse trade in wildlife soon posed a threat to certain species; it was already noticed in early antiquity that species had disappeared due to the extensive trade. This continued more seriously in the industrialized modern era with many incalculable consequences as discussed from socio-theoretical perspectives in Chap. 2. What are the consequences of the wildlife trade and why is it difficult to estimate and dispel these risks? Due to the harmful consequences of the trade several scientists argue that it is time to consider *ecocide* as a fifth International Crime Against Peace. Nonetheless, in reality only a limited regulation of the wildlife trade exists and the development of regulations has been strongly influenced by Western stakeholders in times of imperialism as described in Chap. 3. Who were these moral entrepreneurs and why did they prefer to preserve species and what were the consequences of their efforts? To date, the existing regulation is primarily intended to allow the trade instead of criminalizing it. Yet, the process of criminalization has recently started under pressure from NGOs and other moral entrepreneurs. The United Nations Commission on Crime Prevention and Criminal Justice has agreed that the illegal wildlife trade should be treated as a 'serious crime', an offence punishable by a maximum deprivation of liberty of at least 4 years or a more serious penalty. In this context, the question arises what has been the role of criminology in studying crimes against nature and the wildlife trade specifically. Chapter 4 draws upon the limitations of the discipline of criminology and its confined attention to environmental issues and it will be argued that it is now time for criminologists to cross the borders of orthodox criminology. Furthermore, criminological explanatory models will be introduced that can be applied to study the actors and organization behind the illegal wildlife trade. At the end of the chapter it will be argued that from a green criminological perspective the harm principle should be extended to study a broad area of victims, including animals and ecosystems. Chapter 5 focuses on the qualitative and quantitative research methods used in this study and their limitations. I will describe the coding of wildlife seizures to get an overall view of the visible illegal wildlife trade and explain how my informants were approached, why they were prepared to talk about their illegal business and how I dealt with dangerous situations. After the methodological justification the empirical data description of the EU seizures will be presented in Chap. 6. The diversity and transnational characteristics of the illegal wildlife trade are highlighted by quantitative analyses by asking what kind of illegal wildlife is traded, what are the source countries and major outlets, what kinds of smuggling and laundering methods are used and who are the perpetrators? The quantitative analyses are then used to select the three case studies in this research: the illegal trade in caviar, Barbary macaques and traditional Chinese medicine. These case studies are then qualitatively investigated based on fieldwork in the source countries. In the first case study, I describe how fish eggs became an extremely highly valued product of luxury and how organized crime took advantage of this lucrative caviar market in Chap. 7. This case study provides in-depth information about the social organization, modus operandi, trade routes and consequences based on fieldwork in Russia, Kazakhstan and Azerbaijan. In the second case study, the illegal trade in the endangered Barbary macaques will be discussed based upon the history of keeping pets as described in Chap. 8. Again, based on fieldwork in the primary source country of this monkey species, Morocco, the organization, methods and trade routes of the criminal entrepreneurs will be examined together with the environmental harm of this illegal wildlife trade. After the symbolic use of caviar as a delicacy and the entertainment use of monkeys as pets, the time has come to describe the functional use of parts of endangered species, such as tiger bones and rhino horn, in traditional Chinese medicine. In Chap. 9 the illegal trade in traditional Chinese medicine will be set out based on fieldwork in China. The case study demonstrates how the business is organized, how this is done and what the harmful consequences are. The overarching analysis of the three case studies, in which the similarities and differences are discussed, takes place in Chap. 10, the final chapter. In that chapter, the social construction of the value of wildlife, the global anomie and criminogenic asymmetries that provide opportunities for the illegal wildlife trade, the social embeddedness of wildlife crime, the criminal networks involved, and the ecological interaction will be analyzed to clarify the entire picture of the illegal trade in wildlife. Finally, how the different perspectives of wildlife crimes have changed in their social context and what can be expected in the near future will be discussed. I will end with a brief conclusion to bring this book to a close.

Chapter 1
Wildlife Trade Through the Ages

The distinction between the past, present and future is only a stubbornly persistent illusion.

Albert Einstein

The trade in wildlife is not a new phenomenon. There has always been a market for animals as sources for food and clothing, as companions or pets, or as strange and curious objects (Alexander 1979). The earliest civilizations were linked to the trade in live animals and parts thereof, from the Egyptian pharaohs to aristocrats in the modern era. Ramses II was regularly seen with a tamed lion and Julius Caesar had allegedly received a giraffe from Cleopatra. In dynamic social and cultural contexts the meaning of wildlife changes. While, historically, exotic animals and the products thereof were strongly connected to social elites, currently reptile and bird fairs attract people from all walks of life who are looking for extraordinary animals for entertainment. A broad historical overview of the trade in exotic animals and parts thereof[1] can place the current trade in its socio-historical context. What kinds of wildlife have been traded in the past and for whom was the trade intended? What was the functional or symbolic value of this trade? What can we learn from history in order to understand the present situation of the trade in wildlife? Providing answers to these questions is essential to explain the origin and historical embeddedness of the trade in wildlife in society.

1.1 Ancient Egypt

The demand for wildlife has existed for centuries; ivory may precede even gold as the first globally traded commodity. The ancient Egyptians (±3500–500 BCE) used ivory, from the time of their earliest dynasties, for making jewellery and carvings.

[1] I will use the term 'exotic' species throughout this book. With exotic animal species I mean animals that are native to a foreign country or of foreign origin in character, i.e. animals that are not native or that have been introduced from abroad (Schupplit and Fraser 2000).

D.P. van Uhm, *The Illegal Wildlife Trade*, Studies of Organized Crime 15,
DOI 10.1007/978-3-319-42129-2_1

Ivory was obtained through trade (or looting and tribute) from Nubia, Somalia and Ethiopia (Naylor 2004). The first African explorer in history, Harkhuf, already used the route through Nubia, from Abu Simbel to Kerma to Lower Nubia, to trade ivory in the twenty-third century BCE; the Nile served as a trade route. For centuries this has been the shortest route connecting the natural wealth of Central Africa with the markets of Near Eastern Egypt and the Mediterranean. Other exclusive products such as leopard skins, giraffe tails and ostrich feathers were traded for religious artefacts and medicines for luxury-loving Egyptians (Kirwan 1963). For instance, leopard skins formed a part of the dress of priests (Budge 1934) and ostrich eggs smeared with oil was included in the treatment of a fractured skull (Strouhal et al. 2014).

However, ancient Egypt is best known for the anthropomorphic representation of (exotic) animals as gods. These gods shared the attributes and strengths of these animals. For instance, the sun god Ra was regularly depicted as a lion; Hapi, the son of Horus, was represented as a baboon; while vultures represented a range of female gods, including Isis, Hathor and Moet (Hoage and Deiss 1996; Ikram 2009). Sacred animals were believed to be avatars of a particular god and the spirit of the god could enter their bodies during their lifetime. The ancient Egyptians were fascinated by the nature, strength and diversity of animals and certain sacred animals were mummified so as to provide a safe passage in the afterlife (Ikram 2009). This may explain the special interest in exotic animals by the rulers of Egypt and Mesopotamia.

From 2500 BCE several exotic animals were kept in menageries by the pharaohs, rulers and the wealthy of ancient Egypt (Kisling 2001; Houlihan 1996). Around 1500 BCE Queen Hatshepsut (1508–1458 BCE) sent an expedition to the 'Land of Punt' to catch monkeys, leopards, exotic birds and giraffes for her extensive palace menagerie. Queen Hatshepsut's menagerie is probably the world's oldest established zoo (Mason 1999; Lennard 1996; Alexander 1979). Lions, leopards, hyenas, gazelles, ibex, hares and porcupines were captured and transported in great cages from neighbouring deserts, baboons and giraffes came from the 'incense' countries and the Upper Nile, while bears and elephants came from Syria (Erman 1971). The acquisition and display of these animals were seen as effective ways to represent imperial power over far-flung lands and to enhance prestige (Foster 1998). According to Delumeau (1995), these menageries were the original *Gardens of Eden* and served as a model for 'paradise parks' for ancient royal leaders (Foster 1998). Furthermore, tamed animals were highly popular; small monkeys were seen as ladies' pets while Ramses II (1290–1224 BCE) had, for example, a tame lion who accompanied him to battle and guarded the tent of his royal master (Erman 1971; Kisling 2001). These exotic pets were mummified and buried with the coffin of their owner or interred in a tomb in a separate coffin or sarcophagus (Ikram 2004). The rarer the animal, the more value it conveyed. Keeping exclusive species was a symbol of status, spirituality and power for rulers in Ancient Egypt (Jennison 1937).

1.2 Roman and Greek Antiquity

After 700 BCE, it became relatively common to exhibit exotic animals in menageries and gardens by the elites of the Greek and Roman Empire (±500 BCE–500 CE). Most Greek and Roman temples contained sacred groves, which gave shelter to several exotic species of birds, fish, reptiles and mammals. In these sacred forests they came to worship the gods, to pray or to sacrifice. These 'paradises'[2] consisted of trees, ponds, springs and streams, and wild animal species. Besides praying and sacrificing, these paradises were used by elites for hunting, fishing and entertainment (Hughes 2003). For instance, during a dinner with the Roman orator and politician Hortensius (114–50 BCE) a trumpet was sounded and an actor dressed like Orpheus, with a robe and lute, played a lyre between boars and other wild animals that were attracted by the sound which meant that they would be fed (Kalof 2007; Katharine 2009). Unlike most exotic animals in menageries in ancient Egypt, Roman and Greek menageries were usually private hunting grounds in the context of controlling nature (Kisling 2001). These paradises were restricted to Roman and Greek rulers and elites and were usually surrounded by walls for defence (Hughes 2003).

In addition, the Greeks and Romans captured, tamed and kept an impressive variety of exotic mammal and reptile species in private households, such as monkeys, ferrets, hedgehogs, deer, giraffes, gazelles, captive wild goats, and harmless 'house' snakes. Also birds were kept individually or in aviaries, including peacocks, various pheasants, parrots, cranes, storks, flamingos, rails, crows, starlings, magpies, thrushes and nightingales (Jennison 1937). During the Roman Empire a parrot that could speak Latin was considered to be a very important pet and was more expensive than a slave. The keeping of exotic animals was in particular popular in the richer part of Roman and Greek society. The emperors even possessed elephants and lions (Kisling 2001; Hughes 2003). Elephants were also used by emperors during warfare. The most famous example would be Hannibal who took an army of 37 war elephants across the Alps to battle against the Roman cavalry (Gabriel 2011).

In honour of Alexander the Great (356–323 BCE) around 270 BCE a parade was held including 96 elephants, 300 exotic sheep, 60 goats and eight pairs of ostriches in spectacular armour. The end of the parade consisted of a selection of big cats: 24 lions, 14 leopards and 16 cheetahs. There was even a white bear exhibited (Frede 2007).[3] Alexander the Great became fascinated by unknown species, such as peacocks, during his expedition to the East. It is said that he issued an edict to protect them. He was educated by the famous philosopher Aristotle (384–322 BCE) (Thompson 1907), who taught him the nature of animals, such as the anatomy and

---

[2]The word 'paradise' originates from the Persian pairidaeˆza and means 'a piece of land protected by a wall' (Hughes 2003).

[3]Although there is no consensus as to whether this was a polar bear or an albino brown bear, a Roman emperor later showed a white bear in a pool catching seals and this must have been a polar bear (Hughes 2003).

diet of an elephant (Frede 2007). Other famous emperors include Julius Caesar (100–44 BCE) who was at various times seen with a lynx from Gaul, elephants and a giraffe. The giraffe was allegedly a gift from Cleopatra, from her royal zoo in Alexandria (Hughes 2003).

The trade in exotic species increased significantly with the emergence of the Roman games in the arena. Romans systematically collected wildlife for entertainment, slaughter and display in arenas, theatres and amphitheatres throughout the Roman Empire (Whatmore 2002; Belozerskaya 2006). The high demand for exotic animals was met by special private enterprises. These companies consisted of professional soldiers and hunters, often in collaboration with the indigenous population in the hunting area. Camouflaged pits were dug to capture large animals such as elephants and young animals were taken away from their mother as bait (MacKinnon 2006). It was a private business on which an import tax of 2.5 % needed to be paid (Hughes 2003). At that time the animal trade was becoming a financially lucrative enterprise; a leopard cost 4,000 sesterces (£25,000) and an African lion was worth 600,000 sesterces (£4 million) (Bomgardner 2000). On the other hand, it was a costly and harmful enterprise as well because many animals died during transport (MacKinnon 2006). A large number of wild animals were captured in the North African region under the power of Rome in the second century (Jennison 1937). The structural trade during Roman and Greek antiquity had already resulted in the disappearance of species from their habitat. Themistius, a travelling Aristotelian philosopher during the fourth century CE, complained that in his lifetime elephants in Libya, lions in Thessaly and hippos near the Nile had disappeared (Hughes 2003).

In the amphitheatres gladiators were deployed to fight with wild animals, wild animals devoured prisoners and herbivores, such as giraffes and elephants, and exotic animals were sacrificed for the purpose of entertainment. The events organized by Pompey around 55 BCE were well known for their large-scale massacres. At one of the events 20 elephants, 600 lions and 410 leopards, a Northern European Lynx and a rhinoceros were slaughtered. Pompey's rival, Caesar, had similar numbers of wildlife slaughtered in the arena after celebrations or events (Wiedemann 2002). These huge shows required large amounts of different exotic animals to entertain the public. Lions, leopards, tigers, lynx, hyenas, bears, elephants, giraffes, antelopes and deer, boar, camels, bison, aurochs, hippos, African and Indian rhinos, zebras, Persian wild donkeys, ostriches, crocodiles and occasionally polar bears were exhibited in the arena (Jennison 1937). According to Kalof (2007) the use of exotic animals during the Roman games was important for the rulers to demonstrate their status, power, worship, control over animals and popularity among the Roman social hierarchy. It was also a political arena: applause meant the show was a celebration of the emperor while an unpleased audience berated him (Kalof 2007).

1.3 The Medieval Period

With the fall of Rome in 476 CE, the large Roman games with animal sacrifices disappeared from the scene, but European royalty and nobility took over the practice of keeping exotic animals in menageries (Kisling 2001) in the Medieval period (±500–1500 CE). According to Kalof (2007: 66) "the mixture of secular and religious symbolism was critical in the establishment of royal menageries filled with animals brought back to northern Europe from the Crusades, and as a collection of live trophy animals kept on the grounds of the royal palace, the medieval menagerie continued its tradition as an illustration of the importance of the ruler and the empire". For instance, Charles the Great (742–814) kept exotic animals (e.g. lions, monkeys, bears, falcons) in different places all over his kingdom (Kalof 2007), but probably the most famous is the royal menagerie in the Tower of London that started with exotic animals kept by King John (1166–1216 CE) (Hahn 2003). Besides a real house for the elephant of Henry III, a special Lion Tower was appointed as a menagerie in the thirteenth century with a large variety of exotic animals. Even a polar bear was presented (Carpenter 1994). Furthermore, animal trainers and performers travelled with exotic animals for entertainment. In particular bears and apes were trained to dance and imitate humans (Strutt 1833; Kalof 2007). Yet, in comparison with the Roman spectacles, during the Middle Ages the demand for large numbers of exotic animals was relatively low (Hoage and Deiss 1996).

During the Middle Ages the exclusivity of wildlife increased with the large-scale loss of natural habitat and the relative wildlife scarcity was caused by technological innovations in agriculture (Kalof 2007). Besides live animals, exclusive animal products were an important means of trade, especially from ivory-derived royal or seigniorial gifts (Pluskowski 2004). Elephant ivory was obtained in different quantities from East Africa and India and walrus ivory from Arctic Norway, Greenland and northern Russia (Barnet 1997; Roesdahl 2001). The Vikings and Arabs were the major traders in animals and animal products. The trade routes were long and complex. The Vikings traded, for example, polar bear skins and cubs, walrus ivory, vulture falcons and narwhal tusks from Iceland and northern Greenland. In the ninth century, polar bears and walruses were hunted in the Barents Sea and White Sea of Russia and walrus ivory and live polar bears were traded in Europe (Bruemmer 1998). A major route was from Norway through Halogaland (a major destination for traders), along the North Cape through the White Sea to Bjarmia (Jankuhn 1982). Tusks were converted into a wide range of expensive and exclusive articles or components of artefacts (Pluskowski 2004).[4]

Fur was also an important trading commodity in the Middle Ages. Not only was wearing fur necessary to protect people against the cold of winter, but aristocrat fashion trends also emerged. Wearing animal skins in the Middle Ages was

[4]Narwhal tusks were also used as ivory (Pluskowski 2004).

associated with class, imperialist and patriarchal oppression and was used as a recognition of social differences. In fact, it was prohibited by law for prostitutes to wear fur to distinguish them from 'respectable women', while wearing a coat of fine, rare and small animal pelts was reserved for the aristocracy in England (Baltodano et al. 2009). According to Perrot (1994: 16) in his book 'Fashioning the Bourgeoisie', with the rise of the bourgeoisie and aristocracy, the decline of feudalism and the emergence of fashion, the endless race between desires and signs appeared. Consumer behaviour became fully dependent on fashion trends to underline the social gap between the upper, middle and lower classes. This was illustrated by hundreds of thousands of squirrel furs that were imported from the Baltic in the thirteenth and fourteenth century, while in the fifteenth century this trade declined due to fashion trends tending to favour marten pelts and budge leather (fur made from lambskin) (Dyer 1989). Because the wealth of urban craftsmen and other non-aristocrats had increased, they started to wear cheap squirrel fur and, subsequently, aristocrats moved to more exclusive furs to maintain their social distance (Veale 2003). By the end of the medieval period leopard and cheetah skins were largely available on the European market for aristocrats. These were exported to Northern Europe, such as to England, France, Flanders and Germany, from major Mediterranean outlets such as Mallorca, Valencia and Lisbon. Leopard skins from Asia were also traded through Eastern Europe (Pluskowski 2004). Not only did the trade in exotic furs, exclusive animals and other products thereof symbolized the power and status of the higher classes, but actual fashion trends and a basic need for furs also influenced the demand for exotic items in medieval society.

1.4 Early Modernity

The global trade in wildlife escalated in the early modern period (±1500–1800 CE) with the advent of European imperialism and colonialism in the 'Age of Exploration'. This period characterizes the European exploration, circumnavigation and large-scale trade with exotic areas (Berger 1980). The British East India Company (BEIC), the Dutch East India Company (VOC: *Vereenigde Oost-Indische Compagnie*) and the Dutch West India Company (WIC) were established and European traders focused on Africa, Asia and South America. Although these companies were famous for their trade in spices and slaves, exotic animals and animal products were also traded (Van Gelder 1997; Cheyns 2008).[5] For instance,

[5]Imperial expansion, exploration and global trade resulted in the disappearance and decline of several species. Perhaps the most famous example is the story of the dodo (*Raphus cucullatus*), which became extinct due to Dutch sailors using them as a free source of meat during their voyages (Duffy 2010).

the VOC transported exotic animals such as ostriches, leopards, penguins, monkeys, cassowaries, parrots, cockatoos and deer to Europe (Van Gelder 1997).[6] Imported exotic animals and products served as an endorsement of modern colonial power and became "a symbolic representation of the conquest of all distant and exotic countries" (Berger 1980: 21). Trade from the colonies was primarily destined for (royal) menageries, private collections and private ownership in Europe (Kalof 2007; Collard 2013).

Together with European imperialist exploration activities, the relatively small menageries of the aristocrats and royalties in the Middle Ages expanded during the Renaissance (Kalof 2007). The increasing interest in biological diversity from far-away exotic regions was reflected in the merging of menageries with a variety of curiosities, the so-called curiosity cabinets (Arnold 2006). These curiosity cabinets or 'wonder rooms' consisted of collections of extraordinary and rare objects, including stuffed exotic animals, animal products and living creatures. The quality and number of assembled elements in the collections kept by a number of princes (e.g. Francis I, William IV, the Duke of Bavaria) were of importance and distanced the nobility from the rest of society (Baratay and Hardouin-Fugier 2003). Menageries and curiosity cabinets were restricted to aristocrats and royalty, but due to the increasing desire of aristocrats and royalty to 'appear powerful and cultured' some of these were opened to the public in the seventeenth century. While people were willing to travel long distances for the opportunity to see exotic animals in menageries (e.g. the Tower of London), the animals were also transported throughout Europe to be exhibited (Kalof 2007: 119).[7] According to Herzog (2014) the keeping of exotic animals as pets (e.g. tortoises and squirrels) had also spread from the aristocracy to the middle classes during the sixteenth century. The accumulation of wealth enabled the bourgeoisie to purchase luxury animals (e.g. monkeys and parrots) (Robbins 2002). Nevertheless, the amount of live exotic

[6]For instance, Christoph Carl Fernberger returned by ship from Batavia to Europe in 1627 and he brought a leopard, a cockatoo, three parrots and three monkeys. He left the care of one of the parrots to an old cook, who would receive one hundred thalers if he delivered the animal alive to Europe. Another sailor would provide fifty thalers to take care of the leopard and his servant took care of the other animals (Van Gelder 1997: 210). Another example is large numbers of wild elephants from Ceylon (Sri Lanka) that were traded by the VOC in the seventeenth century. The animals were sold as luxury mounts or beasts of burden, for example, during wars. In a jungle, over the surface of a few square kilometres, triangular palisades were set up where people drove herds of elephants inside. The elephants, preferably males without tusks, were then hunted into smaller compartments. The individual elephants were accompanied by two domesticated elephants to tame them. The elephants were then sold to Indian or European princes for 6,000 to 7,000 guilders per animal.

[7]In the 1600s the elephant 'Hansken' was exhibited in several places in Europe over a period of six years and the rhinoceros Clara was transported in a 'horse-drawn chariot' and presented all over Europe in the 1700s (Kalof 2007).

animals that arrived in Europe in the Early Modernity remained relatively small due to high mortality rates during transportation (Van Gelder 1997).[8]

In addition to live animals, animal products, such as tusks from elephants, were imported on a large scale by the WIC from West Africa to Europe during European imperialism. Between 1675 and 1731 the WIC recorded an imported amount of 2,955,533 lb of ivory (a total value of 2,512,280 guilders), which was 10.3 % of the total cargo (Rijkelijkhuizen 2009). The ivory was mainly used for luxury and fashion products (e.g. lice combs), but elephant products were also used as currency; a good elephant tail had the value of two to three slaves and played a major role in the Portuguese slave trade in West Africa in the early seventeenth century (Runge 1987).

As a continuation of previous fashion trends in the late Middle Ages, fashionable animal products also began to play a larger role in the context of the growing prosperity among the middle classes. For instance, wearing feathers became fashionable, as reflected by the robes and hats of Marie Antoinette, Queen of France from 1774 to 1792. Feathers, wings, heads and, sometimes, complete birds were used as an ornament or jewellery (Boekhout van Solinge 2008). In his book 'Social Theory and Social Structure' in 1968 Merton stated that individuals choose as role models those who occupy higher social ranks. From this perspective the middle class desire to compare themselves to their 'reference groups' from the upper class resulted in the growing demand for animal parts in fashion. In addition, in the seventeenth and eighteenth century the European hunting of whales, mainly bowhead whales, flourished. While the primary reason for the hunting was lubricant oil and whale meat, many other products were made of baleen, the popular corset in particular. In the eighteenth century the VOC started to make high profits from the trade in baleen. Between 1733 and 1738 lists of products sold by the VOC showed 23,691 lb of imported baleen (with a total value of more than 23,246 guilders at an average price of 136 cents per pound). Whaling decreased at the end of the eighteenth century due to naval wars, increasing competition between European nations and, what is noteworthy, declining whale populations in Spitsbergen (Rijkelijkhuizen 2009).

Characteristic of Early Modernity with the advent of European imperialism is that while exotic animals or the products thereof were still a status symbol, the bourgeoisie started to widely copy the fashion trends which were prevalent among the elite and this resulted in larger flows of wildlife to meet this new demand. This continued during Modernity.

[8]Many animals died during the trip, due to temperature changes and the lack of proper food and water. According to the soldier Müller, on a returning ship in 1669 many parrots, cockatoos, seven parakeets, cassowaries, many monkeys, meerkats and a porcupine were transported. All the animals died during the journey, except for two Javanese monkeys, which were in a bent position in their pen and could no longer move (Van Gelder 1997).

1.5 The Modern Era

From the Victorian era (±1800 CE) onwards, it became customary to trade in live exotic animals, including leopards, jaguars, giraffes, rhinos and exotic birds. Due to strengthened colonial relationships, animals were cheaply purchased from locals for the European market and were accessible to the middle classes (Simons 2012). Aristocratic naturalists, painters and officers owned menageries containing exotic animals such as panthers, elephants and lions (Collard 2013; Simons 2012). These animals were also imported from far-reaching colonies for classification and study (Crosby 1986). The rise of the science of natural history (at the time of Darwin's evolution theory) and zoology and, thereby, increasing knowledge concerning the physical and psychological qualities of animals in combination with the discovery of new species resulted in a growing fascination with exotic animals (Simons 2012). For instance, Blyth, an acquaintance of Darwin, extensively traded in different species around 1850 (Brandon-Jones 1997). The trade in live animals was destined for the first public zoos and circuses. The animals were obtained from travelling menageries or merchant shipping (Jacobi 1988). The first official zoos were, unlike the menageries before that time, menageries that were open to the public, including the Tiergarten Schönbrunn in Vienna. Other zoos, developed by aristocrats and traders, include the London zoo in 1828 and the Amsterdam zoo (Artis) in 1838. The first circuses also gained ground in the early 1800s. Subsequently, the popularity of zoos resulted in a decline in menageries (Hoage and Deiss 1996). While the original function of menageries was to symbolize (royal) power, the focus of the (modern) zoo became entertainment, education and, in the late twentieth century, species' conservation by means of breeding programmes (Patrick et al. 2007).

Around the turn of the twentieth century, several traders foresaw the growing demand for certain species in Europe. With technological innovation as a result of the industrial revolution, people succeeded in transferring large numbers of live exotic animals from as far away as New Zealand (Broad et al. 1988a, b, c; Simons 2012). This was the beginning of the specialist animal trade, as we know it today. An example would be the famous animal trader Carl Hagenbeck who became one of the most prominent exotic animal traders in Europe during the early 1900s. Besides animals, indigenous people were traded for human exhibitions (Van Uhm 2015).[9] The extensive trade in exotic animals was illustrated by the low prices for animals, based on sales from the animal trader Jamrach in 1903: elephants £120–150, lions £20–25, tigers £80, wolves £4, hyenas £10–40 (Simons 2012). From 1950 onwards, the market for exotic animals for private exotic animal

[9]In the late Nineteenth century exhibitions of indigenous people became immensely popular in Europe. Between 1870 and 1940, hundreds of groups of indigenous people were traded to Europe for entertainment and science in zoos, circuses, fairs and world exhibitions. These indigenous people were mainly imported from overseas colonies. North American Indians, Bushmen, Hottentots, Zulus and Aboriginals were exhibited in makeshift depictions of their natural habitat (Van Uhm 2015).

ownership was booming (Ryhiner and Mannix 1958). This trend seemed to run hand in hand with the post-war overall growth in the economy and prosperity. The trade in exotic animals has evolved as a trend-sensitive trading market that responds to consumer demand (Vinke 1995). For example, in the 1960s and 1970s, the keeping of a huge diversity of exotic animals by individuals from different classes became a trend. A documentary from that time entitled 'Christian, The Lion at World's End' demonstrates how easily two young students bought a lion cub at the famous department store 'Harrods' and kept it in their small attic apartment in central London. At that point in time, one could purchase monkeys, lions and even elephants in various department stores all over Europe.[10]

Simultaneous with the trade in live exotic animals, the trade in animal products expanded and was also influenced by fashion trends. By 1850, trade in the feathers and skins of exotic birds for the millinery industry was thriving as a continuation of the trend initiated by Marie Antoinette in the eighteenth century and it involved hundreds of thousands of birds as recorded in hunting and trading statistics. During the peak of the 'feather fashion' between 1901–1910, 362,000 lb of exotic feathers were imported by the United Kingdom (UK) alone with an estimated value of £19,923,000 (Doughty 1975). Fifty years later, during the 1960s, the wearing of extraordinary coats made of skins from big cats or bears became fashionable as symbols of wealth and status in Europe. For instance, the US first lady Jackie Kennedy, dressed in a leopard-skin coat, met the US Ambassador in Rome in 1962. Queen Elizabeth II and the film star Elizabeth Taylor also wore similar leopard-skin coats at this time (Lee 2003).[11] Subsequently, 'ordinary' women tended to imitate these role models.

The increased call for exotic animals from the middle classes resulted in growing demand markets and a decline in species. According to Collard (2013) the commercial trade had a devastating effect on species' populations. Between 1950 and 1985 some 200–1,000 tonnes of ivory were exported from Africa each year (Barbier et al. 1990). In the twentieth century, the international demand for ivory led to the extinction of elephant populations in many parts of Africa (Blanc et al. 2003). In addition, large fairs with exotic animals reflected the extended pet market for exotic animals driven by fashion trends and the popularity of reptiles, birds and monkeys. Therefore, several populations of exotic species significantly declined due to the demand for animals as pets (Chap. 8). In the late twentieth century, caviar from sturgeon eggs became a high-prized luxury product for the upper classes in Europe. Between 1998 and 2006 the trade in caviar amounted to more than 1,300 tonnes, while the sturgeon population has declined sharply (Knapp et al. 2006; Schneider 2012) (Chap. 7). Also an increasing demand among the middle classes for alternative medicines, including traditional Chinese medicine (e.g. Patrick 1995), has resulted in pressure on several endangered species (Chap. 9).

---

[10]'Christian, The Lion at World's End.' Scotia American, 1971.

[11]Government licences in the UK showed that 3,000 tiger skins were exported in 1968 (Sharma et al. 2014).

Consequently, well-known species such as the rhinoceros and the tiger are now on the brink of extinction (Still 2003).

Thus the modern era is characterized by technological innovation as an outcome of the industrial revolution that made an extremely large structural trade in wildlife products possible. The twentieth and twenty-first centuries characterize the massive boom in keeping exotic animals as pets and extraordinary animal products being sold over the Internet, at auctions and in pet shops (Collard 2013). Especially the overall growth of the economy and prosperity has resulted in expanding demand markets. The perception of animals has not only changed in the context of the industrial revolution when animals were increasingly regarded as commodities. A contradictory transformation process of animals as 'items' into 'individuals with animal rights' emerged in the twenty-first century (Van Uhm 2015). Elias indicated how standards regarding violence gradually transformed by growing thresholds of shame and repugnance. In his book 'The civilising process' he describes how violent activity was rejected and placed under increasing social control in European society reflected by declining rates of homicide (Elias 1939). Public human torture and execution became outlawed in the context of the development of human rights. The rejection of public violence regarding (exotic) animals can be explained in the context of the development of animal rights. Several animal welfare rights were developed in most Western countries in the late twentieth century (Van Uhm 2015).

1.6 Lessons from the Past

The relationship between humans and animals is as old as the hills and the trade in wildlife has always taken place. Initially, animals and animal products were used as 'basic needs'. The *functional use* of animals in ancient societies can be linked to leather and fur for clothing to provide protection against the cold (e.g. the wearing of bear fur) or animal products as food to survive. Animals were also functionally used in work and warfare, Hannibal crossed the Alps with his war elephants, and ancient societies used products from exotic animals in medicines, such as ostrich eggs against skull fractures. Yet, the *symbolic function* and value of animals and animal products changed in the social and cultural context of history. In ancient Egypt, exotic animals for menageries and ivory for the royal empires already illustrated the fascination with wildlife. Keeping exotic animals or products thereof was a symbol of status, spirituality and power for the pharaohs and wealthy Egyptians. In the Greek and Roman Empires exhibiting exotic animals in 'paradises' (menageries and gardens) became relatively common for the elites to worship their gods, pray and sacrifice or to be used as hunting grounds. The trade increased substantially with the Roman games in the arena used by rulers to demonstrate their status, power, worship, control over animals, and to gain popularity among the Roman social hierarchy. During the Middle Ages the exclusivity of wildlife increased with a substantial loss of natural habitat and wildlife became more scarce. European royalty and nobility took over the practice of exotic animals in menageries as an illustration of the importance of status and empire. The first aristocrat fashion trends emerged for exclusive furs in order to underline social differences. Elite fashion trends copied by the bourgeoisie expanded during early modernity and, simultaneously, menageries were opened to the public. Moreover, in this era the global trade was widely extended with the emergence of European imperialism and colonialism. Exotic animals and products thereof became a symbolic representation of domination over colonies. In the Victorian era, it was not exceptional to keep exotic animals as pets and fashion trends using parts of exotic animals appeared in almost all walks of life. The use of wildlife for *entertainment* emerged, as reflected by the transformation from menageries into public zoos and circuses and exotic pets kept by 'ordinary' people. In the nineteenth and twentieth centuries, the rise of the science of natural history and zoology proved that there were similarities between humans and animals and a fascination for exotic animals was growing. Simultaneously, an emancipation trend towards animals emerged where public violence against animals was increasingly being rejected. In the late twentieth and early twenty-first centuries, the distinction between humans and animals has been losing force in the West since psychological and behavioural connections have been widely accepted. Exotic animals are approached from a sentimental perspective rather than as commodities.

Looking at animals in history, on the one hand the symbolic value has changed in several forms of the wildlife trade. Extraordinary exclusive wild animals and animal products associated with the upper classes have been transformed into a commodity owned by ordinary people. We have also seen a transformation from ancient menageries as symbols of status and domination by the pharaohs and aristocrats, to public zoos for entertainment, education and species conservation. And, currently, the wearing of fur is associated with animal cruelty rather than an upper-class fashion item. On the other hand, symbols of status and luxury are still related to certain wildlife products. Caviar from endangered sturgeons has become a product of luxury and status and fashion still plays an important role in the market for exotic pets and furs.

The historical use of wildlife could be divided into three interrelated pillars. First, the functional use of wildlife such as leather and fur for clothing to provide protection against the cold (e.g. the wearing of bear fur), animals used for work and warfare (e.g. the war elephants of Hannibal) and animal products used in medicines (e.g. traditional Chinese medicine). Second, the entertainment and educational use of wildlife reflected in animals in menageries (e.g. Queen Hatshepsut's menagerie), circuses and zoos (e.g. the Tower of London) and as pets (e.g. large global reptile fairs). Third, the symbolic use of wildlife represented by status (e.g. caviar as a delicacy), fashion trends (e.g. the wearing of feathers) and religion (e.g. leopard skins worn by priests).

The impact of the diverse wildlife trade already became visible in early antiquity. Elephants, lions and hippos disappeared as a result of overexploitation in Roman and Greek times. During the Middle Ages technological innovations in agriculture wiped out forests on a large scale and, subsequently, the exclusivity of wildlife increased. European imperialism and colonialism in the 'Age of Exploration' led to a growth in the global wildlife trade and whale populations at Spitsbergen declined during Early Modernity due to the demand for baleen and lubrication oil. Today the trade in wildlife is seen as a major driver of the global wave of the extinction of species in the twentieth and twenty-first centuries as described in Chap. 2. In the context of the overall growth of the economy and prosperity, large demand markets for exotic animals and products thereof emerged and this was met by trade based on technological innovations in transportation (e.g. rapid airline travel) and communication (e.g. the Internet). Although the impact of intensive trade has become much more visible with thousands of animal species at risk we seem to have learned little from history and the overexploitation of wildlife will continue. Never before have so many exotic animals and products been traded globally.

References

Alexander, E. P. (1979). *Museums in motion: An introduction to the history and functions of museums*. Nashville: American Association for State and Local History.

Arnold, K. (2006). *Cabinets for the curious: Looking back at early english museums*. Aldershot: Ashgate.

Baltodano, M. P., Andrzejewski, J., & Symcox, L. (2009). *Social justice, peace, and environmental education: Transformative standards*. New York: Routledge.

Baratay, E., & Hardouin-Fugier, E. (2003). *Zoo: A history of zoological gardens in the west*. London: Reaktion books.

Barbier, E. B., Burgess, J. C., Swanson, T. M., & Pearce, D. W. (1990). *Elephants, economics and ivory*. London: Earthscan Publications Ltd.

Barnet, P. (1997). *Images in Ivory: Precious objects of the gothic age*. Detroit: Detroit Institute of Arts.

Belozerskaya, M. (2006). *The medici giraffe: And other tales of exotic animals and power*. New York: Little, Brown & Company.

Berger, J. (1980). *About looking*. New York: Random House.

Blanc, J. J., Thouless, C. R., Hart, J. A., Dublin, H. T., Douglas-Hamilton, I., Craig, C. G., et al. (2003). *African elephant status report 2002: An update from the African elephant database*. Gland: IUCN/SSC African Elephant Specialist Group.

Boekhout van Solinge, T. (2008). The land of the orangutan and the bird of paradise under threat. In R. Sollund, R. (Ed.), *Global harms: Ecological crime and speciesism* (51–70). New York: Nova Science Publishing.

Bomgardner, D. L. (2000). *The story of the roman amphitheatre*. London: Routledge.

Brandon-Jones, C. (1997). Edward Blyth, Charles Darwin, and the animal trade in nineteenth-century India and Britain. *Journal of the History of Biology, 30*(2), 145–178.

Broad, S., Luxmoore, R., & Jenkins, M. (Eds.). (1988a). *Significant trade in wildlife: Mammals (Vol. 1)*. Cambridge: IUCN.

Broad, S., Luxmoore, R., & Jenkins, M. (Eds.). (1988b). *Significant trade in wildlife: Reptiles (Vol. 2)*. Cambridge: IUCN.

Broad, S., Luxmoore, R., & Jenkins, M. (Eds.). (1988c). *Significant trade in wildlife: Birds (Vol. 3)*. Cambridge: IUCN.

Bruemmer, F. (1998). Of monstrous moles and unicorn horns. *International Wildlife, 28*(3), 30–38.

Budge, E. W. (1934). *From fetish to God in ancient Egypt*. London: Oxford University Press.

Carpenter, D. A. (1994). King Henry III and the tower of London. *The London Journal, 19*(2), 95–107.

Cheyns, M. (2008). *Zeeuwse schepen voor Azië. Het scheepsbouwbedrijf van de kamer Zeeland van de de VOC in de eerste helft van de 18de eeuw*. Gent: Universiteit Gent.

Collard, R. C. M. S. (2013). *Animal traffic: Making, remaking and unmaking commodities in global live wildlife trade*. Vancouver: University of British Columbia.

Crosby, A. (1986). *Ecological imperialism: The biological expansion of Europe, 900–1900*. Cambridge: Cambridge University Press.

Doughty, R. W. (1975). *Feather fashions and bird preservation: A study in nature protection*. Berkeley: University of California Press.

Duffy, R. (2000). *Killing for conservation: Wildlife policy in Zimbabwe*. Oxford: James Currey Ltd.

Dyer, C. (1989). *Standards of living in the later middle ages: Social change in England c. 1200–1520*. Cambridge: Cambridge University Press.

Elias, N. (1939). *The civilizing process*. Oxford: Basil Blackwell.

Erman, A., & Tirard, H. M. (1971). *Life in ancient Egypt*. New York: Dover Publications.

Foster, K. P. (1998). Gardens of Eden: Exotic flora and fauna in the ancient Near East. In J. Coppock & J. A. Miller (Eds.), *Transformation of middle eastern natural environments: Legacies and lessons* (pp. 320–329). Yale School of Forestry and Environmental Studies: New Haven.

Frede, D. (2007). *A tale of two zoos: A study in watching people watching animals*. Sydney: University of Sydney.

Gabriel, R. A. (2011). *Hannibal: The military biography of Rome's greatest enemy*. Washington: Potomac Books Inc.

Hahn, D. (2003). *The tower menagerie: Being the amazing true story of the royal collection of wild and ferocious beasts*. Eastbourne: Gardners Books.

Herzog, H. A. (2014). Biology, culture, and the origins of pet-keeping. *Animal Behavior and Cognition, 1*(3), 296–308.

Hoage, R. J., & Deiss, W. A. (Eds.). (1996). *New worlds, new animals: From menagerie to zoological park in the nineteenth century*. Baltimore: Johns Hopkins University Press.

Houlihan, P. F. (1996). *The animal world of the pharaohs*. London: Thames and Hudson.

Hughes, J. D. (2003). Europe as consumer of exotic biodiversity: Greek and Roman times. *Landscape Research, 28*(1), 21–31.

Ikram, S. (2004). *Beloved beasts: Animal mummies from ancient Egypt*. Cairo: Supreme Council of Antiqities Press.

Ikram, S. (2009). *Ancient Egypt: An introduction*. Cambridge: Cambridge University Press.

Jacobi, E. F. (1988). *Honderdvijftig jaar Artis*. Amsterdam: Stichting IVIO.

Jankuhn, H. (1982). Trade and settlement in Central and Northern Europe up to and during the Viking Period. *The Journal of the Royal Society of Antiquaries of Ireland, 112*(1982), 18–50.

Jennison, G. (1937). *Animals for show and pleasure in Ancient Rome*. Manchester: Manchester University.

Kalof, L. (2007). *Looking at animals in human history*. London: Reaktion Books.

Katharine, T. (2009). *The Roman garden: Space, sense, and society*. London/New York: Routledge.

Kirwan, L. P. (1963). Land of Abu Simbel. *Geographical Journal*, 261–273.

Kisling, V. N. (Ed.). (2001). *Zoo and aquarium history: Ancient animal collections to zoological gardens*. Boca Raton, Fla: CRC Press.

Knapp, A., Kitschke, C. & von Meibom, S. (Eds.) (2006). *Proceedings of the International Sturgeon Enforcement Workshop to Combat Illegal Trade in Caviar. Prepared by TRAFFIC Europe for the European Commission*. Brussels: Traffic.

Lee, M. (2003). *Fashion victim. Our love-hate relationship with dressing, shopping, and the cost of style*. New York: Broadway Books.

Lennard, J. (1996). The dark business of animal trade. *Americas* 48(5).

MacKinnon, M. (2006). Supplying exotic animals for the Roman amphitheatre games: New reconstructions combining archaeological, ancient textual, historical and ethnographic data. *Mouseion, 3*(6), 1–25.
Mason, P. (1999). Zoos as heritage tourism attractions: A neglected area of research? *International Journal of Heritage Studies, 5*(3–4), 193–202.
Naylor, R. T. (2004). The underworld of ivory. *Crime, Law and Social Change, 42*(4–5), 261–295.
Patrick, H. (1995). Traditional Chinese medicine and public health: The Yin and the Yang. *Journal of the Royal Society of Medicine, 88*(9), 485–486.
Patrick, P. G., Matthews, C. E., Ayers, D. F., & Tunnicliffe, S. D. (2007). Conservation and education: Prominent themes in zoo mission statements. *The Journal of Environmental Education, 38*(3), 53–60.
Perrot, P. (1994). *Fashioning the bourgeoisie: A history of clothing in the nineteenth century*. Princeton: Princeton University Press.
Pluskowski, A. (2004). Narwhals or unicorns? Exotic animals as material culture in medieval Europe. *European Journal of Archaeology, 7*(3), 291–313.
Rijkelijkhuizen, M. (2009). Whales, walruses, and elephants: Artisans in ivory, baleen, and other skeletal materials in seventeenth-and eighteenth-century Amsterdam. *International Journal of Historical Archaeology, 13*(4), 409–429.
Robbins, L. E. (2002). *Elephant slaves and pampered parrots: Exotic animals in eighteenth-century Paris*. Baltimore: Johns Hopkins University Press.
Roesdahl, E. (2001). Walrus ivory in the viking age—and ohthere (Ottar). *Offa, 58*, 33–37.
Runge, H. J. (1987). Vormünzliche Zahlungsmittel: Tiere. *Felle, Zähne, Money Trend, 1*, 22–25.
Ryhiner, P., & Mannix, D. P. (1958). *The wildest game*. New York: J.B. Lippincott Company.
Schneider, J. (2012). *Sold into extinction: The global trade in endangered species*. Santa Barbara: Praeger.
Schupplit, C. A., & Fraser, D. (2000). A framework for assessing the suitability of different species as companion animals. *Animal Welfare, 9*, 359–372.
Sharma, K., Wright, B., Joseph, T., & Desai, N. (2014). Tiger poaching and trafficking in India: Estimating rates of occurrence and detection over four decades. *Biological Conservation, 179*, 33–39.
Simons, J. (2012). *The tiger that swallowed the boy: Exotic animals in victorian England*. Oxford: Libri Publishing.
Still, J. (2003). Use of animal products in traditional Chinese medicine: Environmental impact and health hazards. *Complementary Therapies in Medicine, 11*(2), 118–122.
Strouhal, E., Vachala, B., & Vymazalova, H. (2014). *The medicine of the ancient Egyptians* (Vol. 1). Cairo: The American University in Cairo Press.
Strutt, J. (1833). *The sports and pastimes of the people of England by William Hone*. Dublin: T.T. & J. Tegg & Son.
Thompson, A. W. (1907). *Aristotle 350 BC 'the history of animals'*. London: John Bell.
Van Gelder, R. (1997). *Het Oost-Indisch avontuur: Duitsers in dienst van de VOC*. Nijmegen: Uitgeverij SUN.
Van Uhm, D. P. (2015). Towards moral principles regarding non-human animals: A green criminological perspective. In F. de Jong et al. (Eds.), *Overarching views of crime and deviancy. Rethinking the legacy of the Utrecht school* (565–587). The Hague: Eleven International Publishing.
Veale, E. M. (2003). *The English Fur Trade in the later Middle Ages* (Vol. 38). V. A. Harding (Ed.). Loughborough: London Record Society.
Vinke, C. M. (1995). *Onderzoek naar de organisatiestructuur van de Nederlandse legale en illegale dierenhandel*. Leiden: Rijksuniversiteit Leiden.
Whatmore, S. (2002). *Hybrid geographies: Natures cultures spaces*. London: Sage.
Wiedemann, T. (2002). *Emperors and gladiators*. London: Routledge.

Chapter 2
The Sixth Mass Extinction

Although, historically, it was common belief that Earth's natural resources, such as wildlife, were inexhaustible (Worster 1988), the biosphere and atmosphere subsequently altered due to overexploitation. During the last century, the impact of humans on the world became clear with the reduction of natural resources and the consequences of excessive use. In the last 50 years, humans have consumed more natural resources than in all previous history (EPA 2009). To sustain the United States' (US) levels of consumption for every person on Earth, we would need four additional planets (Wilson 1993: 23). As a result half of the tropical and temperate forests of the world are now gone and one acre per second is disappearing (EPA 2009). Deforestation not only contributes to 25–30 % of the annual greenhouse gasses released into the atmosphere caused by human activity (Worldwatch Institute 2006; FAO 2006), but also to high rates of species extinction and extirpation as tropical forests contain about 75–90 % of all living species on Earth (Terborgh 1993). The impact is immense, especially on tropical rainforests that include the most biodiverse ecosystems containing a large variety of species (Wilson 2002). While these rainforests represent only 6 % of the Earth's surface, they contain more than half and up to two-thirds of all known species; e.g. the Amazon rainforest contains 30 % of all known species (Boekhout van Solinge 2010, 2012). In addition to deforestation and habitat degradation, the trade in wildlife has become the second hazard to biodiversity (Zimmerman 2003).[1] Moreover, the trade in wildlife is considered to be the greatest threat to certain species in particular, transcending degradation and loss of habitat (Oldfield 2003, World Bank 2005). In modern society flows of endangered species have become important to the global economy and are traded as commodities for a wide range of purposes as illustrated in Chap. 1. Animal parts are used as medicines, meat or eggs from animals are served as food, skins are used as leather products and to keep us warm, live animals are kept as pets and so on. Yet, the current size and scale of the trade seems to be more immense than

[1]According to Stiles et al. (2013) the decline of natural range drives the illegal trade as it promotes contact and conflict between animals and humans.

D.P. van Uhm, *The Illegal Wildlife Trade*, Studies of Organized Crime 15,
DOI 10.1007/978-3-319-42129-2_2

ever before and leads to global defaunation. Defaunation is the equivalent of deforestation and the term is used to refer to the loss of species, populations and local declines in the abundance of individuals of wildlife (Dirzo et al. 2014). According to recent studies the scale and impact of anthropocene defaunation and biodiversity losses on ecosystem functions is comparable with other harmful global changes, such as worldwide pollution growth and global warming (Hooper et al. 2012).

2.1 Global Defaunation and Ecological Interaction

After the five mass extinctions on Earth that were caused by meteorite impacts, volcanic activity and large-scale climate change several scientists predict that we are currently at the beginning of the sixth mass extinction (e.g. Leakey and Lewin 1995; May et al. 1995; Pimm et al. 1995; Butchart et al. 2010; Barnosky et al. 2011; Dirzo et al. 2014). Previous extinction waves include generally one half of all animal species when at least one quarter and occasionally even all animal species disappeared (Myers 1990). The first mass extinction at the end of the Ordovician period took place around 450 million years ago and it is believed to be the second largest of the five mass extinctions. The world at that time was inhabited by a large variety of marine invertebrates (e.g. molluscs, arthropods). The cause of the Ordovician mass extinction is believed to consist of alternating glacial and interglacial pulses. Around 85 % of all species disappeared (Jablonski 1991; Sheehan 2001). The second mass extinction occurred 375 million years ago during the Devonian period, known as the 'Age of fishes'. In the Devonian era the first primitive vertebrate (tetrapod) developed the skills to live outside water on land and primitive insects and precursors of amphibians appeared. The period was characterized by the diversity of fish species (e.g. fish with jaws, ancient sharks, bony fish), for instance the prehistoric armoured fishes measuring up to 10 metres from the *Dunkleosteus* genus (Williams 2007). The Devonian extinction is believed to have been caused by oceanic anoxia and global cooling. According to McGhee (1996) around 75 % of all species became extinct. In the early Permian period, 300–250 million years ago, the supercontinent Pangaea was formed and sharks filled the ecological gap left by the extinction of prehistoric armoured fish. Two groups of ancestor mammals (*Synapsids*) and ancestors of reptiles and birds (*Sauropsids*) dominated the land area (Grose 2012). A famous example is one of the largest predators of the early Permian period, the *Dimetrodon*, with a size up to 4.6 m (Berman et al. 2001). The demise of this predator and the end of the entire Permian era 250 million years ago was caused by global warming and volcanic activity. The 'Great Dying' is the most intense extinction wave ever, including the extinction of up to 95 % of all species (Benton and Twitchett 2003). The restoration of species diversity took 10–20 million years and vertebrates became common with large mammal-reptile species, amphibians and the first dinosaurs in the Triassic period, 250 million years ago. Triassic was the first period of the 'Age of the reptiles' (the Mesozoic Era) and, as most marine genera had been wiped out by the last mass extinction, a group of reptiles (e.g. *Ichthyosauria*) explored the ocean (Thorne et al. 2011). In addition, the late Triassic period is famous for the evolution of dinosaurs, such as the *Staurikosaurus*, *Eoraptor* and *Plateosaurus* that became increasingly dominant (Cloudsley-Thompson 2005). It is believed that 200 million years ago sea-level fluctuations (Hallam 1990) and increasing CO_2 levels by seismic activity (Beerling and Berner 2002; Hautmann 2004) caused the fourth mass extinction of 76 % of all species (Tanner et al. 2004). During this fourth mass extinction most mammal-like reptiles and large amphibians disappeared and dinosaurs began to rule the planet. In the Cretaceous period, the 'Age of the Dinosaurs', huge terrestrial dinosaurs (e.g. *Tyrannosaurus rex; Triceratops; Brachiosaurus*) were living next to giant sea reptiles (e.g. *Ichthyosaurs, Plesiosaurs, Mosasaurs*) and flying reptiles (*Pterosaurs*). The most recent mass extinction is believed to have been the result of volcanic activity in combination with the impact of the Yucatan meteorite and, as a result, 80 % of species became extinct (Huynh and Poulsen 2005).

Contrary to the previous mass extinctions, in the current scenario humans seem to be causing the mass extinction by unbalancing nature (Barnosky et al. 2011). For instance by, but not limited to, killing species, introducing non-native species, fragmenting habitats, spreading pathogens, co-opting resources and changing global climate. According to Wilson (1993: xxiv) "We have been too self-absorbed to foresee the long-term consequences of our actions". During the last century, the rate at which species became extinct was about 50–500 times higher than the 'normal' extinction rate as can be derived based on the dating of fossils from the previous mass extinctions.[2] In the last hundred years, the level of species extinction increased by as much as a thousand times (Millennium Ecosystem Assessment 2005). It has been estimated that between 17,000 and 100,000 species vanish from our planet each year (Leakey and Lewin 1995; Dirzo et al. 2014; Wilson 1993). Probably this number is higher as scientists estimate that 86 % of species on Earth and 91 % in the ocean have not yet been discovered (Mora et al. 2011) and each year about 18,000 new species are found (Chapman 2009). Currently, for those that have been discovered as much as 16 to 33 % of all vertebrate species are threatened or endangered (Hoffmann et al. 2010). Based on vertebrate data an estimation of a 28 % decline in the number of individuals across species in the past four decades has been found (Dirzo et al. 2014). The rates of the decline in invertebrates (e.g. insects, worms) would be at least as severe as among vertebrates. According to Dirzo et al. (2014), over the past 40 years invertebrate numbers have decreased by 45 %. For instance, numbers as high as 26–37 % of mammals, 17 % of birds, 38 % of chameleons, 31 % of sharks and rays, 33 % of reef-forming corals and 41–56 % of amphibians experience threat levels (see also Appendix I). Insufficient data makes it impossible to estimate the percentage for the groupings of reptiles and molluscs (IUCN 2014). The largest numbers of threatened species are found in

[2]Generally, recovery from mass extinction episodes occurs on timescales encompassing millions of years.

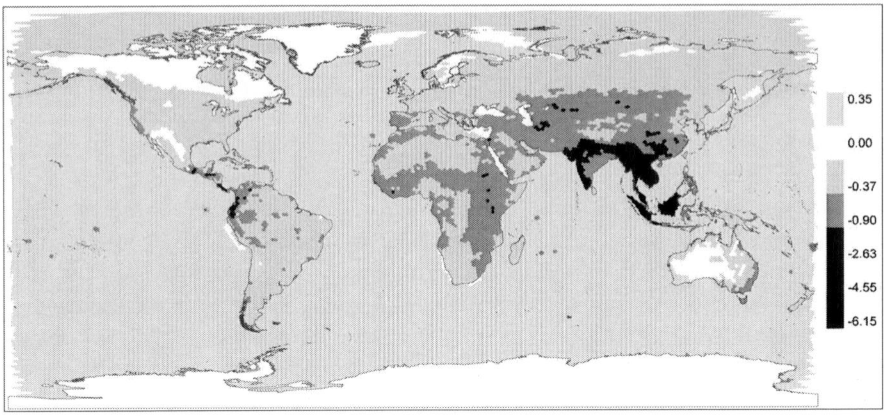

Map. 2.1 Global patterns of global defaunation. *Source* Hoffmann et al. (2010)

Ecuador (2,299), the United States (1,287), Malaysia (1,236), Indonesia (1,225), Mexico (1,091), China (995), India (988), Tanzania (979), Brazil (965) and Madagascar (929) (IUCN 2014). Map 2.1 presents the global patterns of threatened land and marine vertebrates. These threatened vertebrates are mainly found in tropical regions. It is believed that by 2020, 10 million species will have become threatened with extinction (South 2008).

The complexity of the current decline of biodiversity and the effect of defaunation can be demonstrated by the sensibility of ecological interaction between animals and plants. An ecosystem consists of abiotic components (air, water, soil, atoms and molecules) and biotic components (plants, animals, bacteria and fungi). Animals are dependent on plants for food or medicines, but plants are also dependent on animals for reproduction. The distribution of seeds of plant species may take place in an abiotic (by means of wind, water or gravity) or biotic manner (with the help of animals) (Wilson 1993; Tudge 2005; Roosmalen 2008). For example, monkeys and birds are usually important distributors of seeds; toucans disperse the threatened Virola trees and a reduction in toucans will have an effect on its distribution (Kays et al. 2011). Even with abiotic seed dispersal animals often play an important role in ecology as eaters or predators of seeds and seedlings. Besides seed dispersal, changing biodiversity or animal abundance will affect other ecosystem functioning and services too. Dirzo et al. (2014) described how carrions are removed by vultures (Ogada et al. 2012), water stream and quality is restored by amphibians (Whiles et al. 2013), seeds are trampled by mammals (Wright et al. 2002), dung is removed by dung beetles (Slade et al. 2011), carbon cycling is carried out by worms (Barrett et al. 2008), 'herbivory' (the eating of plants) takes place by large mammals, litter respiration and decomposition are organized by seabirds and plants are pollinated by birds (Anderson et al. 2011). If an animal or plant species is removed from or added to an ecosystem or a population is reduced, the consequences could be disastrous for the perennial species and its ecosystem (Wilson 1993; Roosmalen 2008). Especially the disappearance of *keystone species* would have a disastrous impact on perennial species and their ecosystems. A keystone species is a species that has a disproportionately large effect on its environment (Kellert and Wilson 1993; Mills et al. 1993; Power et al. 1996). For example, as a result of a reduction in sea star populations, mussel populations will explode and extrude most other species (Paine 1966) and, vice versa, the reintroduction of grey wolves in Yellowstone National Park has led to the recovery of the entire ecosystem from vegetation to beavers and bison (Ripple and Beschta 2006). Furthermore, the introduction or release of non-native animals (invasive species) could have serious negative effects for the stability of an ecosystem. Although several exotic species have been introduced for the purpose of benefiting agriculture or aquaculture, the side effects of these introductions include a loss of native species and changes to ecosystem functions and services (Moulton and Sanderson 1999; Mooney and Hobbs 2000).

The incalculability of defaunation is reflected in the process of *trophic cascades*. The concept of a trophic cascade arose from fieldwork and experiments by ecologists who observed the power of predators in marine ecosystems (e.g. Paine 1980; Power 1990). A trophic cascade is an ecological phenomenon with reciprocal changes in the predator and prey balance caused by the removal or addition of top predators. This would result in dramatic changes in the structure of the ecosystem. For instance, a decrease in the numbers of cougars will lead to an increase in mule deer densities and, subsequently, to more browsing intensity and a decrease in riparian cottonwood recruitment and bank erosion. Stream bank erosion may result in a decline in both terrestrial and aquatic species that live near the banks (Ripple and Beschta 2006). In practice, many trophic cascades have been initiated by humans who poach or harvest top predators, such as tigers, jaguars and great white sharks (Terborgh and Estes 2013). A dramatic example is the *ecological meltdown* in predatory free forest fragments. A study by Terborgh et al. (2001) proved that a loss of predators unbalanced the ecosystem by an increase in herbivores, a reduction of seedlings and saplings of canopy trees and plants and animal diversity being lost. The survival of specific populations subsequently depends on the correlation between the density and size of a population and its mean individual fitness. In many small populations of endangered species reproduction and survival is limited and this is caused by a mating shortage or a limited genetic variety, the so-called *Allee effect* (Courchamp et al. 2006). This ensures that a small population can extirpate at a higher rate than expected. The anthropogenic component, the ‘water and diamonds paradox’, is applied to the Allee effect by Courchamp et al. (2006: 2405): “water has much value in use but none in exchange, while the opposite is true for diamonds”. The demand for rare endangered species may have a similar effect. The rarity of a species would determine its value on the black market and, therefore, the demand.[3] The 'anthropogenic Allee effect' refers to the additional component of overexploitation due to a high value on the market (Courchamp et al. 2006; Hall et al. 2008). For instance, an increase in the demand for rhino horn may be caused due to its high price on the black market. In combination with a small population, gene pool and distribution range, the future chances of survival of the Javan rhino, one of the most endangered large mammals in the world with a population of less than 50 animals in Java, are extremely low (Brook et al. 2014).

The previous section demonstrates the strong symbiosis between species in ecosystems and, according to several authors, these may become unbalanced or could even collapse as a result of defaunation by the wildlife trade (Lindsey et al. 2012; Myers et al. 2007). The contemporary anthropogenic impact of defaunation is demonstrated by the high numbers of species reduction. Even a small reduction in a certain species due to trade can be fatal in terms of trophic cascades, the ecological meltdown and (anthropogenic) Allee effects. This represents the vulnerability of ecosystems and the incalculability of anthropocene defaunation. While the extent (scale, size) of the wildlife trade and species reduction has for a long time been unclear, with the current high rate of species extinction and the serious deterioration of biodiversity, the risk of a new mass extinction on Earth may become a realistic scenario.

2.2 Creation and Management of Risks

While the previous section underlined the impact of defaunation in the context of ecological interaction and high extinction rates of species on Earth, the overall effects and risks of a decline in species are difficult to estimate. According to the sociologist Ulrich Beck, the risks are part of a new phase of the industrial age, referred to as the *risk society* (Risikogesellschaft). Although in early modernity risks were seen as dangers beyond the control of man and were therefore attributed to fate or control by gods, in modern society emphasis is placed on manageability. Simultaneously, certain developments are becoming less and less manageable (Beck 1986). Giddens explained that the modern world introduces new risks that previous generations 'have not had to face'. The ecological crisis is central to his

[3]The declaration of a species as endangered is believed to prove the rarity of a species and therefore its high value. Paradoxically, this declaration could result in a more desirable item and increased exploitation (Courchamp et al. 2006). After the Roti Island snake-necked turtle (*Chelodina mccordi*) was defined as a rarity, the price reached high prices up to 2,000 USD and the overexploitation led to a near extinction in the wild (Stuart et al. 2006). Courchamp et al. (2006) applied this concept to the Allee effect; 'a positive relationship between any component of individual fitness and either numbers or density of conspecifics' (Stephens et al. 1999). Several processes could simultaneously contribute to the decline in the fitness of an individual species (e.g. its survival probability, the reproductive rate), including the human component of its high value and overexploitation (the anthropogenic Allee effect) (Courchamp et al. 2006).

social analysis of late Modernity and would form an important part of everyday life (Giddens 1991: 4). Environmental risks have become the predominant product, not just an unpleasant, manageable side-effect of the industrial society. Characteristic effects include a decrease in biodiversity, but also large-scale disasters such as global deforestation, CO_2 emissions, soil erosion and widespread pollution have proved that environmental risks are strongly associated with the side effects of Modernity. Despite efforts by governments and science to assess and manage risks, the controllability of problems is limited and the negative effects of modernization come back to haunt us (Beck 1999). These risks are invisible, diffuse and the existing control structures, such as regulating the trade in endangered species or emission certificates, are not sufficient to manage these new risks (Roef 2003). In contrast to earlier threats, the new risks are not bound by location, time or social class, but are all-encompassing and not insured or compensable (Boutellier 2008). The risks and consequences of this modernization are revealed as irreversible threats to the lives of plants, animals and humans (Giddens 1990; Beck 1992).

The significant decline in wild animals is a clear example of these alarming developments and unmanageable risks. As mentioned before, we cannot estimate how much the reduction in biodiversity or defaunation effects society. As described in the previous section, the vulnerability of an ecosystem is presented by ecological interaction or symbiosis between animals and plants. The decline in keystone species may affect several ecosystem functioning and services. Certain trees can disappear with a decline in seed dispersers or water quality will decrease. This may also have indirect negative impacts on CO_2 emissions. Moreover, the diversity of species produces a large collection of genetic material that can be used for the development of new medicines by pharmaceutical industries. Around one out of four drugs originate from the tropical rainforest (Boekhout van Solinge 2011). The disappearance of biodiversity ensures that potential medicines will be lost (Balick et al. 1996; De Vis 2006). A biodiversity loss threatens not only the loss of plant and animal resources, but also traditional community life and cultural diversity with its knowledge of the medicinal value of various native species (Okigbo et al. 2008). The 'red list' of endangered species worldwide is becoming increasingly longer and the effects are becoming more visible (Beck 1992).

Gibbs et al. (2010) underline that the risks for human health, natural resources and the environment should be central in studying environmental issues. They explained that both direct and indirect environmental risks could be approached as the complex interaction between human and natural systems takes place on multiple scales. According to Beck (2006) the new risks that influence the world are characterized by three features: de-localization, incalculableness and non-compensability. First, de-localization: the consequences of the trade in wildlife result not only in a reduction of a population in the source region, but can also affect ecosystems in the region of destination; for example trafficked exotic species may become competitors to local species (Mooney and Hobbs 2000). "Its causes and consequences are not limited to one geographic location or space, they are in principle omnipresent" (Beck 2006: 333). Second, incalculableness: the ecological interaction between humans, animals and plants make ecosystems vulnerable to defaunation. Ecosystems may collapse, fertile soil may disappear and water can lose its purity and clarity as described in Sect. 2.1, with incalculable consequences for life on Earth. "Its consequences are incalculable; at bottom it is a matter of 'hypothetical' risks, which, not least, are based on science-induced not-knowing and normative dissent" (Beck 2006: 334). However, humans change the environment and use resources at unsustainable rates in such a way that currently the side effects (e.g. defaunation, pollution, global warming) are becoming more visible. Third, non-compensability: "the security dream of first modernity was based on the scientific utopia of making the unsafe consequences and dangers of decisions controllable; accidents could occur, as long as and because of the idea that they were compensable" (Beck 2006: 334). The disappearance of species appears to be difficult to compensate. Not only does each species have a unique role in its ecosystem but also genetics and potential medicine will disappear.

In other words, the new environmental risks are not land or border-related, the effect and the duration may be poorly estimated and the causes and consequences of the complexity of the risks are difficult to calculate (Douglas and Wildavsky 1982; Giddens 1990; Beck 2006). The economic success formulas of the social order (private enterprises, the division of labour and increasing scale, unfettered scientific developments) are (partly) the causes of major risks in society (Huls 2009). For instance, fish is systematically caught and processed into food with polluting machines and rainforests are structurally cut down and turned into wood products with inevitable CO_2 emissions. Thus modern industrial societies create emerging issues, manufactured on a large scale by modern technologies that were previously unknown. The consequences of the decline in biodiversity (or global warming) are relatively invisible effects of the risk society that not only affect humans. These are not just individual risks, but risks that we share as a global society in the public interest, so-called social risks (Rademaker 2008).

2.3 The Boomerang Effect

These shared modern risks have become widespread and produce new international inequalities, primarily between the Global South and the industrialized countries in the Global North, and in the second place in the industrialized countries themselves. For instance, according to the outcomes of the United Nations Climate Change Conference in 2010, Western countries have to reduce activities that produce too much CO_2 emissions. Consequently companies transfer their activities to relatively poor countries with limited environmental regulations for factories and low wages; CO_2 emissions are therefore being 'outsourced' by Western companies. Generally, multinational enterprises can develop undisturbed activities due to limited controls in these countries (Rademaker 2008).

Another example of the distribution of inequalities is the exploitation of natural resources, such as mining, oil refining or wildlife poaching, that takes place in relatively poor source countries (e.g. in the last primeval forests of the Amazon and

Congo basin). According to Roe (2002) the general wildlife trade flows are from developing to developed countries. Traffickers exploit poverty and inequality to entice people to poach in territories without a government presence (Haken 2011). In these developing countries, rainforests are inhabited by millions of people who are dependent on wildlife resources of the rainforest, which disappear partly as a result of the wildlife trade (Roe 2002; Boekhout van Solinge 2010). For example, meat from wild animals (including fish) contributes 20 % or more of the animal protein in the diets of forest communities (Bennet and Robbinson 2000). Not only do these activities result in the disappearance of forests and their animal and plant species, but they also ensure that the economic and social value of the land decreases. According to Beck (1992: 38): "Property is being devalued, it is undergoing a creeping ecological expropriation". The destruction of and the threat to nature and the environment result in a continuous devaluation and expropriation of property rights. Damaged ecosystems in a social sense are worthless or have a lower value because the habitat has disappeared and in an economic sense because the natural resources have gone, the land has been cleared and the risk of soil erosion has grown (Beck 1992).

Besides the impact on source regions (often developing countries), destination countries (often industrial states) are affected as well. A lesser known example would be the dangerous side effects of wildlife trafficking, such as outbreaks of zoonotic diseases. Increased human contact with wild animals due to the wildlife trade and habitat fragmentation causes a risk of pathogen exchange (Zommers and Macdonald 2006; Wolfe et al. 1998). When these animals carry microorganisms which could adapt to humans, this may lead to the emergence of new infections. In 2003 the outbreak of Severe Acute Respiratory Syndrome (SARS) coronavirus, a life-threatening form of atypical pneumonia, could be traced back to the relatively small trade in carnivores and bats. Joint teams of epidemiologists from China and the WHO (World Health Organization) discovered that some of the first SARS patients in Guangdong province in China worked in the sale or preparation of wild animals for human consumption. The Chinese authorities responded by imposing a temporary ban on the hunting, sale, transport and export of all wild animals in southern China (Bell et al. 2004; Lau et al. 2005). In 2003, SARS had spread within a few weeks from the Guangdong province of China to infected people in about 37 countries around the world. The first cases of SARS outside China were reported on February 26, 2003 and on May 31, 2003 and there were a total of 8,359 potentially infected cases, with a mortality rate of 14 % outside China. Ultimately, about 10,000 people were infected with 1,000 people dying and major global economic damage being caused. Initially the SARS outbreak was characterized by the scientific uncertainty surrounding the cause of the outbreak and, second, the complicated control of the outbreak through interventions or measures (Smith 2006). The damage was unforeseeable and the outbreak was (almost) uncontrollable. After the SARS outbreak 838,500 wild animals were seized in markets in Guangzhou, where masked palm civets, solar badgers, barking deer, wild boars, hedgehogs, foxes, squirrels, bamboo rats, gerbils, several species of snakes and endangered leopard cats were being sold together with domestic dogs, cats and rabbits (Karesh et al. 2005).

Both the legal and illegal trade in wild birds have also played an important role in the global spread of the highly pathogenic avian influenza (HPAI bird flu) H5N1. Since 2003, 240 people, millions of poultry, and an unknown number of wild birds and mammals have been infected and died, including endangered species (Brooks-Moizer et al. 2008). Avian influenza is a bird disease that causes flu-like symptoms, with drowsiness, watery eyes and swollen throats. H5N1 emerged in eight Asian countries in late 2003 and early 2004. Since then, the virus has spread to other countries in Asia and various countries in Europe (Zommers and Macdonald 2006). The H5N1 subtype of the avian influenza virus spread by migratory waterfowl and the (illegal) trade in wildlife contributed to the global spread of H5N1. An illegal import from Thailand to Brussels included two infected eagles (Yee et al. 2009). The wildlife trade has played a role in the evolution, distribution and transmission of the disease at fairs, exhibitions or during transportation (Zommers and Macdonald 2006).

The most recent large incidence of the transmission of zoonotic diseases is the distribution of the Ebola virus. Already in the early 2000s several human Ebola outbreaks in Gabon and the Republic of Congo were traced to meat from infected Great Apes (Leroy et al. 2004), but the Ebola outbreak in West Africa in 2014 (mainly in Sierra Leone, Liberia and Guinea) highlights the global effect that zoonotic diseases may have. The WHO estimates a total of 23,860 suspected cases and 9,675 deaths, but the WHO believes that this substantially understates the real impact of the outbreak (WHO 2015). Although flights from these areas to non-infected areas were said to be highly controlled, people became infected in the EU and US as well. It can be traced back to the trade in meat from infected fruit bats and monkeys. The virus has spread in a short period of time and has proven to be incalculable and hard to control (EFSA 2014).

An increase in the number of viruses passed from animals to humans that cause serious diseases, such as SARS, Avian influenza and Ebola has been noted (Mensink 2007). The growing volume of the global wildlife trade with rapid and cheap transportation, temporary storage facilities and common network nodes increase the risk of transmitting infectious diseases (Burgos and Burgos 2007). The wildlife trade may also be a factor in the spread of infectious diseases to other pets and wild animals (Bell et al. 2004). Every day mammals, birds and reptiles are traded through trade nodes, where they come into contact with people and native and non-native animal species. The billions of direct and indirect contacts between wildlife, humans and domestic animals, driven by technological improvement in combination with the expanding global size of the wildlife trade and modern transportation with commercial nodes, has increased the risk of the outbreak of life-threatening diseases (Karesh et al. 2005).

However, certain countries or regions are or will be more affected than others because of the spread and growth of risks. This may correspond with class inequalities and social positions relating to a fundamentally different distributional effect. The source countries generally include some of the poorest countries with the richest sources of biodiversity. Several studies have identified African and Southeast Asian countries as the main source countries for illegal wildlife (Rosen and Smith 2010; UNODC 2010; World Bank 2008; Lawson and Vines 2014). Therefore, green crimes could be seen as a new form of colonization: Western companies use natural resources from poor countries and subsequently leave the damage behind (Passas and Goodwin 2005).

The risks of modernization, however, will sooner or later touch upon the producers who are reaping the profits (Beck 1992). Life-threatening diseases cost hundreds of billions of dollars in economic damage, a destabilization of the market and the destruction of livelihoods worldwide. Outbreaks of diseases since the mid-1990s, such as avian influenza, swine fever, bovine spongiform encephalopathy (BSE) and others, have led to many deaths and have cost the economy $80 billion worldwide (Karesh et al. 2005). The *boomerang effect* breaks the pattern of class and national society. The rich and powerful parts of society are also not safe from the ecological (and economic) consequences of the risk society (Beck 1992).

2.4 Nature is Society and Society is Nature

The degradation of natural and ecological resources changes the relationship between nature and society. The destruction of nature has become a part of the social, political and economic dynamics. Giddens explained that ecological degradation derives from the lifestyle patterns being followed in the modernized sectors of the world society. He highlights the interconnection between personal activities and planetary environmental problems (Giddens 1991). Contrary to the perspective of the classical industrial society based on the contrast between nature and society, nature is integrated by culture in the (industrial) risk society. According to Beck (1992) at the end of the twentieth century, nature is society and society is 'nature'.

The central consequence of technological innovation and industrialisation is that in advanced modernity, society with all its subsystems of the economy, politics, culture and the family can no longer be understood as being autonomous of nature. In his article 'Biology and social theory in the environmental debate' (1994) Benton underlined that the dualist strategy of thinking about nature and society as distinct realms insist that society plays an independent role. However, environmental problems are not just problems affecting our surroundings, but—in their origins and through their consequences—are thoroughly social problems, problems of people, their history, their living conditions, their relation to the world and reality, their social, cultural and political situations (Giddens 1991; Beck 1992).

Higgins (2010, 2012) discussed the impact of *ecocide* by referring to anthropogenic environmental degradation. She explains that ecocide is "the extensive damage to, destruction of or loss of ecosystem(s) of a given territory, whether by human agency or by other causes, to such an extent that peaceful enjoyment by the inhabitants of that territory has been severely diminished" (Higgins 2012: 3). The extensive wildlife trade could be defined as a driver of the process of ecocide. She underlines that at certain points in history the world had to change. Each time, humanity would reach a tipping point; after the abolition of slavery, the outlawed apartheid system and criminalized genocide, it would be time for the next stage: to consider *ecocide* as a fifth International Crime Against Peace (Higgins 2010; 2012).[4]

Indeed, the exploitation of natural resources has become a social problem and thus needs to be anticipated in social and scientific thinking (Beck 1992). How can we reduce the risks of a decline in biodiversity and how can we trade sustainably or find alternatives for natural resources? Ecological risks and uncertainties require constant self-reflection. This reflexive modernity can be defined as the process of self-management and self-determination on the basis of continuous detection and a reflection of all types of social information, in this case in the area of the environment (Giddens et al. 1994). Beck speaks of 'organized irresponsibility' in dealing with the environment. Governments are working closely with industry, employers and workers' organizations and the major political parties, each defending their own motives to the core of the social and economic structure. The economic interests that underlie the wildlife trade trump the damage caused by the trade in wildlife (Beck 1992; Hajer and Schwarz 1996). These economic interests have obstructed the criminalization process for a long time as described in the next chapter. Nevertheless, some initiatives by moral entrepreneurs to protect wildlife species have led to the start of the criminalization of the wildlife trade by means of laws and regulations. However, the process of the criminalization of the wildlife trade is not a process of mere registration, regulation and the drafting of laws, but has to be understood as part of the socioeconomic context of European colonialism in Africa and Asia.

References

Anderson, S. H., Kelly, D., Ladley, J. J., Molloy, S., & Terry, J. (2011). Cascading effects of bird functional extinction reduce pollination and plant density. *Science, 331*(6020), 1068–1071.

Balick, M. J., Elisabetsky, E., & Laird, S. A. (1996). *Medicinal resources of the tropical forest: Biodiversity and its importance to human health*. New York: Columbia University Press.

Barnosky, A. D., Matzke, N., Tomiya, S., Wogan, G. O., Swartz, B., Quental, T. B., et al. (2011). Has the Earth's sixth mass extinction already arrived? *Nature, 471*(7336), 51–57.

Barrett, J. E., Virginia, R. A., Wall, D. H., & Adams, B. J. (2008). Decline in a dominant invertebrate species contributes to altered carbon cycling in a low-diversity soil ecosystem. *Global Change Biology, 14*(8), 1734–1744.

Beck, U. (1986). *Risikogesellschaft: Auf dem Weg in eine andere Moderne*. Frankfurt am Main: Suhrkamp.

Beck, U. (1992). *Risk society: Towards a new modernity*. London: Sage.

Beck, U. (1999). *World risk society*. Cambridge: Polity Press.

Beck, U. (2006). Living in the world risk society. *Economy and Society, 35*(3), 329–345.

[4]The four international Crimes Against Peace are 'Crimes Against Humanity', 'Genocide', 'War Crimes' and 'Crimes of Aggression'.

Beerling, D. J., & Berner, R. A. (2002). Biogeochemical constraints on the Tr- JT-J boundary carbon cycle event. *Global Biogeochemical Cycles, 16*, 101–113.

Bell, D., Robertson, S., & Hunter, P. R. (2004). Animal origins of SARS coronavirus: Possible links with the international trade in small carnivores. *Philosophical Transactions of the Royal Society B: Biological Sciences, 359*, 1107–1114.

Bennett, E. L., & Robinson, J. G. (2000). *Hunting of wildlife in tropical forests: Implications for biodiversity and forest peoples*. Washington D.C: International Bank for Reconstruction/The World Bank.

Benton, M. J., & Twitchett, R. J. (2003). How to kill (almost) all life: The end-Permian extinction event. *Trends in Ecology & Evolution, 18*(7), 358–365.

Berman, D. S., Reisz, R. R., Martens, T., & Henrici, A. C. (2001). A new species of Dimetrodon (Synapsida: Sphenacodontidae) from the Lower Permian of Germany records first occurrence of genus outside of North America. *Canadian Journal of Earth Sciences, 38*(5), 803–812.

Boekhout van Solinge, T. (2010). Deforestation crimes and conflicts in the Amazon. *Critical Criminology, 18*(4), 263–277.

Boekhout van Solinge, T. (2011). Etnografie en criminologie in het tropisch regenwoud. *Tijdschrift over Cultuur & Criminaliteit, 0*(1), 70–91.

Boekhout van Solinge, T. (2012). Ontbossing en criminologie. *Groene Criminologie, Justitiële verkenningen, 38*(2), 9–28.

Boutellier, H. (2008). Leven met risico's. In T. Dietz, F. den Hertog, H. van der Wusten (2008). *Van natuurlandschap tot risicomaatschappij—De geografie van de relatie tussen mens en milieu*. Amsterdam: University Press.

Brook, S. M., Dudley, N., Mahood, S. P., Polet, G., Williams, A. C., Duckworth, J. W., et al. (2014). Lessons learned from the loss of a flagship: The extinction of the Javan rhinoceros Rhinoceros sondaicus annamiticus from Vietnam. *Biological Conservation, 174*, 21–29.

Brooks-Moizer, F., Roberton, S. I., Edmunds, K., & Bell, D. (2008). Avian influenza H5N1 and the wild bird trade in Hanoi. *Vietnam. Ecology and Society, 14*(1), 28.

Burgos, S., & Burgos, S. A. (2007). Influence of exotic bird and wildlife trade on avian influenza transmission dynamics: Animal-human interface. *International Journal of Poultry Science, 6* (7), 535–538.

Butchart, S. H., Walpole, M., Collen, B., Van Strien, A., Scharlemann, J. P., Almond, R.E., et al. (2010). Global biodiversity: Indicators of recent declines. *Science, 328*(5982), 1164–1168.

Chapman, A. D. (2009). *Numbers of living species in Australia and the world*. Toowoomba: Australian Biodiversity Information Services.

Cloudsley-Thompson, J. L. (2005). The dinosaurs: Weapons, display and reproduction. *Ecology and Behaviour of Mesozoic Reptiles,* 125–147.

Courchamp, F., Angulo, E., Rivalan, P., Hall, R. J., Signoret, L., Bull, L., et al. (2006). Rarity value and species extinction: The anthropogenic allee effect. *PLoS Biology, 4*(12), e415.

De Vis, S. (2006). *De ontbossing van regenwouden, een economische analyse*. Gent: Universiteit Gent.

Dirzo, R., Young, H. S., Galetti, M., Ceballos, G., Isaac, N. J., & Collen, B. (2014). Defaunation in the Anthropocene. *Science, 345*(6195), 401–406.

Douglas, M., & Wildavsky, A. (1982). *Risk and culture: An essay on the selection of technological and environmental dangers*. Berkeley: University of California Press.

EFSA. (2014). *An update on the risk of transmission of ebola virus (EBOV) via the food chain*. Parma: European Food Safety Authority.

EPA. (2009). *Sustainable materials management: The road ahead*. Ohio: EPA.

FAO. (2006). *Deforestation Causes Global Warming*. Rome: FAO.

Gibbs, C., Gore, M. L., McGarrell, E. F., & Rivers, L. (2010). Introducing conservation criminology towards interdisciplinary scholarship on environmental crimes and risks. *British Journal of Criminology, 50*(1), 124–144.

Giddens, A. (1990). *The consequences of modernity*. Cambridge: Polity Press.

Giddens, A. (1991). *Modernity and self-identity: Self and society in the late modern age*. Stanford: Stanford University Press.

Giddens, A., Beck, U., & Lash, S. (1994). *Reflexive modernization. Politics, tradition and aesthetics in the modern social order*. Cambridge: Polity Press.

Grose, C. (2012). Pangaea and the out-of-Africa model of varicella-zoster virus evolution and phylogeography. *Journal of Virology, 86*(18), 9558–9565.

Hajer, M., & Schwarz, M. (1996). Contouren van de risicomaatschappij. In U. Beck (Ed.), *De wereld als risicomaatschappij*. Amsterdam: Uitgeverij de Balie.

Haken, J. (2011). *Transnational crime in the developing world*. Global Financial Integrity.

Hall, R. J., Milner-Gulland, E. J., & Courchamp, F. (2008). Endangering the endangered: The effects of perceived rarity on species exploitation. *Conservation Letters, 1*(2), 75–81.

Hallam, A. (1990). The end-Triassic mass extinction event. *Geological Society of America Special Papers, 247*, 577–583.

Hautmann, M. (2004). Effect of end-Triassic CO_2 maximum on carbonate sedimentation and marine mass extinction. *Facies, 50*(2), 257–261.

Higgins, P. (2010). *Eradicating ecocide: Laws and governance to prevent the destruction of our planet*. London: Shepheard Walwyn Publishers Ltd.

Higgins, P. (2012). *Earth is our business: Changing the rules of the game*. London: Shepheard Walwyn Publishers Ltd.

Hoffmann, M., Hilton-Taylor, C., Angulo, A., Böhm, M., Brooks, T. M., Butchart, S. H., et al. (2010). The impact of conservation on the status of the world's vertebrates. *Science, 330* (6010), 1503–1509.

Hooper, D. U., Adair, E. C., Cardinale, B. J., Byrnes, J. E., Hungate, B. A., Matulich, K. L., et al. (2012). A global synthesis reveals biodiversity loss as a major driver of ecosystem change. *Nature, 486*(7401), 105–108.

Huls, N. J. H. (2009). *Actie en reactie. Een inleiding in de rechtssociologie*. Boom Juridische uitgevers: The Hague.

Huynh, T. T., & Poulsen, C. J. (2005). Rising atmospheric CO_2 as a possible trigger for the end-Triassic mass extinction. *Palaeogeography, Palaeoclimatology, Palaeoecology, 217*(3), 223–242.

IUCN (2014). *Red List version 2014.3*. Gland: IUCN.

Jablonski, D. (1991). Extinctions: A paleontological perspective. *Science, 253*, 754–757.

Karesh, W. B., Cook, R. A., Bennett, E. L., & Newcomb, J. (2005). Wildlife trade and global disease emergence. *Emerging Infectious Diseases, 11*(7), 1000–1002.

Kays, R., Jansen, P. A., Knecht, E. M., Vohwinkel, R., & Wikelski, M. (2011). The effect of feeding time on dispersal of Virola seeds by toucans determined from GPS tracking and accelerometers. *Acta Oecologica, 37*(6), 625–631.

Kellert, S. R., & Wilson, E. O. (1993). *The Biophilia Hypothesis*. Washington, DC: Island Press.

Lau, S. K. P., Woo, P. C. Y., Li, K. S. M., Huang, Y., Tsoi, H., Wong, B. H. L., et al. (2005). Severe acute respiratory syndrome coranavirus-like virus in Chinese horseshoe bats. *Proceedings of the National Academy of Sciences of the United States., 102*, 14040–14045.

Lawson, K., & Vines, A. (2014). *Global impacts of the illegal wildlife trade: The costs of crime, insecurity and institutional erosion*. London: Chatham House.

Leakey, R., & Lewin, R. (1995). *The sixth extinction*. London: Weidenfeld and Nicolson.

Leroy, E. M., Rouquet, P., Formenty, P., Souquiere, S., Kilbourne, A., Froment, J. M., et al. (2004). Multiple Ebola virus transmission events and rapid decline of central African wildlife. *Science, 303*(5656), 387–390.

Lindsey, P. A., Masterson, C. L., Beck, A. L., & Romañach, S. (2012). Ecological, social and financial issues related to fencing as a conservation tool in Africa. In M. J. Somers & M. Hayward (Eds.), *Fencing for Conservation* (pp. 215–234). New York: Springer.

May, R. M., Lawton, J. H., & Stork, N. E. (1995). *Assessing extinction rates. Extinction rates*. Oxford: Oxford University Press.

McGhee, G. R. (1996). *The late devonian mass extinction: The Frasnian/Famennian crisis*. New York: Columbia University Press.

Mensink, A. (2007). *Infectieziekten en veiligheid. Toekomstige uitdagingen voor maatschappij en beleid*. Bilthoven: Rijksinstituut voor Volksgezondheid en Milieu.

Millennium Ecosystem Assessment. (2005). *Ecosystems and human well-being: Synthesis*. Washington, D.C.: Island Press.

Mills, L. S., Soulé, M. E., & Doak, D. F. (1993). The keystone-species concept in ecology and conservation. *BioScience*, 219–224.

Mooney, H. A., & Hobbs, R. J. (2000). *Invasive species in a changing world*. Washington, D.C.: Island Press.

Mora, C., Tittensor, D. P., Adl, S., Simpson, A. G., & Worm, B. (2011). How many species are there on Earth and in the ocean? *PLoS Biology, 9*(8), e1001127.

Moulton, M. P., & Sanderson, J. (1999). *Wildlife issues in a changing world*. New York: Lewis Publishers.

Myers, N. (1990). Mass extinctions: What can the past tell us about the present and the future? *Palaeogeography, Palaeoclimatology, Palaeoecology, 82*(1), 175–185.

Myers, R. A., Baum, J. K., Shepherd, T. D., Powers, S. P., & Peterson, C. H. (2007). Cascading effects of the loss of apex predatory sharks from a coastal ocean. *Science, 315*(5820), 1846–1850.

Ogada, D. L., Torchin, M. E., Kinnaird, M. F., & Ezenwa, V. O. (2012). Effects of vulture declines on facultative scavengers and potential implications for mammalian disease transmission. *Conservation Biology, 26*, 453–460.

Okigbo, R. N., Eme, U. E., & Ogbogu, S. (2008). Biodiversity and conservation of medicinal and aromatic plants in Africa. *Biotechnology and Molecular Biology Reviews, 3*(6), 127–134.

Oldfield, S. (2003). *The Trade in Wildlife. Regulation for Conservation*. London: Earthscan.

Paine, R. T. (1966). Food web complexity and species diversity. *American Naturalist*, 65–75.

Paine, R. T. (1980). Food web linkage, interaction strength and community infrastructure. *Journal of Animal Ecology, 49*, 667–685.

Passas, N., & Goodwin, N. (2005). *It's legal but it ain't right: Harmful social consequences of legal industries*. Ann Arbor: University of Michigan Press.

Pimm, S. L., Russell, G. J., Gittleman, J. L., & Brooks, T. M. (1995). The future of biodiversity. *Science, 269*(5222), 347–349.

Power, M. E. (1990). Effects of fish in river food webs. *Science, 250*, 811–814.

Power, M. E., Tilman, D., Estes, J. A., Menge, B. A., Bond, W. J., Mills, L. S., et al. (1996). Challenges in the quest for keystones. *BioScience*, 609–620.

Rademaker, P. (2008). Risicosamenleving en duurzaamheid—oxymoron of uitdaging? In T. Dietz, F. den Hertog, & H. van der Wusten (2008). *Van natuurlandschap tot risicomaatschappij—De geografie van de relatie tussen mens en milieu*. Amsterdam: University Press.

Ripple, W. J., & Beschta, R. L. (2006). Linking a cougar decline, trophic cascade, and catastrophic regime shift in Zion National Park. *Biological Conservation, 133*(4), 397–408.

Roe, D., Mulliken, T., Milledge, S., Mremi, J., Mosha, S., & Grieg-Gran, M. (2002). *Making a killing or making a living. Wildlife trade, trade controls and rural livelihoods*. London: IIED, and Cambridge: Traffic.

Roef, D. (2003). Strafrechtelijke verantwoordelijkheid in de risicomaatschappij. In P. L. Bal, E. Prakken, & G. Smaers (Eds.), *Veiligheid of vergelding?* (pp. 33–56). Deventer: Kluwer.

Roosmalen, M. G. M. (2008). *Blootsvoets door de Amazone*. Amsterdam: Uitgeverij Bert Bakker.

Rosen, G. E., & Smith, K. F. (2010). Summarizing the evidence on the international trade in illegal wildlife. *EcoHealth, 7*(1), 24–32.

Sheehan, P. M. (2001). The late Ordovician mass extinction. *Annual Review of Earth and Planetary Sciences, 29*(1), 331–364.

Slade, E. M., Mann, D. J., & Lewis, O. T. (2011). Biodiversity and ecosystem function of tropical forest dung beetles under contrasting logging regimes. *Biological Conservation, 144*(1), 166–174.

Smith, R. D. (2006). Responding to global infectious disease outbreaks: Lessons from SARS on the role of risk perception, communication and management. *Social Science and Medicine, 63*, 3113–3123.

South, N. (2008). Nature, difference and the rejection of harm: Expanding the agenda for green criminology. In R. A. Sollund (Ed.), *Global harms; ecological crime and speciesism*. New York: Nova Science Publishers.

Stephens, P. A., Sutherland, W. J., & Freckleton, R. P. (1999). What is the Allee effect? *Oikos*, 185–190.

Stiles, D., Redmond, I., Cress, D., Nellemann, C., & Formo, R. K. (Eds.). (2013). *Stolen apes—The illicit trade in chimpanzees, gorillas, bonobos and orangutans. A rapid response assessment. United nations environment programme*. Arendal: GRID-Arendal.

Stuart, B. L., Rhodin, A. G., Grismer, L. L., & Hansel, T. (2006). Scientific description can imperil species. *Science, 312*, 1137–1139.

Tanner, L. H., Lucas, S. G., & Chapman, M. G. (2004). Assessing the record and causes of Late Triassic extinctions. *Earth-Science Reviews, 65*(1), 103–139.

Terborgh, J. (1993). *Lebensraum Regenwald - Zentrum biologischer Vielfalt*. Heidelberg: Spektrum Akademischer Verlag.

Terborgh, J., & Estes, J. A. (Eds.). (2013). *Trophic cascades: Predators, prey, and the changing dynamics of nature*. Washington, DC: Island Press.

Terborgh, J., Lopez, L., Nunez, P., Rao, M., Shahabuddin, G., Orihuela, G., et al. (2001). Ecological meltdown in predator-free forest fragments. *Science, 294*(5548), 1923–1926.

Thorne, P. M., Ruta, M., & Benton, M. J. (2011). Resetting the evolution of marine reptiles at the Triassic-Jurassic boundary. *Proceedings of the National Academy of Sciences, 108*(20), 8339–8344.

Tudge, C. (2005) *The Tree. A natural history of what trees are, how they live, and why they matter*. New York: Crown Publishers.

United Nations Office on Drugs and Crime. (2010). *The globalization of crime: A transnational organized crime threat assessment*. Vienna: UNODC.

Whiles, M., Hall, R. O., Dodds, W. K., Verburg, P., Huryn, A. D., Pringle, C. M., et al. (2013). Disease-driven amphibian declines alter ecosystem processes in a tropical stream. *Ecosystems, 16*, 146–157.

WHO. (2015). *Ebola situation report*. Washington, D.C.: WHO.

Williams, N. (2007). Force feeding. *Current Biology, 17*(1), R3.

Wilson, E.O. (1993). Biophilia and the conservation ethic. In S. R. Kellert & E. O. Wilson (Eds.), *The biophilia hypothesis*. Washington, DC: Island Press.

Wilson, E. O. (2002). *The future of life*. New York: Vintage Books.

Wolfe, N., Escalante, A., Karesh, W., Kilbourn, A., Spielman, A., & Lal, A. (1998). Wild primate populations in emerging infectious disease research: The missing link? *Emerging Infectious Diseases, 4*(2), 148–159.

World Bank (2005). *Going, going, gone ...The illegal trade in wildlife in East and Southeast Asia*. Washington, DC: The World Bank.

World Bank. (2008). *What's driving the wildlife trade? A review of expert opinion on economic and social drivers of the wildlife trade and trade control efforts in Cambodia, Indonesia, Lao PDR, and Vietnam*. Washington, DC: The World Bank.

Worldwatch Institute. (2006). *Vital signs 2006–2007*. Washington, DC: Worldwatch Institute.

Worster, D. (1988). *The ends of the Earth: Perspectives on modern environmental history*. Cambridge: Cambridge University Press.

Wright, J. P., Jones, C. G., & Flecker, A. S. (2002). An ecosystem engineer, the beaver, increases species richness at the landscape scale. *Oecologia, 132*(1), 96–101.

Yee, K. S., Carpenter, T. E., & Cardona, C. J. (2009). Epidemiology of H5N1 avian influenza. *Comp Immunol Microbiol Infect Dis* Jul, *32*(4), 325–340.

Zimmerman, M. E. (2003). The black market for wildlife: Combating transnational organized crime in the illegal wildlife trade. *Vanderbilt Journal of Transnational Law, 36*(5), 1657–1690.

Zommers, Z., & Macdonald, D. W. (2006). *T12: The wildlife trade and global disease emergence. In foresight. infectious diseases: Preparing for the future*. London: Office of Science and Innovation.

Chapter 3
Imperialism and Criminalization

In the twentieth century, the damage from unregulated trade became transparent as many species became extinct or were on the brink of extinction. Consequently, various moral entrepreneurs emerged to underline the need for regulation. The effect of these initiatives to protect endangered species was divergent. On the one hand, protecting species was regularly faced with the economic and personal interests of powerful stakeholders stagnating any initiatives. On the other hand, European imperialists enhanced the exclusion of local people in order to protect nature reserves and their species. In the late 1900s, public concern increased and international agreements were signed at the initiative of Western countries. While trading in wildlife was always legal, this trade became slowly criminalized during the twentieth century. The process of criminalization is dependent on the definitions given by social dominant groups in society. It can be divided into primary and secondary criminalization. Primary criminalization refers to the establishment of the penal code and secondary criminalization refers to specific acts by stakeholder practices and the role of the mass media (Hulsman 1986). According to Becker (1963) perspectives of crime are broadly influenced by moral entrepreneurs who advocate that certain behaviour should be criminalized. However, who were these moral entrepreneurs? Why did they prefer to preserve species and what were the consequences of their efforts? The legislative development and criminalization of the trade in wildlife in the twentieth and twenty-first centuries will be discussed in its socioeconomic context in order to understand the European interest in species conservation.

3.1 European Interference in Nature Protection

Although the wildlife trade has always existed as described in Chap. 1, during the last century the impact of the trade became more transparent and a conservation ethic began to take shape. One of the first environmental issues to be addressed

D.P. van Uhm, *The Illegal Wildlife Trade*, Studies of Organized Crime 15,
DOI 10.1007/978-3-319-42129-2_3

includes concerns regarding the overexploitation of wildlife species. Humans became aware of the fact that their activities damaged the environment and that it was a civic duty to protect the environment with its species against this exploitation. The extinction of several species in the nineteenth century, including the sudden or near-extinction of certain species, such as the Passenger Pigeon and the North American Bison were widely noted (Harper 1942). Consequently, around 1900 several organizations around the world, including the Sierra Club in North America, the National Trust in the UK and the Dutch Society for the Conservation of Nature Reserves, were developed for the conservation of species and nature. Membership of conservation organizations was limited to hunters and fishermen and a small group of the social elite (Van der Heijden 2004). This small group of the elites with a passion for natural history and hunting, were often influenced by world views concerning the relationship between humans and nature. Natural history was strongly linked to European exploration, trade and expansion in the world to gain power and access to exclusive exotic products as privileged domains of the aristocracy (see also Chap. 1). This is illustrated by the members and the vice-president of the Fauna Preservation Society in London that included the Secretary of State for the Colonies, Colonial Governors and members of the House of Lords (Jepson and Whittaker 2002).

Historically, European imperialism and wildlife conservation are strongly interconnected (e.g. Grove 1995; MacKenzie 1988). MacKenzie argues that wildlife conservation is linked to the history of hunting as a sport in the colonies. By the beginning of the First World War hunting as a sport had become the norm in the colonies (MacKenzie 1988). Especially with European expansion and the advent of the railways, the sport of hunting became extremely popular. During this period the 'values and abilities embodied in hunting' were seen as role models for children (Jepson and Whittaker 2002). Extensive European hunting led to a reduction in exotic animals in the colonies and, consequently, conservation efforts were developed, because it was important to maintain animals for hunting in the colonies by Western elites (MacKenzie 1988). According to Nadelmann prohibition regimes are introduced for various reasons: "to protect the interests of the state and other powerful members of society; to deter, suppress, and punish undesirable activities to provide for order, security, and justice among members of a community; and to give force and symbolic representation to the moral values, beliefs, and prejudices of those who make the laws" (Nadelmann 1990: 480–481). Many regulations and the first game reserves were developed to protect interests and to introduce the moral values of the Western elites. This resulted in several disadvantages for the local people with regard to restrictions on their natural resources and social differentiation with settler communities.

In 1930, the Fauna Preservation Society reported, based on visits to the British colonies in East and Central Africa, that many species in Africa were heading for extinction. Long-term survival would only be possible by the separation of man and nature through national parks and sanctuaries (Jepson and Whittaker 2002). The role of imperialism in conservation remained strong with the replacement of local communities and restrictions on hunting because of the establishment of many

National Parks and Game Reserves (Ranger 1989; Hutton and Dickson 2000). African tribes were not only removed from their land by force when reserves were created, it also became forbidden for local people to hunt their natural resources in the context of racial separation. Meanwhile hunting for sport, leisure and trade by Europeans was legal and accepted. Western European hunting methods would ensure a quick kill without animals having to suffer, while the 'degrading' African hunting methods with snares and traps were defined as cruel and unsporting. Africans were represented as uncivilized, barbaric and greedy poachers (Duffy 2010). From this perspective it was both a form of conservation of wildlife and conservation of the social order (Dickson 2000; Duffy 2000, 2010). Not only was conservation as a social order of great importance for the European settlers, it also played a social and economic role. According to Carruthers (1989) the establishment of the Kruger National Park played a role in connecting Afrikaans and English speakers and the establishment of 'cross-class alliances among the whites' (Dickson 2000: 165). In addition, the development of the national parks would be influenced by the economic successes of the national parks in the US (Carruthers 1989). Currently 950,000 people visit the Kruger National Park in South Africa each year (Saayman and Slabbert 2004).

In this context the first environmental protection agreements and national parks (e.g. the Kruger National Park in 1926) were developed to reduce environmental degradation, but in particular to control overhunting and poaching (Roe et al. 2002). In Europe the London Convention Designed to Ensure the Conservation of Various Species of Wild Animals in Africa Which Are Useful to Man or Inoffensive was signed in 1900.[1] Although this treaty was important for the colonial states of Africa, it never entered into force (Schneider 2012). Another regulation was the London Convention Relative to the Preservation of Fauna and Flora in their Natural State of 1933 for the protection of African fauna and flora that brought together delegates from colonial powers with African territories. These countries, together with the colonies in Africa, committed themselves to protecting endangered species and to regulating the importation of such animals and the products thereof (Fitzgerald 1989; Jepson and Whittaker 2002). Other countries could accede to this convention. In order to import protected animals or products derived thereof, permits were required under the convention. While the convention came into force in 1936, it was not a great success because of the lack of supervision. Poaching and the trade in products such as elephant tusks and skins proved difficult to subdue as a result of the substantial demand from Europe and North America. Four years later, in 1940, the Washington Convention on Nature Protection and Wildlife Preservation in the Western Hemisphere was established. This convention intended to control the trade

[1]One of the most famous US laws regarding the protection of wildlife is the US Lacey Act dating from 1900, originally focussing on the conservation of wild birds, due to the large domestic trade in feathers for the fashion industry. The domestic trade in native species was restricted and the importation of certain wildlife products was protected by foreign laws and banned. Similar legislation was enacted at the same time in other countries such as Australia (1913) and Canada (1914) (Roe et al. 2002).

in endangered species by creating a licensing system. This convention reflects the modern regulations that followed (Schneider 2012).

While international efforts to reduce the trade in endangered species were obstructed for a long time by strong economic and industrial interests, the motivation changed into enhanced environmental and ecological concerns in the second part of the twentieth century (Nadelmann 1990). On 5 October 1948, 18 governments, 7 international organizations and 107 national conservation organizations came together to create the first global environmental network, called the International Union for Conservation of Nature (IUCN). Its major goal is to protect nature from harmful interventions by human activities (Christoffersen 1994). Public awareness seriously increased in the 1960s and 1970s due to the international wave of environmental protest movements. These were strengthened by authoritative groups (e.g. the Club of Rome) that warned against the impact that economic growth would have on the environment. Apparently, there was a growing concern within the international community about the rate of species extinction (Jenkins 2000). As a result of the increasing attention to declining wildlife in the 1960s and 1970s the IUCN adopted a resolution (Van Male 2003). This resolution led to the agreements entered into force in 1973 between eighty countries on the trade in endangered animal and plant species. This multilateral treaty is the "Convention on International Trade in Endangered Species of Wild Fauna and Flora" (CITES).

3.2 The International Convention

CITES is the governing international legal framework that regulates the trade in wild animals and plants through CITES permits. In 1975, CITES entered into force (Inskipp and Wells 1981). It should be noted that the emergence of CITES was an initiative by the Northern countries, while developing countries hardly realized what was going on (Van Spaandonk 2000). According to Dickson (2003) the convention was developed with little attention being paid to background problems in poor source countries to maintain their natural resources.[2] While several authors see this development as a continuation of the colonial approach to conservation in a post-colonial world of the white man's burden, the notion slowly changed into the idea of conservation for all humans (Dickson 2000).

Currently, 182 countries participate in the convention and have committed themselves to adhering to the rules laid down in the convention. Each country assigns a Management Authority to manage the permit system and a Scientific Authority to identify and administer biological aspects of the convention. The Management Authority is the responsible agency for the implementation of CITES and the issuing of all permits. The Management Authority must report to the CITES

[2]The convention focussed on endangered species instead of background problems in developing countries.

Table 3.1 Numbers of species listed in the Appendices of CITES

	Appendix I	Appendix II	Appendix III
Fauna			
Mammals	300 spp. (incl. 11 popns) + 23 sspp. (incl. 3 popns)	501 spp. (incl. 16 popns) + 7 sspp. (incl. 2 popns)	45 spp. + 10 sspp.
Birds	154 spp. (incl. 2 popns) + 10 sspp.	1278 spp. (incl. 1 popn) + 3 sspp.	25 spp.
Reptiles	80 spp. (incl. 8 popns) + 5 sspp.	673 spp. (incl. 6 popns)	40 spp.
Amphibians	17 spp.	126 spp.	3 spp.
Fish	16 spp.	87 spp.	–
Invertebrates	63 spp. + 5 sspp.	2162 spp. + 1 sspp.	22 spp. + 3 sspp.
Fauna total	**630 spp. + 43 sspp.**	**4827 spp. + 11 sspp.**	**135 spp. + 13 sspp.**
Flora	301 spp. + 4 sspp.	29592 spp. (incl. 162 popns).	12 spp. (incl. 2 popns) + 1 var.
Grand total	**931 spp. + 47 sspp.**	**34419 spp. + 11 sspp.**	**147 spp. + 13 sspp. + 1 var.**

*Explanation of abbreviations: spp.= species; sspp.= subspecies; var. = variety; popn = population
Source 'The CITES species', CITES website, 2013

secretariat and it provides stamps and certificates upon request. Member states are also allowed to develop stricter legislation in their country if they so wish (Van Spaandonk 2000).

The aim of CITES is to ensure that the international trade in wild animals and plants is not a threat to the conservation of species in the wild. CITES regulates the trade in more than 35,000 species, both animals and plants (Table 3.1).

The species covered by CITES are listed in three Appendices:

- CITES Appendix I species are seriously threatened with extinction.[3] The commercial trade in species derived from the wild is therefore strictly forbidden.[4] The trade in captive-bred CITES I animals or plants or parts or products thereof is permitted, subject to compliance with specific conditions.[5] To import CITES I species an import and export or re-export certificate is required.[6] For the inclusion or deletion of a CITES I species a two-thirds majority of CITES states is mandatory.[7]
- CITES Appendix II species are not directly threatened with extinction but consist of vulnerable populations. It is assumed that if the trade is not regulated,

[3]Article II.1, CITES.
[4]Article III.3.c, CITES.
[5]Articles VII.4 and VII.5, CITES.
[6]Article III.3, CITES.
[7]Article XV.1.b, CITES.

these species may become threatened with extinction in the near future.[8] The trade in these animals is permitted if an export permit or re-export certificate is issued.[9] No import permit is required. For the inclusion or deletion of a CITES II species a two-thirds majority of CITES states is mandatory.[10]

- CITES Appendix III includes species where the country of origin will offer protection.[11] Therefore, the trade therein is subject to special procedures and the international trade in CITES III species is only permitted with the appropriate permits or certificates.[12]

Basically, CITES I species[13] are only allowed to be traded in exceptional circumstances. The vast majority of protected species (±34,000) are listed in Appendix II.[14] These are not necessarily threatened with extinction, but are vulnerable and controlled in order to avoid utilization which is incompatible with their survival. International trade may be authorized by the granting of an export permit or re-export certificate. The appropriate Scientific Authority in the country of origin has to determine that trade will not be detrimental to the survival of the species and can establish quotas limiting the amount of trade (ibid.). Appendix II species include 'look-alike' species as well in order to make them easier to control; they are species whose traded specimens resemble those of species listed for conservation reasons (European Commission 2010). However, due to the fact that Appendix II species can be traded without an import permit, it is difficult to identify the legality of the trade by the Management Authority. Appendix III species[15] are protected in at least one country, which has asked other CITES Parties for assistance in controlling the trade and to prevent unsustainable or illegal exploitation. The international trade in Appendix III specimens is permitted only with the appropriate permits or certificates (European Commission 2010).

As shown in Table 3.1, the scope of CITES is very diverse; from live animals and plants to a multitude of products derived thereof (e.g. food products, exotic leather goods and medicines). Every 10 years, species from different Appendices are reviewed as to whether the species in the lists are still justified and every 2½ years CITES members come together at the Conference of Parties (CoP) to make proposals to add new species. These meetings are also attended by, in addition to the CITES Parties, representatives of non-governmental organizations, the private sector and research institutions.

Generally, CITES only protects species that are (possibly) threatened with extinction. This entails that many animal and plant species are not protected by

[8]Article II.2.a, CITES.

[9]Article IV.4, CITES.

[10]Article XV.1.b, CITES.

[11]Article II.3, CITES.

[12]Article V.3, CITES.

[13]CITES Appendix I included 630 animal species and 43 animal subspecies in 2013.

[14]CITES Appendix II included 4,827 animal species and 11 animal subspecies in 2013.

[15]CITES Appendix III included 135 animal species and 13 animal subspecies in 2013.

CITES and can be legally traded without the need for paperwork or permits (Wyatt 2013). It may be that a subspecies or population in a given area is included in one of the appendices only if a corresponding population is threatened with extinction in a specific area. If in the appendix such a case is listed, the population and the specified area are mentioned.

3.3 EU Wildlife Trade Regulations

The European Union implemented the CITES multilateral treaty in 1984 by joint regulations, which applied in all EU countries, including the countries which were not yet CITES Parties at that time. In order to take these changes into account and to fulfil the CITES conditions, new regulations from the European Commission (EC) came into force. The implementation of CITES through EU regulations is known as the EU Wildlife Trade Regulations. These regulations consist of the following EC regulation of the trade in wild animals and plants:

- Council Regulation (EC) No. 338/97 on the protection of species of wild fauna and flora by regulating trade therein (*the Basic Regulation*)
- Commission Regulation (EC) No. 865/2006[16] laying down detailed rules concerning the implementation of Council Regulation (EC) No. 338/97 (*the Implementing Regulation*)
- Commission Implementing Regulation (EU) No. 792/2012 laying down rules for the design of permits, certificates and other documents provided for in Council Regulation (EC) No. 338/97 and Commission Regulation (EC) No. 865/2006 (*the Permit Regulation*).

These regulations ensure the implementation of CITES across the EU and deal with wildlife imports and exports to and from, and within the EU. The regulations describe what are endangered plants and animals and what documents are thereby required for this trade (European Commission 2010). The EC regulations on the trade in protected animal and plant species is directly applicable in all EU Member States and is the legal basis for the implementation of CITES in the EU (Nurse 2015).

The provisions in the EU Wildlife Trade Regulations differ in a number of respects in comparison to the CITES regulation. First, Council Regulation (EC) No. 338/97 regulates the import, export and re-export provisions. It has four Annexes (A–D) which contain non-CITES species as well (Table 3.2).

Second, there are stricter import conditions for species in Annexes A and B than under CITES. An important difference is that an import licence is required for CITES Appendix II species to the EU. Some Appendix II species are listed in

[16]As amended by Commission Regulation (EC) No. 100/2008, Commission Regulation (EU) No. 791/2012 and Commission Implementing Regulation (EU) No. 792/2012.

Table 3.2 Annexes to Regulation (EC) No. 338/97

Annex	Includes
Annex A	• All CITES Appendix I species • Some CITES Appendix II and III species, for which the EU has adopted stricter domestic measures • Some non-CITES species
Annex B	• All other CITES Appendix II species • Some CITES Appendix III species • Some non-CITES species
Annex C	• All other CITES Appendix III species
Annex D	• Some CITES Appendix III species for which the EU holds a reservation • Some non-CITES species

Source Council Regulation (EC) No. 338/97

Annex A and cannot be traded or used for commercial purposes. Furthermore, Annex A and B species are only allowed to be imported into the EU if the recipient is suitably equipped to house and care for the specimens. Finally, Regulation (EC) No. 338/97 provides that the Commission has to establish import restrictions for certain species/countries, even if trade is allowed under CITES.

Because the purpose of CITES and the EU wildlife trade regulations is the conservation of wild species, CITES I species that were born and bred in captivity or were artificially propagated are considered as CITES II species. Concerning EU regulation, captive-bred Annex A species are treated as specimens of species listed in Annex B (European Commission 2010).

Internal EU trade, trade between individual EU Member States, and trade within one EU Member State can take place freely with one single market in the EU without internal border controls. No permits or certificates are compulsory for the internal trade in Annex B, C or D species within the EU and Annex A species that may not, as described above, be commercially used (European Commission 2010). Certain countries require, in addition to CITES-listed animals, permits for exporting all wildlife (De Klemm and Shine 1993).

Criminal sanctions in (the implementation of) CITES is not explicitly present as there are no articles with criminal provisions within the regulation framework; this is dependent on the implementation of CITES through national law (Nurse 2015).[17] If countries sign CITES, they agree to enact the necessary legislation. However, not all Member countries choose a criminal penalty, but may implement civil or administrative sanctions to enforce CITES (Wyatt 2013). Consequently, the sanctions for the illegal trade in wildlife depend on the national law of the Member States within the EU. Table 3.3 provides an overview of measures regarding the enforcement of CITES in the EU Member States. Clearly sanctions vary considerably between EU Member States.

[17]Article 16 Regulation (EC) No. 338/97.

Table 3.3 Overview of measures regarding enforcement of CITES in the EU

Member State	Max. prison sentence	Max. fines in EUR for private persons (fine for legal entities in brackets)
Austria	2 years	1,800,000 (180 daily units)
Belgium	5 years	300,000
Bulgaria	5 years	10,000
Croatia	5 years	13,160 (131,580)
Cyprus	3 years	1,700
Czech Republic	8 years	58,700
Denmark	1 year	Variable
Estonia	5 years	65,000
France	7 years	150,000
Finland	2 years	240 day fines (850,000)
Germany	5 years	1,800,000 (1,000,000)
Greece	10 years	500,000
Hungary	3 years	332 (per specimen)
Ireland	2 years	100,000
Italy	1 year	103,000
Latvia	2 years	28,457 (28,457,000)
Lithuania	4 years	37,650 (1,882,530)
Luxembourg	6 months	25,000
Malta	2 years	4,659 (not specified)
Netherlands	6 years	78,000 (780,000)
Poland	5 years	175,000 (1,250,000)
Portugal	–	2,494 (29,928)
Romania	3 years	3,570 (23,800)
Slovakia	8 years	331,930 (99,582)
Slovenia	3 years	20,856 (125,000)
Spain	5 years	Unlimited
Sweden	4 years	Variable (1,000,000)
UK	5 years	Unlimited

Source Traffic (2014)

3.4 The Effect of Regulation

CITES, as the main multilateral treaty regulating the international trade in wildlife, is seen as the most important instrument for the regulation of the trade in wildlife. While "its aim is to ensure that international trade in specimens of wild animals and plants does not threaten their survival" (Dickson 2003: 24), there is little empirical evidence that trade measures will work whenever a wild species is threatened by trade. According to Dickson (2003) in some cases it could be effective, while in others alternative measures have to be implemented. For instance, the effect of trade bans is debatable (Duffy 2010; Swan and Conrad 2014). According to Hutton and

Dickson (2000) part of the weakness of CITES is that it was not always successful in enforcing its bans on CITES I species and it is often unable to regulate the trade in CITES II species successfully. Jenkins (2000) proclaims that in practice the condition that the CITES II species will not be detrimental to the survival of that species is often violated and,[18] as a consequence, such species have become more endangered, resulting in this species being elevated in CITES (from CITES II to I).

Another limitation of CITES is that it remains a trade agreement that regulates the trade in endangered species. Its purpose is not to ban trade but to regulate the possibilities which are available in the trade in endangered species. Consequently, it has been noticed by Wyatt (2009) that CITES gives little consideration to animal welfare as the focus is on trade. According to Sollund (2011) CITES is designed to maintain trade in wildlife and, therefore, the continued consumption of wildlife. Species' rights or animal welfare issues are not touched upon.

Even more so, the regulation with three Appendices seems to confuse law enforcement and provides opportunities for fraud; CITES Appendix I species are traded as Appendix II species. This may be difficult to detect, as Appendix species may look like non-CITES species, such as elephant ivory (Appendix I), walrus ivory (Appendix II) and mammoth ivory (unprotected). Another example would be the physical difference between a protected and unprotected turtle that may be just a dot on the cheek of the animal (Van Uhm 2012a). According to Hutton and Dickson (2000) in order to avoid these practical bottlenecks, all species of international concern could be included in one Appendix, instead of three different Appendices. According to Dickson a quota for the trade in each species could be issued based on (scientific) research and the registration and identification of individual live animals by means of a chip could reduce the opportunities to 'launder' wildlife.

Another improvement could be to focus on the relationship between CITES and the Convention on Biological Diversity (CBD). While CITES and the CBD aim at the conservation of wild species, the CBD acknowledges a wide range of threats to conservation (e.g. habitat destruction; pollution; climate change), while CITES focuses on a certain aspect: trade (Nurse 2015). A substantial advantage would be the recognition of a social, economic and political context to approach the main goal of conservation (Martin 2000a). According to Cooney (2001) in terms of conservation, the international trade in wildlife is not an isolated problem. "Effective tackling of unsustainable international trade mandates addressing problems of national management of wild species, economic incentives for conservation and sustainable use, and national protection of species from exploitation—all policy areas within the ambit of the CBD" (Cooney 2001: 266). From this perspective, connecting these conventions may lead to better enforcement and regulation (Martin 2000b).

Furthermore, the effectiveness of CITES depends on the Parties that implement its decisions (Martin 2000a; Reeve 2014). According to Martin (2000a: 31–32) CITES suits Parties with strong centralized and efficiently managed wildlife control,

---

[18]Article IV.2, CITES.

where this control is socially accepted. This will be a different situation where wildlife control is not centralized and not socially accepted or where there is weak and inefficient state bureaucracy. Reeve (2014) states that the success of CITES completely depends on the political will of range and consumer states.

Although there are specific criteria for the inclusion of species in the CITES appendices, during this process other factors may also play a role. There is generally a greater focus on mammals and visible species, which include, for example, monkeys or birds instead of insects and unknown species. Furthermore, there may also be political, cultural and emotional considerations (Nadelmann 1990). For instance, the Netherlands tried to get *Merbau* and *Ramin* timber on the CITES II list in 1992. Many developing countries voted against the proposal, with the main argument being the colonial position of the Netherlands (Bastmeijer and Van Kreveld 2008). According to many scholars (e.g. MacKenzie 1988; Wu and Wen 2015) CITES has largely been developed by conservationists from the North, while Southern developing countries see the preservationist approach as a legacy of the colonial period and they suggest that a successful conservation plan must provide benefits for local people in source areas (Hutton and Dickson 2000). Wu and Wen (2015) consider the implementation of CITES as somewhat paternalistic, because it was implemented without concerns about local communities who depend on wildlife for their livelihood.

While there is discrepancy within the EU between the capacity and political will of different Parties to protect species, the effectiveness of CITES is only applicable to international cross-border movements of wildlife; CITES regulates wildlife that commercially enters *international* trade. Internal trade in wildlife within the EU is generally freely available, due to the establishment of one market in the EU whereby no permits or certificates are required for species listed in Annex B, C or D of the EU Wildlife Trade Regulations. Consequently, an attractive market emerged in which priorities in the area of enforcement differ between Member states, cooperation between enforcement is limited and control is difficult due to the internal EU market. Although, theoretically, the EU regulations seem to be stricter for exports or imports into the EU, trade within the EU seems to be, practically speaking, less strict. This makes the EU easily accessible to member states without strict control or low penalties in relation to the illegal trade in wildlife.

3.5 The Further Process of Criminalization

Despite the limitations of laws and regulation, the criminalization of the trade in wildlife is continuous, as demonstrated by other underlying processes presented in this section. Before certain harmful activities are defined as crimes a long process may have been necessary. In the first stage, the targeted activity is regarded as entirely legitimate, whereby states are often the principal protagonists and are aiders and abettors of the activity. For a long period of time the trade in wildlife was perfectly legal. As described in this chapter, the first regulations regarding wildlife trafficking were established in the early twentieth century.

During the second stage, the targeted activity is redefined as a problem by moral entrepreneurs (Nadelmann 1990). The process of the criminalization of the trade in wildlife is traditionally driven by global attention by Western moral entrepreneurs with a dominating influence by environmental organizations (Duffy 2000, 2010). Environmental non-governmental organizations (NGOs) emphasize the rational drivers behind the wildlife trade, such as low probability, low penalties and high profits, or the emotional aspects, such as the harm to animals during poaching, transport or at the final destination (e.g. RSPCA 2004; WWF 2013). The influence of NGOs on the criminalization process is also illustrated by NGOs that financially support and cooperate with law enforcement. In May 2013, for instance, a Memorandum of Understanding was signed by the IFAW (International Fund for Animal Welfare) and Interpol regarding their 10-year relationship.[19]

During the third stage of the criminalization, regime proponents start to agitate actively for the suppression and criminalization of the targeted activity. Usually the regime proponents include government officials (Nadelmann 1990). In addition to the intensified lobbying by several NGOs, prominent persons of a certain status have also contributed to the process of criminalization in the recent years. For instance, Hillary Clinton hosted an event entitled 'Wildlife Trafficking and Conservation: A Call to Action' at the US Department of State on November 8, 2012. During her speech, she proclaims that: "[O]ver the past few years wildlife trafficking has become more organized, more lucrative, more widespread, and more dangerous than ever before. (…) Trafficking relies on porous borders, corrupt officials, and strong networks of organized crime, all of which undermine our mutual security".[20] In 2013, Barack Obama signed the 'Wildlife Trafficking Executive Order' to combat wildlife trafficking. He referred to an escalating international crisis: "The poaching of protected species and the illegal trade in wildlife and their derivative parts and products (…) represent an international crisis that continues to escalate. Poaching operations have expanded beyond small-scale, opportunistic actions to coordinated slaughter commissioned by armed and organized criminal syndicates".[21] The agitation from these officials takes many forms, from diplomatic pressure to propaganda campaigns.

The mass media strengthened the claims by including headlines such as 'Wildlife crime ranks among trafficking in drugs, arms and humans',[22] 'Organised crime sets

---

[19]Note that the independence of the police can thereby be compromised.

[20]US Department of State, 'Remarks at the Partnership Meeting on Wildlife Trafficking', November 8, 2012.

[21]The White House Office of the Press Secretary, 'Executive Order—Combating Wildlife Trafficking', July 1, 2013.

[22]The Guardian, 'Wildlife crime ranks among trafficking in drugs, arms and humans', September 26, 2013.

sights on wildlife'[23] and '$213 billion illegal wildlife and charcoal trade 'funding global terror groups'.[24] Traditionally, the mass media have played a substantial role in the process of criminalization (Brants 2013; Brisman and South 2013, 2014). According to Ferrell et al. (2008: 71) the emotions engendered by media images and collective representations of crime affect individual and collective behaviour. The role of the media is illustrated by the presentation of images of environmental disasters or non-human victims of the wildlife trade (Benton 1998). Such attention may lead to 'moral panic' caused by the aggravating factors of the media, politics and the public (Cohen 1972).

In stage four, the targeted activity becomes the subject of criminal law, and laws and regulations are modified or become stricter. In this context international institutions and conventions start to play prominent roles (Nadelmann 1990). This is illustrated by the agreement of the UN Commission on Crime Prevention and Criminal Justice in April 2013 that illegal wildlife trade should be treated as a 'serious crime' (Article 2b), an offence punishable by a maximum deprivation of liberty of at least 4 years or a more serious penalty. UN countries are encouraged to ensure that they adapt their sentences so that a custodial sentence of 4 years or more can be imposed in the context of the illegal trade in wildlife.[25] This means that the trade in wildlife is transformed into a criminalized industry that is defined as a 'serious crime' in a relatively short period of time. Moreover, it has become a global surrounding problem in the context of side-effects and the involvement of criminal organizations and thus needs to be addressed and studied by criminologists. In the next chapter, criminology's limited attention to environmental issues will be discussed and criminological explanatory models will be introduced to explain and describe the actors, organization and harm of the wildlife trade.

References

Bastmeijer, C. J. & van Kreveld, A. R. (2008). *Kennisdocument soortenbescherming. Strafrechtelijkebescherming van inheemse en uitheemse dier- en plantensoorten in Nederland.* Nijmegen: Wolf Legal Publishers.

Becker, H. S. (1963). *Outsiders: Studies in the sociology of deviance*. New York: The Free Press.

Benton, T. (1998). Rights and justice on a shared planet: More rights or new relations? *Theoretical Criminology, 2*(2), 149–175.

Brants, C. (2013). De sociale constructive van criminaliteit. In M. Boone & C. Brants (Eds.), *Criminologie en strafrecht*. The Hague: Boom Lemma uitgevers.

Brisman, A., & South, N. (2013). A green-cultural criminology: An exploratory outline. *Crime, Media, Culture, 9*(2), 115–135.

[23]BBC, 'Organised crime sets sights on wildlife', February 12, 2014.

[24]The Guardian, '$213 billion illegal wildlife and charcoal trade 'funding global terror groups', June 24, 2014.

[25]CITES, 'CITES Secretary-General welcomes adoption of UN Commission on Crime Prevention and Criminal Justice draft resolution recognizing wildlife crime as a serious crime', April 26, 2013.

Brisman, A., & South, N. (2014). *Green cultural criminology: Constructions of environmental harm, consumerism, and resistance to ecocide*. New York: Routledge.

Carruthers, J. (1989). Creating a National Park, 1910–1926. *Journal of Southern African Studies, 15*(2), 188–217.

Christoffersen, L. E. (1994). IUCN: A bridge-builder for nature conservation. *Green Globe Year Book, 1997*, 59–70.

Cohen, S. (1972). *Folk devils and moral panics: The creation of the mods and rockers*. London: MacGibbon & Kee Publishers.

Commission, European. (2010). *Wildlife trade regulations in the European Union: An introduction to CITES and its Implementation in the European Union*. Luxembourg: Publications Office of the European Union.

Cooney, R. (2001). CITES and the CBD: Tensions and synergies. *RECIEL, 10*(3).

De Klemm, C., & Shine, C. (1993). *Biological diversity conservation and the law: Legal mechanisms for conserving species and ecosystems (No. 29)*. Gland: IUCN.

Dickson, B. (2000). Global regulation and communal management. In Endangered Species (Ed.), *Threatened convention: The past, present and future of CITES, the convention on international trade in endangered species of Wild Fauna and Flora*. London: Earthscan.

Dickson, B. (2003). What is the goal of regulating wildlife trade? Is regulation a good way to achieve this goal? In: Oldfiels, S. (Eds.), *The trade in wildlife. Regulation for conservation*. London: Earthscan Publications.

Duffy, R. (2000). *Killing for conservation: Wildlife policy in Zimbabwe*. Oxford: James Currey Ltd.

Duffy, R. (2010). *Nature crime: How We're getting conservation wrong*. New Haven: Yale University Press.

Ferrell, J., Hayward, K., & Young, J. (2008). *Cultural criminology: An invitation*. London: Sage.

Fitzgerald, S. (1989). *International wildlife trade: Who's business is it?* Washington: World Wildlife Fund.

Grove, R. (1995). *Green imperialism*. Cambridge: Cambridge University Press.

Harper, F. (1942). *Extinct and vanishing mammals of the old world*. New York: American Committee for International Wildlife Protection.

Hulsman, L. H. (1986). Critical criminology and the concept of crime. *Crime, Law and Social Change, 10*(1), 63–80.

Hutton, J., & Dickson, B. (Eds.). (2000). *Endangered species, threatened convention: The past, present, and future of CITES, the convention on international trade in endangered species of Wild Fauna and Flora*. London: Earthscan.

Inskipp, T., & Wells, S. (1981). *Internationale handel in wilde dieren en planten*. Utrecht: Stichting Natuur en Milieu.

Jenkins, R. W. (2000). The significant trade process: Making Appendix II work. In Endangered Species (Ed.), *Threatened convention: The past, present and future of CITES, the convention on international trade in endangered species of Wild Fauna and Flora*. London: Earthscan.

Jepson, P., & Whittaker, R. J. (2002). Histories of protected areas: Internationalisation of conservationist values and their adoption in the Netherlands Indies (Indonesia). *Environment and history, 8*(2), 129–172.

MacKenzie, J. (1988). *The empire of nature*. Manchester: Manchester University Press.

Martin, R. B. (2000a). When CITES works and when it does not. In: Hutton, J. & Dickson, B. (Eds.), *Endangered species threatened convention. the past, present and future of CITES*. London: Earthscan Publications.

Martin, R. B. (2000b). CITES and the CBD. In: Hutton, J. & Dickson, B. (Eds.), *Endangered species threatened convention. The past, present and future of CITES*. London: Earthscan Publications.

Nadelmann, E. A. (1990). Global prohibition regimes: The evolution of norms in international society. *International Organization, 44*(04), 479–526.

Nurse, A. (2015). *Policing wildlife. Perspectives on the enforcement of wildlife legislation*. Basingstoke: Palgrave Macmillan.

Ranger, T. (1989). Whose heritage? The case of Matobo National Park. *Journal of Southern African Studies, 15*(2), 217–249.
Reeve, R. (2014). *Policing international trade in endangered species: The CITES treaty and compliance*. London: Routledge.
Roe, D., Mulliken, T., Milledge, S., Mremi, J., Mosha, S., & Grieg-Gran, M. (2002). *Making a killing or making a living. wildlife trade, trade controls and rural livelihoods*. London: IIED, and Cambridge: Traffic.
RSPCA. (2004). *Handle with care. A look at the exotic animal pet trade*. Horsham: RSPCA.
Saayman, M., & Slabbert, E. (2004). A profile of tourists visiting the Kruger National Park. *Koedoe, 47*(1), 1–8.
Schneider, J. (2012). *Sold into extinction: The global trade in endangered species*. Santa Barbara: Praeger.
Sollund, R. (2011). Expressions of speciesism: The effects of keeping companion animals on animal abuse, animal trafficking and species decline. *Crime, Law and Social Change, 55*(5), 437–451.
Swan, K., & Conrad, K. (2014). The conflict between Chinese cultural and environmental values in wildlife consumption. In *Routledge Handbook of Environment and Society in Asia*. London: Routledge.
Traffic. (2014). *Wildlife trade in the European Union*. Brussels: Traffic Europe.
Van der Heijden, H. A. B. (2004). De milieubeweging in de twintigste eeuw. *Belgisch Tijdschrift voor Nieuwste Geschiedenis, 34*(3), 445–483.
Van Male, B. (2003). *Wild feest: de bestrijding van de handel in bedreigde dier- en plantsoorten is al dertig jaar succesvol dankzij het CITES verdrag., 25*(4), 24–27.
Van Spaandonk, J. A. M. (2000). *Katern CITES. Toelichting op de Overeenkomst inzake de internationale handel in bedreigde in het wild levende dier- en plantensoorten*. Lelystad: Koninklijke Vermande.
Van Uhm, D. P. (2012a). De illegale handel in beschermde diersoorten, *Justitiële Verkenningen* 2 (themanummer Groene Criminologie), 91–100.
Wu, F., & Wen, B. (2015). Nongovernmental organizations and environmental protests. *Routledge Handbook of Environment and Society in Asia.*
WWF. (2013). *Fighting illicit wildlife trafficking: A consultation with Governments*. København: Dalberg.
Wyatt, T. (2009). Exploring the organization of Russia Far East's illegal wildlife trade: Two case studies of the illegal fur and illegal falcon trades. *Global Crime, 10*(1–2), 144–154.
Wyatt, T. (2013). *Wildlife trafficking: A deconstruction of the crime, the victims, and the offenders*. Basingstoke: Palgrave Macmillan.

Chapter 4
Crimes Against Nature

> *A criminology relevant to the [twenty-first century] should have the intellectual breadth and constitutional space to be able to embrace environmental, human and non-human animal rights issues as related projects.*
>
> Nigel South

Since social and professional concerns regarding the environment increased and the impact on humans became clear (Chap. 2), the wildlife trade became slowly criminalized in the past few decades (Chap. 3). While it can be expected that criminologists would study this phenomenon, many criminologists hesitated in discovering this new field for several reasons. In this chapter I will explore the role of criminology in studying crimes against nature and the wildlife trade specifically. I will discuss the limitations of the discipline of criminology and its confined attention to environmental issues. In addition, the role of animals in criminology and relevant criminological concepts are looked at in order to establish a theoretical framework in which actors and crime networks in the wildlife trade chain can be approached. At the end of this chapter the emergence of green criminology will be described including new perspectives on crimes and harms.

4.1 Criminology and Green Crimes

Many scientists warn that the extinction rate of species is higher than ever before and that humankind is principally responsible for the reduction of Earth's resources. As described in Chap. 2, species disappear, ecosystems collapse and the consequences for the world are incalculable, i.e. these environmental problems and conditions are not restricted to one society but have become a worldwide environmental issue with global consequences. Simultaneously, there is increasing social and professional concern about environmental issues under the influence of growing media attention (White 2008). The following question arises: what does criminology have to do with these comprehensive global environmental problems?

D.P. van Uhm, *The Illegal Wildlife Trade*, Studies of Organized Crime 15,
DOI 10.1007/978-3-319-42129-2_4

Traditionally, the central focus of the discipline of criminology is the history of the study of ordinary forms of street crimes and the response thereto. For instance, some major forms of crime that are extensively studied by criminologists from all over the world are robbery and burglary. These crimes involve the shifting of a *possession* of a person (the owner) to another person (the thief), so-called property crime. We perceive it as theft and loss when products unwillingly change ownership, because we have become attached to them (e.g. televisions, computers, mobile phones). Generally, criminologists do not pay attention to environmental problems in society. According to Lynch and Stretesky: "As criminologists we are dissatisfied to be a part of a discipline that has become rather meaningless within the context of the modern world" (Lynch and Stretesky 2014: 2). These authors state that the planet and the natural resources are overexploited and wasted in the context of numerous violations, crimes and unethical practices against the environment, while the discipline of criminology remains focussed on conventional forms of (street-level) crime.

According to White (2011) the consequences of conventional forms of crime offences (e.g. property crime) for the world seem to be relatively limited in the context of the transcending global environmental destruction. However, the attention devoted by the discipline of criminology to these environmental violations, crimes and unethical practices is low: out of 1,000 crime publications only three environmentally related research publications are published in the discipline of criminology (Lynch and Stretesky 2014). Apparently, criminology not only neglects the study of widespread serious crimes and harms against nature, but also fails to take green crimes seriously and leaves research to other disciplines (e.g. conservation biology and ecology). Why do the majority of criminologists fail to address these global environmental problems, while the concerns are so obviously widespread?

An important limitation of criminology is the central focus on crime and law-breaking behaviour (Walklate 2007). In the discipline of criminology law and, in particular, criminal law is used as the main reference point (norm) in defining which human behaviour is criminal. Consequently, many harmful activities, such as the global destruction of the environment, are not criminalized and are therefore not studied by criminologists (White 2008; White and Heckenberg 2014). For instance, most natural resources are (over)exploited without any regulation. Criminology is largely dependent on the legal definitions of criminal behaviour defined by law-makers and politicians. Problematic is that most laws change over the course of time. To be more specific, certain behaviour can be perfectly legitimate in one region or period in time, while being illegal in another. For instance, abortion has long been banned but is now permitted in most Western countries or the use of marijuana that is legal in certain countries, while strictly forbidden in others. Crime is a so-called *social construct* that dependents on the time and place in the context of changing norms and morals (Becker 1963). According to Hulsman (1986) crime has no ontological reality; crime is not the object but the product of criminal policy. As crime depends on the social construction, the objectivity of the discipline of criminology is called into question. Lynch and Stretesky (2014: 7) argue that "the scope of criminology is not objective because it fails to address the nature of acts that ought to be treated criminally because of their characteristics. The legal process of socially constructing crime contains subjective dimensions which criminologists, if they adhere to the principles of scientific investigation, ought to reject". Might it be true that criminology develops its discipline on subjective standards that are being constructed by lawmakers who identify certain harms as crimes? Or do criminologists also explore new forms of harmful behaviour? For instance, Sutherland (1940, 1983) defined the concept of *white-collar crime* as illegal or unethical acts that were not previously criminalized, while in subsequent years it came to be adopted in criminal law. From this perspective is it possible that environmental harmful behaviour becomes a new form of crime in the near future.

Environmental problems seem to be constructed by social processes of public attention influenced by consciousness, opinion and the selection of information. This process of social construction depends on objective and subjective components (White 2007; Brisman and South 2014). From a realism perspective (environmental) problems are actually happening and are objective (Matthews and Young 1986), while constructionists believe that (environmental) problems are completely dependent on human perspectives and priorities (Quinney 1970). Currently, it is believed that social problems are constructed by a combination of these perspectives. Objective environmental problems actually exist and are interpreted through cultural factors (e.g. Hannigan 2006). "The problems may be 'real', but the definition, magnitude, impact, risk and origins (…) are open to interpretation and dispute" (White 2007: 33). Indeed, due to the social construction environmental issues are not always addressed or criminalized. In the last few decades social movements and other moral entrepreneurs played important roles in addressing certain environmental problems in society and warranting social attention (Benton 1998). A combination of scientific evidence, media attention and dramatizing environmental problems influenced the social reality. Consequently, criminologists slowly started to study environmental crimes, while many treaties and regulations have been established with regard to the protection of nature in the last decade (Situ and Emmons 1999; White 2011). Although for a long time several studies from a broad variety of scientific disciplines (e.g. conservation biology and ecology) have addressed green crimes and harms as major global concerns in modern society, criminology seems to lag behind with just a few criminological research studies on environmental issues (Lynch and Stretesky 2014).

Another explanation for the meagre attention from criminology may be that criminal law is mostly applicable to offenders from a socio-economically poor background (the lower classes) instead of powerful and large corporations (Sutherland 1940, 1983; Coleman 1997; Friedrichs 1996; Friedrichs and Rothe 2011). On a regular basis, crimes by corporations or state-owned enterprises with political and economic power are not treated in the same way as street crimes. Orthodox criminology generally devotes attention to crimes of the powerless and ignores *crimes of the powerful*. And offenders of environmental crimes are usually powerful actors with enterprises who are merely subjected to fines or warnings (Lynch and Stretesky 2003; Ruggiero and South 2010, 2013).

It should be noted that besides the focus on crimes by people from the lower classes, a human-centred perspective also limits the focus of criminology as a social science. The victimization of non-human subjects (e.g. ecosystems, animals) in relation to environmental crimes and harms is largely ignored in criminology. Criminologists usually approach the concept of victimization from a human-centred perspective based on interpretations and understandings of humans as victims, instead of ecosystems or animals as victims. For instance, animals are generally regarded as the legal property of humans that can be bred, killed, and tortured by their owners (White 2011; White and Heckenberg 2014).

Finally, criminology devotes little attention to crimes outside the Western world. Western or 'Northern' research themes dominate criminological research influenced by Western governments and law enforcement organizations. The Western bias would be framed in their language (Boekhout van Solinge 2014). However, many crimes are committed outside the Western world and the consequences of these environmental crimes are left behind (Passas and Goodwin 2005). It can be argued that even most victims of crimes live there and that precisely in these areas with relatively weak governments and an ineffective rule of law, investigating crimes is indeed necessary (Boekhout van Solinge 2014).

The meagre attention by criminologists regarding crimes against nature, defined as *green crimes* by South (2004), is demonstrated by the fact that just a small number of criminologists have studied green crimes in general from the 1990s onwards (South and Beirne 1998; Lynch and Stretesky 2003; Beirne and South 2007a; Sollund 2008; White 2008, 2011) and specifically the illegal wildlife trade in the 2000s (Zimmerman 2003; Pires and Moreto 2011; Sollund 2013; Wyatt 2013; Petrossian and Clark 2014). This research aims to contribute to the study of criminology by focussing on endangered live animals and animal products that are being illegally traded. In the next sections criminological research on animals will be discussed together with criminological concepts, which can be used to describe and explain the criminal or harmful acts in the network of the wildlife trade. To come back to the relationship between crime and nature, the green harms of the wildlife trade will be approached from a green criminological perspective. This perspective explicitly places harms against the environment, humanity and non-human animals as a point of departure.

4.2 Animals in Criminology

As described in Chap. 1, the history of the trade in wildlife goes back to ancient civilizations. To understand this long-term relationship between humans and non-human animals in the context of crimes, this section will explore the criminological relationship between crime and animals. What has been written about animals as perpetrators, 'primitive relatives of humans' and victims? How has criminology made use of comparisons with animals, nature and ecological inter-relations? And what kinds of 'animal crimes' have been identified up to now?

When in the ancient Greek, Roman, Teuton, Celtic and Slavic empires animals caused serious damage (e.g. human deaths were no exception), their fate was in the hands of the victim or the family of the victim without a trial. After centuries this changed in the medieval period in Europe under the influence of the Roman Catholic Church. The legal system transformed into an extended punishment system for animals analogous to the human legal system (Hyde 1916). Animals could be punished and prosecuted by the courts when they harmed humans. The prosecutions of domesticated animals were held in secular courts and the animals were exposed to public executions, while wild animals were tried in ecclesiastical courts and punished by curses of malediction (Beirne 1995). A famous case of a trial against domestic animals took place in France in 1457. The indictment against a sow and her six piglets included the murder and partial devouring of an infant. Although the sow was found guilty, her young piglets were pardoned due to their youth and innocence and the 'bad example' shown by their mother as well as a lack of evidence. Consequently, the sow was sentenced to death by hanging (Hyde 1916).

However, there was one recurring problem: animals did not always show up in court. In 1522, during an ecclesiastical court case, rats were charged with destroying several barley crops. The perpetrators were expected on a certain day for the trail. Unfortunately the rats did not appear, but their advocate argued that all rats, instead of some, should be summoned. The argument was accepted and all rats were summoned. Again the rats failed to appear. Their advocate argued that such an emigration required time, and a delay was accepted. Yet, still no rats appeared in court. This time their advocate excused the rats as they were anxious because of the plaintiffs' cats which frightened them. Finally, the "appearance of the rats was adjourned *sine die* and judgment was given by default" (Hyde 1916: 707). These are just two examples of court cases in a period in which a large amount of animals were summoned, such as bulls, asses, wolves, cocks, dogs, snakes, goats, horses, mice, swine and even worms, beetles, termites and leeches. Sometimes animals were even admitted as witnesses in court (Hyde 1916; Evans 1906). These examples illustrate that during the Middle Ages animals entered the area of crime as being rational actors who could be convicted for their (criminal) behaviour.

Centuries later, in 1800, criminologists took the perspective of animals with criminal behaviour to another level: they started to compare criminals with animals (Olson 2013). This perspective was developed in a period when scientific knowledge about animals increased with Darwin as a major explorer of the capabilities of animals. In his book 'The Descent of Man' (1871), he argued: "There is no fundamental difference between man and the higher mammals in their mental faculties". Social Darwinism combined evolutionary biology (evolutionary processes produce the diversity of species) with social science in the context of the 'survival of the fittest' (Spencer 1884). Lombrosian members of the school of anthropology tried to distinguish *Homo criminalis* from *Homo sapiens* in the philosophy of social Darwinism in the 1870s and 1880s. Lombroso's theory of *criminal atavism* tried to explain crime as 'a reversion to a lower state of evolution' with an analogy between the atavist and 'primitive humans', monkeys and apes. Atavists would get a stigmata from degeneration belonging to an earlier, more primitive stage of evolution found in animal characteristics. Lombroso made an analogy between the skulls of criminals and animal anatomy based on autopsies. Criminal atavists would have "ears of unusual size, either occasionally very small, or standing out from the head as do those of the chimpanzee (...) pouches in the cheek like those of some animals; peculiarities of the palate, such as a large central ridge, a series of cavities and protuberances such as are found in some reptiles (...) chin receding, or excessively long or short and flat, as in apes" (Wolfgang 1960: 370–371). Lombroso found characteristics of 'inferior' animals in his skull analyses, such as the overdevelopment of the *vermis* referring to the middle cerebellum of birds: "This was not merely an idea, but a revelation. At the sight of that skull, I seemed to see all of a sudden, lighted up as a vast plain under a flaming sky, the problem of the nature of the criminal—an atavistic being who reproduces in his person the ferocious instincts of primitive humanity and the inferior animals" (Lombroso 1911, quoted in Wolfgang 1960: 369). Criminal tendencies would be instinctual in primitive humans and lower animals that were physically and psychologically less evolved (Lombroso 1911). Lombroso stated that *Homo sapiens* are superior above other hominids, including criminals who might even belong to another human species *(Homo criminalis)* recognized by animal physical characteristics and primitive (animal) instincts. According to Lombrosian followers the biological origin of criminals has to be found in criminal examples of 'lazy beavers', 'rogue elephants', 'thieving monkeys', 'wild goats', 'dangerous cows', 'adulterous bees', 'robber sparrows', 'thieving pigeons and female dogs' and 'murdering hawks and elephants' (Ellis 1890; Hall 1902; Beirne 1995). Several early criminal anthropologists suggested that besides *Homo criminalis*, animals could be 'born criminals' too (Beirne 1995). However, Lombroso's theory to predict crime based on skull shape and other physical characteristics of criminals proved highly controversial (e.g. Gould 1996). Although the biological determinist Lombroso believed in the born criminal, French anthropologists and sociologists who came after him argued from an indeterministic perspective that crime is the result of a learning process (e.g. Tarde 1886). Lombroso's theories were rather naive with many unsubstantiated assumptions. Moreover, Goring challenged Lombroso's statistical methodology and sampling techniques and, based on organized data on more than 3,000 convicts, he refuted most propositions and findings claimed by Lombroso (Wolfgang 1972). Currently, Lombroso's research is seen as being pseudoscientific and highly controversial. However, the border he drew between *Homo sapiens* and *Homo criminalis* is interesting in the context of the current separation between humans and non-human animals or, to be more specific, the border between species in the family of *Hominoidea*: humans versus the great apes (e.g. gorilla, orangutan, chimpanzee). According to the moral philosopher Singer (1975), the distinction between humans and non-human animals would be completely arbitrary, demonstrated by the fact that the DNA of humans appears to be closer to the chimpanzee (>98% similarity of DNA) than the DNA of a chimpanzee to a gorilla. The social construction of this distinction would be based on the presumption that animals are less developed and makes it morally possible to approach animals as primitive creatures that can be treated as products or human property without any feelings (more details in Sect. 4.6).

However, according to Beirne (1995), from the 1920s onwards, for a long time there was no place for animal crimes in criminology. Actually, this is remarkable as the interrelationship between human and non-human animals became more transparent (Benton 1998). This can be partly explained by associations with *biocriminology*[1] and controversial political ideologies of eugenics in the early twentieth century and fascism and national socialism in Nazi Germany. According to these ideologies certain ethnic groups would be degraded and considered intrinsically inferior. An exception would be the use of natural selection based on the Darwinian theory of evolution by social ecologists of the Chicago school. In the book 'City' Park, Burgess and McKenzie explored the principles of a *biotic balance*, interactions between animals and plants in their ecosystem and compared these principles with human interactions in urban areas, using the term 'human ecology' (Park, Burgess and McKenzie 1925). And the ecological approach of social disorganization by Shaw and McKay (1942) in their book 'Juvenile delinquency and urban areas' found that "the effectiveness of social institutions and the desirability of residential and business locations correspond closely to natural, ecological principles that are influenced by the concepts of competition and dominance" (Shoemaker 1996: 101). From this perspective the city was seen as a biotic organism.

Are these examples the only interfaces with criminology? In 1979 the sociologist Bryant concluded that animal crime or *zoological crime* has been completely ignored by scientists. He stated that animals are highly involved in human social relations and that zoological crimes 'may well be the oldest form of sanctioned social norm violation' (Bryant 1979: 409). In his study 'The Zoological Connection: Animal-Related Human Behavior' he described animals as perpetrators, instigators, objects, motivation, instruments, mechanisms for punishment and: victims of crime. According to him at least five categories of animal crimes can be distinguished: animals as personal property, animals as public property, animals as a hazard or nuisance, anti-animal cruelty laws and crimes against ecology (Bryant 1979). First, animals enter the area of criminology as stolen items or assaulted or killed animals as personal property. Animal theft has taken place for centuries, from horse stealing among ancient Indians (Carson 1995) to the taking of deer 'in a search for the authentic Robin Hood in fourteenth century England' (Beirne 1995) and stealing dogs for ransom[2] (Bryant 1979). Second, animals are illegally poached as public property. This category includes offences regarding hunting, fishing and trapping that are regulated by State or Federal legislation. For example, illegal hunting on animals in national parks. Third, animals are studied as a hazard or nuisance in society. With the development of the Dangerous Wild Animals Act in the United Kingdom in 1976, several dangerous animals (e.g. poisonous snakes) were prohibited from being kept as pets (Blackman et al. 1989). And, currently, it is forbidden

[1]Study on biological and hereditary links to antisocial and deviant behaviour.

[2]Animal theft is still a major mode of criminal activity.

to keep dangerous animals (e.g. big cats) as pets in several countries in Europe (Van Uhm 2015). Fourth, animals are protected by animal laws regarding anti-cruelty (Beirne 2009). Since the 1980s moral entrepreneurs and NGOs have underlined animal abuse in agriculture and laboratories and, subsequently, protection by animal law has increased (Van Uhm 2015). In addition, illegal dogfights and cock fighting may belong to these offences as well as bestiality (Bryant 1979). Finally, crimes against ecology usually include illegal poaching or the trade in endangered species. Since CITES came into force, the trade in protected animals has been regulated and more than 35,000 animal and plant species are now protected. A wide variety of offences can be defined in this category, such as the illegal trade in live animals (e.g. reptiles and birds), animal products (e.g. medicines, leather products, food) and plants (e.g. tropical timber, cacti) (Wyatt 2013).

To sum up, just a small number of theories and scientific and pseudoscientific studies in criminology have focussed on crimes in relation to animals. In his article 'The use and abuse of animals in criminology' in the mid-1990s Beirne agreed that criminologists for a long time failed to study animal-related crimes (Beirne 1995, 1999). There have been exceptions, however, e.g. animals as criminals in the medieval period, the comparisons between criminals and animals in the late nineteenth century by Lombrosian members of the school of anthropology, Chicago School theories based on the biotic balance of interactions between animals and plants, and the preliminary identification of crimes against animals in the twentieth century. Since criminologists have studied animal-related crimes to such a limited extent, it would be relevant and meaningful to explore the process of the wildlife trade to find criminological theories that can be applied in the following sections.

4.3 Through Time and Space

The illegal trade in wildlife involves a broad variety of actors from deprived individuals to profitable companies and corrupt government officials. Small and large-scale actors, powerful and poor actors and legal and illegal actors could be involved in the illegal trade in wildlife. To identify the social organization in the illegal wildlife trade the idealized *pipeline model* is used in the case studies to illustrate the different stages, actors and networks in the chain of this illegal (transnational) trade. The pipeline model is based on the movement of products from their origin to the destination. This reflects different steps and actors in the chain (Tremblay et al. 1998; Siegel 2009). According to Elliott (2009) animals or animal products are moved along a line of contacts but key aspects of the movement may be handled by just one or two central players. Pipeline models function as a combination of chain and hub networks where illegal trade persists and flourishes (Arquilla and Ronfeldt 2001; Vander Beken et al. 2004). For example, the pipeline model has been used to sketch the stages in the diamond trade (e.g. Sevdermish et al. 1998; Vander Beken et al. 2004; Siegel 2009) (Fig. 4.1).

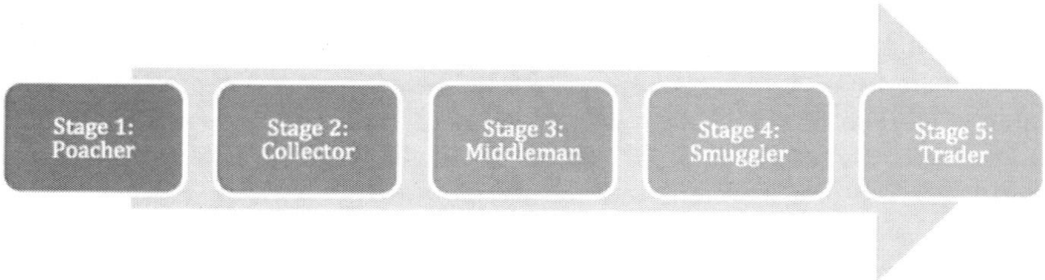

Fig. 4.1 Idealized pipeline model of the illegal wildlife trade

In the first stage of the pipeline model the animals are poached in the source region. Due to the diversity of source countries in the context of their ecosystems and biodiversity, the process of poaching is unique and needs to be studied in the context of its historical and socio-economic situation. The poachers are often local and usually poor people (e.g. farmers or hunters) who are familiar with the area and know how to find specific species (e.g. monkeys, sturgeons, rhinos). The groups of poachers are very different in terms of their degree of organization, from low scale or even individual poachers to a highly professional coordinated network of a number of poachers. The location of poaching is commonly far from urban areas in deep forests, upper river waters and remote plains. Depending on the requested end product, the animal is kept alive or killed. The second stage consists of the gathering of wildlife by collectors. These can be local traders or regional traders from outside the local villages. Sometimes they have a small market shop in a local village or on other occasions they sell the contraband to middlemen in relatively large cities. The middleman in the third stage has a network of people to arrange for the contraband to be transferred to the next destination (e.g. large capitals). Generally, middlemen have contacts with smugglers who transport the illegal wildlife in stage four. The smugglers may be recruited by middlemen and are specialized in smuggling specific products. It is no exception that officials are being bribed during the entire process. In the final stage the products end up in the hands of a national or international trader or a second middleman in a transit or destination area. The animals or products will be sold by a trader or are transferred by a middleman (again) to another region, country or continent. During the last stage wildlife is often laundered on the legal market. The illegal origin of the products has then disappeared (see Sect. 6.6) and they are sold together with legal products in shops, clinics, pet shops and so on.

At each stage several individuals, companies and even states can be involved, and the organization may differ from opportunistic flexible networks to being highly organized and structured. Traditionally, the model has been described as a continuum. This is the ideal situation, 'the metaphor describing the movement of products', and simultaneously, a disadvantage of the pipeline model, because in reality the steps may be less structured (Sevdermish et al. 1998). This is especially the case in criminal networks. Morselli (2009) indicated that many criminal networks are fluid and flexible depending on and changing in new situations over time

(Sect. 4.5). According to Liddick (2011) the chain of the trade, from capture to the market, often covers flexible distribution lines and networks of intermediaries, from harvesters through middlemen and on to wholesalers, exporters, processors and retailers, and may involve intermediate destinations. To understand the illegal wildlife trade, the pipeline demonstrates a structured process while in reality criminal networks function in a more fluid and flexible way. For instance, the poacher can sell the illegal wildlife to a collector, middleman, trader or directly to the client. Or poachers may play a dual role: they can be the same people who sell illegal wildlife on the markets. It totally depends on the relationships between actors in the crime networks. Nor does the model take into account that sometimes products come back to a middleman or products pass certain hubs, instead of a strict trade hierarchy from poacher to consumer. Moreover, the trade hierarchy does not necessarily start with a poacher, as there could be an application from a principal beforehand.

While the economic value of products or animals increases with each step in the pipeline, the *social value* is dependent on the judgement made by subjects. Appadurai (1986) mentions in 'The social life of things' how the value of commodities is embodied in exchanged commodities instead of the forms or functions of trade. The commodities would have 'social lives'. In his book 'The Philosophy of Money' Simmel (1978) explained that value is a judgement made by subjects. In this context the distance between a person and the (economic) object in relation to pure desire is important as "one's desire for an object is fulfilled by the sacrifice of some other object, which is the focus of the desire of another". Certain exchanges of sacrifices demonstrate their social lives (Appadurai 1986: 3–4). For instance, in the context of the illegal trade in endangered species the value increases as the species becomes rarer. Unfortunately, the more an animal is threatened with extinction the higher prices may become on the black market (e.g. with consequences regarding the Allee effect, Sect. 2.1). An example would be the growing price for rhino horn that reaches prices higher than their weight in gold (Van Uhm 2012). Note that this concept of a social life of things will be given an additional meaning as the wildlife trade is also about living beings approached as commodities (Sect. 4.6). In addition, economic objects can be placed in several *regimes of value* in time and space and are dependent on the cultural and historical milieus. According to Appadurai things have no meaning without human transactions, attributions and motivations: "This formal truth does not illuminate the concrete, historical circulation of things. For that we have to follow the things themselves, for their meanings are inscribed in their forms, their uses, their trajectories" (Appadurai 1986: 7). This is illustrated by the demand for the same rhino horn: without the meaning of the use of rhino horn in Chinese culture, the symbolic and moral value of the trade cannot be understood (described in Chap. 9).

Both the wildlife trade chain and the social construction of the value run through time and space. By following the commodities in their historical, cultural and social embeddedness an overview can be provided. However, the pipeline model has to be approached as an idealized model of the criminal network. In each case study I will include a more detailed and complex pipeline model to understand the major flows of the illegal trade. As described in the next section these flows of the illegal wildlife trade cannot be understood without the context of the globalization, global anomies and opportunities for crime.

4.4 Illegal Flows and International Inequalities

Legal and illegal trade flows can no longer be dissociated from trends of globalization. According to globalization scholars (e.g. Aas 2007) the world, including the connection between people and trade goods, has become 'smaller'. Not only has the global exchange of natural resources increased, but advances in transportation and telecommunications and the international transfer of money, the infrastructure of a diversity of lines and faster connections provide opportunities for illegal trafficking (Bauman 1998; Beck 1999). In other words, crime has become globalized. For instance, in Europe due to the Schengen Agreement (1993) internal legal and illegal trade is possible without border controls. To transfer illegal birds from South America to the EU will take only 7 h by plane and once they have arrived in Europe the birds can be relatively easily transported to other Schengen countries. Consequently, criminal networks focus on weak entry points in the EU, such as the East European countries and the Southern parts of Europe.[3] In the context of the reduction of borders and improved infrastructures with further reaching air transportation, opportunities for crime in the wildlife trade are enhanced (Zimmerman 2003; Haken 2011).[4]

As a result of globalization[5] several international inequalities are manifested between developing and developed countries. Basically, prosperity is allocated to powerful industrial states and natural resources from poor source regions are (over) exploited in order to meet the demand from the consumption-driven culture of the rich West (Sect. 2.3). According to Passas (1999) *criminogenic asymmetries* mean that: "structural discrepancies and inequalities in the realms of the economy, law, politics, and culture" provide opportunities for crime. Especially, economic and power inequalities have been spread within and across countries and lead to *global anomie* and, ultimately, economic misconduct or crimes. Global anomie is the

[3]CITES day organized by the National Police in the Netherlands, May 19, 2015.

[4]Especially in combination with high profits and a low risk of detection and conviction (Zimmerman 2003; Europol 2013a, b).

[5]The main driving forces of the globalization of crime include technological drivers, political drivers, enforcement drivers, internal drivers and economic drivers (Galeotti 2004). For instance, advanced technology results in an easy transfer of legal and illegal products (e.g. live animals can be transferred within hours from any part of the world to Europe), criminals respond to political developments (e.g. ethnic tensions, wars), the efforts of the law enforcement authorities (e.g. limited law enforcement regarding environmental crimes, including the illegal wildlife trade), structural changes in crime (e.g. from hierarchical to loose and flexible crime networks) and illegal products are sold abroad for a higher price (e.g. wildlife products have a higher value in the West).

mismatch between group standards and wider social standards, such as relatively poor people who compare their 'needs' with normative frameworks of consumption from richer countries. This *relative deprivation* as a result of economic and power inequalities may lead to crimes (Passas 2000). Many criminologists have conducted research on forms of crime driven by poverty and inequality. For instance, the Dutch criminologist Bonger studied the link between crime and economic and social conditions based on links between bread prices and arrests for theft. He approached crime as a normal response to cultural expectations in the capitalist society as poor people would commit crimes to fight injustice (Bonger 1932). In this context, international (illegal) traders benefit from poverty and inequality to allure people to poach wildlife for small prices (Haken 2011).

The power and economic inequalities seem to affect the normative framework of people (Passas 2000). According to Merton (1938) individual adaptation to pressure is based on the social structure. A discrepancy or an imbalance between the social structure of means and internalized cultural goals referring to success stories of the 'American Dream' would result in *strain*. He argued in his book 'Social structure and anomie' that because not everyone can attain conventional success by working hard, alternative (e.g. illegal) means will be used to achieve the desired goals (Merton 1938). People may search for alternative solutions to become successful, i.e. *innovation* to achieve the culturally approved goal (wealth) by unconventional means (e.g. poaching or trading in illegal wildlife). Especially in times when 'needs' and normative models are harmonized in the globalized world, strain may result in criminal behaviour (Passas 2000).

According to Passas (2002) processes of globalization also intensify the intertwined relationship between the upperworld and underworld. Powerful legal enterprises misuse structural weaknesses in existing regulation in source countries. The economic, political and legal asymmetries between countries have given rise to illicit markets for the uncontrolled exploitation of natural resources by corporations (Passas 2000). According to several authors, legally registered companies are regularly involved in the illegal trade in wildlife (Cook et al. 2002; Lyons and Natusch 2011). Zaitch et al. (2014) highlight that there are common overlaps with political and economic powerful actors involved in the exploitation of natural resources. The interconnectedness between the legal and illegal world consists of a variety of components (Van Duyne et al. 2002). Based on an *antithetical relationship*, when competition between legal and illegal actors is present, an enterprise may choose to include illegal products (e.g. illegal wildlife) for less money than its competitors. The enterprise could even profit from a brand name to sell illegal or counterfeit products (e.g. the illegal use of caviar brands). As a result illegally obtained wildlife often ends up as a legal product in the world economy. A *symbiotic relationship* exists when interests are shared and enhance mutual benefits between the 'underworld' and 'upperworld' (Passas 2002).

Sutherland introduced the concept of *white-collar crime*, referring to "a crime committed by a person of respectability and high social status in the course of his occupation" (Sutherland 1949: 9). The concept of white-collar crimes changed the criminological perspective of crime that was primarily focused on crimes by the poor. He found that white-collar crime cases were only exceptionally adjudged by criminal law; most cases were dealt with by civil and administrative law. Yet, these 'socially injurious acts' would be more harmful than less serious crimes committed by lower classes (Sutherland 1940, 1983). Geis (1992: 9) underlined the opportunities provided for the abuse of power by persons situated in high places. Although criminal law mainly deals with criminals of low status, infringements by highly respected powerful people (in the course of their occupation) or businesses are not considered or dealt with as 'real crimes'. Often these infringements are dismissed with a symbolic fine instead of heavy sentences. Ruggiero and South (2010) transformed the term white-collar crime into *dirty collar crime* to underline the role of legally registered companies in the illegal activities of environmental crime. They described how powerful, state or private, companies conduct illegal activities in the waste and oil industry (Ruggiero and South 2010, 2013). Other authors (e.g. Barrett 1997; O'Hear 2004; Wolf 2011) used the term *green-collar crimes* to refer and synthesize both white-collar crime and environmental justice to examine green crimes. This context of global anomie, power and conceptual interrelation between legality and illegality will be used to understand the mechanisms and organization of the illegal wildlife trade.

4.5 The Organization Behind Crimes

The global anomie based on power and economic inequality also provides opportunities for transnational crime networks. European organized crime groups that were previously involved in the drug trade, fraud, illegal immigration and counterfeit products are currently active in the illegal wildlife trade (e.g. Europol 2011). The increasing involvement of criminal networks and, especially, organized crime in the illegal wildlife trade (Europol 2013a, b) is currently a concern for law enforcement, and has resulted in international resolutions to tackle wildlife crimes (Sollund and Maher 2015, see also Chap. 3).

However, there is no formal definition of organized crime and many concepts of organized crime exist in criminology (Levi and Maguire 2004). According to Siegel (2008: 86) organized crime remains an 'unclear and ambiguous concept'. She explains that it is unclear what is organized (the Italian mafia, the Chinese triads) or disorganized (groups of pickpockets), how many members have to be involved in order to be considered as organized crime and why certain activities are seen as organized (human trafficking) while others are not (cyber crime). The United Nations Convention against Transnational Organized Crime has vaguely defined organized crime as "a structured group of three or more persons, existing for a period of time and acting in concert with the aim of committing one or more serious crimes or offences established in accordance with this Convention, in order to obtain, directly or indirectly, a financial or other material benefit."[6] The term 'serious crime' means conduct constituting 'offences punishable by a maximum deprivation of liberty of at least 4 years or a more serious penalty'.[7] As described in Chap. 3, the UN Commission on Crime Prevention and Criminal Justice agreed that the illegal wildlife trade should be treated as 'serious crime' in 2013. However, Pires and Moreto (2011: 104) astutely noted that *organized* "can simply mean anything from three individuals who are loosely organized together to a vast criminal enterprise that comprises all stages of the wildlife trade (i.e. vertically integrated organizations)".

According to Passas (1995) an indication of organized crime could be the degree of organization and structure. Organized crime would have an element of continuity and resilience, because these groups are of a long-standing nature. And organized crime could be characterized as having a high amount of rationality behind its activities making the crime very calculated. Especially illicit market activities have been linked to organized crime (Fijnaut and Paoli 2004; Spapens 2010). To maintain its power or to complete its mission, organized crime would make it possible to use violence and counterstrategies. Since organized crime operates outside the law there are no legal contracts to guarantee the delivery of the illegally traded product. Organized crime groups use their own internal system to solve conflicts or disputes in illegal activities; they create internal systems of rules and codes of behaviour to run illegal businesses (Siegel 2008; Gambetta 2009).

In addition, criminal networks may vary in their content, form and scope. On the one hand, they could be based on the incentives provided by a once-only collaboration to set up a criminal venture or they could be performed within a bureaucratic-like infrastructure that enforces exclusivity on activities and productivities by members (Morselli 2009). The network can be set up by organizers for a specific purpose (a directed network) or can appear spontaneously to fill a gap in the market (a transaction network) (Arquilla and Ronfeldt 2001). Or criminal networks could be fluid and flexible, based on ad hoc coalitions, or highly hierarchically structured and formal as in a mafia-type network (Blok 2008). According to Williams (2001) particularly illegal enterprises take shape in the light of flexible and fluid crime networks instead of hierarchical, monolithic and highly regulated crime networks. Morselli (2009) argues that the interaction between actors creates a form of flexibility in the network. The flexible order reflects the opportunistic short-term character of crime networks. Illegal enterprises need to react quickly and the hierarchical structures of crime networks would stagnate the anticipation of new developments in the market (Fijnaut and Paoli 2004). However, that does not mean

[6]Article 2.a United Nations Convention against Transnational Organized Crime.

[7]Article 2.b United Nations Convention against Transnational Organized Crime.

that key players have no control over certain links in the chain. The most flexible crime networks are centralized around one or just a small amount of central actors (Morselli 2009).

A severe restriction of certain crime models is that criminal networks are approached from a static model with actors and relations, while Bauman argues that interpersonal relationships in the modern liquid society have become very fragile and perishable. In his book 'Liquid Modernity' he describes how swiftly and temporary relations characterize the modern liquid society (Bauman 2000). Another limitation of these networks and organized crime approaches include the social and cultural context in which networks operate. The social ties between the offenders would play an important role in the context of geographic distance, ethnicity, family, education and age (Bruinsma and Bernasco 2004; Kleemans and Van de Bunt 1999, 2003). According to Van de Bunt et al. (2014: 323) "Criminal activities cannot be separated from the social relations between the participants and the institutional environments in which their interactions take place". 'Partners in crime' are usually bound by social and cultural ties and depend on a high level of 'trust', i.e. informing the police after a 'rip-off' is not recommended. That is why ties based on friendship and family relations are not uncommon in illegal enterprises.

The social embeddedness creates both a breeding ground for (organized) crime and an explanatory framework for criminologists (Van de Bunt et al. 2014). An example would be the social embeddedness of passive or active corruption (Passas 2002). The illegal wildlife trade is regularly associated with corruption (Hoser 1993; Boekhout van Solinge 2014; Lawson and Vines 2014). According to Siegel (2011: 207) "corruption, which in the Western world is commonly considered an abuse of public office for private gains, has elusive meanings in the non-Western world and it is often difficult to achieve moral clarity". The view of corruption in the context of the separation between the public and private sphere ignores social relationships and the cultural aspects of gifts, solidarity and patronage in source countries. Corruption could be seen in source countries as moral and social in their social context (Siegel 2011).

In this research the crime networks involved in the illegal wildlife trade are approached in their socio-economic and cultural context to understand the motivation behind the actors and network structures. In addition, concepts such as the degree of organization, structure, corruption, violence and links with other forms of crime are used to analyse the level of organized crime. After describing social and criminological theories on the social construction of the value of products and the actors and organization of criminal networks, in the next section the emergence of green criminology and new frameworks to approach the consequences and harms of the trade will be discussed.

4.6 The Greening of Criminology

As described earlier, crimes against nature or animal-related crimes are rarely studied by criminologists. Only from the 1990s onwards have criminologists started to focus on green crimes,[8] including the wildlife trade from the 2000s. This emergence of *green criminology* occurred in the context of the increasing social and professional concern regarding the environment in recent years (White 2008). Green criminology cannot be dissociated from important trends in criminology over the past 20 years: increased attention to globalization, corporate crime, victims and unequal distribution of victimization and human rights (South 1998; White 2011). Drawing on its roots from critical criminology, green criminology transcends the borders of orthodox criminology and its definition of crime (Wyatt 2013; Lynch and Stretesky 2014). Traditionally, the field of criminological science focused on crimes such as murder, rape, robbery and burglary. Criminologists examined the motives of the perpetrators, why people commit crimes and how society must punish or repair the damage done. From the perspective of traditional criminology, attention has been solely given to the damage to humans (Schneider 2012). According to Halsey (1997: 217): "Criminologists have failed to explicate the many theoretical and practical implications arising from the continued existence of so many legal yet ecologically damaging practices". With the advent of green criminology the focus of criminology is also on the study of environmental harm in general and the symbiosis between man and nature in particular. Environmental crimes could be seen as side effects of the industrialized society (Chap. 2) with links to legal actors in society (Sect. 4.4) (South 1998). According to Wyatt (2013) the green criminological perspective is often related to international environmental crimes and harms with legal and illegal entrepreneurs and the victimization of the environment, animals and plants. These green crimes and harms cover a wide range of (criminal) activities ranging from forms of pollution (air, water and soil), deforestation (legal and illegal logging), species decline (poaching and overexploitation) and the abuse of animals (vivisection and intensive livestock farming) (Carrabine et al. 2004).

Like other delinquencies, the criminalization of environmental issues is dependent on the social construction of crime as described in Sect. 4.1. Crime is dependent on time and place (Quinney 1970). In addition, Ruggiero and South (2013) argue that the social construction of environmental crime is also dependent on power relations and social inequality within society. Powerful corporations or entities (e.g. the state) would influence environmental crime and harm (Lynch and Stretesky 2003; Pearce and Tombs 1998). These interests of powerful political and economic elites may play a role in minimalizing the regulation of green crimes and excluding environmental harmful activities from criminalization in order to continue environmental destruction (Stretesky et al. 2013; Westerhuis et al. 2013; Zaitch et al. 2014). The social, political and economic interests and conflicting

[8]Lynch (1990) proposed to include environmental issues within the discipline of criminology.

private, state and environmental interests result in a complex field of power relations (White 2011). Consequently, relatively poor countries in Africa, South America and Southeast Asia that own nature-rich areas are being (legally) over-exploited as described in Chap. 2. According to Hall (2013) this demonstrates that environmental harm is unequally distributed (see also Sect. 2.3).

To understand these *criminal* activities, from a green criminological perspective the basic starting point is that something or someone has suffered *harm* (Halsey and White 1998; White 2011). Green criminology elaborates on the concept of 'social harm' beyond legalistic definitions of crime (Hillyard et al. 2004; Hillyard and Tombs 2004, 2007). The social harm principle proposes a rejection of the legal definition of crime and instead focussing on the wider social context of harm (Hillyard and Tombs 2004). Already in the mid-twentieth century Sellin (1938) and Sutherland (1940) criticized the legal approach of crime and Schwendinger and Schwendinger (1970) argued that we have to approach the criminality of activities based on their human rights as the main criteria to define crime. The green criminological study takes this principle of harm to an extended level with environmental harms as a result of activities that have not (yet) been criminalized (Lynch and Stretesky 2003). The degree of harmfulness, however, does not determine if harmful behaviour is criminalized, but depends on the social construction of crime. In many green criminological themes injury is (as yet) hardly formally recognized by criminalization or enforcement. "[A] harms perspective is shaped by shared understandings and scientific knowledge about what constitutes ecological harm rather than being a socially constructed concept defined by politicians as in orthodox criminology" (Stretesky et al. 2013: 71). The comprehensive approach to harm emphasizes green criminology in comparison to orthodox criminology (Beirne and South 2007a; White 2008, 2011). Beirne and South (2007) have further developed the concept of green criminology and focussed in their book 'Issues in green criminology' on this extended harm principle. Green harms should not be considered as activities defined as crimes but have to be related to the norms of society (Nurse 2013). White (2013) has approached environmental harm in terms of *justice* based on environmental justice and harms to humans, conservation, ecological justice and harm to nature, and species justice and harm to animals.

Although the green criminological harm principle goes well beyond the borders of the conventional definition of crime, a limitation is that harm is a very broad concept and is difficult to define: What is harmful for someone could be relatively harmless to somebody else. Is not the concept of harm also socially constructed? Harm is codependent on social and moral norms that change over time. According to critics these harm-based approaches are not relevant as harm cannot be bound or defined. Sellin already argued in 1938 that it is precisely this artificial boundary, based on norms embodied in criminal law, that imposes a limitation on the discipline of criminology (Sellin 1938).

However, the green harm principle is useful to identify the impact or significance of harmful activities to the environment. According to White (2008, 2011), from a green criminological and eco-justice perspective harm includes not only transgressions against humans, but also against the environment and non-human species.

Humans are seen as part of a complex ecosystem and no longer as the central actors; ecosystems, plants and animals can be victims too. It is the assumption that the value of animals and the natural environment is paramount in itself, rather than the value that they may not have to humans (Beirne and South 2007b; Lynch and Stretesky 2007). This should be a dichotomy between the justification of protecting the global environment with its fauna and flora and the future generations. Also to justify the protection of the environment based on the grant-related inherent value of all non-human life on our planet (Benton 1998). This includes not only the abuse of specific non-human animals, but also institutionalized harmful activities (Beirne 2009). From a green criminological perspective this comprehensive harm principle can be distinguished in three major approaches to harm: an anthropocentric, eco-centric and biocentric approach.

From an anthropocentric perspective, humans occupy the central point with a demand for health and well-being. From this view, humans are regarded as the main victims (Cazaux 2003; White 2008). Anthropocentrism is based on the biological, mental and moral superiority of humans in relation to all other (non-human) living beings on Earth; nature is at the service of humankind. Nature is protected where benefits for humans can be derived. Profit maximization, capitalist values and economic interests are the driving forces for the exploitation of nature. From an anthropocentric perspective, humans are separated from the ecosystem and nature is just a tool to satisfy their needs. There is harm if human victims are present (Halsey and White 1998; White 2008). For instance, heavily armed criminal gangs from Chad and Sudan killed soldiers from Chad during their elephant poaching activities; dozens of rangers were killed during certain confrontations (Wyler and Sheikh 2013). After decades of virtually no attention being paid to the illegal wildlife trade as a serious crime, the anthropocentric perspective of humankind is more than obvious in the context of recent links between the wildlife trade and 'terrorism' that pose a hazard to humans. Suddenly large-scale police and investigation entities (e.g. FBI, CIA, Interpol) are starting to explore the field of the illegal wildlife trade in relation to Al-Shabaab and Janjaweed in Africa. It is well noted by Wyatt (2013) that it is ironic that from this perspective, which is focussed on short-term gain, the damage to human livelihood and health that are caused as a direct or indirect effect of the wildlife trade are not recognized. Referring to Chap. 2, harms or risks to humans could be relatively invisible and may include the loss of potential medicine with the reduction of biodiversity, the transfer of zoonotic diseases, the loss of natural resources for local communities and so on. Although humans protect themselves against indirect threats such as avian influenza, humans are regularly unaware of the interconnection with the environment. Herbig (2010) correctly added that with the global disappearance of species also a culturally and emotionally poorer world is left for the next generations.

From an ecocentric perspective there exists a dialectical relationship between humans and nature. Humans are part of the larger natural circle. This relationship is based on the ecological principle of 'everything is related to everything else', a value which is assigned to its inherent nature (Benton 1998). In the context of symbiosis and the ecological interaction between species as described in Chap. 2, the disappearance of keystone species could have a disastrous impact (e.g. the trophic cascade) on perennial species and their ecosystem (Kellert and Wilson 1993; Mills et al. 1993; Power et al. 1996). Historically, several examples demonstrate how humans have induced trophic cascades by the poaching of top predators (Terborgh and Estes 2013). The absence of top predators may even lead to an ecological meltdown on islands with predatory free forest fragments (Terborgh et al. 2001). Accompanied by an (anthropogenic) Allee effect, the extinction rate of endangered species may be higher as a result of the wildlife trade (Courchamp et al. 2006). In addition, the (re)introduction or release of non-native species may cause instability in the ecosystem (Mooney and Hobbs 2000). From this perspective, ecosystems may become unbalanced or could even collapse as a result of the wildlife trade due to the strong symbiosis and ecological interaction between species in ecosystems (Lindsey et al. 2012; Myers et al. 2007). From an ecocentric perspective the ecosystem and its interests are above human interests. Nevertheless, humans are aware of its activities which have an adverse impact on the ecosystem. Humans are socially and ethically responsible for minimizing the damage and preserving the natural balance and the integrity of non-human entities (Halsey and White 1998). Collective human needs may be satisfied subject to the condition that the stability of the ecosystem is maintained. Forests may be used for the benefit of humans, but the side effects thereof, such as climate change and species loss, must be taken into account. The ecosystem with its species is seen from this perspective as a victim with an intrinsic value whose harms must be minimized (White 2011). According to Wyatt (2013) the conservation of ecosystems by national parks could be seen as an example of how humans protect the environment against exploitation. It would combine human enjoyment and the use of the national park with conservation aspects. According to White (2013) ecocentrism tries to approach the balance between the human needs of natural resources for survival and protection to maintain the benign use of the ecosphere. This would be demonstrated by activities such as selective logging techniques to maintain the long-term well-being of ecosystems or hunting quotas in the context of the conservation of animal populations.

Finally, from a biocentric perspective all species are morally and ethically equal. Humankind is not superior in comparison to non-human species and all species have an intrinsic value and must be respected in the context of welfare. A biocentric society is based on laws and mechanisms of a non-human nature. According to Halsey and White (1998) the environment, together with its species, have priority above human interests. From this approach epidemics and natural disasters are a result of overcrowding and industrialization. According to Wyatt (2013) natural areas where no people, besides conservationists, are allowed could refer to a place where non-human animals dominate (e.g. small islands in Panama or New Zealand). This biocentric approach is complemented by *speciesism*, introduced by Ryder (1970), with an emphasis on the animal that is being discriminated against on the basis of 'inferior' intuition by humans. Non-human animals are perceived as being inferior to human species in a similar way that sexism and racism involve prejudice and discrimination against 'other' people (White 2007). The moral philosopher Singer (1975: 495) argued in one of the leading works in the field of animal rights, 'Animal Liberation': "Racists violate the principle of equality by giving greater weight to the interests of members of their own race. Especially when there is a clash between their interests and the interests of those of another race. Sexists violate the principle of equality by favouring the interests of their own sex. Similarly, speciesists allow the interests of their own species to override the greater interests of members of other species. The pattern is identical in each case." Discrimination against or the exploitation of non-human animals is approached based on an anthropocentric perspective with the assumption of the superiority of humans.[9] This discriminatory ideology is reflected in the social legitimation of abusive or exploitative acts towards animals. From this perspective, the use of the word 'animal' contributes to a distinction between humans and non-human species. Currently, several green criminologists use the term 'non-human animals' to underline the invalidity of the distinction between humans and animals (e.g. Sollund 2008; Wyatt 2013; White 2008). However, according to a biocentric perspective the quality of individual lives and the well-being of all species is important (Singer 1975; Regan 1983; Cazaux 2007). Most non-human animals in the trade are killed for manufacturing or are removed from their ecosystem (Wyatt 2013). According to Gonzalez (2003) up to 75 to 90 % of illegally traded parrots will die during transference. According to Wyatt (2013) the victimization is continuous. If the non-human animals survive the transportation they are kept in cages or held in captivity for the remainder of their lives. From a biocentric perspective this would be unacceptable.

These different approaches can be useful to explore the consequences and harms of the wildlife trade (Table 4.1). The distinction between levels of harms is not at all strict. There may be an intertwined connection between anthropocentric, ecocentric and biocentric harms as well as different orders and intentional directiveness. Not only are harms interconnected in several ways, environmental harms are partly determined by transnational transference (Heckenberg 2010). The harms can transfer through the trade process. For instance, the transfer of harms may arise during the (illegal) transportation of the wildlife from abroad into the EU. For example, two eagles infected with avian influenza were hidden in pipes and illegally imported into Belgium from Thailand (Yee et al. 2009). Note that during transfer animals can be transformed into a product (e.g. during the manufacturing stage). However, the extended harms model can be used to explore the interrelation between human activities and nature, and more specifically to approach harms at different levels and to expose the impact or significance of the trade in the three case studies.

Concluding, this chapter has underlined the limited attention of criminology to crimes against nature and has pointed out important theoretical foundations for

[9]To come back to Lombroso, he made a distinction between *Homo criminalis* and *Homo sapiens* and in the early 1900s scientists proclaimed that indigenous people, which were traded together with exotic animals, were an inferior species, in evolutionary terms, to humankind (Dreesbach 2012).

Table 4.1 Perspectives on the relationship between humankind and nature

	Anthropocentric	Ecocentric	Biocentric
Conception of human beings	Biologically, mentally and morally superior to all other entities	Socially and ethically responsible for the integrity of non-human entities	Morally and ethically equal to all other entities
Conception of natural environment	Instrumental use	Dialectical relationship	Intrinsic value
Ideological basis of activity	Self-interest	Socio-environmental interest	Biotic interest
Main object of social world	Maximization of economic freedom in commodity production/consumption	Meeting of collective human needs by maintaining ecosystemic stability	Self-realization based on Gaian biological and ecological concerns
Favoured environmental strategy	Sustainable development Economically efficient use of resources	Bioregionalism Ecological balance	Righteous management Mass preservation of wilderness

Source Halsey and White (1998)

studying wildlife crimes. First, the value of wildlife is dependent on the social construction and, therefore, the meaning of social life. This may explain the increased attributed value of rare endangered animal species. Second, in the context of globalization and global anomie, new illegal international markets have emerged and opportunities for crime are created. The illegal trade in wildlife is no exception to this. The illegal wildlife market will be explored in different stages; from the poaching areas to the final destination. I will thereby describe the actors, the social embeddedness and the organization in the wildlife crime networks. Third, the greening of criminology has led to an extended harm approach in which not only humans are regarded as victims, but also animals and ecosystems can be seen as victims of human activities. From this green harms perspective, the consequences of the wildlife trade will be discussed. These theoretical frameworks form the foundation of this research and provide opportunities to explain the process of the illegal wildlife trade. In the next chapter the underlying research method that is used to uncover the illegal trade in wildlife will be described.

References

Aas, K. F. (2007). *Crime and globalization*. London: Sage.

Appadurai, A. (Ed.). (1986). *The social life of things: Commodities in cultural perspective*. Cambridge: Cambridge University Press.

Arquilla, J., & Ronfeldt, D. (2001). The advent of netwar. In J. Arquilla & D. Ronfeldt (Eds.), *Networks and netwars: The future of terror, crime and militancy*. RAND: Santa Monica.

Barrett, J. F. (1997). Green collar criminals: Why should they receive special treatment. *Maryland Journal of Contemporary Legal Issues, 8*, 107–117.

Bauman, Z. (1998). *Globalization: The human consequences*. New York: Columbia University Press.

Bauman, Z. (2000). *Liquid society*. Cambridge: Polity Press.

Beck, U. (1999). *World risk society*. Cambridge: Polity Press.

Becker, H. S. (1963). *Outsiders: Studies in the sociology of deviance*. New York: The Free Press.

Beirne, P. (1995). The use and abuse of animals in criminology: A brief history and current review. *Social Justice, 22*(1), 5–31.

Beirne, P. (1999). For a nonspeciesist criminology: Animal abuse as an object of study. *Criminology, 37*(1), 117–148.

Beirne, P. (2009). *Confronting animal abuse: law, criminology, and human-animal relationships*. Lanham: Rowman & Littlefield Publishers.

Beirne, P. & South, N. (Ed.) (2007a). *Issues in green criminology. Confronting harms against environments, humanity and other animals*. Cullompton: Willan publishing.

Beirne, P. & South, N. (2007b). Introduction: approaching green criminology. In P. Beirne & N. South, N. (Eds.) *Issues in green criminology*. Cullompton: Willan Publishing.

Benton, T. (1998). Rights and justice on a shared planet: More rights or new relations? *Theoretical Criminology, 2*(2), 149–175.

Blackman, D. E., Humphreys, P. N., & Todd, P. (1989). *Animal welfare and the law*. Cambridge: Cambridge University Press.

Blok, A. (2008). Reflections on the Sicilian mafia: peripheries and their impact on centres. In D. Siegel & H. Nelen (Eds.), *Organized crime: Culture, markets and policies*. New York: Springer.

Boekhout van Solinge, T. (2014). The illegal exploitation of natural resources. In L. Paoli (Ed.). (2014), *The oxford handbook of organized crime*. Oxford: Oxford University Press.

Bonger, W. A. (1932). *Inleiding tot de Criminologie*. Haarlem: Erven Bohn.

Brisman, A., & South, N. (2014). *Green cultural criminology: Constructions of environmental harm, consumerism, and resistance to ecocide*. New York: Routledge.

Bruinsma, G., & Bernasco, W. (2004). Criminal groups and transnational illegal markets. *Crime, Law and Social Change, 41*(1), 79–94.

Bryant, C. D. (1979). The zoological connection: Animal-related human behavior. *Social Forces, 58*(2), 399–421.

Carrabine, E., Iganski, P., Lee, M., Plummer, K. & South, N. (2004). The Greening of Criminology. In *Criminology: A Sociological Introduction*. London: Routledge.

Carson, J.T. (1995). Horses and the economy and culture of the choctaw Indians, 1690–1840. *Ethnohistory*, 495-513.

Cazaux, G. (2003). Agenda voor een ecocriminologie of groene milieucriminologie. *Panopticon, 24*, 226–227.

Cazaux, G. (2007). Labelling animals: non-speciesist criminology and techniques to identify other animals. In P. Beirne & N. South (Eds.). *Issues in green criminology*. Cullompton: Willan Publishing.

Coleman, J. W. (1997). *The criminal elite: Understanding white-collar crime*. New York: MacMillan.

Cook, D., Roberts, M., & Lowther, J. (2002). *The international wildlife trade and organised crime: A review of the evidence and the role of the UK*. Wolverhampton: University of Wolverhampton.

Courchamp, F., Angulo, E., Rivalan, P., Hall, R. J., Signoret, L., Bull, L., et al. (2006). Rarity value and species extinction: The anthropogenic allee effect. *PLoS Biology, 4*(12), e415.

Darwin, C. R. (1871). *The Descent of Man, and Selection in Relation to Sex*. London: John Murray.

Dreesbach, A. (2012). *Colonial exhibitions, 'völkerschauen' and the display of the 'other'*. Mainz: Leibniz Institute of European History (IEG).

Ellis, H. (1890). *The criminal*. New York: Scribner & Welford.

Europol (2011). *Organised Crime Threat Assessment (OCTA).* The Hague: Europol.
Europol (2013a). *Serious and Organised Crime Threat Assessment (SOCTA).* The Hague: Europol.
Europol (2013b). *Threat assessment 2013. Environmental crime in the EU.* The Hague: Europol.
Evans, E. P. (1906). *The criminal prosecution and capital punishment of animals.* London: William Heinemann.
Fijnaut, C., & Paoli, L. (2004). *Organised crime in europe: concepts, patterns, and control policies in the European Union and beyond.* Dordrecht: Springer.
Friedrichs, D. (1996). *Trusted criminals: White collar crime in contemporary society.* Belmont: Wadsworth, Cengage Learning.
Friedrichs, D. O., & Rothe, D. L. (2011). *Crimes of the powerful. Routledge handbook of critical criminology.* London: Routledge.
Galeotti, M. (2004). Introduction: global crime today. *Global Crime, 6*(1), 1–7.
Gambetta, D. (2009). *Codes of the underworld: How criminals communicate.* Princeton: Princeton University Press.
Geis, G. (1992). White collar crime: What is it? In K. Schlegel & D. Weisburd (Eds.), *White collar crime reconsidered.* Boston: Northeastern University Press.
Gonzalez, J. A. (2003). Harvesting, local trade, and conservation of parrots in the Northeastern Peruvian Amazon. *Biological Conservation, 114*(3), 437–446.
Gould, S. J. (1996). *The mismeasure of man.* New York: Norton.
Haken, J. (2011). *Transnational crime in the developing world.* Global Financial Integrity.
Hall, A.C. (1902). *Crime in its relations to social progress (No. 40).* New York: Columbia University Press.
Hall, M. (2013). *Victims of environmental harm: Rights, recognition and redress under national and international law.* Oxford: Routledge.
Halsey, M. (1997). Environmental crime: towards an eco-human rights approach. *Current Issues in Criminal Justice, 8*, 217–242.
Halsey, M., & White, R. (1998). Crime, ecophilosophy and environmental harm. *Theoretical Criminology, 2*(3), 345–371.
Hannigan, J. (2006). *Environmental sociology.* New York: Routledge.
Heckenberg, D. (2010). The global transference of toxic harms. In White, R. (Ed.), *Global environmental harm. Criminological perspectives.* Cullompton: Willan Publishing.
Herbig, J. (2010). The illegal trade as a form of conservation crime: a South Africa criminological investigation. In R. White (Ed.), *Global environmental harm. Criminological perspectives.* Cullompton: Willan Publishing.
Hillyard, P., & Tombs, S. (2004). Beyond criminology? In P. Hillyard, C. Pantazis, S. Tombs & D. Gordon (Eds.) (2004). *Beyond criminology. Taking harm seriously.* London: Pluto Press.
Hillyard, P., & Tombs, S. (2007). From 'crime' to social harm? *Crime, Law and Social Change, 48*(1–2), 9–25.
Hillyard, P., Pantazis, C., Tombs, S., & Gordon, D. (Eds.). (2004). *Beyond criminology. Taking harm seriously.* London: Pluto Press.
Hoser, R. T. (1993). *Smuggled: the underground trade in Australia's wildlife.* Mosman: Apollo Books.
Hulsman, L. H. (1986). Critical criminology and the concept of crime. *Crime, Law and Social Change, 10*(1), 63–80.
Hyde, W.W. (1916). The prosecution and punishment of animals and lifeless things in the middle ages and modern times. *University of Pennsylvania Law Review and American Law Register*, 696–730.
Kellert, S. R., & Wilson, E. O. (1993). *The biophilia hypothesis.* Washington, DC: Island Press.
Kleemans, E., & Bunt, H.G. van de (2003). The social organisation of human trafficking. In H. Van de Bunt, D. Siegel & D. Zaitch (Eds.). *Global organized crime. Trends and developments* (97–104). Dordrecht: Kluwer Law International.
Kleemans, E. R., & Van de Bunt, H. G. (1999). The social embeddedness of organized crime. *Transnational Organized Crime, 5*(1), 19–36.

Lawson, K., & Vines, A. (2014). *Global impacts of the illegal wildlife trade: The costs of crime, insecurity and institutional erosion*. London: Chatham House.
Levi, M., & Maguire, M. (2004). Reducing and preventing organised crime: An evidence-based critique. *Crime, Law and Social Change., 42*(5), 397–469.
Liddick, D. R. (2011). *Crimes against nature. Illegal industries and the global environment*. Oxford: Praeger Publishers.
Lindsey, P. A., Masterson, C. L., Beck, A. L., & Romañach, S. (2012). Ecological, social and financial issues related to fencing as a conservation tool in Africa. In M. J. Somers & M. Hayward (Eds.), *Fencing for conservation* (pp. 215–234). New York: Springer.
Lombroso-Ferrero, G. (1911). *Criminal man: According to the classification of Cesare Lombroso*. New York/London: G.P. Putnam.
Lynch, M. (1990). The greening of criminology: A perspective on the 1990s. *The Critical Criminologist, 2*(3), 1–4.
Lynch, M., & Stretesky, P. (2007). Green criminology in the United States. In P. Beirne & N. South (Eds.), *Issues in green criminology: Confronting harms against environments, humanity and other animals*. Devon: Willan Publishing.
Lynch, M. J., & Stretesky, P. B. (2014). *Exploring green criminology: Toward a green criminological revolution*. Farnham: Ashgate Publishing.
Lynch, J. M., & Stretsky, B. P. (2003). The meaning of green: Contrasting criminological perspectives. *Theoretical Criminology, 7*(2), 217–238.
Lyons, J. A., & Natusch, D. J. (2011). Wildlife laundering through breeding farms: Illegal harvest, population declines and a means of regulating the trade of green pythons (Morelia viridis) from Indonesia. *Biological Conservation, 144*(12), 3073–3081.
Matthews, R., & Young, J. (1986). *Confronting crime*. London: Sage Publications.
Merton, R. K. (1938). Social structure and anomie. *American Sociological Review, 3*(5), 672–682.
Mills, L. S., Soulé, M. E., & Doak, D. F. (1993). The keystone-species concept in ecology and conservation. *BioScience*, 219–224.
Mooney, H. A., & Hobbs, R. J. (2000). *Invasive species in a changing world*. Washington, D.C.: Island Press.
Morselli, C. (2009). *Inside criminal networks*. New York: Springer.
Myers, R. A., Baum, J. K., Shepherd, T. D., Powers, S. P., & Peterson, C. H. (2007). Cascading effects of the loss of apex predatory sharks from a coastal ocean. *Science, 315*(5820), 1846–1850.
Nurse, A. (2013). *Animal harm: Perspectives on why people harm and kill animals*. Farnham: Ashgate.
O'Hear, M. M. (2004). Sentencing the green-collar offender: Punishment, culpability, and environmental crime. *Journal of Criminal Law and Criminology*, 133–276.
Olson, G. (2013). *Criminals as animals from Shakespeare to lombroso* (Vol. 8). Berlin: Walter de Gruyter.
Park, R. E., Burgess, E. W., & McKenzie, R. D. (1925). *The city*. Chicago: University of Chicago Press.
Passas, N. (1995). *Organized crime*. Brookfield: Dartmouth.
Passas, N. (1999). Globalization, criminogenic asymmetries and economic crime. *European Journal of Law Reform, 1*, 399–424.
Passas, N. (2000). Global anomie, dysnomie, and economic crime: Hidden consequences of neoliberalism and globalization in Russia and around the world. *Social Justice, 27*(2), 16–44.
Passas, N. (2002). Cross-border crime and the interface between legal and illegal actors. In P. C. van Duyne, K. von Lampe, & N. Passas (Eds.), *Upperworld and underworld in cross-border crime* (pp. 11–42). Nijmegen: Wolf Legal Publishers.
Passas, N., & Goodwin, N. (2005). *It's legal but it ain't right: Harmful social consequences of legal industries*. Ann Arbor: University of Michigan Press.
Pearce, F., & Tombs, S. (1998). *Toxic capitalism: Corporate crime and the chemical industry*. Aldershot: Dartmouth Pubishing Company.
Petrossian, G. A., & Clarke, R. V. (2014). Explaining and controlling illegal commercial fishing an application of the CRAVED theft model. *British Journal of Criminology, 54*(1), 73–90.

Pires, S. F., & Moreto, W. D. (2011). Preventing wildlife crimes: Solutions that can overcome the 'Tragedy of the Commons'. *European Journal on Criminal Policy and Research, 17*(2), 101–123.

Power, M. E., Tilman, D., Estes, J. A., Menge, B. A., Bond, W. J., Mills, L. S. et al. (1996). Challenges in the quest for keystones. *BioScience*, 609–620.

Quinney, R. (1970). *The social reality of crime*. Boston: Little and Brown.

Regan, T. (1983). *The case for animal rights*. Berkeley, CA: University of California Press.

Ruggiero, V., & South, N. (2010). Green criminology and dirty collar crime. *Critical Criminology, 18*(4), 251–262.

Ruggiero, V., & South, N. (2013). Green criminology and crimes of the economy: Theory, research and praxis. *Critical Criminology*, 21(3), 359–373.

Ryder, R. (1970). Speciesism again: The original leaflet. *Critical Society*, 2, Spring 2010.

Schneider, J. (2012). *Sold into extinction: The global trade in endangered species*. Santa Barbara: Praeger.

Schwendinger, H., & Schwendinger, J. (1970). Defenders of order or guardians of human rights? *Issues in Criminology, 5*(2), 123–157.

Sellin, T. (1938). *Culture conflict and crime*. New York: Social Science Research Council.

Sevdermish, M., Miciak, A. R., & Levinson, A. A. (1998). The diamond pipeline into the third millennium: A multi-channel system from the mine to the consumer. *Geoscience Canada, 25* (2), 71–84.

Shaw, C. R., & McKay, H. D. (1942). *Juvenile delinquency and urban areas*. Chicago: University of Chicago Press.

Shoemaker, D. J. (1996). *Theories of delinquency*. New York: Oxford University Press.

Siegel, D. (2008). Diamonds and organized crime: The case of Antwerp. In D. Siegel & H. Nelen (Eds.). *Organized crime. Culture, markets and policies*. New York: Springer.

Siegel, D. (2009). *The mazzel ritual*. Dordrecht, Heidelberg, London, New York: Springer.

Siegel, D. (2011). Trafficking of 'conflict diamonds'. In C. Smith, S. Zhang, & R. Barberet (Eds.), *Routledge handbook of criminology*. London: Routledge.

Simmel, G. (1978). *The philosophy of money*. London: Routledge.

Singer, P. (1975). *Animal liberation: A new ethics for our treatment of animals*. New York: Random House.

Situ, Y., & Emmons, D. (1999). *Environmental crime: The criminal justice system's role in protecting the environment*. Thousand Oaks: Sage Publications.

Sollund, R. A. (Ed.). (2008). *Global harms; ecological crime and speciesism*. New York: Nova Science Publishers.

Sollund, R. (2013). Animal trafficking and trade: Abuse and species injustice. In D. S. Westerhuis, R. Walters, & T. Wyatt (Eds.), *Emerging issues in green criminology: Exploring power, justice and harm*. Basingstoke: Palgrave Macmillan.

Sollund, R. & Maher, J. (2015) *The illegal wildlife trade. A case study report on the illegal wildlife trade in the United Kingdom, Norway, Colombia and Brazil*. Oslo & Wales: University of Oslo and University of South Wales.

South, N. (1998). A green field for criminology: A proposal for a perspective. *Theoretical Criminology, 2*(2), 211–233.

South, N. (2004). Green criminology. In E. Carrabine, P. Cox, M. Lee, N. South, K. Plummer, & J. Turton (2004). *Criminology: A sociological introduction*. London: Routledge.

South, N. & Beirne, P. (Eds.) (1998). For a green criminology. *Special Edition of Theoretical Criminology* 2(2).

Spapens, T. (2010). Macro networks, collectives, and business processes: An integrated approach to organized crime. *European Journal of Crime, Criminal Law and Criminal Justice, 18*, 185–215.

Spencer, H. (1884). *The man versus the state*. London: Williams and Norgate.

Stretesky, P. B., Long, M. A., & Lynch, M. J. (2013). *The treadmill of crime: Political economy and green criminology*. London: Routledge.

Sutherland, E. (1940). White-collar criminality. *American Sociological Review, 5*(1), 1–12.

Sutherland, E. (1949). *White collar crime*. New York: Dryden Press.

Sutherland, E. (1983). *White collar crime*. New Haven: Yale University Press.

Tarde, G. (1886). *La criminalité comparée*. Paris: Alcan.

Terborgh, J., & Estes, J. A. (Eds.). (2013). *Trophic cascades: Predators, prey, and the changing dynamics of nature*. Washington, DC: Island Press.

Terborgh, J. et al. (2001). Ecological meltdown in predator-free forest fragments. *Science*, 294 (5548), 1923–1926.

Tremblay, P., Cusson, M., & Morselli, C. (1998). Market offenses and limits to growth. *Crime, Law and Social Change, 29*(4), 311–330.

Van de Bunt, H., Siegel, D., & Zaitch, D. (2014). The social embeddedness of organized crime. In L. Paoli (Ed.), *The oxford handbook of organized crime*. Oxford: Oxford University Press.

Van Duyne, P. C., Von Lampe, K., & Passas, N. (2002). *Upperworld and underworld in cross-border crime*. Nijmegen: Wolf Legal Publishers.

Van Uhm, D. P. (2012). Organised crime in the wildlife trade. *Centre for Information and Research on Organised Crime (CIROC) Newsletter*, 10(2): 2–4.

Van Uhm, D. P. (2015). Towards moral principles regarding non-human animals: a green criminological perspective. In F. de Jong et al. (Eds.), *Overarching views of crime and deviancy. Rethinking the legacy of the Utrecht school.* The Hague: Eleven International Publishing, 565–587.

Vander Beken, T., Hansens, J., Black, C., Defruytier, M., De Ruyver, B., & Cuyvers, L. (2004). *Kwetsbaarheid voor georganiseerde criminaliteit*. Een gevalstudie van de diamantsector. Gent: Academia Press.

Walklate, S. (2007). *Understanding criminology*. Maidenhead: Open University Press.

Westerhuis, D., Walters, R., & Wyatt, T. (2013). *Emerging issues in green criminology: Exploring power, justice and harm*. Basingstoke: Palgrave Macmillan.

White, R. (2007). Green criminology and the pursuit of social and ecological justice. In P. Beirne & N. South (Eds.) (2007). *Issues in green criminology*. Cullompton: Willan Publishing.

White, R. (2008). *Crimes against nature: Environmental criminology and ecological justice*. Devon: Willan Publishing.

White, R. (2011). *Transnational environmental crime. Toward an eco-global criminology*. London: Routledge.

White, R. (2013). *Environmental harm. An eco-justice perspective*. Bristol: Policy Press.

White, R., & Heckenberg, D. (2014). *Green criminology: An introduction to the study of environmental harm*. London: Routledge.

Williams, P. (2001). *Transnational criminal networks. Networks and netwars: The future of terror, crime, and militancy.* Rand Corporation Monograph.

Wolf, B. (2011). 'Green-collar crime': Environmental crime and justice in the dociological perspective. *Sociology Compass, 5*(7), 499–511.

Wolfgang, M.E. (1960). Pioneers in criminology: Cesare Lombroso (1835–1909). *The Journal of Criminal Law, Criminology, and Police Science*, 361–391.

Wolfgang, M. E. (1972). Cesare Lornbroso. In H. Mannheim (Ed.), *Pioneers in criminology*. Patterson Smith: Montclair.

Wyatt, T. (2013). *Wildlife trafficking: A deconstruction of the crime, the victims, and the offenders*. Basingstoke: Palgrave Macmillan.

Wyler, L. S., & Sheikh, P. A. (2013). *International illegal trade in wildlife: Threats and US policy*. Washington, D.C.: Congressional Research Service report for Congress.

Yee, K. S., Carpenter, T. E. & Cardona, C. J. (2009). Epidemiology of H5N1 avian influenza. *Comp Immunol Microbiol Infect Dis* Jul, 32(4), 325–340.

Zaitch, D., Boekhout van Solinge, T. & Müller, G. (2014). Harms, crimes and natural resource exploitation: A green criminological and human rights perspective on land-use change. In M. Bavinck, L .Pellegrini & E. Mostert (Eds.). *Conflicts over natural resources in the global south.* London: CRS Press.

Zimmerman, M. E. (2003). The black market for wildlife: Combating transnational organized crime in the illegal wildlife trade. *Vanderbilt Journal of Transnational Law, 36*(5), 1657–1690.

Chapter 5
Enter the Field of Wildlife

After decades of leaving environmental crimes to other disciplines, such as conservation biology, political ecology and development studies, criminologists have started to focus on environmental issues including the illegal trade in wildlife. This study answers the call for empirical research on transnational environmental crimes by exploring the illegal trade in wildlife. However, insights into this type of crime are extremely limited and only very little criminological studies have focussed on this research field. While the EU appears to be one of the foremost demand markets for wildlife (Europol 2011), the global focus of scientists, NGOs and policy makers is on source countries in Africa, Asia and Latin America. This exploratory research is derived from the idea of understanding underlying mechanisms such as the sociocultural context and economic constraints of actors and their organization of the illegal wildlife trade to the EU. In other words:

- Why is there a demand market for wildlife?
- Which actors are involved in the illegal wildlife trade?
- How is the illegal wildlife business organized?
- What are the harmful consequences of the wildlife trade?

To obtain a global overview of this illegal trade, statistical descriptive analyses were carried out on a database with confiscations of illegal wildlife shipments in the EU (Chap. 6). Based on these quantitative analyses, multiple case studies were selected. Case studies as a research design are regularly used in criminological research (e.g. Shaw 1930; Sutherland 1937; Geis 1991). A case study is a detailed, intensive study of research defined as a phenomenon, which manifests itself in social reality. The researcher uses multiple observation techniques and information sources to sketch and understand the complexity of the case study (Leys et al. 2010). The aim is to describe and explain the specific characteristics of the phenomenon. According to Yin (2008) case studies are mainly appropriate to answer how and why questions. In this study both quantitative and qualitative methods were used to explore the case studies. The three case studies were selected subject to three conditions: First, the case studies aim to align top illegal exporters of

D.P. van Uhm, *The Illegal Wildlife Trade*, Studies of Organized Crime 15,
DOI 10.1007/978-3-319-42129-2_5

wildlife to the EU. Second, the illegal trade consists of substantial trade, taking into account the context of the species population. Third, the three case studies guarantee a variation in terms of symbolic, functional and entertaining use of the wildlife trade concerned. An extensive argumentation is made after the quantitative analyses in Chap. 6 (Sect. 6.7). Based on these conditions the following three case studies were selected:

1. The illegal trade in caviar
2. The illegal trade in Barbary macaques
3. The illegal trade in traditional Chinese medicine

To understand the numbers in the statistical analyses and to describe the actors and network structures, qualitative field research has been carried out. Semi-structured interviews were conducted with informants and participant observation has been used regarding the illegal wildlife trade in general, and caviar, Barbary macaques and traditional Chinese medicine specifically (Chaps. 7–9). Finally, secondary data include scientific literature, international police reports, news articles and reports from NGOs.

5.1 Analyzing Seizures

While several studies have been conducted on individual cases of the illegal trade in wildlife (e.g. Wyatt 2009, 2011; Herbig 2010; Lindsey et al. 2012; Pires 2012; Petrossian and Clarke 2014), it remains unclear what kind of major flows in relation to animal species are traded in the illegal wildlife trade. To obtain an overview of the illegal trade to the EU, data relating to confiscations in the EU were obtained from the European Union Trade in Wildlife Information eXchange database (EU-TWIX), a database of information on wildlife seizures in the EU. The data include more than 20,000 shipments ($N = 22,204$) of animals and animal products seized in the EU between 2001–2010. The data were organized into a categorical SPSS (Statistical Package for the Social Sciences) database and analysed. The illegal shipments originated from 207 different countries from all over the world, with a marked concentration in Africa and Southeast Asia. The European Union is defined as members of the European Union in the year 2012. The following countries are included in the analysis: Austria, Belgium, Bulgaria, Cyprus, the Czech Republic, Denmark, Estonia, Finland, France, Germany, Greece, Hungary, Ireland, Italy, Latvia, Lithuania, Luxembourg, Malta, the Netherlands, Poland, Portugal, Romania, Slovakia, Slovenia, Spain, Sweden and the United Kingdom. The data variables include confiscation incidents by: species order, species family, species genus, subspecies, appendices (Appendices I, II, III or unknown: N), Annexes (Annexes A, B, C, D), quantity, relative description code (e.g. caviar, ivory), whether they were alive, dead, or in product form, export volume (reported in individuals or products), measurement unit (e.g. kg, m^3), date of entry, importing country (EU Member States), exporting country, source country, import and export purpose (captive breeding, educational, botanical gardens, hunting trophies, enforcement, biomedical research, (re)introduction, personal, circuses, scientific, commercial trade and zoos), location type (e.g. land boundary), source (wild [W], captive bred [C, D and F], ranch raised [R] and unknown [U]), purpose (e.g. personal use, commercial trade), transport type (air, mail, maritime, pedestrian, rail, river, road, other, unknown), CITES offence, concealment method (e.g. in container, inside vehicle), detection (customs' documentary checks, intelligence/investigation, random control, routine, targeting, tip-off, other, unknown), nationality, job (e.g. animal trader, diplomat) and fine. Since volumes were measured as either specimens or in weight, the data were analysed by incidents to avoid converting weighted products into products.

The variables 'date of entry', 'species class', and 'source country' were recoded as different variables. The variable 'date of entry' was recoded as 'year of entry' (2001–2010) to analyse trends over the years. The species in the variable 'species class' were recoded as the new following umbrella class 'animal groupings': *Mammalia* as mammals, *Aves* as birds, *Reptilia* as reptiles, *Actinopterygii*, *Elasmobranchii* and *Pisces* as fish, instead of *Anthozoa* or *Hydrozoa*[1] the category 'coral' was used for coral, *Bivalvia* and *Gastropoda* as molluscs. The six groupings of animals included for this analysis were mammals (1), birds (2), reptiles (3), fish (4), coral (5) and molluscs (6). These six groupings were chosen because they represent 93 % of all incidents. The variable 'source country' was recoded as the new variable 'source continent'. EU Member States and third countries (outside the EU) were divided by continent, based on 'The World Factbook' of the Central Intelligence Agency (CIA).[2] The following subheadings have been made: North America (1), Central America (2), South America (3), Africa (4), Europe (5), Central Asia (6), South Asia (7), East and Southeast Asia (8), Middle East (9), Australia/Oceania (10) and Antarctica (11) (Appendix II).

Besides descriptive statistical analyses, a chi-squared test (X^2 test) has been used to determine whether a significant difference occurs between expected frequencies and observed frequencies. For instance, whether there is a significant difference in the number of seizures between the CITES Appendices. The statistics from a chi-squared test arise from the assumption of independent normally distributed data.

The reliability of the data is entirely dependent on the accuracy with which EU member states report these data (Blundell and Mascia 2005). For instance, for ten years no single seizure was recorded by Greece and a comparison between seizures in the Netherlands recorded by the Ministry of Economics and EU-TWIX data indicates a discrepancy.[3] Moreover, the confiscations reflect only a part of the illegal trade as a large part of this trade remains unreported or undiscovered, the so-called dark number (Coleman and Moynihan 1996). Law enforcement experts

[1]These classes include also non-coral species.

[2]The World Factbook of the Central Intelligence Agency, accessed in 2012.

[3]Freedom of Information request at the Ministry of Economics in the Netherlands, 2013.

estimate that no more than 10 % of all contraband of wildlife is seized (Stiles et al. 2013). In the absence of more detailed data, the analyses are used to obtain a global overview of the illegal wildlife trade to the EU.

5.2 Chasing the Wildlife

To explore the illegal trade in wildlife based on three case studies, primary data were collected and used from a grounded theory approach whereby theory or concepts are constructed through the analysis of data (Charmaz 2006: 2). I conducted *multi-sited ethnographic research*, a method that is designed to obtain in-depth knowledge of a phenomenon that has barely been explored through different field sites geographically and/or socially. The researcher uses the same qualitative research plan at various local, regional, national or international sites from those many which could potentially be included to obtain an overview of the phenomenon (Hannerz 2003; Siegel 2009). According to Marcus (1995), during the multi-sited research one follows the people, the thing, the story, the biography, the metaphor or the conflict. In this research I follow the illegal wildlife trade along its route. The areas of research covered both origin areas, such as fishing villages and hunting grounds, as well as the final destinations in the markets and restaurants. In total two fieldwork visits to Russia (March and September 2014) and Morocco (March and April 2013) and single fieldwork visits to China (November–December 2013), Kazakhstan (March 2014) and Azerbaijan (September–October 2014) were made.

During my fieldwork I engaged in *participant observations* and stayed in the areas where wildlife was being poached or hunted (e.g. Azrou, Kunming, Dagestan) or in the trading areas (e.g. Marrakech, Guangzhou, Hong Kong, Moscow, Makhachkala, Atyrau, Baku) to interview my informants and to observe the process. I visited several fishing towns, forests, TCM, caviar and animal markets, TCM clinics and hospitals, bars, clubs and restaurants. In these areas I established relationships and met my informants. By observing the process of the illegal trade, through direct, naturalistic observations, it was possible to gain a more in-depth understanding of the general context in which actors operate (DeWalt and DeWalt 2011). For instance, understanding a poacher in Sulak (Dagestan) without a picture of his social economic situation or an interview with an illegal caviar trader without the context of the market would be impossible. In my participant observations both *obtrusive* and *unobtrusive* methods were used depending on the setting. In a covert setting this could be an advantage as people would not be aware that they are being observed by a researcher (Zaitch et al. 2009). For instance, while undercover I observed several markets where traders sold their illegal trade such as wild caviar and raw materials for TCM under the counter (unobtrusive). On the other hand, my main goal was to find important informants who would be able to give me useful and reliable information that required me to be more overt (obtrusive). In addition,

I took photographs with my mobile phone in some settings without drawing too much attention; whilst in other situations I took photographs in order to record the time of the interviews with my informants. This resulted in a continuum between both *insider* and *outsider* experiences.

5.3 Approaching and Understanding Informants

The primary research carried out for this project was in the form of *semi-structured interviews* with persons who are directly involved in the illegal trade in wildlife in order to strengthen, complement and understand the quantitative data. Next to the value of additional and confirmatory information, this qualitative research method creates a link between theory and the actual situation and, moreover, increases the reliability and validity of the research. The method of semi-structured interviews was chosen due to the fact that it accommodates flexibility (Beyens and Tournel 2009), which allows specific issues to be addressed in more detail with a clear focus on the actors, modus operandi and network structures in the illegal trade in wildlife. A framework of themes was developed to support the author during the interviews.

The interviews were mainly held with people who are directly involved in the illegal trade, such as poachers, illegal traders, smugglers and middlemen; these interviewees were the key informants. Other informants include people who are indirectly involved such as legal traders, scientists, journalists, lawyers, officials and representatives of relevant organizations and institutions so as to compare the stories and interpretations of my primary informants involved in the illegal trade. The majority of the conversations took place during fieldwork abroad with a minority in the EU. I have spoken with 67 informants in Russia, Kazakhstan and Azerbaijan, 32 respondents in Morocco and 68 informants in China. These conversations included semi-structured interviews and, sometimes, small chats. For the full list see Appendices VI, VII, VIII and IX.

Many hours were spent day and night in order to analyse the situation and to understand the sociocultural background of the informants; this was achieved with a great deal of help from my interpreters. Although not all my interviews were recorded, after any interview fieldwork notes were made and each conversation was further discussed and analysed in their social context at the end of each day. Moreover, my interpreters were *gatekeepers* and played an important role in building trust with the informants. During my research in China it became clear that one of my interpreters was not only a gatekeeper but was also a consumer of illegal traditional Chinese medicine herself, which gave me the opportunity to understand the illegal use and purchase of TCM.

An important method for finding respondents was through *snowball sampling:* future participants were recruited from among their acquaintances and through the first point of access (Goodman 1961). The focus was on their specific views, modus operandi and network structures regarding illegal wildlife trade to cover the whole spectrum of people who are involved in the illegal wildlife trade. These conversations varied from half an hour to five hours. I decided to send my recordings and files by 'wetransfer'[4] to my e-mail on a weekly basis so as to avoid computer problems and perhaps losing data at border controls. As my data included sensitive information about the role of government officials, I was worried about risking losing these data while passing through border controls.

The informants provided information varying from in-depth interviews to informal chats on street corners during observations. I still keep in touch with several respondents today, while others consisted of only brief contact. During some of these conversations informants suddenly decided to stop talking about their business, while others structurally provided new information. There were places I visited more than once, while other places were just visited for a brief period of time. Varying from very rich neighbourhoods in Baku, Moscow and Atyrau to extremely poor villages such as Kirovskiy, Izberbash and Neftçala near stretches of the Caspian Sea, I usually had appointments in public places, but in certain cases I met the illegal traders at their homes or even at parties (e.g. Astrakhan).

Despite structured plans and schedules, the plans were often subject to change, as unexpected events and twists occurred. Common sense in combination with indispensable luck guided the investigation. Due to limited fixed appointments during my fieldwork, I was quite flexible in my research schedule. For instance, I decided to fly 12 h in advance to another city due to new information that indicated the importance of a specific trade area. In other circumstances I stayed for several weeks, a longer period than expected.

5.4 Access and Building Trust

In contrast to claims made by others, by my predecessors, access to illegal entrepreneurs often went fairly smoothly. I found myself, sometimes to my surprise,[5] in a long conversation for hours with a key informant or, not incidentally, I was invited to have dinner at their homes. While I tried to avoid any undercover research, not all persons that I met knew about my research. In certain situations I introduced myself as a researcher on the wildlife trade in general, while in others they thought I was a buyer or even a seller myself. For instance, during my search for a dealer in illegal rhino horn in Hong Kong, TCM traders thought that I carried a rhino horn for sale in my plastic bag, instead of just a notepad which I usually carried. Apparently a Western white man with a rhino horn for sale or asking questions about this kind of business is not uncommon.

I usually introduced myself as a researcher from Utrecht University and always made it clear that my focus was on (crime) structures instead of the specific

---

[4]Wetransfer is a free service to transfer files by internet.

[5]For instance: without having made an appointment, I stumbled across an illegal entrepreneur at a local cafeteria in the TCM neighbourhood in Anguo, China.

surnames of offenders. I underlined that names were not important to me. Informants regularly asked me, sometimes more than twice, to confirm that no names or companies were mentioned. Of course I respected their wish: the names of informants used in this book were changed. To underline the confidentiality and anonymity it is important to defend my informants against adverse effects and criminal prosecution. Moreover, without this anonymity fewer informants would provide useful information (Zaitch 2002; O'Gorman and Vander Laenen 2009).

Nevertheless, occasionally people were initially suspicious about my background. And people asked several questions about me to the interpreter. For instance in Russia: "*Is he a spy from the US?*" Or in Morocco: "*Is he from the United Nations?*" Sometimes the way in which I was introduced differed from the real situation. For example, "*He is a researcher from a university in the Netherlands who writes about the trade in caviar*", not mentioning that I was primarily interested in the illegal trade. After a while most informants felt more comfortable to speak about illegal aspects.

Besides the illegal trade, I spoke with key informants about other issues such as their family, interests and even sensitive subjects such as politics. For example, during my fieldwork in Russia in March 2014, tempers ran high between the West and Russia regarding the conflict between Russian separatists and political leaders in the Ukraine. Although political discussions can lead to disagreements, they regularly resulted in a more open conversation and even closer contact with the informants.

Just like the role of trust based on the relationship that illegal entrepreneurs have with their colleagues, trust is also very important in conversations with informants. This is a necessity if one talks about illegal business with the informants and, moreover, the illegal circuit operates according to a circle of trust and distrust (e.g. Zaitch 2002).

Although one could argue that it would be more difficult to conduct research if one does not speak the language[6], I believe that in my research in many situations it actually was an advantage to be a *stranger*. As Simmel would say: the wanderer comes today and leaves tomorrow. Generally, people were not afraid that I was an 'official'. An informant explained that he trusted me because I did not look like a government official and that this has worked to my advantage. Key informants provided me with a lot of detailed information about their poaching, smuggling and bribing methods, in the knowledge that I would leave.

Even though I was occasionally seen as a stranger or wanderer, in other situations I was considered to be part of the community. Sometimes informants introduced me after a while as a 'friend' from the Netherlands and on occasion I was invited to their homes. In this role I was more integrated in the community. I found myself in Russian karaoke bars sharing a drink with informants, enjoyed the tea parties in China and had forest walks with poachers in Morocco. I still have contact with several informants who have become acquaintances close to friends.

[6]Understanding the conversations would be valuable, see the limitations Sect. 5.9.

5.5 Talking About Illegal Business

Unexpectedly, most respondents loved to talk about issues related to the illegal trade in wildlife. On the one hand, they dared to speak about it because the illegal trade in wildlife is not yet completely criminalized while, on the other hand, they find excitement in what they do; it is a part of their life. These illegal entrepreneurs even sometimes felt honoured to talk about their business and shared their life stories while presenting me with (digital) photographs of their lives. Of course, there were those who were not keen to speak about their business, others were scared of their higher ranking bosses, but in many cases people started talking about illegal businesses quite easily. They regularly started with stories about others, and eventually admitted that they themselves were also involved. Furthermore, there is a substantial nexus between the legal and illegal trade and people talk about their illegal business in legal matters, such as in teahouses, bars and restaurants. Often the illegal entrepreneurs were also legal entrepreneurs.

In addition, many informants claimed to be irresponsible with the use of many, sometimes justified, *neutralization techniques* (Sykes and Matza 1957). "The whole system is corrupt, why would I stick to the law." "Besides poaching and fishing, we have no other way of surviving." "I have been in this business for years, but the law has recently made it punishable. What else should I do?" Many informants spoke about their hopeless situation, wrong decisions, corrupt politics or an unequal society. On the other hand, other respondents spoke about their business with pride. "Nobody can do something to me." "I am smart enough to work together with officials." "Criminals should be afraid of me." They proclaimed that they are fearless, powerful and intelligent.

Some informants were impressed by the fact that I dared to investigate this subject. Other informants even indicated that it was too dangerous to ask specific questions or to go to certain places (e.g. Dagestan, Russia). However, on most occasions they helped me with information and linked me to other people in the business. On many occasions I was surprised by the extremely detailed information from my informants. Yet, I could not just take all the information for granted. I had to repeat questions to different people and occasionally answers contradicted each other. Each time one gets a small piece of the puzzle that is eventually put together. Activities were mostly cross referenced among various sources to check validity and reliability.

Finally, on some occasions expectations arose among my respondents. Especially in China, in order to build trust I tried to use the cultural practice of *guanxi*[7] and developed social relationships with my informants. For instance, an illegal entrepreneur in Guangzhou wanted to set up a TCM business in the Netherlands and had all sorts of related questions. In this way the conversation had sided interests, because I could help him with general information about regulation

[7]The *guanxi* principle refers to the dynamics of favours and personalized services in Chinese networks and will be explained in more detail in Chap. 9.

in the Netherlands. And on several occasions I brought along gifts and presents for my informants. It also occurred that informants were eager to provide information in the hope of exacting revenge on rivals. For instance, the director of a caviar farm in the Astrakhan region told me about competitors who paid money to officials to fish for sturgeon under the scientific quota size. In such cases I had to be especially careful with the reliability of the information and to check again. Although gossip could play a role in data collection as valuable information, double-checking with other sources is important (Siegel 2009). The use of conflicting information was always a very detailed consideration with regard to all possible arguments from different sources.

5.6 Dangerous Situations and Ethical Dilemmas

Does every criminologist have dirty hands? Among criminologists there is a discussion about appropriate research methods to study illegal business where the safety of the researcher is at stake (Siegel 2005, 2009). During my research I was very discreet with the information which I handled so as to avoid dangerous situations. As a precaution I recorded spoken messages on my phone and computer with information about my work and underlined that I did not want to be involved in illegal forms of trade. I was just conducting research on the illegal trade in wildlife and had no intention of becoming involved. While I was occasionally really 'close' to people involved in the illegal business, it was important to remain peripheral (Zaitch 2002). Since sentences of several years imprisonment can currently be imposed for trading in rhino horn, caviar or tiger bones, I had to be careful in order not to become involved in illegal activities. Also because I found myself in secluded places with people who have no reservations in resorting to violence. I always clarified that I was there for research activities and not for 'problems' regarding the illegal business.

Although several criminologists warn against dangerous situations during fieldwork (e.g. Williams et al. 1992; Ferrell and Hamm 1998), in most cases I felt relatively safe. Only on a few occasions did I feel that I was in a sensitive situation. For instance, illegal caviar traders in Izberbash in Dagestan (Russia) who tried to persuade me to start a business line in illegal caviar from Makhachkala to the Netherlands. Or my informant 'Ali' in Baku who decided, after hours of talking about caviar lines from Azerbaijan to the EU, to focus more on the market in the Netherlands. He asked me to help him with information about enforcement in the Netherlands. I had anticipated this question by giving him general information about law enforcement in the Netherlands, such as public organizations involved in the law enforcement of the trade in caviar.

However, I received a great deal of tips, advice and warnings from informants to avoid dangerous situations. Nevertheless, there were situations on the edge of safety. For instance, a rhino horn dealer in Anguo (China) told me to go with him to discuss his business in private. In a very small room in a small backstreet alley I was suddenly among four large men who were armed and who were clearly not waiting for people who were snooping around. They wanted to know my exact background, why I asked such questions and why I was there. In all honesty I was glad that they allowed me to go after answering these questions. And my Chinese interpreter indicated during a *tuk tuk* ride that he was firmly convinced that we were being followed by people involved in the business.

Not only people involved in wildlife crimes but officials could also be unhappy with researchers from the West who are looking for information relating to this illegal trade. Especially since officials also play a role in the illegal trade in wildlife. For instance, similar questions were asked during road controls in Dagestan where military personnel in balaclavas and with kalashnikovs were ready to intervene. Or Chinese local officials who arrived after a call from a hotel in a small town in China to check who I was and what I was doing. This makes sense considering the background of well-known cases in Russia and China where researchers and journalists are occasionally arrested or forcibly asked to leave a specific area. Also at border crossings (e.g. the Dagestan-Azerbaijan border or that of Astrakhan-Kazakhstan) people responded to my arrival with suspicion. At the border between Dagestan and Azerbaijan I was taken to a special room to answer questions about my background and, last but not least, to pay an amount of money (a bribe) to get out of Russia.

It also happened that a potentially dangerous situation was created by the intervention of the police. In Fez (Morocco) after talking for an hour and a half with one of my key informants, he was arrested in broad daylight at the entrance of the famous Medina. Apparently, my informant was wanted by the police. My interpreter and I were forced to keep our distance. The informant was taken to the police station and we were interrogated and asked for our passports after which we were allowed to leave. This was not the only time my informant was arrested. Several weeks later it turned out that another informant had been arrested in Oujda: when we called him the police answered his phone. The day later he was released and we could speak to him again. However, I never ended up in serious trouble, mainly due to carefully considering the interests depending on the setting (i.e. going a step further or just retreating), but perhaps the most important reason was common sense. In certain situations, I decided to leave early to avoid risky situations, while in others I stayed for a long time.

An important ethical issue is that as a researcher you will disappear at a certain point in time, but the interpreter will remain having gained a great deal of information about illegal practices. Leaving potentially dangerous situations on time, leaving room for the interpreted translations and making agreements in advance covered any potential risks. Second, according to Zaitch (2002) it is of great importance to protect your informants as long as one is not directly confronted with serious violent crimes or lives being placed at risk. In all other cases I kept my informants confidential; all real names were removed in notes and computer files. Furthermore, several informants were already introduced with false names or nicknames. Third, talking to illegal wildlife entrepeneurs in their social environment and, simultaneously, having contact with officials could be dangerous or unethical (Bovenkerk 1998), due to having access to sensitive information from informants *and* the police. Because of the latter point, I decided to talk mainly to people involved in the illegal trade instead of the police in the source countries.

5.7 Literature, Police Reports and News Articles

Various sources of information were used to support the primary data in this research. Relevant literature about the wildlife trade from a historical, ecological, sociological, juridical and criminological perspective were studied. Besides relevant scientific literature regarding the wildlife trade, scientific literature about crime networks, legal entrepreneurs in illegal businesses and green crimes in general were studied. Although scientific literature about the illegal wildlife trade is limited, international police reports, news articles, reports from several NGOs and data from wildlife trade databases were more than welcome. The secondary data has been used to sketch the background and context of the forms of the trade in wildlife. News articles were analysed from several Chinese, Russian, Moroccan, Dutch and English newspapers regarding illegal wildlife-related cases. The searches consisted of terms related to the illegal trade in wildlife in general or caviar, Barbary macaques and TCM specifically. Newspapers were also analysed as to their validity and reliability. In spite of the ability to look in various police records in the Netherlands, most of them include limited information and were not very informative. This has to do with the fact that illegal wildlife trade cases were scarce and, moreover, the cases often involve flukes rather than extensive studies.

5.8 Triangulation, Validity and Reliability

In this research the first step has been to statistically describe and interpret the available data on seizures. This presents the visible global flows of the illegal trade in wildlife. Due to the large dark number in the illegal wildlife trade, these data are initially simply used as an indication. Three case studies were chosen based on quantitative data in combination with secondary data. Subsequently, the case studies were qualitatively researched based on fieldwork in several countries abroad. To present the explanations, interpretetations and statements, quotes are extensively used throughout the text. However, the statements from the informants should not be interpreted as ‘scientific truths’ (Decorte and Zaitch 2010; Siegel 2013). To increase the validity and realibility the information from different sources is always compared with interviews, quantitative and secondary data. Combining different data sources and both qualitative and quantitative research contributes to internal validity and reliability. The external validity and reliability is approached due to the large database of more than 20,000 confiscations ($N = 22{,}204$) in the EU together with the large number of informants (more than 150). This data triangulation and methodological triangulation substantially strengthen the scientific value of this research.

5.9 Limitations and Difficulties

Several limitations and difficulties were also noticed during my research. The results of the quantitative research are completely dependent on the accuracy with which EU member states report their data. Moreover, the confiscations reflect only the visible illegal wildlife shipments recorded by the Member States. It is plausibel that the confiscations are just the tip of the iceberg, since a large part of the trade remains unreported or undiscovered. It is estimated that no more than 10 % of the illegal trade is confiscated. Only a part of these confiscations are recorded in the EU-TWIX database. It would be likely that certain flows of illegal wildlife are invisible in the seizures because they are not detected at all. Although the numbers give an overview of the market, it is unclear what the story behind the numbers is.

To understand the actors and networks behind the figures, qualitative research is examined on the basis of semi-structured interviews with people involved in the illegal trade. Although it is necessary to speak to persons who are involved in order to understand the illegal trade, there are several limitations to this research method. First, conflicting information demanded many double checks that were sometimes impossible. A very detailed consideration of all possible arguments from different sources was necessary to understand the underlying story. Second, in certain situations it was not possible to record the interviews; I had to reconstruct the information. It was a great advantage that my interpreter helped me to clarify the information in the context of the sociocultural backgrounds of the informants. Third, one is completely dependent on the availability of informants. Sometimes it was straightforward and sometimes difficult to find the right people who were willing to talk about their illegal business. In certain regions of Russia people were afraid to talk because of possible threats from higher bosses. Fourth, there is a risk of over-involvement (Zaitch 2002). There were situations during my research that I must underline that I had to be peripheral. Especially since I occasionally participated in other activities with the people who were involved in the illegal trade and informants became acquaintances close to friends. Fifth, there were dangerous situations during my fieldwork research. For instance, people involved in the illegal trade in caviar are linked to forms of excessive violence and even murder. Although there were situations on the edge of safety, I never ended up in real trouble, mainly due to carefully considering the interests involved, but probably also because of the use of common sense. Sixth, while I experienced the company of my interpreters during my fieldwork as positive (e.g. gatekeeper, analyses of interviews), it can be seen as a limitation on the research, since I was dependent on translation by the interpreter. To overcome this limitation, at the end of each day I summarized and analysed the interviews together with my interpreter to make sure that I understood the information in a proper manner. Finally, the Western perspective of the research should not be underestimated. Conducting research abroad requires a good understanding of the social and cultural background of the country or region. For instance, the catching of sturgeon cannot be understood without understanding the political socioeconomic situation of minority groups in Dagestan. Another example is the use of illegal traditional Chinese medicine in China. The function cannot be understood without the sociological and cultural history of TCM.

In the next chapter (Chap. 6) quantitative descriptive analyses based on seizures in the EU will be made in order to obtain an overall picture of the illegal trade in wildlife. Concerning these quantitative analyses three case studies are selected and explored based on qualitative multi-sited ethnographic research in the following chapters. In Chap. 7 the illegal trade in caviar will be discussed, in Chap. 8 the illegal trade in Barbary macaques will be described and in Chap. 9 the illegal TCM trade will be outlined. In the last chapter the case studies will be analytically compared as to their similarities and differences and criminological analyses will be made to understand the future of the illegal trade in wildlife.

References

Beyens, K., & Tournel, H. (2009). Mijnwerkers of ontdekkingsreizigers? Het kwalitatieve interview. In T. Decorte & D. Zaitch (Eds.), *Kwalitatieve methoden en technieken in de criminologie* (pp. 200–232). Leuven: Acco.

Blundell, A. G., & Mascia, M. B. (2005). Discrepancies in reported levels of international wildlife trade. *Conservation Biology, 19*(6), 2020–2025.

Bovenkerk, F. (1998). Fenomeenonderzoek; of hoe de etnografische criminologie haar onschuld verliest. *Justitiële verkenningen, 24*(8), 27–34.

Charmaz, K. (2006). *Constructing grounded theory: A practical guide through qualitative analysis*. Thousand Oaks: Sage Publications.

Coleman, C., & Moynihan, J. (1996). *Understanding crime data: Haunted by the dark figure*. Buckingham: Open University Press.

Decorte, T., & Zaitch, D. (Eds.). (2010). *Kwalitatieve methoden en technieken in de criminologie*. Leuven: Acco.

DeWalt, K. M., & DeWalt, B. R. (2011). *Participant observation: A guide for fieldworks*. Lanham: AltaMira Press.

Europol (2011). *Organised Crime Threat Assessment (OCTA)*. The Hague: Europol.

Ferrell, J., & Hamm, M.S. (1998). *Ethnography at the edge. Crime, deviance and field research*. Boston: Northeastern University Press.

Geis, G. (1991). The Case Study Method in Sociological Criminology. In J. R. Feagin et al. (Ed.), *A Case for the Case Study*. Chapel Hill: The University of North Carolina Press.

Goodman, L. A. (1961). Snowball sampling. *Annals of Mathematical Statistics, 32*(1), 148–170.

Hannerz, U. (2003). Being there… and there… and there! Reflections on multi-site ethnography. *Ethnography, 4*(2), 201–216.

Herbig, J. (2010). The illegal trade as a form of conservation crime: A South Africa criminological investigation. In R. White (Ed.), *Global environmental harm. Criminological perspectives*. Cullompton: Willan Publishing.

Leys, M., Zaitch, D., & Decorte, T. (2010). De gevalstudie. In T. Decorte & D. Zaitch (Eds.), *Kwalitatieve methoden en technieken in de criminologie*. Leuven: Acco.

Lindsey, P. A., Masterson, C. L., Beck, A. L., & Romañach, S. (2012). Ecological, social and financial issues related to fencing as a conservation tool in Africa. In M. J. Somers & M. Hayward (Eds.), *Fencing for conservation* (pp. 215–234). New York: Springer.

Marcus, G. E. (1995). Ethnography in/of the world system: The emergence of multi-sited ethnography. *Annual Review of Anthropology, 24*, 95–117.

O'Gorman, A., & Vander Laenen, F. (2009). Ethische aspecten van het kwalitatief onderzoek. In T. Decorte & D. Zaitch (Eds.), *Kwalitatieve methoden en technieken in de criminologie* (pp. 261–314). Leuven: Acco.

Petrossian, G. A., & Clarke, R. V. (2014). Explaining and controlling illegal commercial fishing an application of the CRAVED theft model. *British Journal of Criminology, 54*(1), 73–90.

Pires, S. F. (2012). The illegal parrot trade: A literature review. *Global Crime, 13*(3), 176–190.

Shaw, C. R. (1930). *The jack-roller: A delinquent boy's own story*. Chicago: University of Chicago Press.

Siegel, D. (2005). *Russische bizniz*. Amsterdam: Meulenhoff.

Siegel, D. (2009). *The mazzel ritual*. Dordrecht, Heidelberg, London, New York: Springer.

Siegel, D. (2013). *Mobiel banditisme. Oost-en Centraal-Europese rondtrekkende groepen in Nederland*. Apeldoorn: Politie en Wetenschap.

Stiles, D., Redmond, I., Cress, D., Nellemann, C., & Formo, R. K. (Eds.). (2013). *Stolen apes—The illicit trade in chimpanzees, gorillas, bonobos and orangutans. A rapid response assessment. United Nations Environment Programme*. Arendal: GRID-Arendal.

Sutherland, E. (1937). *The professional thief. By a professional thief*. Chicago: University of Chicago Press.

Sykes, G.M., & Matza, D. (1957). Techniques of neutralization: A theory of delinquency. *American Sociological Review*, 664–670.

Williams, T., Dunlap, E., Johnson, B. D., & Hamid, A. (1992). Personal safety in dangerous places. *Journal of Contemporary Ethnography, 21*(3), 343–374.

Wyatt, T. (2009). Exploring the organization of Russia Far East's illegal wildlife trade: Two case studies of the illegal fur and illegal falcon trades. *Global Crime, 10*(1–2), 144–154.

Wyatt, T. (2011). The illegal trade of raptors in the Russian Federation. *Contemporary Justice Review, 14*(2), 103–123.

Yin, R. (2008). *Case study research: Design and methods*. Los Angeles: Sage.

Zaitch, D. (2002). *Trafficking Cocaine: Colombian Drug Entrepreneurs in the Netherlands*. The Hague: Kluwer Law International.

Zaitch, D., Mortelmans, D., & Decorte, T. (2009). Participerende observatie in de criminologie. In T. Decorte & D. Zaitch (Eds.), *Kwalitatieve methoden en technieken in de criminologie* (pp. 261–314). Leuven: Acco.

Chapter 6
The Numbers of the Trade

In this chapter[1] the illegal trade in wildlife, with a focus on the trade in animals and animal products, is approached and propositions are discussed based on quantitative analyses of confiscations in the EU. While several studies have previously been conducted to analyse confiscations of wildlife in the US by using the US Fish and Wildlife Service (FWS) Law Enforcement Management Information Systems (LEMIS) database (e.g. Rice and Moore 2008; Schlaepfer et al. 2005; Stiles and Martin 2009; Petrossian et al. 2016), or global wildlife confiscations published by Traffic[2] (e.g. Rosen and Smith 2010) and the WCMC-CITES trade database (e.g. Wyatt 2013), there are no studies that have analysed overall wildlife seizures in the EU. Therefore, this exploratory quantitative study fills this gap by identifying illegal wildlife imports into the EU. According to Momii (2002) the EU is believed to account for one-third of the demand for the global illegal wildlife trade. The EU is the foremost destination market for wildlife in the world, coordinated by well organized, loose networks based in the EU and in the source regions (Europol 2011). The nature of the illegal wildlife trade in relation to the EU is approached by quantitative analyses of wildlife confiscations in the EU over a 10 year period. This chapter describes the diversity and transnational characteristics of the trade by asking what kind of wildlife is illegally traded, what are the source and destination countries, what kinds of smuggling and laundering methods are used and who are the offenders. Based on the quantitative analyses three case studies were selected to investigate qualitatively.

[1]Parts of this chapter have been published in the article: Van Uhm, D.P. (2016a). Illegal trade in wildlife and harms to the world. In Spapens, A.C.M., White, R. & Huisman, W. (Eds.) Environmental Crime in Transnational Context. Farnham: Ashgate publishing.
[2]Traffic is the international organization dedicated to ensuring that the trade in wildlife is not a threat to the conservation of nature.

D.P. van Uhm, *The Illegal Wildlife Trade*, Studies of Organized Crime 15,
DOI 10.1007/978-3-319-42129-2_6

6.1 A Multi-billion Dollar Industry

Estimates of the value of global crimes are usually uncritically reproduced, because they are assumed to have been generated by experts (Andreas and Greenhill 2010). The figure of $20 billion that is often quoted to indicate the illegal wildlife trade was initially the estimated value of the *legal* trade in wildlife by Traffic in the 1990s (ibid.) and Interpol has been incorrectly quoted as a source for this illegal wildlife trade figure (Søyland 2000). Based on a calculation method used for decades by Traffic the global and EU value of the wildlife trade is estimated in this section.[3] The value of the *legal* global international wildlife trade, including non-CITES species, is conservatively estimated to be about €86 billion per year, based on the figures of declared import values in 2010 (UN Comtrade and FAOSTAT database). Table 6.1 shows that the EU had, as a global top importer by value, an estimated declared import value of €38 billion.

According to Traffic this calculation method is far from a complete representation of the value of the wildlife trade either globally or in the EU; however, it serves as an indication of its scale (Engler and Parry-Jones 2007). The results are substantially influenced by the retail value of the fur and fish industry. The true scale and value of the wildlife trade are unknown, because much of the trade that is carried out through informal networks, and is not documented or captured in government statistics (World Bank 2008; Broad et al. 2003).

The *illegal* wildlife trade is said to be in the financial top three illegal enterprises worldwide, along with the global drug trade and the trade in illegal arms (ECOSOC 2003; UNODC 2012), with an estimated value of between $10 billion and $25 billion annually (Liddick 2011; McMurray 2008; Interpol 2012; Gagnier 2013). Although these numbers are highly debatable since they refer to very rough estimates and incorrect quotes of Interpol, the illegal wildlife trade is estimated to be approximately one-fourth of the legal trade based on several segment studies (Søyland 2000; European Commission 2006; Schneider 2008). Even though this figure, which is quoted on several occasions in renowned reports, must not be regarded as accurate and applicable to all sectors, it could give an indication of the value of the illegal wildlife trade. This would mean that if there is an assumed legal wildlife trade of €86 billion, the illegal wildlife trade would be roughly estimated at €21.5 billion worldwide from which €9.5 billion relates to the EU (Table 6.1). It is noteworthy that this seems to be reasonably close to the estimated values mentioned above.[4]

---

[3]UN Comtrade categories including live primates, live birds of prey, live psittaciformes 'incl. parrots, parakeets, macaws and cockatoos', live reptiles 'e.g. snakes, turtles, alligators, caimans, iguanas, gavials and lizards', live ornamental fish, fur skins and artificial fur, manufactures thereof *minus* artificial fur and articles thereof, reptile skins, raw, coral, shell, cattle bone, etc., unworked, and waste, natural pearls not permanently mounted or set, meat and edible offal of reptiles, incl. snakes and turtles, fresh/chilled/frozen, snails, edible (except sea snails).

[4]Perhaps both the legal and illegal trade increased in value to such an extent that the present value of illicit trade is comparable to the value of the legal trade in the 1990s.

Table 6.1 Estimate of global and EU wildlife trade values

Commodity	Estimated global value (EUR)	Estimated EU value (EUR)
Live animals		
Primates	100 million	18 million
Birds of prey	4 million	0.2 million
Cage birds	8 million	0.2 million
Reptiles	29 million	7 million
Ornamental fish	270 million	94 million
Animal products		
Mammal furs	5 billion	490 million
Reptile skins	280 million	97 million
Corals and shells	109 million	16 million
Natural pearls	57 million	9 million
Game meat	509 million	166 million
Reptile meat	3 million	0.3 million
Edible snails	77 million	16 million
Fish (excluding aquaculture)	80 billion	37 billion[a]
Total legal trade	**86 billion**	**38 billion**
Estimated illegal trade (25 %)	**21.5 billion**	**9.5 billion**

[*]Estimate of wildlife trade values in 2010
[a]Estimate for all European countries
Source UN Comtrade and FAOSTAT database 2012

Table 6.2 presents several other rough estimates of the illicit trade in specific wildlife. The illegal trading of ivory would include more than $100 million (EIA 2004). The unregulated and unregistered fish trade is estimated to be between $10 billion and $23 billion per year (Pitcher et al. 2002). The illegal trade in caviar is thought to be several times greater than the value of the legal trade in 2005: €244 million (Engler and Parry-Jones 2007). The illegal trade in birds is estimated to be worth around €10 million per year (Traffic 2008). And the illegal rhino trade would be worth more than $8 million while the illegal trade in tiger parts amounts to $5 million (UNODC 2010).

Table 6.2 Estimates of illegal wildlife trade values

Illegal trade	Profit (p/y)	Source
Ivory	>100 million dollars	EIA (2004)
Caviar	>244 million dollars	Traffic (2007)
Rhino horns	>8 million dollars	UNODC (2010)
Tiger parts	<5 million dollars	UNODC (2010)
Fish	10–23.5 billion dollars	Pitcher et al. (2002)
Birds	12.5 million dollars	Traffic (2008)

While from this perspective the illegal wildlife industry seems to be a multi-billion dollar industry, all figures remain approximations, as crime cannot be captured in numbers. Law enforcement experts estimate that no more than 10 % of all contraband wildlife is seized (Stiles et al. 2013). Thus the confiscations reflect only a fraction of the illegal trade as a large part of the trade remains unreported or undiscovered, the so-called dark number (Coleman and Moynihan 1996).

6.2 Animal Species

To obtain an overview of the illegal trade to the EU, data on confiscations in the EU were obtained from the European Union Trade in Wildlife Information eXchange database (EU-TWIX), a database of information on wildlife seizures in the EU. The data includes more than 20,000 illegal *wildlife* shipments ($N = 22{,}204$) of animals and animal products seized in the EU between 2001–2010. These shipments originated from 207 different countries all over the world, with a marked concentration in Africa ($N = 5{,}219$) and Southeast Asia ($N = 3{,}964$). Although several studies have focussed on individual cases of the illegal trade in wildlife (e.g. Wyatt 2009, 2011; Herbig 2010; Lindsey et al. 2012; Pires 2012; Petrossian and Clarke 2014), it remains unclear what kinds of major flows there are in relation to animal species traded illegally. To gain more insight, Fig. 6.1 presents the common animal groups confiscated during seizures in the EU between 2001–2010.

The wildlife confiscations were analysed according to the animal groups: mammals, birds, reptiles, fish, coral and molluscs. The species classes were recoded as the new following umbrella groups: *Mammalia* as mammals ($N = 3{,}814$), *Aves* as birds ($N = 1{,}490$), *Reptilia* as reptiles ($N = 7{,}303$), *Actinopterygii* ($N = 1{,}870$), *Elasmobranchii* ($N = 12$) and *Pisces* ($N = 1$) as fish ($N = 1{,}883$), instead of *Anthozoa* (4,465) or *Hydrozoa* ($N = 114$)[5] the category 'coral' was used for coral ($N = 4{,}385$) and *Bivalvia* ($N = 1{,}074$) and *Gastropoda* ($N = 1{,}735$) for molluscs ($N = 2{,}809$). There is a significant difference in the number of seizures between the various groupings ($X^2(9) = 24{,}025$, $p < 0.05$). These six groupings were chosen because they represent 93 % of all incidents.

It was not live animals but animal products which made up the majority of the seizures (82 %), compared to the seizures involving live animals (15 %). There is a significant difference in the number of seizures between live and dead confiscations ($X^2(2) = 23{,}603$, $p < 0.05$).[6] The 3,405 confiscations of *live* animals consisted of 64 % reptile, 26 % bird and 5 % mammal-related seizures. Only 1 % of all confiscations consisted of live amphibians, including poison dart frogs and salamanders.[7] 70 % of the seizures were related to CITES II species, compared to 27 %

[5]This category has been chosen due to the animal classes also including non-coral species.

[6]Categories include: 'live', 'dead' and 'unknown'.

[7]Including 59 % *Dendrobatidae* and 21 % *Ambystomatidae*.

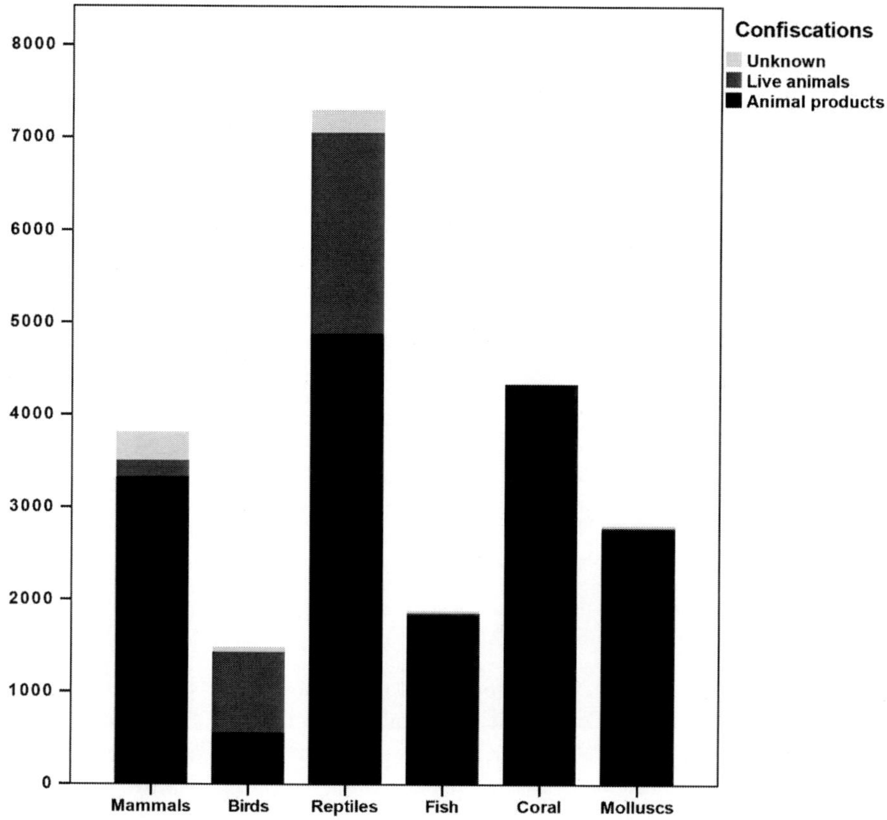

Fig. 6.1 Illegal wildlife groups. *Source* Personal analyses of the EU-TWIX database, 2001–2010

CITES I and 3 % CITES III species. There is also a significant difference in the number of seizures between CITES appendices ($X^2(2) = 8.5 \times 10^6$, $p < 0.05$).[8] Table 6.3 demonstrates that most confiscations involving the illegal trade in the six animal groupings are related to animal products ($N = 17{,}751$), such as ivory from elephants and medicines from several mammal species, small and large leather products from snakes and crocodiles, caviar, coral and shells. Live animal confiscations ($N = 3{,}268$) mostly included tortoises (16,104 animals), chameleons (2,597 animals), parrots (3,197 animals), falcons (241 animals) and monkeys (235 animals) (see also Appendix III).

Although much attention is given to the illegal trade in mammal species (e.g. elephants, rhinos, tigers), it is reptiles that dominate the figures with one-third of the total wildlife confiscations, followed by coral and mammals. It is not surprising that in terms of live animals, reptile and bird-related confiscations are common as the

[8]Categories include: 'CITES I', 'CITES II' and 'CITES III'.

Table 6.3 Wildlife seizures by animal groupings

Animal groupings	Total seizures	Live seizures	Number of animals	Species	Product seizures	Description	Species
Mammals	**3,814** (*100 %*)	**178** (*5 %*)	**367**	Monkeys, big cats	**3,327** (*87 %*)	Ivory and medicine	Elephants, big cats
Birds	**1,490** (*100 %*)	**877** (*59 %*)	**4,063**	Parrots, falcons	**559** (*38 %*)	Bodies and feathers	Falcons, parrots
Reptiles	**7,303** (*100 %*)	**2,171** (*30 %*)	**30,299**	Tortoises, chameleons	**4,883** (*67 %*)	Small and large leather products	Snakes, crocodiles
Fish	**1,883** (*100 %*)	**22** (*1 %*)	**784**	Sea horses, sturgeons	**1,835** (*98 %*)	Caviar and bodies	Sturgeons, sea horses
Coral	**4,385** (*100 %*)	N/A	**N/A**	N/A	**4,385** (*100%*)	Coral	Stony coral, black coral
Molluscs	**2,809** (*100 %*)	**20** (*1 %*)	**814**	Giant clams, sea snails	**2,762** (*98 %*)	Shells and bodies	Sea snails, giant clams
Total	**21,684** (*100 %*)	**3,268** (*15 %*)	**36,327**		**17,751** (*82 %*)		

Source Personal analyses of the EU-TWIX database, 2001–2010

EU was already known in the 2000s to be one of the largest markets in the world for wild birds and reptiles (FAO 2011; Engler and Parry-Jones 2007). In the next subsections, the major illegal wildlife categories will be discussed: mammals, birds, reptiles, fish, coral and molluscs.

6.2.1 *Mammals*

The mammal confiscations ($N = 3,814$) consisted mainly of mammal products (>85 %), including ivory from elephants and animal products used for traditional Chinese medicine.[9] Medicine, dominated by traditional Chinese medicines (TCM), is the largest of all the categories in terms of quantity; more than 50,000 medicines were confiscated between 2001–2010, including 7,200 big cat products, 4,600 musk deer products, 3,100 bear products, 1,900 saiga antelope products and 1,028 rhino products known to be used in TCM. Europe is clearly a major market for TCM (Nooren and Claridge 2001). The illegal trade in TCM to the EU will be discussed in more detail in Chap. 9. In addition, hundreds of seizures of ivory in the EU indicate a demand market for ivory. The illegal trade in ivory seems to have increased since the CITES Standing Committee approved the sale of African

[9] The 3,814 confiscations of mammal products consisted of 42 % *Elephantidae*, 16 % *Felidae*, 9 % *Ursidae*, 8 % *Moschidae* and 4 % *Bovidae*.

government-owned ivory stocks to China and Japan in the late 2000s. In 2008, 108 tonnes of ivory seized or collected by Botswana, Namibia, South Africa and Zimbabwe were sold to China and Japan. These legal ivory stocks on the market provided opportunities to launder illegal ivory (Gabriel et al. 2012; Underwood et al. 2013; EIA 2013a, b). Ivory is usually related to status and due to the increased economic prosperity in China, more people can afford these luxury products.[10] Besides the demand market for TCM and ivory, the EU functions as a transit hub for rhino horn, pangolins and ivory from Africa to Asia (Milliken 2014; Lawson and Vines; Traffic 2014). For instance, Europe accounts for one-third of all global ivory seizures, with Belgium, France, Portugal and the UK as key transit countries (Traffic 2014). In addition to mammal products, old world monkeys were mainly found in the seizures of live mammals ($N = 178$) including 367 live animals.[11] The most confiscated live mammals in the EU were Barbary macaques (*Macaca sylvanus*) and vervet monkeys (*Chlorocebus aethiops*). During the 2000s a substantial illegal trade in Barbary macaques from Morocco into the EU has been noticed. This is confirmed in the seizures of live mammals; the most confiscated endangered live mammal in the EU is the Barbary macaque (Van Uhm 2014a). The illegal trade in Barbary macaques will be discussed in Chap. 8.

6.2.2 Birds

Seizures of live birds ($N = 877$) dominate the 1,490 bird-related seizures (±60 %), consisting mainly of parrots and falcons.[12] In 877 seizures more than 4,000 live birds were confiscated and the most confiscated bird species in the EU was the African grey parrot (*Psittacus erithacus*), the eastern rosella (*Platycercus eximius*) and the rose-ringed parakeet (*Psittacula krameri*). The EU is well known for its demand market for CITES birds; between 2000 and 2003 the EU imported 2.8 million wild CITES birds, representing 93 % of imports registered worldwide (FAO 2011). However, from 2006 legal wild bird imports became drastically reduced because of a European import ban and protection measures in response to the growing threat of avian influenza (Cooney and Jepson 2006; Nijman 2010).[13] According to the Crime Squad in the Netherlands, the prices for rare bird species

---

[10]For instance, the so-called Hanko (a family stamp carved from ivory) is a 'must have item' for every family. To deceive customs officials the Hanko is regularly painted (EE4).

[11]The 178 confiscations of 367 live mammals consisted of 45 % *Cercopithecidae* and 14 % *Felidae*.

[12]The 877 confiscations of 4,063 live birds consisted of 61 % *Psittacidae* and 6 % *Falconidae*.

[13]2005/94/EC.

have increased considerably since the import ban.[14] Criminal groups may have filled the gap immediately with the illegal trade in birds (Van Uhm 2012b).[15] The 559 seizures of confiscated bird products were mainly related to stuffed birds and the feathers of hawks, eagles and parrots.[16]

6.2.3 Reptiles

Most seized live animals in the EU were reptiles (30,299 animals),[17] of which 61 % were tortoises and turtles, including 3,180 spur-thighed tortoises (*Testudo graeca*), 2,168 Horsfield's tortoises (*Testudo horsfieldii*) and 1,569 Kleinmann's tortoises (*Testudo kleinmanni*). Interpol had already mentioned in the Noah report (1996) that Europe is highly involved in the illegal trade in spur-thighed tortoises from Morocco as a traditional supplier. Certain populations of spur-thighed tortoises have suffered over a 90 % decline in Morocco (Van Dijk et al. 2004). The impact of illegal trade to the EU is illustrated by the fact that the wild population of Kleinmann's tortoises consists of only 7,470 individuals, while within 10 years at least 20 % of the total population was intercepted (see also Perälä 2003). Reptile-related confiscations ($N = 7{,}303$) include 4,883 reptile product seizures (±65 %).[18] The EU is well known as the world's largest importer of reptile skins according to value (Engler and Parry-Jones 2007). The value has been estimated to be over €100 million based on imports of reptile skins in 2005 (Liddick 2011). Indeed, a substantial number of reptile products were seized, including 19,404 lizard, serpent and crocodilian leather products (e.g. briefcases, furniture, suitcases, belts and braces). More than 10 million reptiles are killed for the largely unregulated leather industry every year. According to Liddick (2011) commercial enterprises falsify the number of reptile skins, the origin or use of illegal wild skins and they launder them through registered farms (Liddick 2011; UN 2012).

[14]For instance, a Dutch smuggler of ten hummingbirds and two sunbirds in his underpants was arrested at Schiphol airport during a 100 % control on a flight from Surinam; the birds were worth thousands of euros. Currently increasing numbers of illegal birds are found all over the European market.

[15]According to an illegal bird trader in the Netherlands a new trend in the illegal bird trade is the smuggling of eggs instead of live birds (ET5).

[16]The 559 confiscations of bird products consisted of 30 % *Accipitridae* and 10 % *Psittacidae*.

[17]The 2,171 confiscations of 30,299 live reptiles consisted of 63 % *Testudinidae*, 9 % *Chamaeleonidae* and 9 % *Emydidae*.

[18]The 4,883 confiscations of reptile products consisted of 22 % *Pythonidae*, 14 % *Elapidae*, 9 % *Boidae* and 8 % *Crocodylidae*.

6.2.4 Fish

The largest part (>95 %) of the seizures regarding fish (N = 1,883) consisted of fish products. Caviar from sturgeons dominates the seizures of fish products.[19] More than 16 tons of caviar were seized between 2000–2010 in the EU, as one of the main destination markets for illegal caviar. Most of the confiscated caviar in the EU originates from the following sturgeon species: the Baltic sturgeon (*Acipenser sturio*), the Beluga (*Huso huso*) and the Russian sturgeon (*Acipenser gueldenstaedtii*). The demand for original wild caviar is fuelled by smuggled caviar from the Caspian Sea to the EU (Van Uhm and Siegel 2016). Some 90 % of the global caviar trade during the last century originated from the Caspian Sea (Engler and Parry-Jones 2007). Since the sturgeon population has significantly declined, prices for caviar have reached extremely high prices, with up to €20,000 per kilo for wild Beluga caviar (Van Uhm and Siegel 2016). The illegal trade in caviar will be discussed in Chap. 7. Only 1 % of the fish confiscations were related to live fish, including mainly sea horses for medicine and sturgeons for breeding facilities.[20]

6.2.5 Coral

Coral confiscations (N = 4,385) were the runners-up in the seized wildlife groups. These corals consist mainly of stony star or hard coral-related seizures. Interestingly, most corals were not specified in specific families or species within that order. Ninety percent of the coral seizures were labelled as *Scleractinia*.[21] The EU is, besides the US, known to be a major importer of hard corals and the trade is mainly linked to the collection of coral for shaping aquaria (Jones 2013). Each year tonnes of coral are confiscated in the EU and the demand is often related to the rare, slow-growing and long-living corals. As corals play an important role in the marine ecosystem, the effects of their decimation could be substantial (NOAA 2010). Imports of illegal corals in the EU were dominated by famous coral export countries, such as Indonesia and the Philippines (Green and Shirley 1999; Wood et al. 2012).

[19]The 1,835 confiscations of fish products consisted of 85 % *Acipenseridae* and 12 % *Syngnathidae*.

[20]The confiscations of live fish consisted of 61 % *Syngnathidae*.

[21]The confiscations of corals consisted of 90 % *Scleractinia*—most seizures were not specified in families: 80 % unknown, 4 % *Faviidae* and 4 % *Acroporidae*.

6.2.6 *Molluscs*

Even less known in the wildlife trade are the illegally imported molluscs. Within the mollusc confiscations (N = 2,809), the most seizures were queen conchs (*Strombus gigas*) and small giant clams (*Tridacna maxima*). Almost all seizures (98 %) were related to mollusc products, in other words shells and 'bodies'. The largest category consisted of shells, whereby true conchs and giant clams dominated the confiscations.[22] Despite fishing bans and regulations, substantial amounts of queen conchs and giant clams are fished illegally for tourism and the aquaria industry (CITES 2003; DeBoer and Barber 2010). Although large numbers of confiscations include one or two molluscs that may be associated with tourists, abalones appear to be currently threatened by illegal commercial crime groups (Tailby and Gant 2002; Goga 2014).

Apparently, the EU market consists of a large demand for exclusive species (e.g. caviar, exotic animals, coral) and critically endangered species are at the top of the list, since they can be sold for extremely high prices (Engler and Parry-Jones 2007). An exclusive pair of parrots can be sold for over €50,000,[23] while the price of a kilo of rhino horn exceeds the price of a kilo of gold (Van Uhm 2012a). The EU demand is influenced by trends and the development of relatively new markets. While traditional well-known wildlife demand markets were identified in the EU seizures (e.g. ivory, reptile leather products, caviar, live reptiles and birds), the analyses of confiscations demonstrate relatively lesser-known flows in corals, shells and, incidentally, live mammals.[24]

6.3 Source Countries

Generally, the source countries for the trade in wildlife include some of the poorest countries with the richest sources of biodiversity. The wildlife trade appears to flow from developing to developed countries (Roe et al. 2002; Duffy 2010). Countries with rich biodiversity density on average experience lower development levels and higher levels of corruption; the *resource curse*. From this perspective 'the presence of many natural resources correlates with crime and violence' (Boekhout van Solinge 2014: 501). Several studies identified African and Southeast Asian countries as the main source countries for illegal wildlife (Rosen and Smith 2010; UNODC 2010; World Bank 2008; Lawson and Vines 2014). The confiscation data of more than 20,000 seizures (N = 22,204) in the EU confirmed that illegal wildlife

---

[22]The 2,809 confiscations of molluscs consisted of 63 % *Strombidae* and 37 % *Tridacnidae*.

[23]EU-TWIX directory of prices 2013.

[24]Due to the relatively high economic prosperity level of EU citizens, it is plausible that currently more people can afford these luxury products. The impact is demonstrated by a large variety of species in the illegal trade on the brink of extinction.

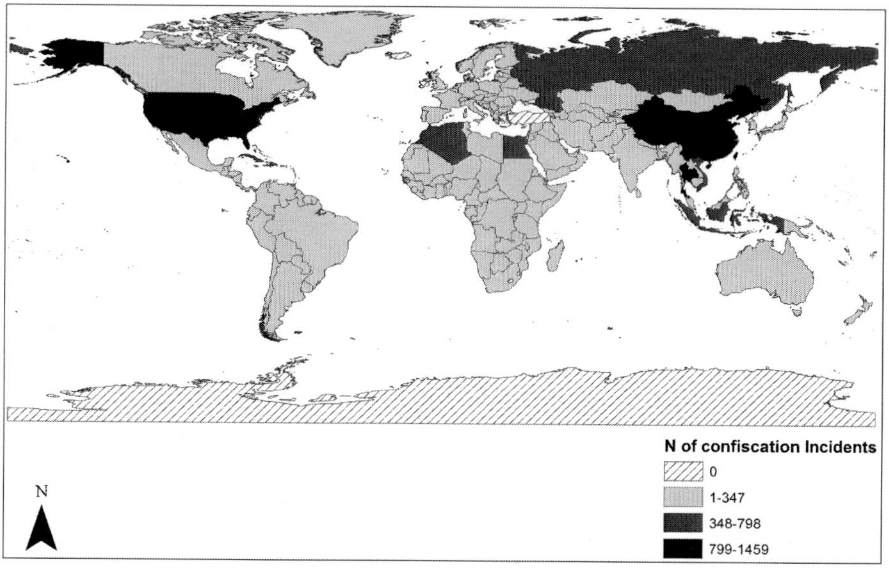

Map 6.1 Export countries for illegal wildlife. *Source* Personal analyses of the EU-TWIX database, 2001–2010

shipments originated mainly from African and Southeast Asian countries (Map 6.1). A marked concentration of seizures in Africa (N = 5,219) and Southeast Asia (N = 3,964) has been identified with a significant difference in the number of seizures between the continents ($X^2(10) = 15{,}124$, $p < 0.05$).[25]

The recorded illegal wildlife shipments in the EU were from 207 countries (see also Appendix IV). There is a significant difference in the number of seizures between the source countries ($X^2(206) = 1.29 \times 10^8$, $p < 0.05$). The top illegal exporters of wildlife shipments from Africa are Morocco (N = 612), Egypt (N = 531), Algeria (N = 446), South Africa (N = 315) and Nigeria (N = 310). The North African countries seem to play an important role in the illegal wildlife trade to the EU because of their geographical advantages (Map 6.1), since the southern coastline of Europe could easily be used to smuggle wildlife over the sea into the EU. For example, the Strait of Gibraltar is well known as the main port between Africa and the EU for the illegal drug trade (cocaine, heroin, cannabis and synthetic drug precursors) and migration (UNODC 2006; Europol 2011; Carpenter 2012), as well as the illegal wildlife trade (Highfield and Bayley 1996; Cowdrey 2002). According to Interpol (1996) Morocco has always been an important transit country

[25]Categories include: North America, Central America, South America, Africa, Europe, Central Asia, South Asia, East and Southeast Asia, Middle East, Australia/Oceania and Antarctica.

for wildlife and appears to be the main country of origin worldwide for illegal shipments of reptiles, especially spur-thighed tortoises (Interpol 1996). The Moroccan border is one of the most used smuggling routes for wildlife to Europe and Morocco is still the main country of origin worldwide for illegal shipments of reptiles to the EU. According to the EU confiscation data 540 illegal shipments (88 % of the total seizures) from Morocco to the EU consisted of live animals:

- 2,107 reptiles; mainly spur-thighed tortoises (*Testudo graeca*) and common chameleons (*Chamaeleo chamaeleon*)
- 49 birds; mainly African grey parrots (*Psittacus erithacus*)
- 41 mammals; all of them Barbary macaques (*Macaca Sylvanus*)

The confiscations of live animals from Algeria included 976 reptiles (mainly spur-thighed tortoises) and 31 birds (mainly African grey parrots). The illegal trade from Egypt is dominated by small numbers of coral probably from tourists who, consciously or not, bring them back home. The confiscations from South Africa and Nigeria are mainly related to elephant ivory, including thousands of tusks and carvings. According to several studies (Lemieux and Clarke 2009; Nowell 2012; UNEP 2013) these countries are well-known source countries for ivory.

Southeast Asia is identified as both a major hub of the illegal wildlife trade and home to a unique variety of endangered species. Even Singapore, which is a highly urbanized country, has the reputation of being an important player in the (illegal) wildlife trade (Sodhi et al. 2004). The main Southeast Asian source countries for illegal wildlife based on seizures are Thailand ($N = 1{,}263$), China ($N = 845$), Vietnam ($N = 688$), Indonesia ($N = 434$) and the Philippines ($N = 172$). In comparison to the African illegal exporters, the Southeast Asian countries are more specialized in the illegal trade in *wildlife products*, such as medicine, leather products, corals and molluscs. For instance, the demand for TCM has spread around the world caused by globalization and the expansion of Chinese diasporas. This trend is confirmed by increasing TCM exports from China (Engler and Parry-Jones 2007; Xueyan 2007) and the number of seizures each year (Traffic 2013). According to Felbab-Brown (2011) China ranks as the number one market for illegal wildlife. According to the confiscation data in the EU, 96 % of the 845 seizures that originate from China are related to animal products dominated by medicine. The seizures of medicine include:

- 244 seizures of medicines from mammals; mainly leopards (*Panthera pardus*) saiga antelopes (*Saiga tatarica*) and tigers (*Panthera tigris*)
- Ten seizures of medicines from fish; seahorses (*Hippocampus* sp.)
- Six seizures of medicines from reptiles; Indian cobras (*Naja naja*)

While Thailand and Vietnam seem to be also major exporters of illegal shipments of TCM (EU-TWIX seizures) and are well-known illegal exporters (Nooren

Table 6.4 Wildlife seizures by country

Continent	Country	Total seizures	Live seizures	Product seizures	Main trade
Africa		**5,219**			
	Morocco	**612**	**540** (*88%*)	**72** (*12%*)	Live tortoises, chameleons, monkeys
	Egypt	**531**	**24** (*5%*)	**507** (*95%*)	Stony corals, clams
	Algeria	**446**	**385** (*86%*)	**61** (*14%*)	Live tortoises, chameleons, monkeys
East and Southeast Asia		**3,964**			
	Thailand	**1,263**	**22** (2%)	**1,241** (*98%*)	Reptile leather products, bodies
	China	**845**	**32** (*4%*)	**813** (*96%*)	TCM, derivatives
	Vietnam	**688**	**25** (*4%*)	**663** (*96%*)	Reptile bodies, corals
Other important exporters	**USA**	**1,457**	**66** (*5%*)	**1,391** (*95%*)	Reptile leather products, shells
	Russia	**798**	**19** (2%)	**779** (*98%*)	Caviar, bear skins

Source Personal analyses of the EU-TWIX database, 2001–2010

and Claridge 2001), the main trade from these Asian countries involves leather products from reptiles to the EU. The seizures from Thailand and Vietnam consisted of 1,051 reptile confiscations, including 454 Indian cobra (*Naja naja*) and 77 reticulated python (*Python reticulatus*) confiscations. According to Nijman (2010) snake, lizard, and crocodilian skins consist of a significant amount of the trade from Southeast Asia, with the EU as a major importer. For instance, Indonesia, with the biodiversity hotspot Borneo, is one of the main source countries for wild pythons in the skin trade (Kasterine et al. 2012). According to Wood et al. (2012) Indonesia is also the main supplier of the trade in live corals. Indonesia has accounted for an average of 70 % of the trade in live corals in the past decade. Together with the Philippines, these two countries are the main exporters of molluscs (Venkatesan 2010). The EU confiscations confirm that these countries are important illegal exporters of corals and shells to the EU, with substantial numbers of coral (N = 301) and mollusc seizures (N = 140).

While most illegal shipments originate from African and Southeast Asian countries, the US and Russia are noteworthy (Map 6.1 and Table 6.4). The top six illegal exporters consist of the *United States of America* (N = 1,457), Thailand (N = 1,263), China (N = 845), *Russia* (N = 798), Vietnam (N = 688) and Morocco (N = 612). However, the illegal trade in wildlife coming from the United States of America and Russia is not regularly mentioned by wildlife studies. The seized illegal wildlife trade from the US is mainly related to leather products from pythons, alligators and crocodiles. The confiscations from the US consist of 805 reptile-related seizures, including seizures of large leather products ($N = 278$) and seizures of small leather products ($N = 269$).[26] According to several studies (Cowdrey 2002; Engler and Parry-Jones 2007) skins of reptiles are imported, processed, re-exported for manufacture, and then imported into the EU, passing through different transit countries in order to launder illegally caught reptiles. The illegal trade from Russia is dominated by caviar: over 40 % of all EU seizures of caviar (more than 3.5 tonnes) originate from Russia. While the annual value of the caviar exported legally by Russia is estimated to be between 40-100 million dollars, the *illegal* Russian export of caviar is estimated to be no less than 250-400 million dollars (Pikitch et al. 2005; Schneider 2012). According to the confiscation data in the EU, of the 798 seizures that originated from Russia, 579 seizures (73 %) were related to caviar from mainly the following species:

- Baltic sturgeon (*Acipenser sturio*)
- Starry sturgeon (*Acipenser stellatus*)
- Russian sturgeon (*Acipenser gueldenstaedtii*)
- Beluga (*Huso huso*)
- Siberian sturgeon (*Acipenser baerii*)

The analyses of seizures from source countries also present certain noteworthy results. While Turkey is a well-known transit country for Caspian caviar to the EU, no seizures from Turkey are recorded in the EU-TWIX database (Map 6.1), probably due to insufficient seizure information from Greece and Bulgaria. In addition, it is remarkable that Brazil, home to the world's biodiversity hotspot the Amazon, and the Republic of the Congo with the Congo basin occupy respectively the 22nd and 19th place when it comes to exporters in the illegal trade in wildlife to the EU.

6.4 Destination Countries

The EU is an important destination and transit market for the trade in wildlife. While the EU ranks as the top importer of wildlife according to value[27] (Engler and Parry-Jones 2007; Traffic 2014), the EU is simultaneously one of the major outlets of the *illegal* wildlife trade (Europol 2013a, b). As the EU has expanded, the size of the EU demand market for wildlife has also increased. Although the EU advocates environmental governance and sustainable use, the substantial demand market for wildlife appears to be a stimulator of the illegal trade, threatening species and ecosystems (Engler and Parry-Jones 2007). Large airports in Europe (e.g. Schiphol, London, Frankfurt) and major harbours (e.g. Antwerp, Rotterdam, Hamburg) seem

[26]Including 429 seizures from *Crocodylia* and 233 seizures from *Serpentes*.

[27]The legal trade in wildlife in the EU had an estimated declared import value of 38 billion, 44 % of the global import value (86 billion), see Table 6.1.

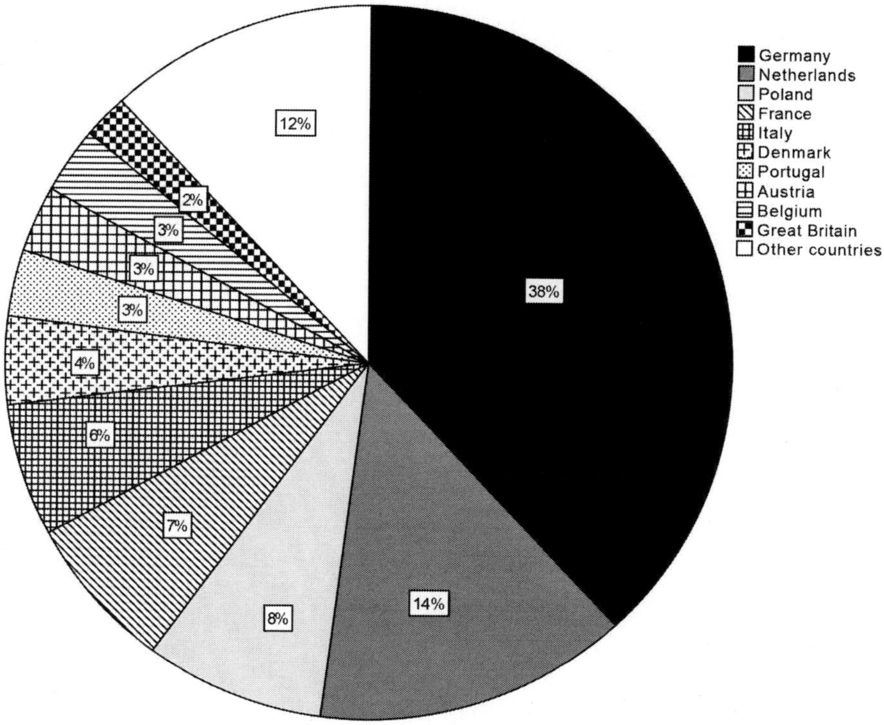

Fig. 6.2 EU destination countries for illegal wildlife. *Source* Personal analyses of the EU-TWIX database, 2001–2010

to play a substantial role as main entry points to enter the EU for the illegal wildlife trade. In addition, the EU appears to play an important role as a trade hub. For instance, the EU functions as a transit point for the illegal wildlife trade, such as ivory and rhino horn, from Africa to Asia (mainly China) and the Middle and Far East (IFAW 2013; European Commission 2014).

The free trade agreement between European countries offers unhindered trade and suitable transhipment locations for illegal wildlife within the Schengen area (Cowdrey 2002; Wyler and Sheikh 2008).[28] The recorded illegal wildlife shipments in the EU were destined for 89 countries, with a significant difference in the number of seizures between the destination countries ($X^2(88) = 2.86 \times 10^8$, $p < 0.05$). However, certain countries appear to have a more prominent role in the illegal trade in wildlife (see Appendix V), since more than half of all confiscations were seized in Germany and the Netherlands (Fig. 6.2). The top import countries of seized illegal shipments to the EU are Germany (N = 7,266), the Netherlands (N = 2,590),

[28]The Schengen area consists of 26 members with 10,000 km of land borders, 50,000 km of sea borders and 2,000 official crossing points.

Poland (N = 1,599), France (N = 1,229) and Italy (N = 1,037). While it may indeed be the case that the seizures reflect increased efforts and a commitment towards enforcement, both Germany and the Netherlands are well known as main transit countries for illegal wildlife (Zembla 2001).

Since the late 1990s Germany has become renowned as being the largest black market hub for birds of prey. From Germany the birds would be smuggled to the Middle East where there is a substantial demand for birds of prey (Holden 1998). Secondly, Germany is well known as a major EU importer of caviar. Almost 250 tonnes of caviar from wild sturgeons were imported by Germany between 1998–2006 (Engler and Knapp 2008). Besides birds of prey and caviar from wild sturgeons, the German confiscations consist mainly of leather products from reptiles, coral, shells and live reptiles.[29]

From the early 1990s onwards, several reports (e.g. internal police reports) have mentioned the Netherlands as a major player in the international trade in illegal wildlife (e.g. CRI 1992; RRD 1995; Interpol 1996; Holden 1998; Cowdrey 2002; KLPD 2005; Van Uhm 2009; Kemner 2010; Liddick 2011). High numbers of live birds such as parrots and falcons are smuggled into the Netherlands through the Czech Republic and Germany. These birds are 'laundered' by forged identification rings to suggest a captive-bred origin, while the birds are in reality from the wild (KLPD 2005). According to the internal report 'Noah' (Interpol 1996) a handful of Dutch persons were identified as key actors in the illegal trade in wildlife in the late 1990s, involving both reptiles and exotic birds. These Dutch actors are also settled in countries such as Indonesia, Madagascar, Nicaragua and Spain. From these countries the Dutch actors operate and organize the illegal trade in wildlife, while they still use their Dutch infrastructure. Besides the role of the Netherlands as an international hub for the illegal reptile and bird trade worldwide, a substantial amount of the illegal trade in TCM within the EU appears to be mainly imported and distributed by the Netherlands (Holden 1998; LNV 2000; Kemner 2010). In addition, a large number of seizures consisted of TCM, live birds and reptiles. Reptile leather products and corals were also well represented.[30]

A possible explanation for the role of Germany and the Netherlands in the international illegal wildlife trade could be the geographically central location of both countries in Western Europe. Second, the national economic and logistic infrastructure include major airports (Schiphol, Frankfurt) and main harbours (Rotterdam, Hamburg). Third, the strong historical trading position in Europe and strong ties with former colonies in Africa, Southeast Asia and Latin America. Although Germany and the Netherlands are prominent based on seizures, various reports indicate the important role of East and South EU border countries in the illegal wildlife trade to Europe. For instance, live reptiles usually enter the EU from

[29]The confiscations in Germany included 1,909 seizures of corals, 1,093 seizures of shells, 717 seizures of small leather products, 713 seizures of caviar and 483 seizures of live animals (mainly reptiles and birds).

[30]The confiscations in the Netherlands included 2,695 medicines and 1,904 live animals (mainly birds and reptiles), 5,502 corals and 3,079 leather products.

Morocco through Spain or from Libya via Egypt through Greece; birds are often smuggled via Turkey through Bulgaria; and caviar smugglers use the borders of EU countries, such as Poland, Ukraine, Bulgaria and Greece.[31]

6.5 Smuggling and Laundering

According to Interpol's Wildlife Smuggling Concealment Case Study Handbook (2010) various modi operandi are used in the illegal wildlife trade. Body packing has been used for smuggling; eggs in underwear, iguanas hidden in prosthetic legs and birds in leg bags. Containers are used for the transportation of illegal wildlife; ivory in hidden compartments, frogs in film canisters and smoked monkeys hidden under declared food imports. Parrots have been smuggled behind the backseats of personal vehicles, pangolins as cargo and wildlife could also be hidden in the tyre well of a vehicle. Methods of disguise involve seahorses declared as plant material, stony coral camouflaged with spray paint, rhino horns disguised as wood products and reptiles declared to be didgeridoos (Interpol 2010).

Crime investigation demonstrates that crime networks dealing with the smuggling of wildlife use a modus operandi similar to that of drug traffickers (Warchol et al. 2003; Elliott 2011; South and Wyatt 2011; Van Uhm 2012b). There have been accounts of customs officers in airports stopping smugglers with birds literally strapped to their legs, with reptiles in their underpants and turtles in their luggage (Schneider 2012). In addition, wildlife is smuggled along with other contraband (e.g. Speart 1993; Wyler and Sheikh 2008). Dead animals are used to conceal drugs, live animals are used as drug carriers, or animals or products thereof are used as barter (Chiszar et al. 1992; Renctas 2001; Zimmerman 2003; South and Wyatt 2009; Sollund and Maher 2015). For instance, cocaine was smuggled wrapped in condoms and stuffed into boa constrictors (ECOSOC 2002), exotic birds have been confiscated in shipments of methamphetamine pills and elephant tusks have been seized with hashish inside (Wyler and Sheikh 2008). Furthermore, the same routes are used as those that are used in the drugs, human and weapons trade (e.g. Zimmerman 2003; Nellemann et al. 2014). In Brazil around 40 % of the wildlife smuggling rings (350–400) are suspected of being involved in other illegal businesses (e.g. drugs and precious stones) (Renctas 2001), while in 1993 in the US one-third of the cocaine confiscations were reported to be associated with wildlife imports (Alacs et al. 2010). However, this interconnection is only incidentally confirmed by seizures in the EU.

In 35 % of the illegal shipments, the method for smuggling wildlife was registered in the EU-TWIX database between 2001–2010. The wildlife was hidden 'in container', 'in freight', 'in personal baggage', 'in postal or express—courier parcel', 'in premises', 'inside vehicle', 'modification of the appearance of specimen',

[31]CITES day organized by the National Police in the Netherlands, May 19, 2015.

'not concealed' and 'under travellers' clothing'. Almost 95 % of the illegal shipments ($N = 7{,}835$) were hidden in personal baggage, parcels, freight loads or vehicles:

- Personal Baggage ($N = 5{,}173$) is the most practical method for transporting small types of animals or products, such as reptiles, birds, amphibians, caviar, shells, coral or carvings.
- Parcel ($N = 1{,}022$) is mainly used for sending products, such as caviar, carvings of ivory or bone, leather products, medicines and coral.
- Freight ($N = 668$) is primarily used for transporting live corals and reptiles.
- Vehicles ($N = 513$): special secret compartments in vehicles mainly contain hidden reptiles, birds and caviar.

There are seven types of transport recorded: 'air', 'mail', 'maritime', 'pedestrian', 'rail', 'river' and 'road', with a significant difference in the number of seizures between the transport methods ($X^2(8) = 6.89 \times 10^7, p < 0.05$).[32] The most common transport method for the illegal trade recorded in the EU-TWIX database was by air: 67 % ($N = 12{,}760$) of the confiscations. Illegal traders also used roads ($N = 780$) by means of cars, trucks or as pedestrians, the sea or rivers ($N = 347$) by boat and the railway ($N = 74$) by train. Sending illegal wildlife products via a parcel has probably increased with the advent of the internet. According to the EU-TWIX support officer the probability of detection is relatively small as customs officials may physically check as few as two percent of all packages (EE4).

Five different CITES offences were recorded: 'falsified documents', 'counterfeit documents', 'providing false documents to obtain CITES documents', 'invalid documents' or 'no documents', with a significant difference in the number of seizures between the CITES offences ($X^2(6) = 5.42 \times 10^7, p < 0.05$).[33] While most of the illegal shipments (98 %) were confiscated because of a lack of CITES documents ($N = 10{,}142$), invalid, falsified or counterfeit CITES documents ($N = 177$) were encountered as well. For instance, traders forged CITES certificates with wrong dates, species or quantities.

Another example is counterfeit/falsified/invalid documentation provided in order to obtain CITES documents. These methods are used to launder the illegal origin of the illegal wildlife. Laundering in criminology refers to the process by which money obtained from illegal business activities is transformed into legitimate money (Levi and Reuter 2006). According to Reuter (2004: 1) 'money laundering is the conversion of criminal incomes into assets that cannot be traced back to the underlying crime'. The origin of the money obtained from illegal activities needs to be disguised as deriving from legal activities and financial institutions then accept

[32]Categories include: 'air', 'mail', 'maritime', 'pedestrian', 'rail', 'river', 'road', 'unknown' and 'other'.

[33]Categories include: 'falsified documents', 'counterfeit documents', 'providing false documents to obtain CITES documents', 'invalid documents' or 'no documents', 'unknown' and 'other'.

the money without suspicion.[34] In laundering wildlife the illegal origin of an animal or animal product is concealed; the wildlife is declared as being a legally obtained product in order to obtain documents that prove its legality.[35] According to Europol (2011) groups in North West Europe cooperate with breeders in other Member States to launder 'wild caught' animals, using false documents to trade them as being captive-bred on the legitimate market. Promoted as biodiversity conservation, many wildlife breeding farms have been established during the last few decades. However, there are strong indicators that many wildlife breeding farms are used to launder illegally caught wildlife (Lyons and Natusch 2011; Cook et al. 2002).[36]

In addition, there seems to be an illegal market in CITES certificates (sometimes purchased from corrupt officials) and the mark characteristics of captive-bred animals. For example, there is an illegal trade in rings for captive-bred birds. Initially leg rings may only be fitted to birds in the first days of life to demonstrate the legality of a bird. However, birds are illegally caught and rings can be quite easily obtained and fitted illegally around the leg of the bird to mark its legality for sale (Van Kreveld 2007). Another example is CITES certificates that are reused multiple times for different animals. Theoretically, CITES certificates should be sent back to the CITES authority if the animal dies. However, in practice this hardly happens. In addition, import certificates for products are used several times for different orders; a small amount of products are legally ordered, half are returned, yet the import certificate is used to launder illegal CITES products.[37] Finally, mislabelling is a method which is used to launder wildlife. For instance, documentation shows a species that is legal to be traded, while the wildlife is actually another species. The illegal wildlife then enters the legal sphere by appearing to be legitimate (Wyatt 2013).

---

[34]For instance, the laundering of drug money is done by purchasing real estate with this illegally obtained money and this property is then sold to obtain legitimate money. In other words, the money has to be paid in cash and with the sale of the real estate the money will be back in the economy as legitimate money.

[35]CITES I species that were born and bred in captivity or were artificially propagated are considered as CITES II species and are allowed to be traded under Annex II conditions. According to EU wildlife regulations captive-bred Annex A species are treated as specimens of species listed in Annex B. This provides a loophole for illegal trade, as the issuance of an import or export permit may be less strict (Lyons and Natusch 2011).

[36]CITES trade data show large fluctuations between years in amounts of captive-bred and wild-caught specimens traded. Specimens declared as captive-bred are exported by a CITES country to a non-CITES country, after which they are then re-exported to another CITES country or surveys and site visits and interviews demonstrate the contrary; no capability of captive-bred farming in commercial quantities or unclear registration (Traffic 2012).

[37]A remarkable example is a bird sanctuary in the Netherlands which, until recently, had a contract with the government and was paid to take care of birds that had been confiscated by the authorities. Unfortunately, more than 50 % of the birds were not present at the sanctuary and very high mortality rates among the birds led to a police investigation that indicated involvement in the illegal trade in birds, including different kinds of parrots (Van Uhm 2016c).

6.6 The Actors Involved

Different types of offenders have been identified in the illegal trade in wildlife, from perpetrators operating individually to highly organized networks that control some or all facets of a particular trade. A range of offenders could be involved along the illicit chain of the trade in wildlife, from local poachers, middlemen and smugglers to state or private corporations and corrupt officials (Kazmar 2000; Zimmerman 2003; Wyatt 2013; Sollund 2013). According to Wyatt (2013) some offenders might be considered to be 'blameless' such as poor local people who kill endangered species for food, while transnational crime groups oversee the whole process and make the really high profits.

There appear to be three types of illegal traders which have been regularly found:

1. Small-scale illegal traders
2. Legal traders involved in illegal trade
3. Criminal organizations

Based on the seizures of wildlife in the EU-TWIX database, incidents vary from one single product to high numbers of illegal trade in cargo. While tourists can unknowingly bring illegal souvenirs, such as shells or coral, from their holiday destination or small-scale illegal opportunists may smuggle a relatively small amount of wildlife to reduce their holiday costs, legal enterprises and crime groups are also involved in the illegal wildlife trade smuggling substantial amounts of highly profitable wildlife across the borders of the EU (Traffic 2014).

In 993 cases the offenders' profession was recorded in the EU-TWIX database. These jobs consist mainly of animal traders ($N = 141$), businessmen ($N = 113$), liberal professionals ($N = 71$), unemployed ($N = 68$), and zoo or wildlife park owners ($N = 64$). There is a significant difference in the number of seizures between the jobs ($X^2(34) = 1{,}278$, $p < 0.05$). Generally, animal traders deal in illegal live birds and reptiles, businessmen are in the caviar business, and liberal professionals trade illegally in ivory carvings and derivatives (Table 6.5).

On a regular basis legally registered companies operate illegally and commit environmental crimes (see also Sect. 4.4). Ruggiero and South (2010) used the term *dirty collar crime* to illustrate that in many European countries corporate entrepreneurs benefit from legal structures to mismatch quantities or falsify the certification of waste. According to Naylor (2004) the illegal wildlife trade has always been operated by the same actors who run the legal business with the same infrastructure. A large number of investigations have demonstrated the involvement of legal enterprises in the illegal trade in wildlife (e.g. Cook et al. 2002; KLPD 2005; Vinke and Vinke 2010; Lyons and Natusch 2011). Indeed, the EU seizures present a large proportion of perpetrators (>30 %) who trade legally in wildlife, which seems to confirm the backgrounds of these 'green collar crime'.[38] For

[38]In an analysis of perpetrators in the Netherlands (KLPD 2005), half of the studied perpetrators were demonstrated to be certified legal wildlife traders.

Table 6.5 Job and main trade of perpetrators

	%	Main trade	%
Animal trader	14.2	Live reptiles and birds	46.8
Businessman	11.4	Caviar	33.6
Liberal profession	7.2	Ivory carvings and derivatives	31.0
Unemployed	6.9	Live reptiles	32.4
Zoo/Wildlife park owner	6.5	Live birds and mammals	73.4
Pensioner/Retired	5.9	Live reptiles and reptile products	43.1
Public service administrative professional	4.8	Ivory carvings, derivatives and coral	37.5
Student	4.5	Live reptiles	37.8
Armed forces	4.4	Reptile products and coral	72.1
Antique dealer	4.3	Ivory carvings	27.9

Source Personal analyses of the EU-TWIX database, 2001–2010

instance, these perpetrators include animal traders, zoo or wildlife park owners, antique dealers, fashion trading companies, breeders, food traders and TCM suppliers.[39] Moreover, illegal wildlife is also destined for legal enterprises such as reptile meat and caviar for restaurants, big cats for circuses and primates and bears for wildlife film producers.

While the previous examples demonstrate the intertwined relationship between the legal and illegal wildlife trade, the involvement of organized crime in the wildlife trade has been put forward as well. Several UN reports suggest the extensive involvement of traditional organized crime, such as Chinese, Japanese, Italian and Russian organized crime groups, in the illegal wildlife trade in the early 2000s. Chinese Triads, such as the Wo Shing Wo group and 14K, were connected to smuggling ivory, rhino horn and shark fin. The Neapolitan Mafia was said to be behind the illegal trading of endangered parrots and Russian organized crime seemed to be involved in the illegal trade in caviar as well as tiger and bear poaching (Søyland 2000; ECOSOC 2002, 2003; Wyler and Sheikh 2008; Van Uhm 2012b). According to Kazmar (2000) the Yakuza has been involved in trading in illicit whale meat and the Colombian Medellin cartel would be involved in the illegal trade in parrots and reptiles. The Cali drug cartel in Colombia would smuggle mixed shipments of wildlife and drugs into the US (ECOSOC 2002). The cartels would exchange drugs for endangered species resulting in cashless transfers (Kazmar 2000). More recent reports indicate that Chinese organized crime groups in Hong Kong are involved in the trade in TCM with derivatives of illegal species to several companies across the EU (Europol 2011), an Irish mobile organized crime group (the Rathkeale Rovers) has been active in stealing more than 100 rhino

[39]For example, confiscations from animal traders (14.2 %), zoo or wildlife park owners (6.5 %), antique dealers (4.3 %) fashion trading companies (2.9 %), breeders (1.4 %), food traders (1.1%) and TCM suppliers (0.5%).

Table 6.6 Significant trade from five countries

	Trade	Species	N>50	N
China	Medicine	Seahorse	24	16,916
		Tiger and leopard	19	4,784
		Musk antelope	18	3,184
		Saiga antelope	8	1,655
		Rhino	3	1,028
	Pieces of ivory	Elephant	17	5,482
	Shark fins	Shark	N/A	N/A
Japan	Whale meat	Whale	N/A	N/A
Italy	Live parrots	Parrot	N/A	N/A
Russia	Caviar	Sturgeon	2	2,590*
Colombia	Reptiles	Reptile skins	3	9,594
	Birds	Parrot	N/A	N/A

* Note that there are dozens of significant caviar seizures recorded in kilos
Source Personal analyses of the EU-TWIX database, 2001–2010

horns from European museums and selling them to Southeast Asian dealers (Ayling 2013; Van Uhm 2012b) and crime groups involved in high-level drugs trafficking in Brazil, Colombia and Mexico are illegally supplying illegal wildlife species to the EU (Europol 2011). By making significant wildlife seizures (>50 items) in the EU from China, Japan, Italy, Russia and Colombia a link may be found pointing to the possible involvement of these criminal organizations. In making large seizures it is generally expected that the following will be found: TCM, shark fins or ivory in connection with China, whale meat on its way to Japan, parrots to Italy, caviar from Russia and a connection with Colombia in relation to reptiles and birds.

Large seizures in Table 6.6 represent significant illegal TCM and ivory shipments connected to China, substantial caviar shipments from Russia and a large-scale reptile skin trade from Colombia. The involvement of Chinese organized crime in the TCM and ivory trade, the trade in caviar by Russian organized crime and the trade in reptile skins by Colombian criminal groups are all plausible. The data present no indicators of large-scale parrot or whale meat operations by Italian and Japanese organized crime.[40] According to Europol (2013b), the role of organized criminal groups in wildlife trafficking within the EU is increasing. Major organized criminal groups may participate in the wildlife trade because of the high profits, the low risk for smugglers when bringing wildlife into a country and the ability to incorporate this type of trade with other types of contraband (Zimmerman 2003; Schneider 2012).[41]

[40]The Port of Rotterdam is used to transfer tonnes of whale meat from Iceland to Japan ('Geen doorvoer walvisvlees via haven Rotterdam', Havenbedrijf Rotterdam, June 26, 2013).

[41]Several reports indicate that the same routes which have been established for other types of illegal commodities are used to transfer illegal wildlife.

6.7 Selection of the Case Studies

As shown, the illegal wildlife trade differs as regards its purposes (from animals as pets to animal products for the manufacturing industry), exclusivity (from a few euros for a live reptile to thousands of euros for a kilo of caviar) and size (from small numbers of shells to containers of TCM). Based on the quantitative analyses three case studies were selected according to three criteria. First, the case studies focus on the top exporters of illegal shipments of wildlife to the EU. Second, they involve substantial trade taking into account the context of the species population. Third, the three case studies should ensure a variation in the purpose of the illegal trade (symbolic, functional, entertainment). As most illegal shipments of wildlife to the EU were from Africa and Asia, the case studies were selected from these regions. The first case study is related to illegal shipments from the top exporter Russia. The main illegal trade from this country is linked to the category fish, in particular the illegal trade in caviar to the EU. Substantial amounts of caviar, as extremely exclusive and valuable luxury food products, are destined for upper-class society in Europe. The sturgeon is one of the most endangered animal groups worldwide as a result of the overexploitation of the species for caviar. The illegal trade in caviar to the EU will be described in Chap. 7. The second case study focuses on Morocco, the main African exporter of wildlife based on EU seizures. A specific species of monkeys, Barbary macaques, appears to dominate the live mammal confiscations with 25 %. Only 5,000–6,000 Barbary macaques remain in the wild, partly as a result of the illegal trade to the EU to meet the demand for exotic pets. The illegal trade in Barbary macaques to the EU will be described in Chap. 8. The third case study is based on illegal trade from China as a major exporter of illegal shipments of medicine to the EU. Medicine is the largest category among all classes in terms of quantity, mainly related to the illegal trade in traditional Chinese medicine to the EU. Products of seized TCM include parts of well-known endangered species, such as the threatened tiger and rhinoceros. The illegal trade in TCM to the EU will be described in Chap. 9. These case studies vary not only in terms of their purposes, live animals and animal products, exclusivity and species, but also their origin from different parts of the world. The illegal trade in caviar is mainly related to Russia (and Kazakhstan and Azerbaijan), the trade in Barbary macaques to Morocco and the trade in TCM to China. This ensures that this research framework includes the main continents of origin (Africa and Asia) and demonstrates the large variety of the black market.

However, based on seizures it is difficult to provide information about the sociocultural and economic context of the actors and the organization of the illegal trade. To get more in-depth information about these aspects, the three case studies based on qualitative research will provide specific details from people directly involved in the illegal wildlife trade.

References

Alacs, E. A., Georges, A., FitzSimmons, N. N., & Robertson, J. (2010). DNA detective: A review of molecular approaches to wildlife forensics. *Forensic Science, Medicine and Pathology, 6*(3), 180–194.

Andreas, P., & Greenhill, K. M. (Eds.). (2010). *Sex, drugs, and body counts: The politics of numbers in global crime and conflict*. Ithaca: Cornell University Press.

Ayling, J. (2013). What sustains wildlife crime? Rhino horn trading and the resilience of criminal networks. *Journal of International Wildlife Law & Policy, 16*(1), 57–80.

Boekhout van Solinge, T. (2014). The illegal exploitation of natural resources. In Paoli, L. (Ed.), *The Oxford Handbook of Organized Crime*. Oxford: Oxford University Press.

Broad, S., Mulliken, T., & Roe, D. (2003). The nature and extent of legal and illegal trade in wildlife. In S. Oldfield (Ed.), *The trade in wildlife, regulation for conservation*. London: Earthscan.

Carpenter, A. (2012). *Security and Europe's Sea Ports: Threats and Issues Facing Maritime Gateways to Europe. Paper Presented at the Policing and European Studies Research Conference*. Cambridge: Cambridge Scholars Publishing.

Chiszar, D., Smith, H. M., & Costain, W. D. (1992). *Reptiles in association with illicit drugs*. Colerado: University of Colerado.

CITES. (2003). *Review of significant trade in specimens of Appendix-II species* (Resolution Conf. 12.8 and Decision 12.75).

Coleman, C., & Moynihan, J. (1996). *Understanding crime data: Haunted by the dark figure*. Buckingham: Open University Press.

Commission, European. (2006). *Study on the enforcement of the EU wildlife trade regulations in the EU-25*. Brussels: European Commission.

Commission, European. (2014). *Communication from the commission to the Council and the European Parliament*. Brussels: European Commission.

Cook, D., Roberts, M., & Lowther, J. (2002). *The international wildlife trade and organised crime: A review of the evidence and the role of the UK*. Wolverhampton: University of Wolverhampton.

Cooney, R., & Jepson, P. (2006). The international wild bird trade: What's wrong with blanket bans? *Oryx, 40*(01), 18–23.

Cowdrey, D. (2002). *Switching channels. Wildlife trade routes into Europe and the UK. A (Report WWF/Traffic)*. Wolverhampton: University of Wolverhampton.

CRI. (1992). *Milieuhandhaving en natuurbescherming; criminaliteitsbeeld van en om de handel in bedreigde plant en diersoorten*. The Hague: Centrale Recherche Informatiedienst.

DeBoer, T. S., & Barber, P. H. (2010). Isolation and characterization of 9 polymorphic microsatellite markers for the endangered boring giant clam (Tridacna crocea) and cross-priming testing in three other Tridacnid species. *Conservation Genetics Resources, 2* (1), 353–356.

Duffy, R. (2010). *Nature crime: How We're getting conservation wrong*. New Haven: Yale University Press.

Economic and Social Council United Nations. (2002). *Progress Made in the Implementation of Economic and Social Council Resolution 2001/12 on Illicit Trafficking in Protected Species of Wild Flora and Fauna*. Report of the Secretary-General.

Economic and Social Council United Nations. (2003). *Illicit Trafficking in Protected Species of Wild Flora and Fauna and Illicit Access to Genetic Resources* (E/CN.15/2003/8).

EIA. (2004). *The enforcement imperative*. EIA: Combating the Illegal Trade in Ivory. London.

EIA. (2013a). *Blood ivory. Exposing the myth of a regulated market*. London: EIA.

EIA. (2013b). *Hidden in plain sight: China's Clandestine Tiger Trade*. London: EIA.

Elliott, L. (2011). *Transnational environmental crime: Applying network theory to an investigation of illegal trade, criminal activity and law enforcement responses*. Canberra: The Australian National University.

Engler, M., & Knapp, A. (2008). *Briefing on the evolution of the Caviar Trade and Range State Implementation of Resolution Conf. 12.7 (Rev. CoP14). A Traffic Europe Report for the European Commission.* Brussels: Traffic.

Engler, M., & Parry-Jones, R. (2007). *Opportunity or threat: The role of the European Union in Global Wildlife Trade.* Traffic Europe.

Europol (2011). *Organised crime threat assessment (OCTA).* The Hague: Europol.

Europol. (2013a). *Serious and organised crime threat assessment (SOCTA).* The Hague: Europol.

Europol. (2013b). *Threat assessment 2013. Environmental crime in the EU.* The Hague: Europol.

FAO. (2011). *International trade in wild birds, and related bird movements, in Latin America and the Caribbean. Animal Production and Health Paper No. 166.* Rome: FAO.

Felbab-Brown, V. (2011). *The disappearing act: The illicit trade in wildlife in Asia.* The Brookings Institution: Washington D.C.

Gabriel, G., Hua, N., & Wang, J. (2012). *Making a killing: A 2011 survey of ivory markets in China.* Yarmouth Port: International Fund for Animal Welfare.

Gagnier, R. (2013). *Illicit trade in wildlife and the economics of agricultural and wildlife smuggling.* New York: Novinka.

Goga, K. (2014). The illegal abalone trade in the Western Cape. *Institute for Security Studies Papers, 261*, 12.

Green, E., & Shirley, F. (1999). *The Global Trade in Coral. WCMC Biodiversity Series No. 9. World Conservation Monitoring Centre.* Cambridge: World Conservation Press.

Herbig, J. (2010). The illegal trade as a form of conservation crime: A South Africa criminological investigation. In White, R. (Ed.), *Global environmental harm. Criminological perspectives.* Cullompton: Willan Publishing.

Highfield, A. C., & Bayley, J. R. (1996). The trade in tortoise-derived souvenir products in Morocco. *Traffic Bulletin, 16*(1), 33–35.

Holden, J. (1998). *By Hook or by Crook: A reference manual on illegal wildlife trade and prosecutions in the United Kingdom.* Sandy: Royal Society for the Protection of Birds.

IFAW. (2013). *Criminal nature: The global security implications of the illegal wildlife trade.* Yarmouth Port: International Fund for Animal Welfare, Report.

Interpol. (1996). *Project NOAH (internal report).* Lyon: Interpol.

Interpol. (2010). *Wildlife smuggling concealment—Case study handbook.* Lyon: Interpol.

Interpol (2012). *World Model UN 2012.* Lyon: Interpol.

Kasterine, A., Arbeid, R., Caillabet, O., & Natusch, D. (2012). *The trade in South-East Asian python skins.* Geneva: International Trade Centre (ITC).

Kazmar, J. (2000). The international illegal plant and wildlife trade: Biological suicide, *U.C. Davis Journal of International Law and Policy, 6*(105), 105–129.

Kemner, J. (2010). *Illegale handel in exotische diersoorten uitgestorven?.* Amsterdam: Bureau Milieu Criminaliteit.

KLPD. (2005). *Analyse CITES-criminaliteit.* KLPD: Een analyse van de illegale handel in CITES-soorten. Zoetermeer.

Lawson, K., & Vines, A. (2014). *Global impacts of the illegal wildlife trade: The costs of crime, insecurity and institutional erosion.* London: Chatham House.

Lemieux, A. M., & Clarke, R. V. (2009). The international ban on ivory sales and its effects on elephant poaching in Africa. *British Journal of Criminology, 49*(4), 451–471.

Levi, M., & Reuter, P. (2006). Money laundering. *Crime and Justice, 34*(1), 289–375.

Liddick, D. R. (2011). *Crimes against nature. Illegal industries and the global environment.* Oxford: Praeger Publishers.

Lindsey, P. A., Masterson, C. L., Beck, A. L., & Romañach, S. (2012). Ecological, social and financial issues related to fencing as a conservation tool in Africa. In M. J. Somers & M. Hayward (Eds.), *Fencing for conservation* (pp. 215–234). New York: Springer.

LNV. (2000). *Voortgangsrapportage CITES.* The Hague: LNV.

Lyons, J. A., & Natusch, D. J. (2011). Wildlife laundering through breeding farms: Illegal harvest, population declines and a means of regulating the trade of green pythons (Morelia viridis) from Indonesia. *Biological Conservation, 144*(12), 3073–3081.

McMurray, C. (2008). Testimony of Claudia McMurray to the U.S. House of Representatives Committee on Natural Resources (5 March) Hearing on Poaching American Security: Impacts of illegal wildlife trade, before the committee on natural resources. Washington (DC), USA: House of Representatives. In Williams, H.O., & Grante, V.T. (Eds.), *Illegal trade in wildlife.* New York: Nova Science Publishers.

Milliken, T. (2014). *Illegal trade in ivory and rhino horn: An assessment report to improve law enforcement under the wildlife TRAPS project.* Cambridge: Traffic.

Momii, M. (2002). *A comparative study of wildlife law in the UK and Japan and the differences in a cultural context.* University of Kent, Doctoral Thesis. Kent: University of Kent.

Naylor, R. T. (2004). The underworld of ivory. *Crime, Law and Social Change, 42*(4–5), 261–295.

Nellemann, C., Henriksen, R., Raxter, P., Ash, N., & Mrema, E. (Eds.). (2014). *The environmental crime crisis—Threats to sustainable development from illegal exploitation and trade in wildlife and forest resources. A UNEP Rapid Response Assessment.* Nairobi and Arendal: United Nations Environment Programme and GRID-Arendal.

Nijman, V. (2010). An overview of international wildlife trade from Southeast Asia. *Biodiversity and Conservation, 19*, 1101–1114.

NOAA. (2010). *Strategic plan for deep-sea coral and sponge ecosystems: Research, management, and international cooperation.* Silver Spring: NOAA Coral Reef Conservation Program.

Nooren, H., & Claridge, G. (2001). *Wildlife Trade in Laos: The End of the Game.* Gland: IUCN-The World Conservation Union.

Nowell, K. (2012). *Wildlife crime scorecard.* Gland: World Wildlife Fund.

Perälä, J. (2003). Testudo kleinmanni. In *IUCN 2012. IUCN Red List of Threatened Species. Version 2012.2.* Gland: IUCN.

Petrossian, G. A., & Clarke, R. V. (2014). Explaining and controlling illegal commercial fishing an application of the CRAVED theft model. *British Journal of Criminology, 54*(1), 73–90.

Petrossian, G. A., Pires, S. F. & Van Uhm, D. P. (2016). An overview of seized illegal wildlife entering the United States, *Global Crime, 17*(2): 181–201.

Pikitch, E. K., Doukakis, P., Lauck, L., Chakrabarty, P., & Erickson, D. L. (2005). Status, trends and management of sturgeon and paddlefish fisheries. *Fish and Fisheries, 6*(3), 233–265.

Pires, S. F. (2012). The illegal parrot trade: A literature review. *Global Crime, 13*(3), 176–190.

Pitcher, T. J., Watson, R., Forrest, R., Valtýsson, H., & Guénette, S. (2002). Estimating illegal and unreported catches from marine ecosystems: A basis for change. *Fish and Fisheries, 3*, 317–339.

Renctas. (2001). *1st national report on the traffic of wild animals.* Brasilia: Renctas.

Reuter, P. (2004). *Chasing dirty money: The fight against money laundering.* Washington, D.C.: The Peterson Institute for International Economics.

Rice, S. M., & Moore, M. K. (2008). Trade secrets: A ten year overview of the illegal import of sea turtle products into the US. *Marine Turtle Newsletter, 121*, 1–5.

Roe, D., Mulliken, T., Milledge, S., Mremi, J., Mosha, S., & Grieg-Gran, M. (2002). *Making a killing or making a living. Wildlife trade, trade controls and rural livelihoods.* London: IIED, and Cambridge: Traffic.

Rosen, G. E., & Smith, K. F. (2010). Summarizing the evidence on the international trade in illegal wildlife. *EcoHealth, 7*(1), 24–32.

Regionale Recherche Dienst. (1995). *Eindrapportage Team HID. Project Wildlife Criminaliteit.* Rotterdam: RRD.

Ruggiero, V., & South, N. (2010). Green criminology and dirty collar crime. *Critical Criminology, 18*(4), 251–262.

Schlaepfer, M. A., Hoover, C., & Dodd, C. K. (2005). Challenges in evaluating the impact of the trade in amphibians and reptiles on wild populations. *BioScience, 55*(3), 256–264.

Schneider, J. L. (2008). Reducing the illicit trade in endangered wildlife: The market reduction approach. *Journal of Contemporary Criminal Justice, 24*, 274–295.

Schneider, J. (2012). *Sold into extinction: The global trade in endangered species.* Santa Barbara: Praeger.

Van Uhm, D. P., & Siegel, D. (2016). Zwarte kaviaar. Criminele netwerken, illegale handel en de bedreiging van de steur. *Justitiële verkenningen, 30*(2), 54–70.

Sodhi, N. S., Koh, L. P., Brook, B. W., & Ng, P. K. (2004). Southeast Asian biodiversity: An impending disaster. *Trends in Ecology & Evolution, 19*(12), 654–660.

Sollund, R. (2013). Animal trafficking and trade: Abuse and species injustice. In D. S. Westerhuis, R. Walters, & T. Wyatt (Eds.), *Emerging issues in green criminology: Exploring power, justice and harm*. Basingstoke: Palgrave Macmillan.

Sollund, R., & Maher, J. (2015) *The illegal wildlife trade. A case study report on the illegal wildlife trade in the United Kingdom, Norway, Colombia and Brazil.* Oslo & Wales: University of Oslo and University of South Wales.

South, N., & Wyatt, T. (2011). Comparing illicit trades in wildlife and drugs: An exploratory study. *Deviant Behavior, 32*(6), 538–561.

Søyland, S. (2000). *Criminal organisations and crimes against the environment—A desktop study.* Turin: United Nations Interregional Crime and Justice Research Institute.

Speart, J. (1993). War within. *Buzzworm, 5*(4), 36–45.

Stiles, D., & Martin, E. (2009). The USA's ivory markets-how much a threat to elephants? *Pachyderm, 45*, 67–76.

Stiles, D., Redmond, I., Cress, D., Nellemann, C., & Formo, R. K. (Eds.). (2013). *Stolen Apes—The Illicit Trade in Chimpanzees, Gorillas, Bonobos and Orangutans. A Rapid Response Assessment. United Nations Environment Programme*. Arendal: GRID-Arendal.

Tailby, R., & Gant, F. (2002). *The illegal market in Australian Abalone*. Canberra: Australian Institute of Criminology.

Traffic. (2008). *The illegal trade in wild birds for food through South-east and Central Europe.* Brussels: Traffic Europe.

Traffic. (2012). *Captive bred, or wild taken?* Cambridge: Traffic International.

Traffic. (2013). *China's wildlife enforcement news digest* (September 2013). Beijing: Traffic.

Traffic. (2014). *Wildlife trade in the European Union.* Brussels: Traffic Europe.

UN. (2012). *Improving international systems for trade in reptile skins based on sustainable use.* Geneva: UN.

UNEP. (2013). *Elephants in the Dust–The African Elephant Crisis. A Rapid Response Assessment.* United Nations Environment Programme, GRID-Arendal.

Underwood, F. M., Burn, R. W., & Milliken, T. (2013). Dissecting the illegal ivory trade: An analysis of ivory seizures data. *PLoS ONE, 8*(10), e76539.

United Nations Office on Drugs and Crime. (2006). *Organized crime and irregular migration from Africa to Europe.* UNODC.

United Nations Office on Drugs and Crime. (2010). *The globalization of crime: A transnational organized crime threat assessment.* Vienna: UNODC.

United Nations Office on Drugs and Crime. (2012). *Wildlife and forest crime analytic toolkit.* New York: United Nations.

Van Dijk, P. P., Corti, C., Mellado, V. P., & Cheylan, M. (2004). *Testudo Graeca. The IUCN Red List of Threatened Species 2004.* Gland: IUCN.

Van Kreveld. (2007). *Gekweekt met de vangkooi. Verkenning naar illegale praktijken in de handel in wilde Europese vogels in Nederland.* Nijmegen: Stroming.

Van Uhm, D. P. (2009). *Illegale dierenhandel en de rol van Nederland. (Masterthesis Criminology).* Utrecht: Utrecht University.

Van Uhm, D. P. (2012a). De illegale handel in beschermde diersoorten, *Justitiële Verkenningen* 2 (themanummer Groene Criminologie), 91–100.

Van Uhm, D. P. (2012b). Organised crime in the wildlife trade. *Centre for Information and Research on Organised Crime (CIROC) Newsletter*, 10 (2): 2–4.

Van Uhm, D. P. (2014). *Illegal trade in Barbary Macaques*. Utrecht: Utrecht University.

Van Uhm, D. P. (2016a). Illegal trade in wildlife and harms to the world. In Spapens, A.C.M.,

Van Uhm, D. P. (2016b). De verwevenheid tussen de onder- en bovenwereld in de wildlife handel. *Cahiers Politiestudies, 38*(1), 41–54.

Venkatesan, V. (2010). Marine ornamental molluscs. *National Training Programme on Marine Ornamental Fish Culture*, 27–32.

Vinke, T., & Vinke, S. (2010). Do breeding facilities for chelonians threaten their stability in the wild? *Schildkroïen im Fokus, Bergheim* 1: 1–18.

Warchol, G. L., Zupan, L. L., & Clack, W. (2003). Transnational criminality: An analysis of the illegal wildlife market in Southern Africa. *International Criminal Justice Review, 13*(1), 1–27.

Wood, E. M., Malsch, K., & Miller, J. (2012). International trade in hard corals: Review of management, sustainability and trends. *Proceedings of the 12th International Coral Reef Symposium* (pp. 9–13). Australia: Cairns.

World Bank. (2008). *What's driving the wildlife trade? A review of expert opinion on economic and social drivers of the wildlife trade and trade control efforts in Cambodia, Indonesia, Lao PDR, and Vietnam*. Washington, DC: The World Bank.

Wyatt, T. (2009). Exploring the organization of Russia Far East's illegal wildlife trade: Two case studies of the illegal fur and illegal falcon trades. *Global Crime, 10*(1–2), 144–154.

Wyatt, T. (2011). The illegal trade of raptors in the Russian Federation. *Contemporary Justice Review, 14*(2), 103–123.

Wyatt, T. (2013). *Wildlife trafficking: A deconstruction of the crime, the victims, and the offenders*. Basingstoke: Palgrave Macmillan.

Wyler, L. S., & Sheikh, P. A. (2008). *International illegal trade in wildlife: Threats and US policy*. New York: Novinka Books.

Xueyan, L. (2007). Promoting sustainable use of Chinese traditional medicines. In *The state of wildlife trade in China. Information on the trade in wild animals and plants in China*. Beijing: Traffic China.

Zembla. (2001). *De Madagascar-connectie*. Documentary on May 24, 2001.

Zimmerman, M. E. (2003). The black market for wildlife: Combating transnational organized crime in the illegal wildlife trade. *Vanderbilt Journal of Transnational Law, 36*(5), 1657–1690.

Chapter 7
Black Caviar

Caviar. World famous as a delicacy, yet consisting of mere fish eggs. Once food for the poor but today only accessible to the upper classes of society. Currently, prices in Western Europe range from €2,000 or 6,000 per kilo, to sometimes €25,000 per kilo for extremely rare varieties (Liddick 2011: 77–78; Neve et al. 2012: 34). The first case study[1] will present how fish eggs became an extraordinary highly valued luxury product and how organized crime took advantage of this lucrative market. Rumours abound that up to 90 % of the caviar that is currently being sold has been extracted from illegally caught sturgeons (Nellemann et al. 2014). Next to the extremely high prices paid for caviar, the phrase caviar mafia is not shunned.[2] How much of this alarming news is based on reality? And what are the consequences of this trade? Based on fieldwork in Russia, Kazakhstan and Azerbaijan in 2014, this chapter examines the actors involved and provides insights into the social organization, modus operandi and trade routes. At the end, the consequences of the harmful trade in caviar will be discussed.

7.1 History of the Valuation of Caviar

Sturgeons are one of the most ancient species of the animal kingdom. It is estimated that these 'living fossils' of the order *Acipenseriformes* appeared 250 million years ago (Shadrina 2007; Nikolaev et al. 2009). They survived the dinosaurs and several mass extinctions, while their eggs were appreciated and consumed in many ancient

[1]Parts of this chapter have been published in two publications: Van Uhm, D.P. and Siegel, D. (2016). The illegal trade in black caviar. *Trends in Organized Crime,* 19(1): 67–87; Siegel, D. and Van Uhm, D.P. (2014). Zwarte kaviaar. Criminele netwerken, illegale handel en de bedreiging van de steur. *Justitiële verkenningen*, 30(2): 54–70.

[2]In this case study the term 'mafia' is used as an emic concept, i.e. how local people perceive and categorize the world (Kottak 1996).

D.P. van Uhm, *The Illegal Wildlife Trade*, Studies of Organized Crime 15,
DOI 10.1007/978-3-319-42129-2_7

cultures (Saffron 2002). The ancient Egyptians and Phoenicians prepared sturgeon eggs with salt and vinegar around 2400 BCE (Shadrina 2007)[3] and the Greeks were also no strangers to caviar as a delicacy. Aristotle described ancient feasts where caviar was served on platters garnished with flowers (Gordon 2002).[4] However, the real exclusivity of caviar was formed centuries later, when Russian Tsars imposed a caviar tax on sturgeon fishing.

According to Simmel (1978) in his book 'The Philosophy of Money' the value of an object is more a judgement about an object rather than an inherent quality. The value will increase as the meaning of the object develops in a certain social context. For instance, products like tea and sugar became symbols of the participation of the working classes as 'higher standards' of living (Mintz 1985). Luxury goods can become status symbols for the elite, but they can also manifest themselves as 'national symbols'. Objects can develop their value in the context of historical and sociological processes. Nowadays caviar, alongside *vodka* and *matryoshka dolls*, is seen as a typical Russian product (Siegel and Van Uhm 2014).[5] From this perspective the symbolic value will be constructed in changing historical and social circumstances.

Caviar first gained popularity in the Middle Ages because fish and fish products were sanctioned as foods that could be consumed during religious fasts when it was forbidden by the Russian Orthodox Christian church to eat meat. The Russian word for caviar is *ikra* (икра), which literally means fish roe. During this period of time the Church governed even minor aspects of Russian life and by sanctioning caviar during the fasting days, it was easier for the poor to follow the religious demands. This strict regime led to a great consumption of fish among the Russian population (Saffron 2002: 47–53).

In the thirteenth century Russia suffered a humiliating defeat by Genghis Khan, and the Mongols controlled the fishery and water trade routes to the Black and Caspian Seas. Khan developed his capital north of the city of Astrakhan (Russia) as the crossroads of the Great Silk Road between China and Europe. Around the fourteenth century European traders first encountered caviar when Venetian ships entered the Black Sea. They took caviar along with other foods back to Europe. To preserve the fish eggs large amounts of salt were added. In the fifteenth century, each year two shiploads of caviar were imported by Venetian traders from the Mongols (Saffron 2002: 54).

In 1556, Ivan the Terrible (1530–1584 CE) forced the Mongols out of Astrakhan and regained control over sturgeon fisheries in the Volga. At that time, fishermen supplied sturgeon to the court of the Tsar, where caviar was served at receptions for

[3]Images of sturgeons were found in Egyptian temple carvings in Luxor (Saffron 2002).

[4]The Greek writer Claudius Aelianus described 'a colossal lake in the land of the Caspians inhabited by huge fish with pointed noises' and in ancient China a legend said that sturgeon can transform into dragons (Shadrina 2007: 55).

[5]In Judaism and Islam caviar was considered to be unclean. This changed in 1981, when Ayatollah Khomeini announced that caviar was *halal*, perhaps in order to bolster Iran's competitive position on the world market against Russia. Many Iranians still avoid eating caviar (Saffron 2002).

foreign diplomats (Saffron 2002). Caviar was still extremely rare in Europe. The exclusivity of caviar in the sixteenth century was illustrated by Shakespeare describing the food as a 'metaphor for obscurity' (Saffron 2002: 47). In 1704, Tsar Peter the Great (1672–1725 CE) established a 'Fishery Head Office' in Astrakhan and decreed a state monopoly on fishing (Shadrina 2007). He organized the delivery of so-called *troitshnaya* caviar, i.e. caviar transported to St. Petersburg by *troika* (a sled drawn by three horses), within three days. The sturgeon trade had increased into a substantial industry to supply the demand. At that time it was sold relatively cheaply in markets and taverns in towns and cities all over Russia. During a certain period in time caviar was even considered as a dish for the poor.

The Don and Volga Cossacks dominated sturgeon fishing in Russia for a long time. While the European-oriented Tsar Peter the Great allowed them a number of privileges, such as the exclusive rights to catch sturgeons to encourage the production of caviar, the Cossacks became associated with criminality in the seventeenth and eighteenth century. However, relations between the Cossacks and the Russian Tsars have always been complicated. Some of their *atamani* (leaders) were known to be bandits, while others were known as pirates, such as the legendary Stepan Razin (Siegel 2005).

In the eighteenth century caviar was transformed from a Russian dish to exclusive food for the European upper classes. One of the important foreign investors in the history of caviar was Ioannis Varvarkis, a Greek sea captain and trader who obtained official documents for tax-free fishing in the Caspian Sea from Catherine the Great. Around 1780, he developed a fishing business in Astrakhan and, subsequently, began to promote the consumption of caviar to the European upper classes. He started to export caviar on a large scale by camel caravans and wooden sailing ships to Europe (Saffron 2002). His trade marked the beginning of a process of transformation, as a result of which sturgeon eggs were no longer regarded as peasant food, but came to be seen as a globally recognized symbol of wealth and power.

The popularity of caviar increased due to two important developments: the industrial revolution with improved methods of transportation and the emergence of a new class of consumers willing to pay for new exotic and exclusive products. At the beginning of the twentieth century, only wealthy Russians could afford to eat caviar (Saffron 2002), while in Europe eating caviar became a trend among the *nouveaux riches* of the Belle Époque, alongside champagne and oysters. Caviar derived its allure in Europe from the association with Russian aristocrats.[6] This was a drastic change in comparison to the nineteenth century when Russian farmers fed their pigs with caviar.

During the First World War, after the Bolshevik Revolution of 1917, the Communist regime of the Soviet Union owned all the fishing rights in the Caspian Sea. Quota limits for sturgeon were introduced, certain fishing gear became

[6]From 1896 to 1914 the annual sturgeon catch reached 350,000–390,000 tonnes in the northern Russian part of the Caspian Sea, as well as in Azerbaijan and Turkmenistan.

prohibited and foreign entrepreneurs were not allowed near the sturgeon fishery. Probably due to the Bolshevik Revolution and the World Wars the sturgeon stocks partially recovered (Birstein et al. 1997; Ruban and Khodorevskaya 2010). During the time of the Soviet Union the catch never reached the level of the beginning of the century (Barannikova et al. 1995). The Soviet Union ended up controlling 90 % of the world production of caviar (Saffron 2002). Only 10 % of its produced caviar was exported; during the 1980s over 2,000 tonnes of caviar was produced each year, while 140 tonnes were for export (Taylor 1997).

This total control over caviar production guaranteed the value of the product. At the same time, caviar was the food of the *nomenklatura* and a lucrative black market emerged. In Soviet times, corruption and the abuse of power were regarded as inevitable consequences of the socialist economy and the lines between legal and illegal were often blurred (Siegel 2005). According to the Russian sociologist Simis, Soviet citizens needed two things to survive in the Soviet system: money and connections to the underground business world (Simis 1982). "Caviar became an underground currency, a luxurious way of greasing palms and extracting favors" (Saffron 2002: 116). The positive side of the Soviet monopoly was that the fishery was closely monitored: with an eye on a balanced population, sturgeon fishing was outlawed in the Caspian Sea as early as 1962 (Vaisman 1997; Ruban and Khodorevskaya 2010).

As a result of the dissolution of the Soviet Union, people were met with mass unemployed. An important cause of the unemployment in Russia, Azerbaijan and Kazakhstan was the total collapse of the agricultural sector that was built on the *kolkhoze* structure, bearing the essence of the Soviet philosophy. The fishing industry was part of this and, therefore, fishers became unemployed and these 'ordinary people' often resorted to poaching. During the Soviet Union almost 70 % of Dagestan's industry consisted of the catching and processing of fish. After the dissolution they had no other way to feed their families (Raymakers 2002).

In the 1990s the caviar trade fell into the hands of *brakonieri* (poachers) who started to fish for sturgeon on a massive scale. Consequently, enormous amounts of cheap caviar appeared on the Russian market and the price of caviar decreased significantly, which in turn led to an increase in demand—from outside the production countries—from around 300 to 450–500 tonnes per year (Taylor 1997). In this way, cheaper caviar became available to the 'ordinary citizen', alongside top quality caviar.[7]

The Soviet authorities guarded the production of caviar in a way which was comparable to how De Beers protected its diamond mines. Production was centralised under a highly efficient state monopoly. However, after the fall of Communism the caviar trade was privatized. In the first years after the dissolution,

[7]Caviar also became a sought-after commodity in barter transactions. A German firm in Kazakhstan, for instance, signed a contract to build 40 houses in exchange for 24 tonnes of caviar. In Astrakhan, promises were made to construct roads in exchange for caviar, but the caviar ended up in Alaska and no roads were ever built (Taylor 1997).

sturgeons were overfished and caviar was exported in extremely large quantities. Under pressure from environmental groups steps were taken to regulate the fishing for sturgeon.

7.2 The Collapse of the Soviet Union and Emerged Regulations

With the collapse of the Soviet Union existing management and control systems disappeared; until that time the catching of sturgeons in the open sea was strictly prohibited by Soviet legislation in 1962 (Vaisman 1997; Ruban and Khodorevskaya 2010). After the dissolution a new period emerged with the formation of independent states in the 1990s. This political transformation in the Caspian region offered opportunities for the poaching of sturgeons on a huge scale without any restrictions (Birstein et al. 1997; Shadrina 2007). Due to concerns over the impact of overexploitation and unsustainable harvesting, a proposal to include all sturgeon species in the CITES Appendices was put forward by Germany and the US at the 10th Conference of Parties (CoP-10) in Zimbabwe in 1997. CITES has been signed by the following countries around the Caspian Sea: Russia, Kazakhstan, Iran and Azerbaijan, with the exception of Turkmenistan. The proposal was improved and implemented in 1998. Since then, all 27 species of *Acipenseriformes*, 25 sturgeon and 2 paddlefish species, have been protected (Pourkazemi 2006; Raymakers 2006).

All species have been listed in the Appendices of CITES, including two species listed in Appendix I (EC 338/97, Annex A), which prohibits the commercial trade in wild species. The international caviar trade of Appendix II species (EC 338/97, Annex B) is only allowed when shipments are accompanied by the appropriate CITES permits, issued by the relevant national CITES Management Authorities (Oldfield 2003; European Commission 2010). The only exception is a maximum amount of 125 g of labelled caviar (CITES II/Annex B sturgeon) per person to be used for non-commercial purposes.[8] Furthermore, caviar containers are required to bear non-reusable labels and the caviar must be packaged in such a way as to permit visual evidence of any opening of the container. The label for containers must include the following information:

1. Standard species code (three-letter code for the identification of sturgeon species, hybrids and mixed species).
2. Source code of the caviar (caviar from wild [W], captive-bred [C] and from sturgeon born in captivity and where at least one parent originated in the wild [F]).
3. Code for the country of origin (ISO code).

---

[8]Conf. 13.7 (Rev. CoP14).

4. Year of harvest.
5. Official registration code of the processing plant.
6. Lot identification number (the caviar tracking system used by the processing or (re-) packaging plant).

For example, the label with the CITES code: 'HUS/C/RU/2015/0001/0024' means that the caviar is from a Beluga sturgeon (*Huso Huso*) bred in captivity (C) from Russia (RU), produced in 2015 from processing plant 0001 with lot identification code 0024. Since 2006, also repackaged caviar within the EU must be affixed with a non-reusable label, and repackaging companies must be registered by CITES authorities.[9] As the EU is considered to be one domestic market, shipments of caviar from sturgeons in Annex B do not require CITES documents, but do require CITES labels (Jahrl 2013).

Due to large amounts of illegal fishing and the decline in sturgeon populations, in June 2001 the CITES Committee threatened, during its forty-fifth meeting in Paris, to impose a complete export ban on caviar and sturgeon products for the countries surrounding the Caspian Sea, unless "they implemente[d] a series of time-sensitive measures designed to stem the alarming depletion of sturgeon stocks in the region" (Gordon 2002: 13).[10] Subsequently, Russia, Azerbaijan and Kazakhstan committed themselves to a range of measures, such as export quotas, to reduce overfishing. The restrictions had a substantial impact on the local economy as the profits from the caviar industry ran into millions (Raymakers 2002), but these restrictions were not enough to ensure the survival of sturgeons according to several environmental groups. For instance, proposals to transfer the critically endangered Beluga sturgeon from Appendix II to Appendix I were ignored by CITES (Gordon 2002).

In Russia, the punishment for the illegal fishing of sturgeons is a fine of up to 500,000 roubles or 3 years imprisonment, including the seizure of equipment and vehicles used during poaching and compensation for the damage to the species (Maltsev 2009). Since 2007, when the sturgeon population had declined significantly, Russia completely banned wild sturgeon harvesting under pressure from different international organizations. All Caspian countries joined this ban in 2014 (Nellemann et al. 2014). According to the United Nations, "no sector of the illegal fauna or flora trade has been criminalized to the extent of that of sturgeon and caviar" (Wyler and Skeikh 2013). However, the ban did not remove the opportunity for smuggling illegal caviar and strict quotas on sturgeon fishing were blatantly ignored (Zabyelina 2013). The population of sturgeons in the Caspian Sea has declined dramatically, despite the regulations and measures taken.

[9]Commission Regulation (EC) No. 865/2006.

[10]The fifth state, Iran, was allowed to continue its export without CITES restrictions as the country was said to strictly control the catch (Gordon 2002).

7.3 The Disappearance of a Prehistoric Fish

Sturgeons are prehistoric fish of the *Acipenseridae* family, and have been living for 250 million years in Earth's waters. A total of 27 species of sturgeon have been identified, including the genera *Acipenser*, *Huso*, *Scaphirhynchus* and *Pseudoscaphirhynchus*. Sturgeons are large archaic fish (50 cm–6 m; 0.5 kg–1.5 tonnes) that feed themselves on small animals and plants and, generally, migrate upriver for breeding. Their population is particularly vulnerable, because of their slow growth and late sexual maturity (up to 25 years). The Beluga sturgeon is the largest freshwater fish worldwide[11] and may reproduce only every four to 8 years (Raspopov 1993). Nowadays, the largest population of sturgeons exists in the Caspian Sea (Jahrl 2013) (Illustration 7.1).

During the twentieth century, sturgeons from the Caspian Sea were excessively exploited for caviar (Pikitch et al. 2005); about 90 % of the global trade in caviar comes from the Caspian Sea (Engler and Parry-Jones 2007; Pourkazemi 2006; Raymakers 2006).[12] Due to the overexploitation of sturgeon as a result of the caviar industry, 85 % of the sturgeon species are threatened with extinction in comparison to 44 % in 1996 (Bronzi and Rozenthal 2014). Sturgeons, as one of the oldest families of fish, have become the most endangered group of animals on the IUCN Red List of endangered species. 27 species of sturgeon are listed on the Red List, including 63 % which are classified as Critically Endangered and four species are possibly extinct (IUCN 2010) (Appendix X).[13]

The main commercial species for the production of caviar are Beluga (*Huso huso*), Russian (*Acipenser gueldenstaedtii*), Persian (*Acipenser persicus*) and Stellate sturgeon (*Acipenser stellatus*), all critically endangered and with decreasing populations. 'Beluga' caviar from the Beluga is well-known for being the most expensive caviar. Other traditional caviar includes 'Oscietra' from Russian and Persian sturgeon and 'Sevruga' caviar from Stellate sturgeon (Knapp et al. 2006). While most inhabitants of coastal areas of the Caspian Sea are well aware of the decrease in fish populations, surveys have revealed that some people, particularly in cities, perceive the threats posed to the decline of the sturgeon population and the potential risk of their extinction as propaganda (Raymakers 2002).

However, according to several scientists, populations of wild sturgeons have declined substantially during the last few decades, because of a variety of activities, such as habitat destruction, environmental degradation, overexploitation and the illegal trade (Birstein 1997; Khodorevskaya et al. 1997; Stone 2002; Pourkazemi 2006; Shadrina 2007; IUCN 2010). Habitat destruction has contributed to the decline in sturgeons as illustrated by the loss of 70 % of the spawning grounds in

[11]The largest Beluga ever caught was as big as 28 ft and weighed 4,570 lb (Saffron 2002: 33).

[12]Between 1999 and 2004 the Caspian Sea provided 89 % of the reported exports worldwide, followed by the Amur River (5 %), the Danube River/Black Sea (5 %) and North American rivers (2 %) (Raymakers 2006).

[13]17 critically endangered; 2 endangered; 4 vulnerable; 2 near threatened; 2 least concern.

Illustration 7.1 Caspian Sea, Baku, Azerbaijan 2014

the Caspian basin due to the installation of hydroelectric power stations since the 1950s (CITES 2000). In addition, the World Bank has estimated that 1 million m^3 of (untreated) industrial wastewater is discharged into the Caspian Sea each year (US Department of Energy 2000). In spite of the contamination of waters and the building of dams, it is assumed that the illegal poaching of sturgeons is the greatest threat to the survival of the species (Vaisman 1997; Knapp et al. 2006). The overexploitation of sturgeons in the 1990s and 2000s resulted in a substantial decline in the wild population of sturgeon in the Caspian Sea (Engler and Knapp 2008). It is estimated that sturgeon populations have decreased by 70 % in the last century (Jahrl 2013).

To increase the sturgeon population, every year fingerlings are said to be released in the Caspian Sea. According to Gesner et al. (2010), in Russia 25 million sturgeons were released between 1979 and 1980, 35 million between 1981 and 1985, 40.8 million between 1986 and 1990, 42 million between 1991 and 1995 and 28 million between 1996 and 1998. According to a manager of one of the main sturgeon aquaculture companies, there is a state programme whereby a company which extracts oil and is responsible for harm to the environment has to compensate by financially contributing to the production and release of fingerlings. He explained that in Russia federal and commercial companies work together in the production and release of around 1 million sturgeons each year (RT6). According to the director of the Scientific Sturgeon Institute in Astrakhan, this is the solution for the survival of sturgeon in the Caspian Sea (RE1).

7.4 From Fishery to Aquaculture

After the dissolution of the Soviet Union, caviar became a main source of foreign currency in former Soviet countries; the industry would be worth millions of dollars. Europe has become the largest importer of caviar, both in terms of quantity and value in the 2000s (Engler and Parry-Jones 2007). During the 1990s, European imports of caviar increased 1.5–2 times (De Meulenaer and Raymakers 1996). Between 1998 and 2006, 45 % (591 tonnes) of the global trade of more than 1,300 tonnes was destined for the EU and 24 % for the US (313 tonnes) (Knapp et al. 2006; Schneider 2012).[14] More than 97 % of the caviar imports of the EU were sourced from the wild (Engler and Knapp 2008). According to Traffic (2009), Germany (233 tonnes) and France (231 tonnes) were major outlets and France, Switzerland and Germany were important re-export countries between 1998 and 2006. The countries bordering the Caspian Sea have been the source of over 90 % of the caviar in the global trade during the 2000s. The world's largest exporters were Iran (438 tonnes), Russia (138 tonnes), Kazakhstan (95 tonnes) and Azerbaijan (35 tonnes) (Traffic 2009).[15]

Due to the overexploitation, the annual export quotas for sturgeons have declined from over 250 tonnes in 1999 to 110 tonnes in 2005 (Knapp et al. 2006). Simultaneously, the price of imported wild caviar increased from €264 in 1999 to €1,359 in 2006 (Engler and Knapp 2008: 28). Since it is prohibited to catch wild sturgeon in the Caspian Sea, the legal caviar is said to come from captive-bred sturgeon. While the recorded trade in wild caviar has sharply declined since 1999, the trade in caviar from aquaculture has slowly increased. Although during the previous 10 years the production of caviar from wild sturgeons has been near zero (confirmed by CITES quotas), the caviar produced from farmed sturgeons has increased. The total amount of produced caviar is estimated to be 350–400 tonnes, including 100–150 tonnes of illegal caviar obtained from poaching (Bronzi and Rozenthal 2014). The decrease in catches of sturgeons is believed to be caused by the decline of sturgeon species and the illegal catching of sturgeons (Pourkazemi 2006).

[14]In 1998, almost 99 % of the total supply of caviar originated from seven countries, including Russia (121 tonnes, 44 %), Iran (42 %) and Kazakhstan (9 %). More than 50 % of the trade was destined for the EU alone with France (19 %) and Germany (17 %) as the major outlets (Raymakers 2002).

[15]However, there were discrepancies between reported imports and reported re-exports. For instance, Russia recorded 74 t of re-exported caviar, while only 28 t were imported. Apparently misreporting occurs at a certain point in the trade (Engler and Knapp 2008).

7.5 Contraband to Major Outlet Europe

In Soviet times, almost 70 % of Dagestan's industry consisted of the catching and processing of fish. As a result of the collapse of the Soviet Union high numbers of workers, fishermen and fish experts became unemployed. These ordinary people had to resort to the poaching of sturgeons in order to feed their families (Vaisman 1997).[16] Consequently, the illegal trade has become many times greater than the legal trade during the previous 20 years (Ruban and Khodorevskaya 2010). It is estimated that since 1991 poachers catch an average of 14,930 tonnes of Russian sturgeons each year, far exceeding legal fishing numbers. In the first year after the dissolution of the Soviet Union, the poaching of sturgeon populations reached as high as 25,000 tonnes per year (without the catching of Beluga) (Ruban and Khodorevskaya 2010). The annual income from the illegal poaching of sturgeons and the trade in sturgeon products would be as high as 10 billion USD (Shadrina 2007).

Several estimations have confirmed the high level of the illegal, uncontrolled trade. In 2000, Traffic estimated that the illegal caviar trade from the Caspian Sea and Volga River was 6–10 times greater than the legal catch and no more than 15–20 % of the catch of sturgeons has been registered in official reports (Speer et al. 2000: 2). The Fish and Wildlife Service has estimated that over 50 % of the global caviar trade was illegal in 2000 (FWS 1998). Wildlife experts estimate that the illegal poaching of sturgeons from 2004 to 2006 in the Caspian Sea region was around 10,000–12,000 t each year. In Russia, 2,700 t of sturgeons were caught illegally in 2004, an equivalent of the production of around 550 t of caviar (UNEP 2010). CITES (2001) discovered that out of every tonne of fish caught legally, at least 5 tonnes were poached. Currently, according to recent market research in Russia by Food Market (2013), experts claim that the illegal volume of caviar exceeds the legal volume by 10 times. The head of the Russian fishing agency's PR centre has stated that the illegal trade constitutes 97–98 % of the Russian market (Food Market 2013).[17] The most recent estimation of the global illegal caviar trade by Bronzi and Rozenthal (2014: 1538) is 100–150 tonnes of the total of 350–400 tonnes (between 25 and 43 % of the total amount). Concluding, while the actual illegal trade remains undetected, these estimates suggest that the illegal trade is a substantial fraction of the legitimate trade, as amounts of illegal caviar are believed to dominate the caviar trade.

[16]The illegal caviar trade also took place in the Soviet Union. In 1978 in Sochi the director of the "Okean" caviar shops and his subordinates were arrested for caviar and sturgeon contraband. High-ranking officials were involved in an abuse of power and corruption (Zabyelina 2013).

[17]The origin of these estimations of illegal caviar is often the Caspian Research Fishery Institute. According to the authors these rates are calculated using mathematical models based on the difference between the expected level of catch and the real catch. However, the founding principles of the estimation methodology are questioned by many experts (Lagutov 2007: 243).

The EU seems to be not only a major importer of legal caviar, but also one of the most important illegal markets (Engler and Parry-Jones 2007). This is illustrated by 16 tonnes of illegal caviar seized by European law enforcers between 2000 and 2010. While the EU makes stringent demands on export countries, illegal caviar is still quite easily obtained within the EU (Shadrina 2007). It has been estimated that 80–90 % of the caviar being sold in Europe has been extracted from illegally caught sturgeons (Neve et al. 2012). A wide range of caviar dealers, fashionable restaurants and Russian shops in Europe are being supplied with illegal caviar from the Caspian Sea (e.g. EN1; RM3; RS13; RS14).

In total 10 tonnes of caviar were confiscated between 2001 and 2010 in the EU with a peak during the early 2000s, both in volume and incidents. Numbers of seizures in previous reports presented lower volumes (e.g. Engler and Parry-Jones 2007; Knapp et al. 2006; Engler and Knapp 2008), because many seizures were recorded in the EU-TWIX database after these publications. While confiscation incidents seem to be quite stable from 2007 onwards, the volume of confiscated caviar in 2009 was remarkably high (Fig. 7.1).

One confiscation of 1 tonne of caviar from Azerbaijan to Germany had a significant influence on the total volume in 2009. However, the confiscations are an

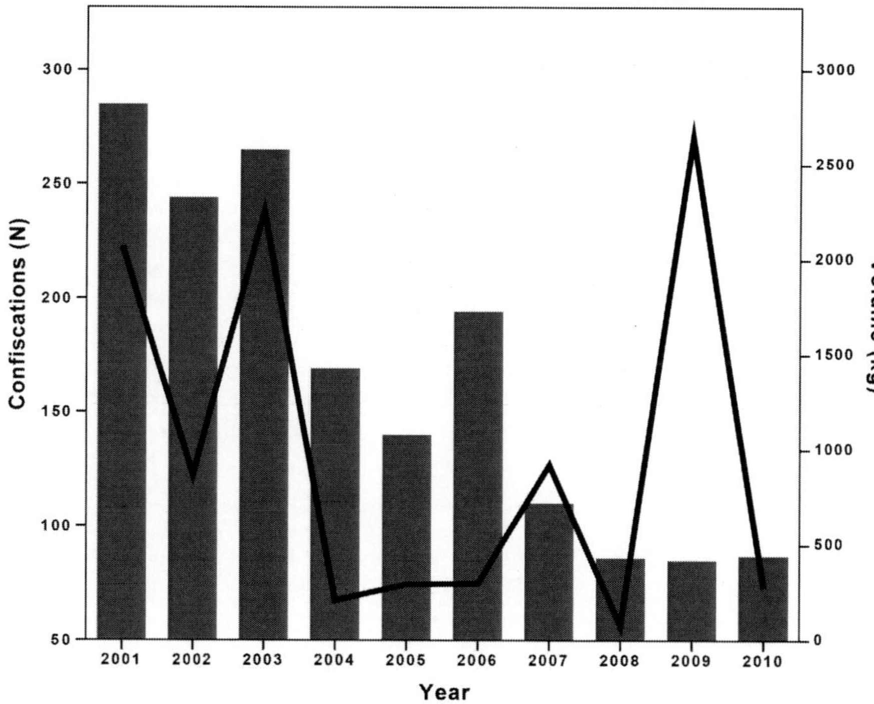

Fig. 7.1 EU confiscations of illegal caviar. *Source* Personal analyses of the EU-TWIX database, 2001–2010

underestimation, as certain seizures are not recorded in the database. For instance, in 2005 two businessmen smuggled more than 1.4 tonnes of caviar into the EU (European Commission 2006), while the volume for 2005 in the database does not reach 1 tonne of seized caviar. The 1,665 seizures of illegal caviar in the EU[18] between 2001 and 2010 indicate that the size of the batches of contraband vary from a few hundred grams to 1.2 tonnes of caviar, with an average of several kilos ($M = 7.7$, $SD = 55.9$). The decrease in confiscations from 2001 could probably be explained by the reduction of wild sturgeons and the decline in exports of wild caviar to the EU. Over the period 1999–2010, the four main 'caviar' species (*Huso huso, Acipenser gueldenstaedtii, Acipenser persicus, Acipenser stellatus*), all critically endangered, were under review by the United Nations Environment Programme (UNEP) and all presented a decrease in exports of wild-sourced caviar (UNEP 2010).

The majority of the illegal caviar originates from countries surrounding the Caspian Sea and more than 40 % of all seizures are from Russia ($N = 579$, 41 %).[19] The annual value of exported caviar by the leading exporter Russia is estimated to be between 40 and 100 million dollars, while the illegal Russian export of caviar is estimated to be no less than 250–400 million dollars (Pikitch et al. 2005; Schneider 2012). Between 1999 and 2006, customs violations associated with the illicit trade in caviar over the Russian customs frontier included almost 10 tonnes of caviar (9,789 kg salted caviar and 22 kg fertilized caviar) (Lyapustin et al. 2007). Recent research on the illegal trade in caviar estimates that as much as 190 tonnes of caviar come from Russia alone (Food Market 2013).[20]

Other major countries of origin for seized illegal caviar are Azerbaijan ($N = 190$, 13 %) and Kazakhstan ($N = 68$, 5 %),[21] with Ukraine ($N = 199$, 14 %) and Poland ($N = 75$, 5 %) as important transit countries. The averages of the quantities to be smuggled are around several kilos from the main departure countries, Russia ($M = 4.8$; $SD = 33$), Ukraine ($M = 6.8$; $SD = 77$), Azerbaijan ($M = 5.2$; $SD = 65$), Poland ($M = 16.9$; $SD = 50$) and Kazakhstan ($M = 1.0$; $SD = 2$), while certain seizures contain large quantities. Germany ($N = 832$, 53 %), France ($N = 293$, 19 %) and Italy ($N = 77$, 5 %) appear to be major outlets in the EU for illegal caviar (Fig. 7.2). For decades, these countries have been well-known to have substantial demand markets for legal and illegal caviar in the EU (Raymakers and Hoover 2002; Knapp et al. 2006; Traffic 2009). For instance, Hamburg, with its free

[18]The number of EU seizures can be found in the EU-TWIX database.

[19]Seizures of caviar in the United States between 2003 and 2012 indicate that more than 30 % originates from Russia (Fish and Wildlife Services database 2013).

[20]In the first half of 2010 in the Republic of Dagestan there were 300 registered criminal cases under Article 256 of the Criminal Code (the illegal harvesting of aquatic biological resources) and Article 175 (the purchase or sale of property knowingly obtained through criminal activity). Only 4 criminal cases were registered by the Fisheries Inspection of Dagestan (Nellemann et al. 2014).

[21]In 2013, 347 crimes related to sturgeon poaching were registered in Kazakhstan over a period of 10 months, showing a 40 % increase compared to 2012. During 2012–2013, only 466 of the 991 criminal cases related to sturgeon poaching were brought to court (Nellemann et al. 2014).

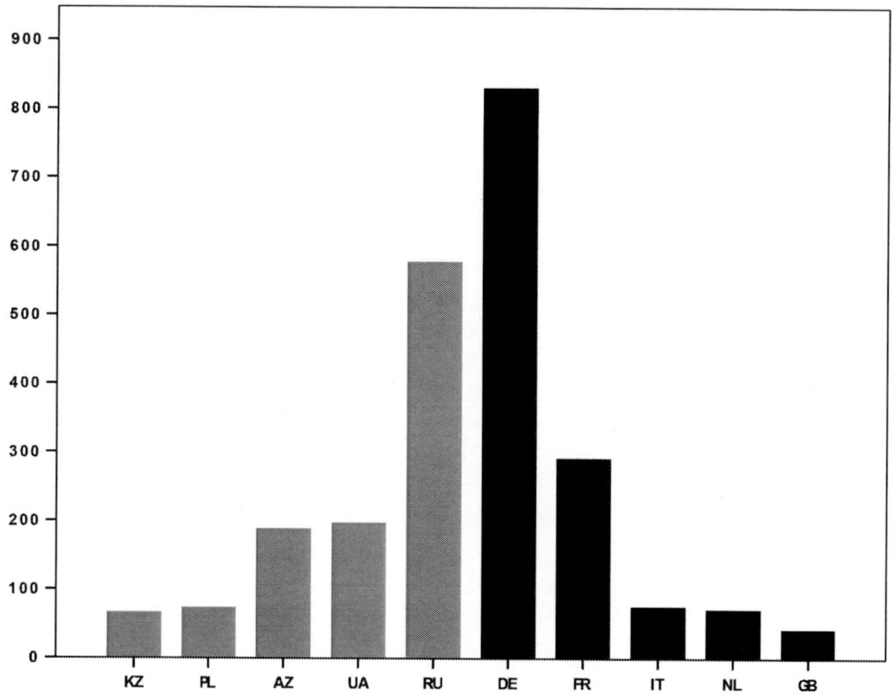

Fig. 7.2 Origin and destination countries for illegal caviar. Export-country codes: Kazakhstan (KZ), Poland (PL), Azerbaijan (AZ), Ukraine (UA), Russia (RU). **Import-country codes: Germany (DE), France (FR), Italy (IT), the Netherlands (NL), Great Britain (GB). *Source* Personal analyses of the EU-TWIX database (seizures), 2001–2010

port, has been the world's biggest clearinghouse for caviar and offers all kinds of opportunities for illegal caviar to enter Europe (Neve et al. 2012) and France is well-known as the leading national caviar demand market in Europe (Monfort 2002; Talishli 2006).

While it is clear that there is a significant illegal trade in caviar in the Caspian countries, as well as a substantial demand market in the EU, the question remains: who are the actors involved in the social organization of the illegal trade in caviar? Before the caviar enters the EU, a complex process precedes, as sturgeons have to be poached, caviar extracted, produced into the final product and smuggled to the destination countries (Schneider 2012). The supply chain usually has flexible distribution lines and networks of poachers through intermediaries to producers and retailers (Haken 2011). In this supply chain a distinction can be made between source countries, transit countries and exporting countries and different actors—poachers, producers, middlemen, smugglers and sellers—who form a distribution network that connects the source and destination (Schneider 2012).

7.6 *Brakonieri* in the Caspian Delta

The brakonieri will exist until the last sturgeon is caught (RT5)

Since the 1990s, the caviar trade has become extremely profitable and entire coastal communities around the Caspian Sea have become involved in illegal sturgeon fishing and the production of caviar. Not just legitimate businesspeople, but especially *brakonieri* (браконьер) started to fish for sturgeons. According to Raymakers (2002) the profile of poachers has changed during the last decades. Until the late 1980s, sturgeons were illegally caught by legal fishermen who had a licence, but not to catch sturgeons in particular. The sturgeons were at that time mainly sold for their meat (RE1). The poachers sold their sturgeons in black markets and thereby exceeded their quota. The local poachers of today are often jobless, without a licence, and are dependent on the illegal catch to feed their families (Raymakers 2002; Ruban and Khodorevskaya 2010).

Several criminologists have conducted research on forms of 'crime to survive'. A person who does not get what he needs (necessities) is a frustrated person and will be easily provoked to rage or crime ('a hungry man is an angry man'). Bongerian theories of crime—for example, the links between bread prices and arrests for theft (Bonger 1932)—may be applicable in understanding the illegal catching of sturgeons. If certain social structures are inherently inadequate, individuals will search for alternatives to satisfy their needs (e.g. illegal fishing). According to Agnew (1992), insufficient resources to achieve positively valued goals result in strain. The relative deprivation will be constructed in a situation where extremely economically poor individuals compare their situation to others who are leading a better life.

Local fishermen in small communities in the Caspian delta have been living for decades from fishing as a source of food and income (Duffy 2010). The fishermen live in very poor villages in small barracks without paved roads which are sometimes only accessible by boat (e.g. personal observation, March 22, 2014, Lagan; September 26, 2014, Sulak), while during Communism in the Soviet Union they were relatively wealthy (RF5; RF7). The majority of poachers are poor citizens from Dagestan and Kalmykia who live day by day and commit 'crimes' without opportunities for a better life (Shadrina 2007). Poverty and unemployment are important push factors that led these local people into poaching (e.g. Knapp et al. 2006). "People are very poor in the Astrakhan delta, Lagan and Dagestan. They are scared, because the police can send you to jail, but if you catch one (big sturgeon with eggs) you have made a living for years" (RF9). This is similar to finding a diamond in Africa. If you are lucky, you will be blessed for life (Siegel 2009).

During the 1990s, with the collapse of the USSR, there was almost no control, and local fishermen became specialized in catching sturgeons. According to interviews held with local fishermen in small villages in the Astrakhan delta,[22]

[22]Kirovskiy, Poldnevoye and Gandurino.

Table 7.1 Types of sturgeon poachers

Type	Equipment	Method
Local independent fisherman	Different kinds of nets and ropes and small boats (limited range)	Poaching for fish, including sturgeons, in the delta (close to the village) with nets with or without a licence. They poach for the subsistence of their family
Professional groups (4–7 people)	Super light boats with Japanese engines and navigation systems, sometimes helicopters (broad range)	Poaching at night on the Caspian Sea with highly sophisticated equipment. They focus on sturgeons for caviar

Kalmykia[23] and Dagestan[24] (Russia), Atyrau[25] (Kazakhstan) and Baku and Talysh[26] (Azerbaijan), there seem to be two types of poachers: local fishermen and professional poachers (e.g. RF1; RF3; RF4; RF7; RF11; RF13) (Table 7.1). The first type consists of local fishermen who poach to feed their families or poach opportunistically. Currently, it is forbidden to catch sturgeons and in order to fish for ordinary fish on a commercial scale one needs a special permit from the Volga-Caspian territorial administration 'Rosrybolovstvo'. Only with this documentation granting permission is one allowed to fish in the Caspian Sea during the fishing season. The process of commercial fishing has become determined by how much of what kind of fish one can catch and where to catch. Prohibited fishing gear (gillnets) and a violation of the quotas is defined as poaching (RF5; RT10; RT11).

Although poaching occurs all the year round, the poaching season starts in April as sturgeon are then spawning. Local fishermen in Lagan (Kalmykia) explained how they evade law enforcement: "We have the required documents to enter the Caspian Sea. In the Caspian nobody knows what we are doing. The guards only check one or two ways to the Caspian Sea in Lagan; the main gates. We use, when necessary, one of the other 15 ways to return to Lagan" (RF9). To catch sturgeons, special nets are used which are placed on migration routes; small fish can pass through the 120 mm holes in the nets measuring 16 × 2 m, but Russian sturgeons and Beluga become stuck. Another poaching method is the use of ropes with hooks. If the sturgeon swims near the rope it is caught. "We do not place any bait on the fishing hooks, we place strands of hooks and lines about 1 cm from the bottom. Any fish that swims along them will inevitably get snagged by the hooks" (RF9).

The second type consists of highly organized and equipped groups of 4–7 people entering the Caspian Sea (RT7; RM7; RS15; RP1). According to a police spokesman in Dagestan: "poachers used to travel in old rickety *Vikhr* boats, but these days the mafia is well organized and use state of the art means of transport",

[23]Lagan.

[24]Sulak, Kaspiysk and Izerbash.

[25]Pakywa.

[26]Salyan and Neftçala.

so that they are better equipped than the government guards. People borrow money to buy a *Baida* (байда), a super light boat made out of aluminium, worth 10–15,000 dollars and instal two Japanese engines worth 30,000 dollars. The poachers also acquire other fishing gear such as a 'Garmin', a navigation system worth 200–500 dollars (RM6). According to a middleman in Astrakhan: "I work with these local guys. (…) They prepare in advance, using GPS to hide their boats in the reed bushes. They have lots of such secret places, which cannot be revealed without knowing the definite coordinates of the hidden boat. They come there at night, often using oars or paddles, so as not to attract the attention of the coastguards and the fish inspectorate, and no light, by pure GPS. (…) They find their hidden boat, armed with fuel and powerful motors, change the boat and go to take out the harvest" (RM2). These poachers are specialized in poaching sturgeons for their caviar on the open sea. They use mid-water floats (not visible on the surface) and GPS to find the nets to collect the sturgeons exclusively in remote areas of the open sea or lower parts of the delta without human settlements and a lack of control. They take out the nets with fish, get out the caviar and throw any sturgeons without caviar back into the water, as the meat of the fish is too cheap in comparison to the caviar; in 500 kg of sturgeon they find only two or three fish with caviar (RM2; RF10; RF11).

Every shift gives the team about 5,000 USD of pure profit. If they take the fish itself, they can get 1,500 USD more. If they hear any noise, they will start to throw all the fish back into the water in order to get rid of the evidence. "A Baida has a small draft, its length on average is about 10 m. The design and shape of the boat are such that it can withstand a sea wave. (…) The speed is more than 100 km/h, even when a loaded Baida is loaded to up to half a ton. Most of the inside space of the boats is occupied by fuel barrels, as the boats consume extreme amounts of diesel" (RM3). The poachers hunt at night because they are afraid of the police that patrol with boats and helicopters during the months of April and May. After the boats pass, they will return to get the sturgeons (RM2; RM3). A poacher in Poldnevoye described a controversial method of poaching. He explained that grenades are used by organized poachers from abroad to bomb certain upriver places with high quantities of sturgeon. Consequently, the sturgeons come to the surface and are easy to catch. According to him these poachers "have no respect, they destroy everything" (RF5).

In contrast to local fishermen, militias of the republics regularly protect professional poachers. These poachers pay 'taxes' to gain access to the Caspian Sea in Dagestan (and to be left alone), and are forced to hand over a certain percentage depending on the size of the catch (RM3; RM6; RS15; RF11; RU3). A poacher in the Babayurt area of Dagestan highlighted the mutual benefits in their symbiotic relationships with officials: "We poach in groups of four people and work together with the police and inspectors. They know what is going on and of course we pay them an amount of money to poach the sturgeon" (RF10). Especially Sulak in Dagestan is a famous poaching town (Illustration 7.2). A smuggler in Makhachkala described the situation as follows: "It is like the mafia, the cooperation between poachers and police officials in Dagestan. They have the power" (RU3). Sometimes

Illustration 7.2 Poaching town Sulak, Dagestan, Russia 2014

there are entire detailed agreements between the poachers and the police. "We mark our boat with a white dot so that they can see during a helicopter patrol that we have paid some bribes. Then they do not control the boat" (RF10). This example demonstrates how the interests of the local crime groups and the police come together for their mutual benefit (Passas 2000).

Professional poachers are usually part of a criminal organization and may be heavily armed (Sellar 2014). A former enforcement officer from the CITES anti-smuggling, fraud, and organized crime unit mentioned that: "One night, they (fishery protection officers) pulled alongside a poacher's vessel but before they could board it, a hand grenade was thrown into their patrol boat. They had to dive overboard to escape the explosion and the poachers escaped" (EE9). According to a poacher in Poldnevoye, not all the local poachers use hand grenades but some of them have automatic firearms to protect them from being shot by the police (RF5). Such conflicts result in an increasing level of armament on both the side of the poachers and the police.

Russian poachers also enter the territorial waters of neighbouring Caspian countries, such as Kazakhstan and Azerbaijan (RF3; RF6; RF10; RF13). "In 2013 a caviar deal was made and a helicopter near Atyrau was used to transfer illegal caviar to the Kazakh border. Two persons with a suitcase of money took the caviar and flew directly in the direction of the border" (RF6). In the same year, Kazakhstan control officials detained five boats with 212 kg of sturgeon in their territorial waters. Fifteen foreign nationals, including five citizens of the Republic of Azerbaijan and 10 from the Russian Federation, were arrested (Ministry of Internal Affairs of the Republic Kazakhstan 2014). According to Lagutov (2007: 244) numerous boats with poachers from Dagestan, Kalmikiya and Azerbaijan are active in the Kazakhstan region. While every year there are arrests of sturgeon poachers, it is believed that only poor fishermen who fail to pay protection money are caught and end up behind bars (Talishli 2006).

After the sturgeons are caught and the eggs are extracted, the caviar has to be prepared. Countless fishermen know how to prepare the sturgeon eggs, because caviar was commonly used in the 1990s. Many Russian families had litre bottles with caviar in the fridge and knew how to prepare caviar. "We fed our chickens with black caviar during the Soviets. It was cheaper at that time. In Soviet times it was 20 roubles a kilo" (RF5). Currently, caviar is prepared secretly in the kitchens or basements of local people mainly outside the fishing season. This happens in small underground factories (RF3; RF5; RM2; RM4; RS13; RS14). "We catch fish in the river (Caspian delta) and have small factories to produce the caviar. Sometimes the production occurs in an ordinary kitchen or a special area for the production of caviar has been created in the basement" (RS10). Fresh eggs from the sturgeons are first extracted by cutting the body of the female sturgeon. The next step is to clean the eggs by the use of a colander and to wash the caviar with water to remove all slime. Finally, in the last stage, it is mixed with salt and (sometimes) spices (RT6). "It is an underground circuit. Some houses in this area are small caviar factories. They make illegal caviar at home" (RF7). In Moscow these small caviar factories are also present. Sometimes unprepared caviar is smuggled to the big cities where the caviar is prepared (RS10). This caviar prepared secretly at home can then be sold to middlemen in the network.

7.7 Intermediation and Negotiation

Besides poverty as a push factor, globalization also provides opportunities for illegal businesses (Aas 2007). At the beginning of the 1990s, a new type of businessman was born in Russia: "an entrepreneur who accumulated a lot of money in the period of privatization" (Siegel 2009: 191). These businessmen or middlemen also became involved in the international trade in illegal caviar. A substantial part of the illegal caviar is now smuggled to European or American black markets instead of the traditional Russian demand market. This extended transnational demand market requires the development of better structures for the international illegal trade (Raymakers 2002).

Middlemen operate as intermediates between poachers and international traders in the wildlife operations (Nichol 1987; Wyatt 2013). According to respondents, middlemen play an important role in the illegal caviar trade, as they collect caviar from the poachers and work for one of the criminal groups (RS10; RS11; RU1; RM3). As soon as the amount of extracted caviar is ready, it is promised to these middlemen (Raymakers 2002). Collecting caviar occurs on both a small and large scale. A local fisherman in Lagan admitted that he sometimes catches sturgeons and secretly brings them home. “When I find caviar I sell it and do not give it to my boss. I am not crazy. I know where to find a middleman” (RF9). On the other hand, middlemen in organized criminal networks control their activities: “The middleman arranges for money, boats, nets, fuel and gear and they fix a price for the fishermen. (…) They arrange illegal transfers to Moscow, St. Petersburg or Europe. (…) A relatively small amount is paid to the fishermen, while the middlemen can re-sell the caviar for a high price to us” (RS10). The middleman arranges appointments, makes deals and has direct contacts with illegal actors (e.g. poachers and smugglers) and legal actors (e.g. shopkeepers, restaurants and officials) (RF3; RS15; RM4).

Since they have contacts in the upperworld and underworld, middlemen are key players in the network (Passas 2002). For instance, at the Prazhskaya market in Moscow and the Rahot market in Atyrau (Kazakhstan) (Illustration 7.3), one middleman is the central supplier of illegal caviar in the market with dozens of kilos

Illustration 7.3 Caviar market, Atyrau, Kazakhstan 2014

in stock. If someone wants to buy a large quantity, the middleman is informed and an appointment will be made. According to a middleman in Moscow: "Before I can deliver high amounts of caviar, I first need more information about your background. (…) I also arrange for large quantities of caviar to be delivered abroad, such as the Netherlands (…) of course for additional costs" (RM5). Other respondents underlined the power of middlemen as part of mafia groups who control the caviar markets in Moscow (RM3; RS13). "There is no law at the market, the mafia groups dominate the (caviar) markets in Moscow" (RM3).

To run a successful criminal enterprise social ties are required. According to Van de Bunt et al. (2014) kinship, friendship and ethnicity are important social ties in criminal networks. Three middlemen explained that to be successful means that one has to build up a network, maintain several relationships and keep a close eye on competitors. While family ties and connections with Russians in destination countries are useful in the context of trust, they also collaborate with Polish and German traders (RM1; RM5; RM7). "To have connections with Russians in countries abroad is useful to deliver the trade (…) my boss has such connections, those are often friends, acquaintances or Russians who he met during his business trips." This middleman in Moscow underlined that foreign dealers are important, as they 'know the system abroad' (RM5).

Family ties can also provide a secure network, as highlighted by a middleman in Baku (Azerbaijan). He took the ability to promote to a higher position in the network where he started to work with family members: "In the first ten years of my life I was a poacher until I became a middleman in the illegal caviar trade. (…) As middleman you can earn real money with connections with poachers, people at the airport, smugglers and traders abroad (…) with the profit I bought two apartments for my sons in Russia. They are now my business partners" (RM7). These examples illustrate how social ties are fundamental for middlemen to operate successfully.

The symbiotic relationship of the middleman in Baku with people from the upperworld is highlighted by the fact that he cooperates with airline employees, customs officials and the local police. "Everybody knows him (the middleman), he is the guy with links with someone higher up" (RS10; RS11). According to Passas (2002) especially ties with legal actors are important as they can profit by selling illegal products for less money or use their legal company to shadow the illegal businesses. In Atyrau, Makhachkala and Baku middlemen also regulate paperwork or a lack of control at the airport. For instance, they can arrange, for additional costs, that buyers are not controlled at the airports. "I have a phone number of an official at the border control at the airport of Atyrau. Do not worry, he arranges everything so that you can fly to Russia or to Europe (…) of course he will receive a commission" (RM4). This demonstrates the mutual relationship between middlemen and officials in the caviar trade. According to middlemen in Baku, Izberbash, Astrakhan and Atyrau these bribes are necessary to facilitate the smuggling process (RM3; RM6; RM7).

7.8 Hide the Eggs

The smuggling part of the chain contains a relatively high risk of being caught during border controls. Based on confiscations, more than 90 % of the illegal shipments of caviar are transferred without documents. For instance, in 2010, 28 kg of caviar were smuggled in a petrol tank from Russia to Belgium by a 36-year-old man from Poland. According to the EU seizures, most illegal traders were Russian ($N = 85$, 23 %), French ($N = 76$, 20 %) and Polish ($N = 31$, 8 %) nationals involved in the illegal trade. According to Raymakers (2002: 21) Polish traders are involved in the illegal business, as Poland is traditionally used as a transit country to smuggle caviar from Russia to the EU. Already in the early nineteenth century the 'Polish connection' was well-known as a smuggling route (Saffron 2002). They repackaged the caviar in tins and jars which imitated the original packaging (e.g. Taylor 1997; Raymakers 2002). Figure 7.3 shows that businessmen, liberal professionals and food traders together amount to 56 % of all perpetrators. In addition, relatively many food handlers, truck drivers, armed forces personnel and officials were detected and involved in the illegal trade as well. Businessmen smuggle an

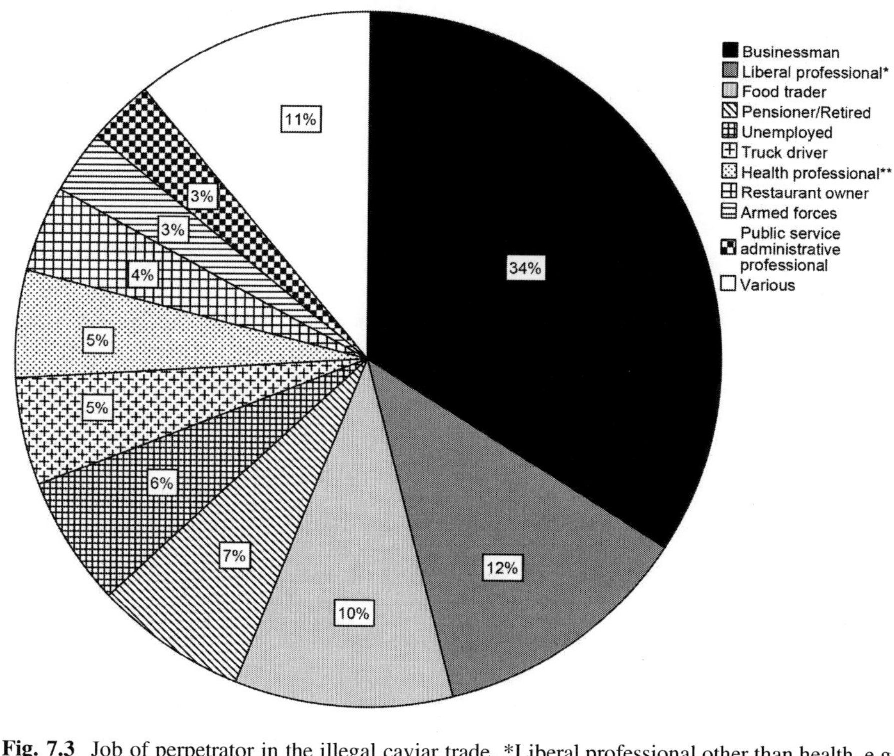

Fig. 7.3 Job of perpetrator in the illegal caviar trade. *Liberal professional other than health, e.g. barrister, notary, architect, etc. **Health professional other than veterinary and traditional medicine. *Source* Personal analyses of the EU-TWIX database, 2001–2010

Table 7.2 Types of caviar smugglers

Type	Method	Transport	Amount
Tourist	Unaware of the regulation —hidden in their (hand) luggage	Aircraft	Several tins of caviar (> 125 g)
Opportunist truck drivers or former residents	Hide the caviar between other products	Road (by car or truck)	Several kilos of caviar (3–5 kg)
Smuggler in criminal network	Hide the caviar in special compartments, falsified labels	Road (by car or truck), cargo, helicopter	Large amounts of caviar (>5 kg)

average of 9 kg of caviar ($M = 8.9$, $SD = 33$, $N = 36$), detected liberal professionals (other than health, e.g. barrister, notary, architect, etc.) smuggle smaller quantities of around 2 kg ($M = 2.0$, $SD = 4$, $N = 13$) and food traders smuggle around 5–6 tins of caviar.

Smugglers of caviar can be divided into three types (Table 7.2). The first type is the 'tourist', who buys caviar as a souvenir. For instance, under this category are well-known artists who buy their caviar at the Dorogomilovsky market in Moscow: "Rich people, movie stars and famous artists buy their caviar at the Dorogomilovsky market. (…) This market is very famous and expensive; last year caviar was sold for 94,000 (roubles) per kilo, but now it may be 70,000 (roubles) per kilo. However, it is real wild-caught caviar from the Caspian, the best you can get in Moscow" (RS13). This group is mostly unaware of the rules regarding the trade in caviar and try to bring back home more than 125 g.

The second type is the 'opportunist', mainly truck drivers or former residents, who try to sell several kilos of caviar in the country of destination to make some profit or to compensate for the fuel used. An Iranian greengrocer in the Netherlands smuggles 3 kg of wild caviar from Iran to the Netherlands at least each year: "Besides the fact I really like caviar, especially from Iran, I sell it to friends and acquaintances to reduce the fuel costs" (ET1). They sell their caviar bought in markets to Russian shops, restaurants or acquaintances and friends.

The third type is the 'well-organized smuggler' who is part of a criminal network and uses sophisticated methods. This type smuggles, on a regular basis, multiple kilos of illegal caviar from the source region to the destination in Russia or abroad. "Sometimes we smuggle 10 kg, sometimes 40 kg by car to Europe. (…) We know how we can outsmart the officials" (RM3). These smugglers are well organized and use sophisticated methods, such as forged and falsified labels, or, as was often mentioned, bribed officials to avoid confiscation. "Four cars drive in convoy. The front one is the scout. If the police are not bribed or able to be bribed, he warns the other three cars to take an alternative route to Moscow" (RF11). In 2010, in a crackdown on illegally smuggled caviar in the Caspian delta, Astrakhan poachers were detected with "professional canning equipment and produced tins of unlicensed black caviar under the label of *OAO Russkaya Ikra*". The illegal caviar was smuggled by a group of smugglers from Astrakhan to St. Petersburg and included the involvement of a traffic police officer (Zabyelina 2014). According to traders at the Teply Stan market (Moscow), police officers at the Polish border are bribed to pass the caviar into the EU. They are part of their informal network (RS13). The organizations even deliver caviar to one's door and large quantities could be smuggled after a number of successful agreements: "Of course this relationship is based on trust. Suppose we would do business for the first time, then I would first sell you 3 kg, the next time the same again, and if all goes well, we can do serious business. There must be trust" (RM5).

There are some practical advantages to caviar in comparison to smuggling live exotic animals, as caviar is compact and easy to hide between other products (Moreto and Lemieux 2014). Different smuggling methods include small fridges in trucks, special boxes in trucks, special compartments in cars (e.g. under the floor of the car, under the seats, in compartments behind the bumper), hidden compartments in (hand) luggage or unaccompanied baggage, postal services, caviar hidden by the flight crew, hidden in private jets, boats and cruise ships (e.g. to harbours in Bulgaria) (Knapp et al. 2006; Reijngoud 2014). Even a funeral van was recently used to smuggle 500 kg of black caviar, worth an estimated £100,000. "The van's driver explained to the police patrol he was hurrying to deliver the body of a woman. (…) The coffin was searched. Inside, there was no dead body but only thermopacks with black caviar hidden under the funeral wreathes."[27]

According to illegal traders in Russia, the caviar is usually transported over land with cars and trucks. The smugglers hide the caviar in special compartments in their cars or in small fridges in the trucks (RS1; RM3; RS15). For instance, crates at the bottom of trucks where caviar is covered with other products. Smuggling occurs on a regular basis according to a smuggler in Moscow at the Dorogomilovsk market: "In cars we smuggle from Astrakhan to Moscow around 40 kg each time. (…) We smuggle the caviar in these plastic buckets of 1 kg in a hidden compartment in refrigerated trucks from the Astrakhan delta, Dagestan and Azerbaijan. Every day a truck arrives with smuggled caviar to supply the market" (RU2). A seller at another market in Moscow confirmed that: "Every morning at 6 o'clock a truck arrives at the back of the Typlistan market with smuggled caviar. From here a part of the caviar is retransferred to the EU" (RS13). Based on the author's observations, in many markets in big cities such as Moscow, Astrakhan, Makhachkala, Baku and Atyrau one could indeed quite easily buy smuggled 'wild' caviar.

Besides cars and trucks, many cases of smuggled caviar by flight crew are known. A famous well-known caviar trader and today's royal supplier in the Netherlands started his caviar business in the 1980s by buying leftovers from flight attendants and repackaging and selling them on the European market (ET2). In 1999, two businessmen were convicted of smuggling a thousand pounds of caviar illegally by paying airline employees to bring suitcases full of caviar into the US

[27] 'Police stop funeral van for breaking speed limit to find caviar inside coffin', Tass, October 27, 2015.

through Kennedy Airport to their traders (Gordon 2002).[28] According to traders at the markets, this is still a commonly used smuggling method (RM6; RM7).

7.9 Trading, Counterfeiting and Laundering

Trading in caviar is connected to several actors using different methods to make money out of this luxury product. In particular, the embeddedness of the illegal trade on legal markets is characteristic of the caviar trade market. Illegal enterprises shape the underworld of the black market and bring together a number of entrepreneurs. The first category: "the Russian shopkeeper, buys the illegal caviar, packages it in tins and sells it under the counter in his shop" (RS1). Generally, it is a substantial investment with a risk for an ordinary seller when he buys several kilos of illegal caviar. Caviar does not remain fresh for long and it is not possible to store it in a fridge for a long time, so one should have a steady market (RS6; RS11; RS15).[29] However, based on the author's observations, in almost every market in the big cities (e.g. Moscow, Astrakhan, Makhachkala, Baku, Atyrau) one can buy illegal wild caviar packed in plastic boxes of 1 kg hidden in plastic bags under the counter. The tins in front of their table are just for advertisement. They sell the illegal caviar in portions of half a kilo or more. These sellers have large quantities of empty cans and provide them together with large orders to the EU (RS4; RS6; RS11; RS15).[30] Several Russian shopkeepers in Europe explained that truck drivers from Russia and Azerbaijan regularly deliver wild caviar in 3-l bottles (e.g. ES1; ES2; ET8).

The second category includes restaurants or cooks who buy caviar and serve it to their clients. They are often tied to regular suppliers and buy the caviar through the 'back door' (RS1). A trader in Moscow explained that the police only incidentally control restaurants, while markets do have regular controls on several products (RS13). According to a head chef in the Netherlands, upper-class clients in his restaurant ask specifically for wild caviar. He orders wild caviar from Kazakhstan from a caviar trader who supplies both captive-bred and (illegal) wild caviar. The caviar dealers do have courier services that carry out home deliveries (EO1).

---

[28]Private aircraft are also used in the illegal trade in caviar. According to a Dutch law enforcer, in April 2013 border force officers from the 'small ports team' intercepted a private aircraft at Farnborough Airport on arrival from Ukraine. Despite the passenger stating that he had nothing to declare, a search of the luggage revealed one kilo (two 500 g unlabelled tins) of Russian caviar. As no CITES documentation had been obtained the goods were seized from the importer. There have been a number of similar seizures from private jets (Reijngoud 2014).

[29]Organized criminal groups also supply Moscow's supermarket chains with illegal caviar (Zabyelina 2014). In 2009, four offenders sold 3.1 t of unlicensed caviar worth RUB 93.5 million (USD 2.8 million) to supermarkets in Moscow.

[30]Sometimes, the sellers allow one to taste their caviar, while others only show their caviar if one really wants to buy it (RS14).

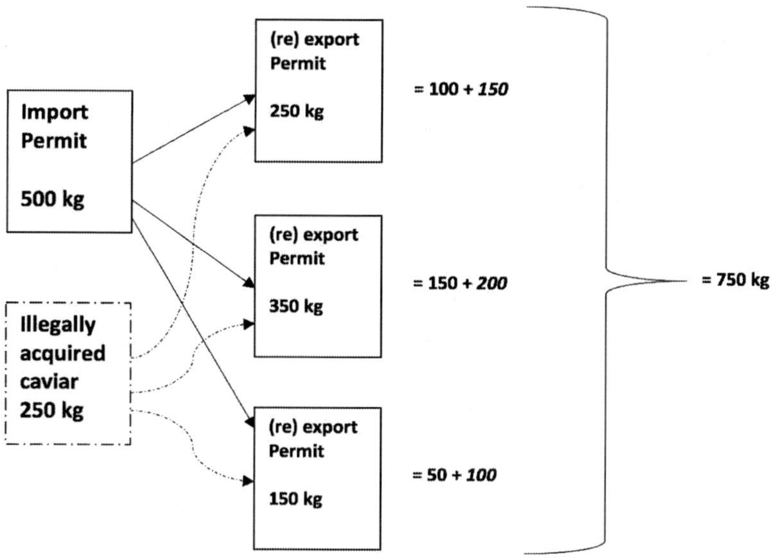

Fig. 7.4 Laundering illegally obtained caviar using CITES permits

The third category consists of legal enterprises that use their legal company to shadow or launder illegal caviar. First, the legal enterprises may reuse CITES certificates. The dealer orders a small batch of legal caviar, sends half of it back, and then uses his import licence to sell the illegal caviar (Knapp et al. 2006). According to a Dutch police investigation in 2009 named 'Platina', this was an important modus operandi (EP1). For instance, a caviar trader does have an import permit for 500 kg of caviar, but uses this permit to (re-)export an additional amount of 250 kg of illegally obtained caviar (see Fig. 7.4). Enterprises in the EU repack legal caviar together with additional illegal caviar (AID 2009).

Second, enterprises falsify CITES documents. According to Vaisman and Raymakers (2001) in 80 % of the surveyed shops in Moscow the certificates were obviously forged, e.g. the amount had been changed from 20 to 200 or the date had been updated (Illustration 7.4). In 2005, an investigation revealed that at least 1.4 t of caviar was smuggled by two caviar businessmen into the EU market in a single year. The caviar was sold illegally in the EU using falsified documents (European Commission 2006). For example, documents were detected from the non-existent *Russian Ministry of Fishery* or the country of origin had been changed (Vaisman and Raymakers 2001; Lawson 2002; Van Uhm and Siegel 2016). In particular, caviar shipments from Kazakhstan entering the EU were regularly accompanied by counterfeit or altered documents. The genuine documents were allegedly issued corruptly, as the documents were detected with non-existing export companies and exports took place accompanied with unrecorded CITES papers. According to Sellar (2014) criminals were not only replacing the issued documents but local officials also determined that they were *bona fide*. They were probably working

Illustration 7.4 Falsification of labels and CITES documents

together with the local Kazakh mafia (Sellar 2014). This was confirmed by informants in Atyrau who referred to government agencies in the illegal trade. The local CITES authority would provide documents for illegal caviar bought at the Rahot market in Atyrau (RS6; RS8; RM4).

Third, enterprises falsify the labels of caviar tins.[31] For instance, the lids of illegal caviar tins and jars imitating well-known brands such as *Russkaya Ikra* (Vaisman and Raymakers 2001). The falsified labels may also indicate another country of origin or company (Illustration 7.4). Imitated lids of illegal caviar tins and jars are usually distinguished from the genuine lids by incorrect spelling or poor grammar (Vaisman and Raymakers 2001). Based on the author's observation of the illegal lids of jars in Baku (Azerbaijan), the net weight was not mentioned on the lid because the bottom of the jar was concave and the incorrect spelling of 'consern fisheries Azerbaijan government' was noticeable (personal observation, September 27, 2014). A middleman in Baku presented several lids of counterfeit caviar brands from Azerbaijan and Russia. He explained how, in this way, locally poached and produced caviar from Azerbaijan is sold as Russian caviar (RM7). Mislabelled caviar is also detected in the EU. According to a law enforcer: "The trade in empty caviar tins and jars, lids and labels is flourishing in Europe" (EP1). Several authors mentioned illegal caviar from Russia smuggled through Dagestan and Azerbaijan to Iran where it is repacked together with legal Iranian caviar and sent to destinations such as Europe (e.g. Zabyelina 2014). For instance, in 2006 1.6 tonne caviar from Kazakhstan were confiscated in the Netherlands because the tins were originally from Astrakhan (Russia). The tins were exported as being Kazakhstan caviar as the quota in Russia was already full (AID 2009).

[31]The results of a study of the caviar market in New York City (Doukakis et al. 2012) show that the level of mislabelled caviar is at least 10 % (in comparison to a previous study which showed 19 %).

Illustration 7.5 Aquaculture in the river, Ikryanoye, Russia 2014

Although aquaculture is mentioned as being the solution to the decline in the sturgeon population, it could also be a risk to wild sturgeons (Kecse-Nagy 2011; Jahrl 2013; Sellar 2014). Sturgeon farms are cropping up all over the world, sometimes in unexpected places, such as the Bulgarian stretch of the River Danube, close to the mouth of the River Kura (Azerbaijan), or the Caspian delta (Russia), where sturgeons are also found in the wild (personal observation of a farm in Ikryanoye, March 17, 2014; a farm in the Babayurt region, September 24, 2014; and a farm in Neftçala, September 28, 2014) (Illustration 7.5). Sturgeon farms are expensive to run, require highly trained staff and it takes a long time before sturgeons can spawn (Knapp et al. 2006; Zabyelina 2013).[32] In comparison to the price of 'wild' caviar it still means that farming is non-competitive (Nikolaev et al. 2009). Various respondents called for attention to the mixing of legal and illegal caviar (e.g. RT7; RM5; RM7; RS10; RS11).

According to Levi and Reuter (2006) money laundering involves the transformation process of illegally obtained money into legitimate money. In the trade in caviar, illegally obtained caviar is mixed with legal caviar or transformed into legal caviar as demonstrated by the following examples. To launder illegal caviar into

[32]'The sturgeon has seen more years when it first spawns than many fish see in a lifetime' (Carey 2005).

legal caviar various methods are used. For instance, wild-caught sturgeons for breeding purposes are not released or caviar from wild sturgeons will be sold as having been produced in fish farms. In 2009, the German authorities confiscated caviar labelled as farmed caviar where isotope analysis found that the caviar had originated from the Caspian Sea. The permitted caviar farming was used to launder illegally sourced caviar into legal caviar (NWCU 2013). Recent research in Bulgaria and Romania has also suggested the involvement of aquaculture operations in the Danube region in laundering wild caviar originating from the Caspian region (Kecse-Nagy 2011; Jahrl 2013). During an observation at a farm on a tributary of the Volga in Ikryanoye ('caviar town') only two female sturgeons were spotted in 30 compartments (personal observation, March 17, 2014). The director underlined that there must be around 300 sturgeons per compartment and the farm would produce 0.5 tonnes of caviar each year. Moreover, they would extract caviar from 250 females in 2 h, in their own words, but there was no table or place for extracting caviar and, perhaps more remarkably, they shared their premises with local fishermen. In answer to the question of whether farms could be used to launder wild sturgeons, the director of this farm said convincingly: "It is 100 % possible that farms in Russia have such a laundering system" (RT7).

A trend in the opposite direction has also been observed by several informants: 'wild caviar is wanted' because it is rare and therefore special. The idea has taken hold that wild caviar, which is supposed to be 'pure and all-natural', is of a higher quality than caviar from cultured sturgeon (e.g. RS10; RS11). Moreover, wild caviar is illegal and therefore hard to get. The principle that 'what is banned or unavailable is always attractive' plays a major role here. However, the consequence is that caviar from cultured sturgeon is now increasingly being sold as 'illegal' wild caviar, simply because it fetches a higher price. In keeping with this 'reverse laundering scheme', caviar dealers are encouraged to sell legal caviar as if it were illegal products; it has been 'blackwashed'. This is a fairly new mechanism: legal caviar extracted from cultured sturgeons is being sold as illegal caviar. This means, in practice, that caviar can initially be laundered in a farm, while on arrival in Europe the caviar is blackwashed to meet the demand for wild caviar.

The ban on fishing sturgeon in the Caspian Sea left several loopholes, such as laundering opportunities and fishing quotas for scientific research. Some commercial farms have documents to fish for sturgeons under the scientific quota (RE1). For instance, a famous caviar company in Atyrau caught wild sturgeon under the pretence of scientific purposes (RT9). According to sturgeon expert Vaisman: "Local authorities set quotas for themselves and procure caviar for supposedly scientific purposes, when in fact these are commercial hauls". This is especially since it is undertaken by commercial fishing companies on behalf of the research facilities. These commercial fishing companies were more than willing to sign these agreements as the fish they kept could be processed for meat and eggs into caviar (Sellar 2014). According to the director of a farm: "A couple of years ago two well-known sturgeon farms bribed officials to catch the wild sturgeons under the scientific quota. (…) These used the catch for the illegal trade (…) too often an official is involved" (RT7). Statistical data covering several years after the ban demonstrates that 600 t of caviar from sturgeon were fished out of the Caspian Sea for 'scientific purposes' (Zabyelina 2014). Although aquaculture could be the solution to the survival of the sturgeon, loopholes seem to offer relatively new opportunities to launder wild caviar in the trade. This embeddedness of the illegal trade in caviar on legal markets is underlined by many sellers of caviar at the local markets (e.g. Astrakhan, Atyrau, Baku) (e.g. RS9; RS10; RS11).

7.10 Away from the Caspian

The Caspian Sea is well-known to be the main source of illegal wild caviar (Engler and Parry-Jones 2007). While the Caspian delta near Astrakhan belonged to one of the traditional illegal poaching places, currently many respondents highlighted other 'hotspots'. A middleman in Astrakhan underlined that: "Nowadays, most illegal sturgeons originate from Dagestan and Baku, not from Astrakhan, because it is easier to catch over there" (RM3). A well-known smuggling route from the Caspian Sea to Europe is by surface transport (road and rail) through Moscow, Ukraine or Belarus to Eastern Europe, mostly via Poland (Raymakers 2002). Around 80 % of the seized caviar in Poland (710 kg) between 2000 and 2002 originated from Russia or was smuggled into Poland through Ukraine. The caviar was destined for Western Europe (Theile et al. 2004). According to illegal traders in Russia, caviar is usually smuggled by road from the Caspian Sea to Moscow where the caviar is collected by middlemen and then smuggled through Belarus to Poland where it enters the EU (RT1; RS13; RM5). "There is no border control between Russia and Belarus, we use this border and enter the EU by bribing Polish border officials. They are close friends" (RM5). They deliver the wild caviar to several restaurants and traders in Germany (RM5; RS13; ET3).

Traditionally, Hamburg (Germany) is an important transit hub (Taylor 1997) where caviar is re-exported and laundered (Neve et al. 2012). A convicted caviar trader in Hamburg explained that large volumes of caviar are arranged by order, while small quantities can be sold immediately (ET4). This smuggling route is confirmed by an illegal trader in the East of the Netherlands, whereby Russian caviar is smuggled from the Caspian Sea hidden in refrigerated trucks into the EU. He explained that he orders his caviar from a German trader who works together with a network of Russian entrepreneurs that deliver wild caviar to several German cities, such as Hamburg, Berlin and Düsseldorf. The smugglers drive from Düsseldorf across the border to enter the Netherlands (ET3).

In addition, substantial amounts of caviar are smuggled from Russia to Turkey mostly by road according to trade experts from Turkey.[33] The 'Dagestan caviar

[33]From 2000 until the beginning of 2014, from the 28 seizures with 1,615 kg of caviar, 16 confiscations (1,272 kg) were by truck or car, 7 by aircraft (114 kg), 1 by ship (4.5 kg) and 7 outside border control (227 kg).

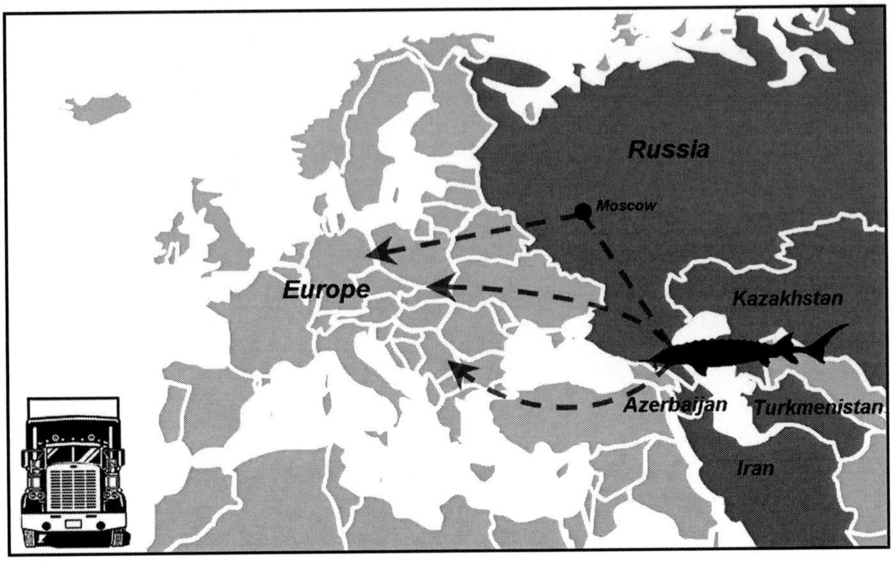

Map 7.1 Smuggling routes for caviar. *Source* Interviews and personal analyses of confiscations in the EU

mafia' started to use this smuggling route from Dagestan through Azerbaijan and Turkey as a result of growing resistance by border guards' forces and the blocking of illegal caviar channels in the late 1990s (Raymakers 1999; Vaisman and Raymakers 2001).[34] This trade route (Russia–Turkey–EU) is still regularly used proclaimed the director of the scientific and educational centre for sturgeon breeding in Astrakhan (RE1). Both middlemen in Baku and Atyrau underlined the involvement of Turkish businessmen (RM4; RM7). "There are a lot of Turkish businessmen in the illegal caviar business. They arrive in Turkey and have the right contacts to transport the caviar to Europe. They also launder the caviar and transfer it to Europe or North America" (RM7).[35] An important middleman in Baku (Azerbaijan), who is responsible for smuggling large batches of caviar from Azerbaijan to the EU through Turkey and through Dagestan to Moscow, explained: "The caviar is mainly smuggled by car across the border of Georgia through Turkey to the EU or to Moscow through Dagestan. (…) However, I also have contacts to send it by plane" (RM7). There were strong indicators that the caviar is packed into Turkish-made cans and exported to the EU as 'Turkish caviar' (Raymakers 1999; Vaisman and Raymakers 2001). Based on export data Turkey exported dozens of tonnes of caviar, while sturgeon are caught only occasionally in Turkey (AID 2009) (Map 7.1).

---

[34]The smuggling route from Azerbaijan by surface transport through Turkey from where large quantities are exported to Western countries had already been noticed in 1999 (Raymakers 2002).
[35]Note that no shipments of illegal caviar from Turkey were seized in the EU.

The majority of caviar smuggled by air seems to arrive in Germany, France and the UK,[36] from where it is spread all over Europe. An important loophole is the United Arab Emirates (European Commission 2006). A sturgeon expert in Astrakhan explained that: "They became one of the biggest exporters of caviar. They bought Russian caviar from the mafia and used falsified labels. They said that they produced caviar on a huge scale for the world market (…) while in reality it came from the black market" (RE1). According to Lowther et al. (2002) the prosecution of the US Caviar and Caviar in 2001 demonstrated that an US label company based in the United Arab Emirates was involved in applying counterfeit labels to illegal caviar worth millions of dollars for the markets in Europe, Asia and North America. Vaisman and Raymakers (2001) highlight the illegal trade route from Kazakhstan to the United Arab Emirates as well. Organized crime groups in Dubai would be responsible for coordinating the illegal trade by forging documents and making false declarations to obtain re-export certificates (Zabyelina 2013).

Other smuggling lines include from Moscow by surface transport (train, car, truck and commercial ship) to St. Petersburg from where it is shipped to large harbours in Western Europe, e.g. Antwerp and Rotterdam (Raymakers 2002). According to a smuggler from Makhachkala the involvement of train conductors is useful to avoid baggage checks during her trip by train to Kiev. In Kiev, the caviar is picked up by an acquaintance (the middleman) of hers and she returns to Dagestan: "The train conductor is a friend of my uncle and I know Serhiy in Kiev through a friend (who is also involved). We have been doing successful business for a long time" (RU3). Crossing the Black Sea by boat seems to be a smuggling route as well. Based on recent research, Bulgaria and Romania were in the world's top-10 of caviar exporting countries; the area seems to be a potential trade route for caviar from the Caspian region into the EU (Jahrl 2013).[37]

7.11 The Caviar Mafia

The collapse of the Soviet Union and worldwide globalization has resulted in the rise of a large black market for caviar dominated by criminal networks (Birstein et al. 1997; Saffron 2002; Sellar 2014).[38] According to several reports the Russian *mafiya* (русская мафия) is heavily involved in the caviar trade (e.g. Vaisman 1997; ECOSOC 2002, 2003; Wyler and Sheikh 2008; Sellar 2014), the trade in sturgeon

[36]Based on confiscations in the EU-TWIX database between 2001 and 2010.

[37]Noteworthy is that many indicators refer to smuggling by road, while the recorded seizures indicate that caviar is largely smuggled by plane (62 %) in comparison to road (6 %), mail (4 %) and rail (2 %). Probably, this is due to the higher probability of detection and control during border controls at airports.

[38]At the end of the 1990s, approximately 3,500 tonnes of illegally caught sturgeon were transported to Moscow every year and this happened under the protection of Chechen organized crime (Taylor 1997).

Table 7.3 Prices of illegal caviar on the market

Caviar	Price/kg (Makhachkala)	Price/kg (Atyrau)	Price/kg (Baku)	Price/kg (Astrakhan)
Beluga	**€740** (±37,000 RUB)	**€820** (±210,000 KZT)	**€850** (±850 AZN)	**€1,000** (±50,000 RUB)
Oscietra	**€500** (±25,000 RUB)	**€550** (±140,000 KZT)	**€620** (±620 AZN)	**€760** (±38,000 RUB)

Source Prices based on the author's observations and interviews

in Azerbaijan is controlled by organized crime (e.g. Shadrina 2007) and the Kazakh mafia dominates the trade in caviar in Atyrau (e.g. Glenny 2008). In addition, several European traders are believed to be representatives of Caspian-based organized crime networks (Sellar 2014).

The socioeconomic degradation in the Caspian region (Azerbaijan, Kazakhstan, Russia, Turkmenistan), caused by a combination of factors, such as the complete collapse of the agriculture sector and the disappearance of the centralised principles of the former Soviet Union economy, have resulted in many opportunities for criminal networks. The high levels of unemployment in Russia, Kazakhstan and Azerbaijan and the devaluation of the Russian rouble had substantial implications on people's livelihood.[39] Consequently, entire coastal communities around the Caspian Sea have become involved in illegal sturgeon fishing and the production of caviar. According to estimates during the 2000s, Russia lost up to $400 million each year to the poaching of sturgeons and the Russian Interior Ministry estimated that the income of the black market for caviar and sturgeon fish was comparable to the profits from the illegal drugs trade (Shadrina 2007).[40]

Furthermore, restrictions on exports and fishing bans in the Caspian Sea have increased the price of caviar on world markets (Raymakers 2006; Zabyelina 2014). At the beginning of the 1990s caviar was on the market on a huge scale: "20 years ago we were selling caviar for less than 50 dollars per kilo. It was even difficult to sell the caviar. Now it is different" (RF7). The current prices of poached caviar vary between 500 euro per kilo in Dagestan, 550 euro in the Ural region, 620 euro in Baku and 760 euro in the Volga delta (Table 7.3). These prices increase when the caviar is moved through the process. According to a seller in Makhachkala with every step the price increases up to the final price at the local market or in the classy

[39]In the late 1970s the currency was one USD for 0.75 RUR, in 2001 the currency dropped by 40 times with one USD for 30 RUR (Raymakers 2002), while currently (2015) one USD is worth 45 RUR.

[40]Based on a large-scale operation in 2003 where police officers intercepted 1,200 incidents of poaching within a month, confiscated 180 poaching boats, 10,000 m of nets, 400 hooks and lines, 1,236 kg of sturgeon caviar, 170 kg of sturgeon fish and almost 135 tonnes of other seafood (with an estimated value of 81,724,000 roubles). 73 people were caught while they were illegally fishing and 5,000 criminal cases were commenced.

restaurants up to €15,000 per kilo (RS15). Profits for smugglers moving the contraband from the Caspian coast to the federal centre could reach 200–3,000 dollars (Zabyelina 2014). These high prices for caviar attract organized crime (Duffy 2010).

While the precarious living conditions of Caspian locals and increasing prices on the black market play a role in the level of poaching in the region, the emergence of organized crime was also driven by the potential of corruption (Raymakers 2002; Sellar 2014). According to Siegel (2011) corruption has an elusive meaning in non-Western countries. From a non-Western perspective corruption is culturally seen as a part of maintaining social relations instead of an abuse by public officials. A police officer in Makhachkala (Dagestan) described it ironically: "I am famous for being a fascist, because I do not take bribes" (RP3). He referred to the high level of corruption in the trade in caviar in Dagestan. In Dagestan, several high-level officials had their own trawlers in the past, such as the Procurator of the Republic, the Minister of Internal Affairs, the Chief of the Water Police and the Chief of the Fish Inspectorate (Vaisman 1997).

Poachers still regularly work together with the police in the Dagestan region. Currently, senior government officials, fishery inspectors, police services and other agencies would all have a stake in the business and poachers pay taxes to enter the Caspian Sea together with a percentage of the catch (RF10; RF11; RM3; RM6). Every illegal boat trip appears to cost around 1,500 USD to bribe officials in Russia.[41] According to several respondents, corruption is the main problem and the bottleneck in enforcing the regulation on the protection of sturgeons. "If you have 10 kg of caviar, you have to pay your protector 1 and 1 kg to the police. Everything is based on sharing and corruption" (RM4). This clearly demonstrates that corruption is embedded in the trade in caviar and reflects one of the links between the upper and underworld (Passas 2000). Coastguards, the police and even customs officials at the airport may have a share in the market. For instance, in 2006, the head of the Internal Affairs Directorate (UVD) of Astrakhanskaya Oblast Col was arrested during a highway control with 91 kg of illegal black caviar hidden in his car, or in 2011, 935 kg of illegal sturgeons were confiscated from an inspector of the FSB (Russian Federal Security Service) (Zabyelina 2013). Illustrative is the author's observation of a wild-caught sturgeon prepared by a cook next to the Coastal Guards who claimed to have total control over the poachers in Neftçala (personal observation, 28 September 2014). Militias of the republics or mafia groups sometimes even protect the poachers during conflicts with the federal authorities. Criminal groups in Dagestan use 'security vessels' to escort the poachers and to distract the police stated a middleman in Izberbash (RM3; RM6).

Most legal and illegal fishermen enjoy such protection or *krysha* (literally a 'roof'). *Krysha* (Крыша) is the name for various transitional forms of protection

---

[41]Taking into consideration that an average team makes about 12 trips per month, it results in about 18,000 USD of corrupt money on a monthly basis, which amounts to about 144,000 USD of corrupt money per 8-month season.

(Volkov 2002). The protection industry in the post-Soviet republics ranged from *militseiskaya krysha* (protection by the police) to *kriminalnaya krysha* (protection by criminal organizations) (Varese 2001: 59–72). The *krysha* model played a major role in post-Communist developments, especially in the integration of the criminal and the legal economy. It refers to protection against petty thieves, but also against competitors and 'amateur extortionists' (Siegel 2005). A poacher in Pakywa explained the role of *kriminalnaya krysha*: "The middle enforcers, captains and lawyers, they all have a powerful person from the mafia standing behind their back and taking care of them. (…) If we have sturgeons on my boat and the police arrive, I call a certain person from the local mafia to say that the police have arrived. I give the phone to the police officer, he then talks to the person and they tell the police to calm down and then the police let me go. (…) Sometimes we have to pay the police with caviar" (RF7). Poachers in Astrakhan and sellers in Moscow confirmed that in Russia *krysha* is active on the caviar markets: "The mafia is behind the sales of all illegal caviar on the markets in Moscow. They determine what happens" (e.g. RS11; RS14).

It is plausible that organized crime took over the control of former state companies and controlled local councils, government agencies and bodies that were arms of the state (Sellar 2014). This is partly confirmed by interviews with informants in these source countries (e.g. RF9; RF11; RM3; RM4; RS9; RU3; RE1). However, it was not always clear who belonged to the caviar mafia. The fishermen reported that the police and dealers consisted of the caviar mafia, while the traders referred to the poachers and the police. Many locals used the term to consider the entire business in the hands of the Russian mafia. The illegal market is at least well organized, as is illustrated by its participants that arrange for sales channels, transport, and bribes to be paid along the way to traffic police and customs officers (RM2; RM3; RM7). Some criminal organizations are highly organized and violent, they involve a range of legal actors, such as corrupt officials (Shadrina 2007; Zabyelina 2014; Sellar 2014). According to a middleman in Izberbash (Dagestan), given the low salary of a coast guard (averaging around 4,000 roubles per month), the temptation is always there to accept bribes (RM6). Low wages traditionally lead to high levels of corruption (Van Rijckeghem and Weder 2001).

The organization of one trade line is as follows: the process starts with bribing officials to enter the Caspian Sea to poach sturgeons. Then poachers enter the Caspian Sea (under the protection of the water police). These poachers sell the caviar to my informant. He subsequently contacts his boss who has the necessary connections with an international trader in Germany; there are several agreements relating to the price and quality. Then he makes sure that a truck driver will transfer the caviar from Astrakhan across the Russian border through Poland into the EU. This again happens with the help of bribed customs officials. Then the caviar is sold in Germany or repacked and laundered into legal caviar. This whole process is under the control of two key players in the criminal network (RM2) (see Fig. 7.5 for other flows).

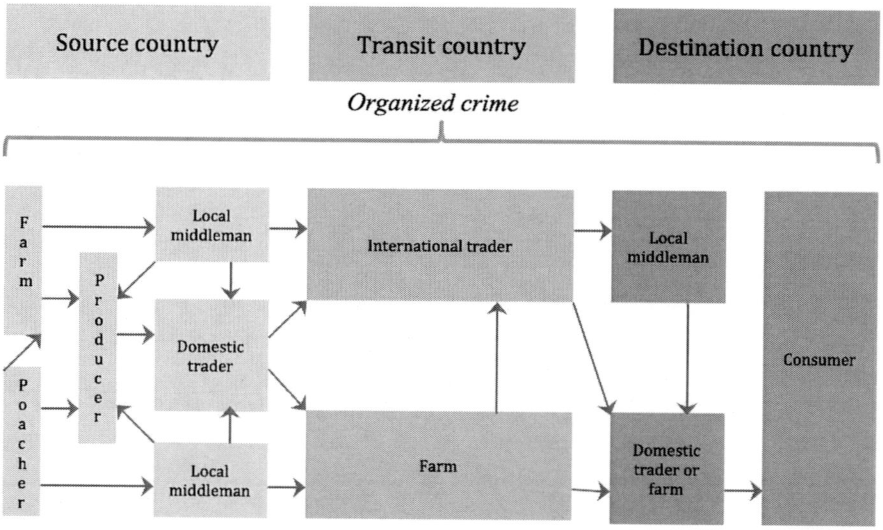

Fig. 7.5 Supply chain (simplified) of the illegal trade in caviar

Besides illegal caviar businesses, the criminal groups also seem to be embedded in legal enterprises. According to several informants, some 10 years ago the directors of farms in Russia were the 'big fish' in the illegal trade in caviar (RT7; RM3; RS10; RS11). This fits within the context of the collapse of the Soviet Union in the early 1990s, when the Russian mafia largely assumed the role of transferring economic assets into private hands. The mafia had taken over this responsibility from the state. During the late 1990s and early 2000s legal institutions and enforcement mechanisms were built and strengthened in Russia. This has resulted in the transformation of criminal organizations into legal business enterprises (Volkov 2002; Dubinsky 2006). This is illustrated by the response from the manager of a sturgeon farm to the question whether they were not afraid that thieves would steal their caviar, as the storage was not subject to sufficient security; he smiled and said: "No, the criminals are afraid of us!" (RT6). Sellar (2014) notes in his book 'The UN's lone ranger' that KGB officers agreed that storing millions of roubles worth of caviar without visible security indicates that security is being provided by the mafia. The director of a farm near Astrakhan explained that in the 2000s, criminals who bought their caviar on the black market invested their money in developing farms. Within a day, kilos of caviar were delivered, but nowadays it is sometimes much more difficult to obtain caviar. For instance, during the Winter Olympic Games in Sochi (2014), the director phoned all her contacts to arrange for some caviar, but it was impossible to obtain it (RT7).

According to a middleman in Baku not only local mafia but also a quasi-state company is predominantly responsible for illegal poaching (RM7). Sellar (2014) explained that the quality of the caviar from the mafia is believed (by restaurant owners) to be better in comparison to the state company. The state company is reluctant to issue receipts and there were impressions that any deal with them took place under the table (Sellar 2014). The middleman underlined: "The main caviar trade in Azerbaijan, you know, is in the hands of this quasi-state company. They do the big business" (RM7). According to the CIA this company, that controls the caviar production in Azerbaijan, was previously controlled by the Russian mafia (WikiLeaks 2010). The company was taken over by a relative of a government official. No company in Azerbaijan is allowed to fish for wild sturgeon, according to the manager of enforcement at the Ministry of Environment (RE4). However, according to employees of this quasi-state company, they fish every year for sturgeon and sell caviar from wild sturgeon (RT13; RT14). Employees even showed price lists of wild caviar for sale (personal observation, September 30, 2014).

Due to the cooperation and agreements between poachers, traders and officials in the caviar trade, conflicts and the use of violence and counterstrategies are not uncommon. The caviar business is sometimes described as 'sturgeon wars' (e.g. Shadrina 2007). There are numerous reports of gunfights between fishery inspectors, border guards and poachers in Dagestan and Kazakhstan (Lagutov 2007: 242). For example, in 1996 the fishing boat 'Kamilia' was intercepted by coast guards in Dagestan during the transfer of poached sturgeons to two heavy Kamaz trucks. While the coast guards tried to stop the activity, corrupt water militias, armed with sub-machine guns, opened fire on the guards and the trucks—guarded by private militias—disappeared. Thereafter, the Kamilia was on several occasions detected with illegal caviar on board, while no legal action was taken against the poachers. According to local poachers they indeed protect themselves against attacks from the police (RF11; RF13). Another example was in November 1996, when the living quarters in the city Kaspiysk where the families of the coast guards lived were bombed by the caviar mafia, in response to the activities of the coast guard (Vaisman 1997). Over 100 people lived in the bombed building, including the Commander of the locally based coast guard, who had been allegedly threatened by 'sturgeon pirates'. A total of 67 people, including 21 children, were killed during the attack on the nine-storey apartment building. The victims consisted mainly of Russian border guards and their families (Committee on Natural Resources, US House of Representative 2008). The border guards would have discovered a caviar smuggling network (Zabyelina 2013). A year later, explosives were found before they had exploded in another building in Kaspiysk. Local officials described the situation as an on-going war with the caviar mafia (Vaisman 1997).

In 2000, a senior official of the 'Izberbash unit' was kidnapped in exchange for seized boats belonging to poachers and in 2001 a crowd of at least 100 poachers and their families stormed a coast guard station in Dagastan (Russia). It was described as a well-organized attack because their boats had been confiscated. Both the Dagestan police spokesman and the presidential spokesman said the attack came as a result of fishing federal restrictions on sturgeon and the caviar trade. "There is a so-called caviar mafia here and we have to fight all the time", admitted one of the coast guards (Saradzhyan 2001). According to a middleman and former caviar smuggler in Izberbash: "The mayor was heavily involved in the caviar trade and he wanted to dominate the caviar trade at that time. This was, of course, not accepted" (RM6). Also the use of hand grenades by poachers against fishery protection officers in the mid-2000s was described in several sources (e.g. Knapp et al. 2006). According to a poacher in Poldnevoye: "Some local poachers use hand grenades, also to bomb certain upriver places to get sturgeons to the surface. (…) Others have automatic firearms to protect themselves from being shot by the police" (RF5).

Furthermore, in April 2005, a week before the start of the fishing season, the Director General of 'Kaspryba' was shot at the entrance to his office in the centre of Astrakhan; he was hit by several bullets to the head and back. According to several journalists his death was related to his commercial fish activities.[42] Also in the very heart of Moscow violence in relation to the trade in caviar has recently been found. For example, in 2008 in the district Khoroshovo-Mnevniki, a scientist was kidnapped because he discovered a way of producing artificial black caviar that would be indistinguishable from wild caviar. "They put a hat on my head, wrapped it with tape and started punching me, they broke my ribs, sprained my hands and bashed my head" (Orlandi 2008). There are also many dangers at sea: apart from collisions, the fishermen are sometimes kidnapped by criminals from Kazakhstan (Van Uhm and Siegel 2016).

Not only in Russia, but also in European countries violence and counterstrategies are being used by criminal groups. In the UK, a raid in London by the National Criminal Intelligence Service (Operation Ribbon) found links between the illegal caviar trade and murder, extortion and corruption by the Russian mafia (Duffy 2010; Schneider 2012). In the Netherlands, there are also indications that the Russian mafia is involved in the caviar trade (AID 2009). In the early 2000s a large volume of illegal caviar from Russia was confiscated. According to several Dutch (former) officials, the Russian mafia arrived at the national CITES office in Dordrecht (the Netherlands) to claim their caviar and threatened the employees (EN1; EN5). On another occasion, Russian criminals in a black Mercedes were seen shadowing the house of an inspector (AID 2009). According to the inspector: "There was a lot of Russian caviar seized, nearly 10,000 kg. Although the papers were clearly not in order, the CITES authority in Geneva approved the documents. The head of the CITES office said that the documents were real, while the papers could not yet have been received. The same afternoon, I was on the train home and got a call from my neighbour who said there were people sitting in a black Mercedes in front of my house and they were taking photographs. I asked her to give me the registration number and got in touch with my colleagues in the police. It turned out to be the same Russians who were involved in this illegal shipment. They were threatening me in front of my own home" (EN1).

Finally, sometimes associations with other forms of crime were highlighted. In one case in December 2005 a Polish network smuggled caviar several times a month from Azerbaijan. "They intercepted two Polish guys with 68 kg of caviar on

[42] 'Осетровая война', Ogoniok, 2007; 'Прокуратура легла на кавказский след', Kommersant, April 26, 2005.

the 29th of December. It was the sixth journey they had made in one month. They were in possession of three mobile phones. They had contacts in France who were also involved in smuggling tabaco. They had between 200 and 300 clients," said a crime environment expert from Europol (EP3). In 2003, German customs officials stopped a Lithuanian lorry driver with 27 kg of caviar in hidden compartments together with 97.5 kg of illegal tobacco hidden in the front wheels (Theile et al. 2004). In another case, an anonymous source indicated that in 2006 a French prosecutor dropped the charges in a large-scale prosecution involving a Russian criminal organization, which besides being involved in the caviar trade was also involved in the trade in oil, timber and nuclear waste in exchange for weapons. "The prosecutor felt threatened by the Russians" (EP2). Exchanging caviar for other contraband has also been found in relation to stolen Western Mercedes cars. 500 g tins of caviar would be an appropriate medium of exchange for the Russian mafia (AID 2009). For instance, a 500 g tin for a stolen Western Mercedes car (Neve et al. 2012). Finally, caviar from Dagestan is not incidentally smuggled together with weapons to Moscow. "Caviar and arms, such as kalashnikovs, are smuggled to Moscow together. Dagestan is the place where you can do this business" (RM3). While previous examples seem to confirm an interrelation between other illegal contraband, based on my interviews the actors involved focus in particular on caviar. However, the majority of the illegal trade in caviar seems to be well organized and mostly takes place under the umbrella of organized crime with the support or protection of corrupt (highly placed) defence and law enforcers.

7.12 Conflicts and the Caspian Ecosystem

While the sturgeon, as one of the few animals still alive today, stems from the time of the dinosaurs, currently the sturgeon is one of the most endangered groups of animals on the Red List of endangered species due to overexploitation driven by organized crime (IUCN 2010). Although there is a wide range of harmful activities because of sturgeon fishing, not all of these forms of harm are defined as crime. From a green criminological perspective the central question of whether something may be harmful is indeed relevant (White 2008). According to Courchamp et al. (2006) in small populations of endangered species reproduction and survival is limited. This is caused by a mate shortage or a limited genetic variety whereby a population can extirpate at a high rate. In addition to the decline in the sturgeon population, a substantial lower proportion of female sturgeons in the Caspian Sea has been noticed. While the natural sex ratio should be 1:1, female sturgeons make up only 15–17 % of the total sturgeon population in Russia due to the focus on the eggs for caviar (Vaisman and Raymakers 2001). The anthropogenic factor includes an additional component to the Allee effect because the high market value can lead to overexploitation as has occurred with the sturgeon (Courchamp et al. 2006). Sturgeons can take up to 25 years to reach sexual maturity (Raspopov 1993). In the context of low population numbers, the recovery of some species could take over a century (Secor et al. 2000).

From an ecocentric perspective, the overexploitation of sturgeon has put substantial pressure on the marine ecosystem. Species interact in complex ways and the survival of indigenous species, such as sturgeon in the Caspian Sea, is an indicator of a healthy ecosystem. If a species is declining, the balance in the ecosystem may be affected (Kellert and Wilson 1993). Species may play an important role in managing an ecosystem, for example by spreading seeds, as well as maintaining populations of smaller fish, such as crustaceans and molluscs in the case of sturgeons. Especially keystone species are crucial in order to maintain a healthy ecosystem. Although it is not clear whether sturgeon species in the Caspian Sea play a role as keystone species, the Atlantic sturgeon (*Acipenser oxyrinchus oxyrinchus*) and lake sturgeon (*Acipenser fulvescens*) are considered to be keystone species (Rossum 2013; US Environmental Protection Agency 2009). In one of the world's most precious and unique ecosystems, the Caspian Sea, the extinction of the sturgeon could possibly lead to the disappearance of other species and even the collapse of the ecosystem. Note that there is also an ecocentric side-effect of farming non-native sturgeon as this may lead to non-native escape and threats to native species. These examples have been recorded in Europe and South America (Arndt et al. 2002; Bauer et al. 2002; Pikitch et al. 2005).

Furthermore, due to the excessive and commercial fishing of sturgeon, there is currently a total ban on fishing for wild sturgeon in the Caspian Sea. This criminalization of fishing for sturgeon can lead to 'protest fishing', where local fishermen continue to fish because they believe it is their right to do so. These fishermen continue to poach sturgeon because a main source of their income is gone (Nurse 2015). Especially in Dagestan, the ban can have enormous consequences for fishermen's families and entire villages that have lived for centuries on sturgeon fishing and selling caviar. Moreover, it is no exception that the authorities enforce the ban by military means. Inspectors in the Caspian Sea area usually carry automatic rifles, which has led to violent clashes with fishermen who have also armed themselves to gain access to fishing grounds (Hauck 2007). In addition, the involvement of organized crime groups in the illegal trade in caviar is not exceptional and can also result in state-security threats (Wyler and Sheikh 2008).

Thus, the illegal caviar trade not only harms humans, for example in relation to violence and the disappearance of natural resources of livelihood for local fishermen, but also harms the sturgeon as a species (biodiversity/welfare) and its natural environment (ecosystem).

7.13 Summary

Caviar has a long and rich history, from the food of the poor to a luxury product for the upper classes in Europe. Historically, the symbolic value of caviar is determined in the context of changing social, political and environmental circumstances.

The poaching exploded in the 1990s with the dissolution of the Soviet Union, due to which poor local people became unemployed and resorted to poaching. The caviar trade developed into a profitable market dominated by organized crime that effectively takes advantage of informal ties with government officials. Legal companies are used in particular to shadow illegal activities or to launder wild caviar from poachers. This confirms the interconnectedness of the upperworld and underworld in the caviar business. Criminogenic factors such as scarcity, the exorbitantly high price for caviar, social instability and corruption in the countries of origin, limited control, and certificates that are susceptible to fraud make this type of criminality extremely attractive for organized crime. The consequences include not only the possible extinguishing of this ancient fish, but the trade can also become extremely harmful to local people and the Caspian ecosystem as a whole, including its species.

References

Aas, K. F. (2007). *Crime and globalization*. London: Sage.

Agnew, R. (1992). Foundation for a generalism strain theory of crime and delinquency. *Criminology, 30*(47), 47–88.

AID. (2009). *Tactische analyse Kaviaar. Dienst opsporing informatie and analyse*. The Hague: Ministerie van Landbouw, Natuur en Voedselkwaliteit.

Arndt, G. M., Gessner, J., & Raymakers, C. (2002). Trends in farming, trade and occurrence of native and exotic sturgeons in natural habitats in central and Western Europe. *Journal of Applied Ichthyology, 18*(4–6), 444–448.

Barannikova, I. A., Burtsev, I. A., Vlasenko, A. D., Gershanovich, A. D., Makarov, E. V., & Chebanov, M. S. (1995). Sturgeon fisheries in Russia. In A. D. Gershanovich & T. I . J. Smith (Eds.), *Proceedings of International Symposium on Sturgeons, 6–11 September 1993* (pp. 124–130). Moscow: VNIRO Publishing.

Bauer, O. N., Pugachev, O. N., & Voronin, V. N. (2002). Study of parasites and diseases of sturgeons in Russia: A review. *Journal of Applied Ichthyology, 18*(4–6), 420–429.

Birstein, V. J., Bemis, W. E., & Waldman, J. R. (1997). The threatened status of acipenseriform species: A summary. In V. J. Birstein, W. E. Bemis, & J. R. Waldman (Eds.), *Sturgeon biodiversity and conservation* (pp. 427–435). Netherlands: Springer.

Bonger, W. A. (1932). *Inleiding tot de Criminologie*. Haarlem: Erven Bohn.

Bronzi, P., & Rosenthal, H. (2014). Present and future sturgeon and caviar production and marketing: A global market overview. *Journal of Applied Ichthyology, 30*(6), 1536–1546.

Carey, R. A. (2005). *The philosopher fish: Sturgeon, caviar, and the geography of desire*. Berkeley: Counterpoint Press.

CITES. (2000). *Sixteenth Meeting of the CITES Animals Committee Shepherdstown (United States of America) 11–15 December 2000. Implementation of Resolution Conf. 8.9 (Rev.)*. Acipenseriformes.

CITES. (2001). Willdife: Sturgeons. *Official Newsletter of the Parties Issue Number 8*. CITES.

Courchamp, F., Angulo, E., Rivalan, P., Hall, R. J., Signoret, L., Bull, L., et al. (2006). Rarity value and species extinction: The anthropogenic allee effect. *PLoS Biology, 4*(12), e415.

De Meulenaer, T., & Raymakers, C. (1996). *Sturgeons of the Caspian Sea and the international trade in caviar*. TRAFFIC International.

Doukakis, P., Pikitch, E. K., Rothschild, A., DeSalle, R., Amato, G., & Kolokotronis, S. O. (2012). Testing the effectiveness of an international conservation agreement: Marketplace forensics and CITES caviar trade regulation. *PLoS ONE, 7*(7), 1–9.

Dubinsky, I. V. (2006). How bad boys turn good: The role of law in transforming criminal organizations into legitimate entities by making rehabilitation an economic necessity. *DePaul Business & Commercial Law Journal, 5*, 379–425.

Duffy, R. (2010). *Nature crime: How we're getting conservation wrong*. New Haven: Yale University Press.

Economic and Social Council United Nations. (2002). *Progress made in the implementation of economic and social council resolution 2001/12 on illicit trafficking in protected species of wild Flora and Fauna.* Report of the Secretary-General.

Economic and Social Council United Nations. (2003). *Illicit trafficking in protected species of wild Flora and Fauna and illicit access to genetic resources* (E/CN.15/2003/8).

Engler, M., & Knapp, A. (2008). *Briefing on the evolution of the caviar trade and range state implementation of resolution Conf. 12.7 (Rev. CoP14). A Traffic Europe Report for the European Commission.* Brussels: Traffic.

Engler, M., & Parry-Jones, R. (2007). *Opportunity or threat: The role of the European union in global wildlife trade.* Traffic Europe.

European Commission. (2006). *Study on the enforcement of the EU wildlife trade regulations in the EU-25*. Brussels: European Commission.

European Commission. (2010). Wildlife trade regulations in the European union: An introduction to CITES and its implementation in the European union. Luxembourg: Publications Office of the European Union.

Food Market. (2013). *Russian market of Sturgeon caviar*. Saint-Petersburg: Agriconsult.

FWS. (1998). *New caviar import measures protect imperiled sturgeon*. Washington: Fish and Wildlife Service.

Gesner, J., Freyhof, J., & Kottelat, M. (2010). *Acipenser gueldenstaedtii. The IUCN red list of threatened species 2010.* Gland: IUCN.

Glenny, M. (2008). *McMafia: A journey through the global underworld*. Toronto: House of Anansi Press.

Gordon, M. (2002). *Such stuff as dreams are made on: The story of caviar, from prehistory to the present*. Harvard: Harvard University.

Haken, J. (2011). *Transnational crime in the developing world.* Global Financial Integrity.

Hauck, M. (2007). Non-compliance in small-scale fisheries: A threat to security. *Issues in Green Criminology*, 270–289.

IUCN. (2010). *Sturgeon more critically endangered than any other group of species*. IUCN.

Jahrl, J. (2013). *Illegal caviar trade in Bulgaria and Romania—Results of a market survey on trade in caviar from sturgeons (Acipenseridae)*. Vienna: WWF Austria & Traffic.

Kecse-Nagy, K. (2011). *Trade in sturgeon caviar in Bulgaria and Romania overview of reported trade in caviar, 1998–2008.* Budapest: Traffic.

Kellert, S. R., & Wilson, E. O. (1993). *The biophilia hypothesis*. Washington, DC: Island Press.

Khodorevskaya, R. P., Dovgopol, G. F., Zhuravleva, O. L., & Vlasenko, A. D. (1997). Present status of commercial stocks of sturgeons in the Caspian Sea basin. In V. J. Birstein, J. R. Waldman, & W. E. Bemis (Eds.), *Sturgeon biodiversity and conservation* (pp. 209–219). Netherlands: Springer.

Knapp, A., Kitschke, C., & von Meibom, S. (Eds.). (2006). *Proceedings of the International Sturgeon Enforcement Workshop to Combat Illegal Trade in Caviar. Prepared by TRAFFIC Europe for the European Commission.* Brussels: Traffic.

Kottak, C. P. (1996). *Mirror for humanity: A concise introduction to cultural anthropology*. New York: McGraw-Hill.

Lagutov, V. (Ed.). (2007). *Rescue of sturgeon species in the ural river basin*. Dordrecht: Springer Science & Business Media.

Lawson, T. (2002). *Traded towards extinction? The role of the UK in wildlife trade*. WWF.

Levi, M., & Reuter, P. (2006). Money laundering. *Crime and Justice, 34*(1), 289–375.

Liddick, D. R. (2011). *Crimes against nature. Illegal Industries and the Global Environment*. Oxford: Praeger Publishers.
Lowther, J., Cook, D., & Roberts, M. (2002). *Crime and punishment in the wildlife trade*. Godalming: World Wildlife Fund.
Lyapustin, S. N., Vaisman, A. L., & Fomenko, P. V. (2007). *Wildlife trade in the Russian far East: An overview*. Moscow: Traffic Europe-Russia.
Maltsev, S. A. (2009). Conservation of the sturgeon fish in lower Volga. In *Biology, conservation and sustainable development of sturgeons*. Dordrecht: Springer Netherlands.
Ministry of Internal Affairs of the Republic Kazakhstan. (2014). *Information on the work being done to combat illicit trafficking of fish and fish products*. Kazakhstan: Ministry of Internal Affairs.
Mintz, S. W. (1985). *Sweetness and power*. New York: Viking.
Monfort, M. C. (2002). *Fish roe in Europe: Supply and demand conditions*. Turin: Food and Agriculture Organization of the United Nations, GLOBEFISH, Fishery Industries Division (FAO).
Moreto, W. D., & Lemieux, A. M. (2014). From CRAVED to CAPTURED: Introducing a product-based framework to examine illegal wildlife markets. *European Journal on Criminal Policy and Research, 21*(3), 303–320.
National Wildlife Crime Unit. (2013). *Strategic assessment 2013*. London: NWCU.
Nellemann, C., Henriksen, R., Raxter, P., Ash, N., & Mrema, E. (Eds.). (2014). *The environmental crime crisis—Threats to sustainable development from illegal exploitation and trade in wildlife and forest resources. A UNEP rapid response assessment*. Nairobi and Arendal: United Nations Environment Programme and GRID-Arendal.
Neve, R., Liezen, J., Nieuwdorp, A., Redder, K., van der Zon, G., & Stokman, A. (2012). *Milieucriminaliteit in Nederland. Een inventarisatie voor het Nationaal dreigingsbeeld 2012*. Zoetermeer: KLPD.
Nichol, J. (1987). *Animal smugglers*. New York: Facts on File Publications.
Nikolaev, A. I., Andrianov, D. P., Burtsev, I. A., Kopylenko, L. R., Kotenev, B. N., & Safronov, A. S. (2009). International trade in caviar and business perspectives in Russia. In R. Carmona, et al. (Eds.), *Biology, conservation and sustainable development of sturgeons* (pp. 321–337). Netherlands: Springer.
Nurse, A. (2015). *Policing wildlife. Perspectives on the enforcement of wildlife legislation*. Basingstoke: Palgrave Macmillan.
Oldfield, S. (2003). *The trade in wildlife. Regulation for conservation*. London: Earthscan.
Orlandi, F. (2008). A new chapter in the caviar wars. *East Magazine, Russia, 2*, 31–36.
Passas, N. (2000). Global anomie, dysnomie, and economic crime: Hidden consequences of neoliberalism and globalization in Russia and around the world. *Social Justice, 27*(2), 16–44.
Passas, N. (2002). Cross-border crime and the interface between legal and illegal actors. In P. C. van Duyne, K. von Lampe, & N. Passas (Eds.), *Upperworld and underworld in cross-border crime* (pp. 11–42). Nijmegen: Wolf Legal Publishers.
Pikitch, E. K., Doukakis, P., Lauck, L., Chakrabarty, P., & Erickson, D. L. (2005). Status, trends and management of sturgeon and paddlefish fisheries. *Fish and Fisheries, 6*(3), 233–265.
Pourkazemi, M. (2006). Caspian Sea sturgeon conservation and fisheries: Past present and future. *Journal of Applied Ichthyology, 22*(s1), 12–16.
Raspopov, V. (1993). Growth rate of Caspian Sea beluga. *Journal of Ichthyology, 33*(9), 72–84.
Raymakers, C. (1999). Trade in sturgeons from the Caspian Sea. In *Proceedings of the Symposium on the Harvest Trade and Conservation of North American Paddlefish and Sturgeon, May 7–8, 1998, Chattanooga, TN*. Washington: Traffic North America.
Raymakers, C. (2002). *Study on the social and economic aspects of illegal fishing in the Caspian Sea*. Brussels: Traffic Europe.
Raymakers, C. (2006). CITES, the convention on international trade in endangered species of Wild Fauna and Flora: Its role in the conservation of Acipenseriformes. *Journal of Applied Ichthyology, 22*(s1), 53–65.

Raymakers, C., & Hoover, C. (2002). Acipenseriformes: CITES implementation from range states to consumer countries. *Journal of Applied Ichthyology, 18*(4–6), 629–638.
Reijngoud, J. (2014). *Smuggling methods; methods of concealment of caviar.* Weiteveen: ReijngoudConcept.
Rossum M. K. (2013). *Written Testimony Regarding H.R. 1900, Natural Gas Pipeline Permitting Reform Act Submitted by Maya K. van Rossum, the Delaware Riverkeeper to the House of Representatives Committee on Energy and Commerce, Subcommittee on Energy and Power July 9, 2013.* Washington, D.C.: United States House of Representatives.
Ruban, G. I., & Khodorevskaya, R. P. (2010). Caspian Sea sturgeon fishery: A historic overview. *Journal of Applied Ichthyology, 27*(2), 199–208.
Saffron, I. (2002). *Caviar. The strange history and uncertain future of the world's most coveted delicacy.* New York: Broadway Books.
Saradzhyan, S. (2001). *Caviar Mafia invades Caspian Guard station.* Moscow.
Schneider, J. (2012). *Sold into extinction: The global trade in endangered species.* Santa Barbara: Praeger.
Secor, D., Arefiev, A., Nikolaev, A., & Sharov, A. (2000). Restoration of sturgeons: Lessons from the Caspian Sea sturgeon ranching programme. *Fish and Fisheries, 1*(1), 215–230.
Sellar, J. M. (2014). *The UN'S lone ranger: Combating international wildlife crime.* Dunbeath: Whittles.
Shadrina, E. (2007). The great Caspian caviar game. *Security Index: A Russian Journal on International Security, 13*(1), 55–78.
Siegel, D. (2005). *Russische bizniz.* Amsterdam: Meulenhoff.
Siegel, D. (2009). *The mazzel ritual.* Dordrecht, Heidelberg, London, New York: Springer.
Siegel, D. (2011). Trafficking of 'conflict diamonds'. In C. Smith, S. Zhang, & R. Barberet (Eds.), *routledge handbook of criminology.* London: Routledge.
Siegel, D., & Van Uhm, D. P. (2014). Zwarte kaviaar. Criminele netwerken, illegale handel en de bedreiging van de steur. *Justitiële verkenningen, 30*(2), 54–70.
Simis, K. M. (1982). *USSR: the corrupt society. The secret world of soviet capitalism.* New York: Simon and Schuster.
Simmel, G. (1978). *The philosophy of money.* London: Routledge.
Speer, L., Lauck, L., Pikitch, E., Boa, S., Dropkin, L., & Spruill, V. (2000). *Roe to ruin: The decline of sturgeon in the Caspian Sea and the road to recovery.* New York: Natural Resources Defense Council, WCS.
Stone, R. (2002). Caspian ecology teeters on the brink. *Science, 295*, 430–433.
Talishli, V. (2006). *Caviar, the other black gold.* Indianapolis: Indiana University.
Taylor, S. (1997). *The historical development of the caviar trade and the caviar industry. IUCN Sturgeon Stocks and Caviar Trade Workshop, 9–10 October.* Bonn, Germany. Gland: IUCN.
Theile, S., Steiner, A., & Kecse-Nagy, K. (2004). *Expanding borders: New challenges for wildlife trade controls in the European union.* Brussels: Traffic Europe.
Traffic. (2009). *Fact sheet: Black gold: The caviar trade in Western Europe.* Brussels: Traffic Europe.
United Nations Environment Programme. (2010). *Review of four sturgeon species from the Caspian Sea basin. A report to the european commission.* Cambridge: UNEP-WCMC.
US Environmental Protection Agency. (2009). *Detroit river-western lake Erie basin indicator project.* Lake Sturgeon Population. Environmental Protection Agency.
Vaisman, A. (1997). *Sturgeon catch and trade in the Russian part of the Caspian Sea.* Brussels: Traffic Europe.
Vaisman, A., & Raymakers, C. (2001). The status of sturgeon resources in Russia. *Traffic Bulletin, 19*(1), 33–44.
Van de Bunt, H., Siegel, D., & Zaitch, D. (2014). The social embeddedness of organized crime. In L. Paoli (Ed.), *The oxford handbook of organized crime.* Oxford: Oxford University Press.
Van Rijckeghem, C., & Weder, B. (2001). Bureaucratic corruption and the rate of temptation: Do wages in the civil service affect corruption, and by how much? *Journal of Development Economics, 65*(2), 307–331.

Van Uhm, D. P., & Siegel, D. (2016). The illegal trade in black caviar. *Trends in Organized Crime, 19*(1), 67–87.

Varese, F. (2001). *The Russian Mafia*. Oxford: Oxford University Press.

Volkov, V. (2002). *Violent entrepreneurs. The use of force in the making of Russian capitalism*. Ithaca and London: Cornell University Press.

White, R. (2008). *Crimes against nature: Environmental criminology and ecological justice*. Devon: Willan Publishing.

WikiLeaks. (2010). *Azerbaijan: Who owns what Vol. 2—The minister of emergency situations, beluga caviar, and fruit juice (C-RE9-02494; C-RE9-02493; C-RE9-02492)*. Retrieved from https://www.wikileaks.org/plusd/cables/10BAKU127_a.html.

Wyatt, T. (2013). *Wildlife trafficking: A deconstruction of the crime, the victims, and the offenders*. Basingstoke: Palgrave Macmillan.

Wyler, L. S., & Sheikh, P. A. (2008). *International illegal trade in wildlife: Threats and US policy*. New York: Novinka Books.

Wyler, L. S., & Sheikh, P. A. (2013). *International illegal trade in wildlife: Threats and US policy*. Washington, D.C.: Congressional Research Service report for Congress.

Zabyelina, Y. G. (2013). *The state and transnational organized crime: A case study analysis of criminal opportunities in the Russian federation and the United States (Doctoral dissertation)*. Trento: University of Trento.

Zabyelina, Y. G. (2014). The 'fishy' business: A qualitative analysis of the illicit market in black caviar. *Trends in Organized Crime, 17*(3), 181–198.

Chapter 8
Monkey Business

The previous case study discussed the essence of the caviar trade, in which ordinary fish eggs are transformed into a highly valued luxury product that has attracted criminal networks. Besides caviar as a delicacy for the upper classes, animals in the illegal wildlife trade are also destined for the pet industry. Exotic pets may be attractive because of their cuddly exterior and due to their rarity. Thus these animals are more valuable because they raise the status of their keepers or due to the mere fact that they are entertaining. The second case study[1] focuses on the other branch of the wildlife trade: the trade in Barbary macaques as pets. Why is there such a demand for monkeys as pets? And how have these pets ended up in the hands of criminal entrepreneurs? This second case study has investigated the actors that are involved and provides insights into the social organization, modus operandi and trade routes. The information is based on fieldwork in Morocco in 2013. This is followed by a green criminological exploration of the harms that are caused by the trade in the small population of Barbary macaques.

8.1 History of Keeping Monkeys

Keeping animals as pets is a worldwide phenomenon. According to Westgarth et al. (2010) there is an animal in around half of all worldwide households. Certain authors suggest that keeping pets is even universal, but varies among human cultures (Serpell and Paul 2011; Shipman 2010). While the Kîembu people of Kenya live together with dogs to guard against animals and strangers, Jared Diamond observed Amazon tribes keeping captured wild animals as companions, such as sloths kept by the Matse, capybaras by the Txicao and coatis by the Ache

[1]Parts of this chapter have been published in two publications: Van Uhm, D.P. (2016b). Monkey business: the illegal trade in Barbary macaques. *Journal of Trafficking, Organized Crime and Security, 2*(1): 36–49; Van Uhm, D.P. (2014). *Illegal trade in Barbary macaques.* Utrecht: Utrecht University.

D.P. van Uhm, *The Illegal Wildlife Trade*, Studies of Organized Crime 15,
DOI 10.1007/978-3-319-42129-2_8

(Herzog 2014). In Western societies the worldwide demand for exotic animals is increasing as described in Chap. 2.[2] Each year, an estimated 4 million birds, 640,000 reptiles, 40,000 primates and 350 million tropical fish are traded primarily to Europe and the US (Chomel et al. 2007). A substantial proportion of the animals for this trade are caught in the wild. For instance, 90 % of marine ornamental fish are believed to be wild-caught (Chapman et al. 1997; Cato and Brown 2003) and 80 % of green tree pythons from Indonesia are illegal wild–caught animals (Lyons and Natusch 2011).

An example of an exotic pet that has been associated with humans for thousands of years is the Barbary macaque (*Macaca sylvanus*). These monkeys have been found mummified in Egyptian pyramids (Goudsmit and Brandon-Jones 1999) and petrified in Pompeii (Bailey et al. 1999). They were kept as pets by ancient Romans and Greeks (Hughes 2003) and were frequently found in early Etruscan art (McDermott 1936). In the medieval period they were desired animals among the nobility (Sax 2001). Illustrations of Barbary macaques at the Iron Age Navan Fort in Northern Ireland (McCormick 1991) and fossils in Carrickfergus represent imported domestic macaques that have been found (Taub 1978). Clerics wanted to keep them in their home for display in front of their window in a way to impress the 'passing rabble' with the glory of their possessions. In the thirteenth century the opening of trade routes with the Near East led to the widespread introduction of monkeys in Western Europe. Barbary macaques were common at that time in the Mediterranean basin. Canons of Notre Dame kept them in their cloisters and monkeys were displayed at courts to demonstrate a sign of wealth and social status (Janson 1952). Keeping exotic animals as pets spread from the aristocracy to middle and lower class citizens during the sixteenth century (Thomas 1984). Shakespeare's references to monkeys were presumably linked to Barbary apes that were kept as pets by Italian courtesans (Kantha 2014).

The initial introduction of Barbary macaques in Europe (Gibraltar) was probably by the Moors who occupied southern Iberia and kept them as pets (Jackson 1987). Consequently, knowledge about apes in European literature between 1700–1900s was mainly based on Barbary macaques (O'Flaherty and Shapiro 2002) and the word 'monkey' may have been first used to refer to Barbary macaques (Sax 2001). The Barbary macaque has also become a symbol that has a social value in political debates between countries. According to a Gibraltarian tale Spanish groups ascended the Rock of Gibraltar to ambush the British town of Gibraltar in the

[2]There has been growing concern regarding the increase in exotic animals being kept as pets. Many exotic animals are ill-equipped to live in close contact with humans and knowledge about the behaviour or ecology of the species by 'pet owners' is often lacking (Duarte-Quiroga and Estrada 2003; Engebretson 2006; Soulsbury et al. 2009). Certain exotic species, such as venomous snakes, spiders or large carnivores may pose a risk to physical human health (Nyhus et al. 2003) whereas others can pose a risk of disease, such as salmonella or Ebola (Ward 2000; Allela et al. 2014). Further concerns include exotic pets from the wild that may contribute to species extinction (Wright et al. 2001) and the threat of released or escaped exotic animals to native flora and fauna (Reed 2005; Perry et al. 2006).

eighteenth century. However, they came across a group of sleeping Barbary macaques that called the alarm to awake the British soldiers. The troops were able to respond to the attack and since then Gibraltar has been in British hands. It is said that Winston Churchill declared that as long as there are Barbary apes on the Rock of Gibraltar, Gibraltar will remain British (Fuentes 2013).

From the 1960s and 1970s onwards, the popularity of keeping exotic pets increased, partially popularized by celebrities, and Barbary macaques were offered for sale in department stores (e.g. Harrods in London) all over Europe (e.g. Bierman and Smith 2000; Sanglim 2014). The popularity of keeping exotic animals as pets resulted in a high demand for eccentric and unusual species in Europe. At that time it was relatively common and socially accepted to keep primates as pets. Thousands of monkeys were brought from Africa, Asia and Latin America to answer the demand in Europe (Broad et al. 1988). Barbary macaques from Morocco still fuel the demand for monkeys in the EU. For example, on a weekday at the famous Djemaa el-Fna Square in Marrakesh there are a variety of merchants with exotic animals. Between snake charmers, storytellers, acrobats, tooth pullers, musicians and water sellers in traditional costumes a range of wild animals impress European tourists. Pythons, tortoises, eagles, chameleons and Barbary macaques are sold as pets (personal observation, 12–13 and 17–18 March 2013).

The demand for extraordinary items has been historically linked to keeping exotic animals as status pets (Chap. 1) and due to the decline in species certain exotic animals are more exclusive than before. Status pets refer mostly to animals which are not native to the region in which they are kept (Fuentes 2013). Similar to caviar, the value of an object or subject is related to the valuation (Simmel 1978). Since only a small population of wild Barbary macaques remains in fragmented parts of Morocco and Algeria, the monkeys are endangered and very highly valuable. According to Simmel (1978) the desire for scarcity creates value for items. From this perspective, endangered animals, such as the Barbary macaque, may be regarded as status symbols or may become fashionable 'accessories', with the scarcest species at the top of demand lists with extraordinary high prices (Courchamp et al. 2006). A famous example is the chimpanzee Bubbles kept as a pet by Michael Jackson in the 1980s (Vigo 2010). He took him along on tour to Japan and Bubbles lived indoors wearing a diaper (Shaw 2003). Celebrities still make the news with their pet monkeys.[3]

Several sociologists have emphasized the effect of role models on civilians. People are exposed to and copy the behaviour of role models' attitudes and values (e.g. Sutherland et al. 1992; Akers 2013). This may result in specific animals becoming fashion trends in the context of values, beliefs and dynamics (Traffic 2011). After the first 'Harry Potter' feature film in the early 2000s, there was a great demand for the protected Snowy Owl and this was visible in seizure data (Van Uhm 2009), while the 'Night in the Museum' films resulted in an increased demand for monkeys as pets (McLennan 2012). The attractiveness of exclusive animals is demonstrated by large

[3]Such as the chimpanzee owned by Kim Kardashian or Justin Bieber's illegal capuchin monkey.

animal fairs with thousands of colourful birds and reptiles (Laufer 2010; Smith 2011). Ferrell (2013: 352) underlines the harmful effects of the *culture of consumption*, "an increasingly globalized consumerist way of life defined by advertised meaning, constructed need, cycled fashion, and conspicuously acquired status". This demand for extraordinary species in the context of their rarity and fashion trends may result in the overexploitation of species in a relatively short period of time. However, where does the fascination for monkeys as pets come from?

Monkeys look like babies. According to Jane Goodall (2014), the world's most famous expert on chimpanzees, monkey infants are 'irresistibly cute', and it might seem that raising one would be just like raising a human child. 'We're looking for a baby monkey to love and spoil (…) we are unable to have any more children and have a void in our hearts. We need a baby to love!'[4] Serpell and Paul (2011) argue that keeping exotic pets by humans could be explained, on an evolutionary basis, by a signal of parental capabilities. Around 90 % of pet owners in the US consider their animals to be part of the family and 75 % consider their pets to be akin to children (Serpell and Paul 2011). Although no studies have been conducted on pet owners' ability to have children, several studies argue that men with pets are attractive to women (e.g. Gueguen and Ciccotti 2008). Pet keeping would be relevant in order to develop parental skills and empathy in the preparation to care for human babies (Bradshaw and Paul 2010). From this point of view, keeping animal species as pets that are (genetically) comparable to humans, such as monkeys, would make sense. Furthermore, some couples who remain childless find a replacement in keeping a monkey as a pet. From this perspective, the baby monkey will replace the role of a human baby. This could explain, to some extent, the integration of macaques in family life (Green 1999; Laufer 2010). However, the most important driver would be keeping a monkey as social pet for entertainment. For instance, families keep macaques as playmates for children or for general companionship (Fuentes 2013). Herzog explains (2014: 298): "Relationships between pets and keepers are typically characterized by affection and are relatively long-lasting as opposed to transient". While human infants grow, mature and become independent, monkeys remain relatively small, fluffy and depended on food given by the pet owner; they are considered to be an eternal baby.

This would explain why humans anthropomorphise their (monkey) pets (Serpell 2003). Anthropomorphism is the ascription of human form or characteristics or mental states onto non-human species. This is illustrated by the fact that many pet owners give their pets birthday presents (Serpell and Paul 2011) and numerous reports indicate the breastfeeding of pets alongside their human infants (Serpell 1996). This is especially applicable to animals that look like humans or are genetically comparable, such as monkeys (Fox 2006). Human and non-human primates have a special relationship due to biological, phylogenetic, and behavioural overlaps (Corbey and Theunissen 1995). Primates, including humans, share several components such as "grasping hands, relatively large brains, an emphasis on

[4]"The Perils of Keeping Monkeys as Pets", National Geographic, September 16, 2003.

visual signalling, extended infant dependency, and behaviourally dynamic social complexity" (Fuentes 2007: 1). Therefore, monkeys are regularly integrated into human family life and wear clothes, sleep in cribs and eat at the dinner table. According to a macaque smuggler and owner: "They bring out the emotions that a newborn child does (…) He slept in bed with my daughter, whom he considered his mom" (Laufer 2010). Not incidentally, seized Barbary macaques that were included in family life wore suits and slept in cribs next to their human 'owners' (EE2).

The habit of keeping Barbary macaques has existed for a long time and is attributable to several factors. The combination of a fascination for the exotic, the exclusivity of Barbary macaques, the exercise of parental skills and the anthropomorphism of monkeys may drive the demand market. Fuentes (2013) distinguished three forms of keeping macaques as pets. Status pets as an indicator of the affluence of their owner; this category is often encountered in the history of keeping macaques as pets. Food pets that are kept until they reach a particular size to be ready to be eaten. This is rarely seen regarding Barbary macaques. And social pets for entertainment; the latter is the most common reason for keeping Barbary macaques whereby they become part of the family. However, in previous decades the demand market was disturbed due to the substantial decline in Barbary macaques that has led to the current trade regulations.

8.2 Protection Measures and Criminalization

Although in the past Barbary macaques were traded legally, in the late twentieth century the trade slowly became criminalized. After 1975 several researchers (Taub 1977; Deag 1977; Fa 1984) raised concerns regarding the declining population. Simultaneously, protective measures were proposed by NGOs, such as the World Wildlife Fund (WWF) or the IUCN (Fa 1984). During that time social and moral norms were subject to change and, under pressure from several moral entrepreneurs, the trade in Barbary macaques became restricted by regulation. Currently, the trade in wild Barbary macaques without proper documents is forbidden. The IUCN has classified the Barbary Macaque as 'endangered' on the Red List of Threatened Species and the Barbary macaque has been listed in Appendix II of CITES (EC 338/97, Annex B) since 1975 (Butynski et al. 2008).[5]

In 2000, the European Community suspended imports of Barbary macaques from Algeria and Morocco under the provisions of Article 4.6b of EC Regulation 338/97 because this trade was deemed to have a harmful effect on the status of the species, i.e. for conservation reasons, and this was reconfirmed in 2006 (Regulation

[5]While the populations of great apes on the CITES I list, such as chimpanzees *Pan troglodytes* (population: between 299,700–431,100), orangutans *Pongo pygmaeus* and *Pongo abelli* (population: 54,000 and 6,600) and bonobos *Pan paniscus* (population: 15,000–20,000) (Stiles et al. 2013; Oates et al. 2008), are estimated to be larger, the Barbary macaques still remain on the CITES list II.

(CE) No. 605/2006) (Butynski et al. 2008). The criminalization process proceeded with a prohibition on keeping monkeys as pets in several European countries during the 1990s and 2000s. Consequently, the legal situation within the EU on the keeping of Barbary macaques as pets varies considerably between individual Member States. For instance, Bulgaria,[6] Sweden,[7] Belgium,[8] the Netherlands,[9] Italy, Portugal, Latvia, Lithuania, Estonia, Hungary and Andalucía, an autonomous community in Spain,[10] have implemented bans on the keeping of primates as pets. Denmark prohibits the importation and private keeping of all primates, except marmosets and tamarins, while Austria and Poland prohibit the private keeping of great apes (RSPCA 2012; Endcap 2012).[11]

The Barbary macaque is also protected by national legislation in Morocco and Algeria; this means that their capture, possession, sale and hunting are prohibited (Royaume du Maroc 2012). The export of Barbary macaques is regulated by a system of permits, but enforcing the legislation thereon is inadequate and illegal trade is a serious problem (Butynski et al. 2008). Law No. 29-05 provides for measures to regulate the possession of this species for cultural purposes, particularly in Marrakesh, through a certificate of ownership per specimen (Royaume du Maroc 2012). At the famous Djemaa el-Fna Square in Marrakesh, macaques are kept for pictures to be taken with tourists, to perform with trainers and (illegally) for sale.

8.3 The Final Countdown?

In the Pleistocene period, the Barbary macaque inhabited parts of Europe and virtually all of North Africa. Based on fossil findings the distribution ranged from southern England in the north to Turkey and the Mediterranean coast from Syria to Morocco (Lindburg 1980; Camperio Ciani 1986). Since then the Barbary macaque has disappeared from the northern coasts of the Mediterranean, Sardinia and, in the last few centuries, from Turkey (Mouna and Camperio Ciani 2006). While the species was once widespread throughout North Africa from Libya to Morocco, its

[6]Articles 21 and 27(1), Animal Protection Law, 2008.

[7]Föreskrifter om ändring i Djurskyddsmyndighetens DFS 2005:8 föreskrifter och allmänna råd (DFS 2004:16) om villkor för hållande, uppfödning och försäljning m.m. av djur avsedda för sällskap och hobby. June 28, 2005.

[8]Arrêté royal du 7 décembre 2001 fixant la liste des animaux qui peuvent être détenus. December 7, 2001.

[9]Flora and Fauna Act 1998.

[10]DECRETO 42/2008, de 12 de febrero, por el que se regula la tenencia de animales potencialmente peligrosos en la Comunidad Autónoma de Andalucía. 12 February 2008.

[11]In the UK a licence is required to keep primate species listed in the Dangerous Wild Animals Act (1976) as pets (DEFRA 2009); between 2,500–7,500 may be kept by private individuals in the UK alone (Soulsburry et al. 2009).

Table 8.1 Barbary macaque population

Location	Population	Year of survey	Source
Morocco	17,000	1974	Taub (1975)
	10,000	2002	Camperio Ciani et al. (2003)
	6,000–10,000	Unknown	Ross (2004)
	5,000	–	Camperio Ciani (2006)
Algeria	≥4,500	1974	Taub (1975)
Global	≥21,500	1974	Taub (1975)
	10,000–16,000	1992	Lilly and Mehlman (1993)
	≥15,000	Unknown	Von Segesser et al. (1999)
	10,000	2003	Modolo (2005), Camperio Ciani (2003)
	5,000–6,000	2009	Majolo et al. (2013)

current distribution is limited solely to small relict patches of forest and scrub, in the rocky and mountainous parts of the Rif and the Atlas Mountains (Morocco) and in parts of the Tellian Atlas (Algeria) (Fa et al. 1984; Camperio Ciani 1986; Scheffrahn et al. 1993; Menard and Vallet 1993). These wild macaque populations are separated by large distances caused by habitat degradation in North Africa (Waters 2011). The Middle Atlas Mountains house the largest population of wild Barbary macaques (Mouna and Camperio Ciani 2006). A semi-wild population of around 200 macaques live in the Upper Rock Nature Reserve of Gibraltar in Europe (Fa 1981).

Table 8.1 illustrates that the total population size of Barbary macaques decreased from an estimated 21,500 individuals in 1974 (Taub 1977, 1978) to 15,000 in the 1990s (Von Segresser et al. 1999), 10,000 in 2003 (Modolo et al. 2005; Camperio Ciani 2003), and 5,000–6,000 in 2009 (Majolo et al. 2013). The numbers of macaques in Morocco are currently estimated to be around 5,000 individuals, whereas in comparison to 1975 it was about 17,000 (Butynski et al. 2008; Radhakrishna et al. 2012). Overall, the population of Barbary macaques is estimated to have declined at a rate exceeding 50 % over the last three generations (24 years). According to the IUCN this decline is expected to continue in the future (see also Appendix XI) (Butynski et al. 2008).

An 8-year-long census and habitat evaluation in the Middle Atlas found that the decline in the Barbary macaque population is mainly attributed to the loss of habitat (Camperio Ciani et al. 2005). Already in 1978 the destruction of native forests was found to be the chief reason for their species decline in Morocco and Algeria (Taub 1978). Since 1994 the primary habitat of the macaques, the cedar forests, have significantly reduced due to forest degradation (Camperio Ciani 1998; Camperio Ciani et al. 2005). While the main threat to the Barbary macaque populations is habitat loss caused by intensive (illegal) logging, land clearance for agriculture, charcoal production and overgrazing by livestock (Fa 1984; Camperio et al. 2005), the illegal trade in macaques for the pet trade has become one of the greatest threats to the survival of the species (Radhakrishna et al. 2012). From the late 1990s onwards, zoological parks and sanctuaries in Europe started to notice a significant increase in the number of Moroccan Barbary macaques being offered for shelter, after being seized by law enforcement authorities in France, Belgium, Spain, Italy and the Netherlands. This trend is probably connected to the demand for Barbary macaques as pets (Van Lavieren 2008). Although the Barbary lion (*Panthera leo leo*) and, possibly, the Barbary leopard (*Panthera pardus panthera*) have already become extinct in the wild due to overhunting (Burger and Hemmer 2006), currently the Barbary macaque is on the brink of extinction.

8.4 Macaques as Laboratory Animals

In the twentieth and the beginning of the twenty-first century macaque species are the most traded protected mammals in the world; within the EU, more than 80 % of traded CITES mammals were macaques between 2001 and 2010. The legal trade in macaques is mainly related to the demand for laboratory animals, such as the crab-eating macaque (*Macaca fascicularis*) and the Rhesus macaque (*Macaca mulatta*) (CITES 2011).[12] Macaques are popular as laboratory animals as they are genetically very similar to humans. Their neurological, reproductive and immunological systems are analogous to human systems. Up to the mid-1970s large numbers of Rhesus macaques were imported into Europe for the production of the polio vaccine, until a significant decline in the population made it necessary for them to be extensively replaced by crab-eating macaques (Mack and Mittermeier 1984; Fitzgerald 1989). Historically, macaques were important in the establishment of the aetiology of polio, yellow fever and prion diseases, and currently they serve as models for more than 70 human infectious diseases (Gardner and Luciw 2008).

In the 1990s, Barbary macaques were also obtained from the wild for biomedical research. However, sometimes hunters misused the obligatory certificates to catch additional macaques for the retail trade. According to a former poacher: “This was the beginning of the large-scale illegal trade in Barbary macaques. Sometimes ten monkeys were captured, while only one was needed for biomedical research and the remaining monkeys were sold for the pet industry” (MF1). He explained that the monkeys were regularly poached using documents provided for catching monkeys for biomedical purposes, while some were illegally traded on the black market. This legal–illegal interface illustrates how legitimate structures have been used to set up illegal activities (Passas 2002).

Currently, capturing Barbary macaques for biomedical research is no longer legal because the species is excluded from the list for biomedical research primate species. The legal trade in Barbary macaques is only possible with CITES documents provided by the CITES authority in the source country. According to trade statistics between 2001–2010, dozens of ‘captive-bred’ Barbary macaques were

[12]UN Comtrade database and WCMC database, 2012.

traded for circuses or travelling exhibitions, regularly confiscated macaques are moved from Morocco and Algeria to Spain, while only two live Barbary macaques from the wild were legally exported from Algeria to Italy (CITES trade database). This contradicts accounts by traders in Morocco who suggest that sometimes CITES documents are provided to people who have bought a wild macaque on the illegal market.

8.5 Full Shelters and Illegal Trade

From the late 1990s onwards, European sanctuaries addressed the growing number of seized Barbary macaques being offered for shelter. Based on confiscations in the EU this trend continued in the 2000s with the Barbary macaque being the most seized CITES mammal in the EU, accounting for almost 25 % of all live mammal-related seizures between 2001 and 2010 (EU-TWIX database). Most macaques are confiscated in Spain because of the lack of CITES documents which are needed to transfer them from Morocco to Spain (ibid.).

According to data on confiscations from the CITES management authorities of Belgium, France, Italy and the Netherlands and the 'Seprona' Police (a unit of the Spanish Guardia Civil) from Spain, the actual number of confiscations is substantially higher than is presented in the EU-TWIX database. Between 2006 and 2010, 159 Barbary macaques were confiscated in the respective countries with a peak of 50 seized macaques in 2008. The same trend is observed in the figures from the EU-TWIX database and the numbers of requests for shelter (Fig. 8.1).

Poachers of and traders in Barbary macaques confirmed this peak as well; in the late 2000s the trade was flourishing with annual numbers of 500–600 illegally traded Barbary macaques from the Azrou area (MF2; MT7; MT9; MT10). "At that time everyone seemed to be involved in the business. Truckloads of monkeys left the Azrou area around 2008 and 2009" (MT3). Law enforcement experts estimate that no more than 10 % of all contraband is seized (Stiles et al. 2013). According to this information around 500 Barbary macaques, based on the 50 animals that were confiscated, were indeed being illegally traded in 2008 and roughly 200 Barbary macaques are traded nowadays. The decrease in this trade (and the confiscations) from 2008 onwards is possibly caused by the economic crisis in Europe with a lesser demand for monkeys (MT9; MS5).

The majority of the Barbary macaque confiscations ($N = 35$, 92 %) originate from Morocco, followed by Algeria ($N = 3$, 8 %).[13] This was to be expected because the last remaining population lives in areas in Morocco and Algeria

[13]During this 10-year period, 49 seizures of 55 Barbary macaques occurred in the EU with 92 % originating from Morocco and 8 % from Algeria.

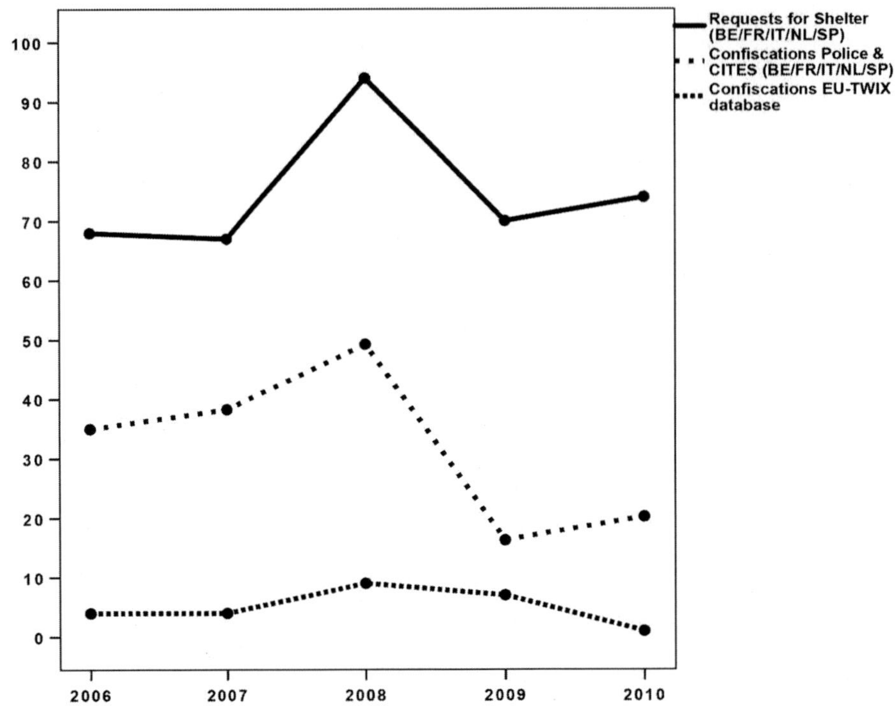

Fig. 8.1 EU confiscations of and shelter requests for Barbary macaques. *Source* Personal analyses of the EU-TWIX database 2001–2010; Seprona Guardia Civil 2013 seizures; CITES Belgium, France, Italy and the Netherlands seizures

(Radhakrishna et al. 2012). The average amount of smuggled Barbary macaques discovered is one monkey per confiscation ($N = 49$; $M = 1.1$; $SD = 0.3$). Furthermore, transit or destination countries for the illegal trade in Barbary macaques are Spain ($N = 42$, 86 %), Belgium ($N = 5$, 10 %), France ($N = 1$, 2 %) and Italy ($N = 1$, 2 %) (Fig. 8.2). Due to its geographic location, Spain, in addition to being a destination country, is mainly an important transit country. France seems to be an important outlet as the French police have stated that they have confiscated approximately 50 macaques in France each year in the late 2000s (Van Lavieren 2008). Respondents confirmed that Belgium, France and Italy are well-known demand markets for Barbary macaques (MF2; MT2; MT5; MS2; MS5; ME1). In the past it has been claimed that in 2 years 500 macaques were smuggled into France (Van Lavieren 2008); however, due to the low confiscation numbers, it is hard to confirm this information based on seizures.

At least the figures on confiscations confirm that in the context of a small remaining wild population, there is a relatively large illegal market for Barbary macaques. Based on numbers from sanctuaries in Belgium, France, Italy, the Netherlands and Spain, 219 Barbary macaques were rescued between 2006

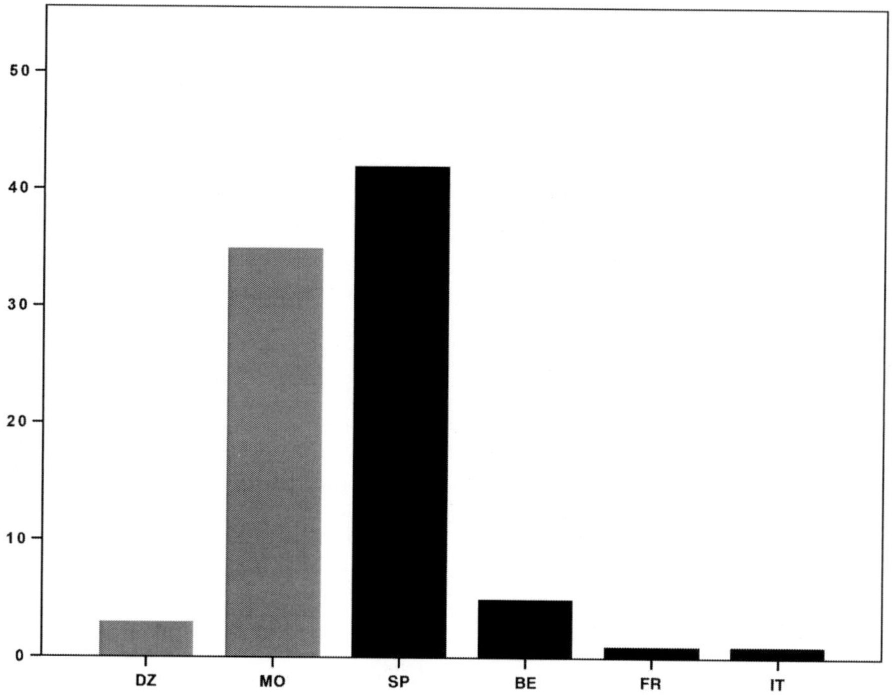

Fig. 8.2 Origin and destination countries for illegal Barbary macaques.*Export country codes: Algeria (*DZ*), Morocco (*MO*).**Import-country codes: Spain (*SP*), Belgium (*BE*), France (*FR*), Italy (*IT*). *Source* Personal analyses of the EU-TWIX database (seizures), 2001–2010

and 2010.[14] The seized monkeys are generally housed and rehabilitated by zoos and sanctuaries, such as the European sanctuary run by AAP.[15] This is one of the few sanctuaries in Europe that provides shelter for Barbary macaques. A large proportion of rescued macaques originate from private (pet) owners (65 %) or have been found wandering as stray animals (24 %). Other purposes for this illegal trade include circuses, gifts to private owners and zoos (Kranendonk et al. 2013). In addition, Van Lavieren (2008: 125) referred to cases where Barbary macaques were used as 'fighting monkeys' in tower block basements and served as a 'substitute for guard dogs'. While it is unknown how many Barbary macaques are left with their owners or are euthanized after border controls, there are strong indications that customs officials sometimes do not confiscate these animals due to a lack of rescue facilities. In the latter case, customs officials prefer to accept a bribe instead of confiscation when there is no shelter (ME1).

[14]As rescued macaques are occasionally moved to another shelter in the EU, double counting may explain the higher number of rescued animals compared to seizures.

[15]http://www.aap.nl.

8.6 Poaching Young Macaques

The illegal trade in Barbary macaques (المكاك البربري-) flows through the supply chain from poachers to the final consumers. Similar to the trade in caviar this supply chain usually has flexible distribution lines with both small scale and relatively large criminal networks involved. The first step in the operation is the poaching of the Barbary macaques. According to multiple respondents, the small Berber town of Azrou and its surroundings (Middle Atlas in Morocco) is the centre of the illegal trade in Barbary macaques (e.g. MT1; MT4; ME1; MS1; MS3). Although poaching occurs all year round, the main season for poaching starts in the spring (April) as there are many infant monkeys. This is the start of the birth season from April to June (Deag 1984). A poacher in Azrou explains: "There is a demand for young monkeys for two reasons. First, young monkeys get used to people better than older ones and, secondly, they are easier to smuggle in suitcases or bags" (MF2). The monkeys are often sold before they become 1-year-old (Van Lavieren 2008). This may explain the significant decrease in the numbers of juvenile macaques and females in the Middle Atlas between 2007 and 2009 (Haut Commissariat aux Eaux et Forêts et à la Lutte Contre la Désertification 2012).

The poachers are usually relatively poor local specialists from Berber villages in the Azrou area in Morocco (Illustration 8.1). This region is home to Morocco's earliest inhabitants, the Berber tribes, who have been living on herding for centuries (Wagner 1993).[16] They live in small villages in the middle or around the cedar forests (personal observation, March 15 and 28–29 April 2013). Similar to the poachers of caviar, the illegal hunters are mainly poor people without sufficient economic resources. This crime (of poaching) seems to be linked to poverty and social injustices (Bonger 1932). A difference is that poachers of Barbary macaques regularly do not hunt monkeys to feed their family, but merely for additional earnings. They commit crimes to obtain a supplementary income. According to one poacher: "It is not our daily business. (…) It is just carried out because people ask for it. As long as they pay us we meet their needs" (MF2). While situational incentives may play an important role (e.g. they live nearby or in the poaching area), they catch monkeys in particular due to the demand from middlemen or tourists driven by economic gains.

An exception is Barbary macaques poisoned by local people in Ouzoud because of nuisance. A local guide explained that many tourists come to see the waterfalls. These tourists feed the macaques and the monkeys have become a scourge

[16]The Berbers are indigenous people of North Africa. The Romans would have first used the name Berber to mean barbarians. The Berbers call themselves 'Imazighen' which means free people. The Barbary Coast was named after the Berbers because a great deal of piracy took place against ships sailing to the Mediterranean Sea.

Illustration 8.1 Poaching area Azrou, Morocco 2013

for local people (MO2; MO). In addition, there are rumours that African migrants who are staying temporarily in tents in the Rif mountains in order to reach the EU occasionally hunt the monkeys as food (MP2). These two examples illustrate other hazards in the context of poaching Barbary macaques.

However, the major group consist of specialist poachers in Azrou that will operate anywhere for between €50–100 per monkey. They act quickly on the orders received and can even deliver more than 10 monkeys a week at short notice. According to a former poacher in Azrou: "They [poacher friends] work with four guys, everybody knows who they are. (…) This group sells around 50 monkeys each year based on fixed prices. Only 750 Dirham (€75) for a monkey, these are special prices, tourists pay more" (MF2). The poachers work in groups of 4–8 people.

Three major poaching methods for capturing the monkeys have been described by (former) poachers in Azrou (MF1; MF2):

1. Poachers (6–7 people) isolate female macaques with infants from the group by trained dogs. They goad them from the dense forest into a solitary tree, then saw the branches and harass the mother with sticks and stones, until the babies are dropped.

2. Poachers place grids on the ground and wait until macaques walk over them. They then pull on a rope that is connected to a net that hangs from trees and it falls to the ground so that the monkey is caught in the net.
3. Poachers entice Barbary macaques with fruit or coconuts, until they are close enough to catch them.

Other methods used to capture Barbary macaques include food in clay pots with a small opening, in such a manner that the monkey can grasp for the food, but is unable to retrieve its hand, or enticing the monkeys with bread dipped in wine to sedate them (Van Lavieren 2008). Then the monkeys are trapped in cages behind the house of one of the poachers, until they are sold (MT10).

Since everyone knows the poachers, they have made agreements with other local people to poach outside the tourist spots in the Cedar Forest in Azrou and not to disturb financial benefits in relation to (eco-)tourism. These agreements can be understood as the poachers originate from the same small Berber villages. Therefore, guides, lumberjacks and forest rangers are involved in the illegal trade and obtain 100 Dirham (±€10) commission if they refer potential buyers of macaques (MF1; MT9; MM1). Based on the author's observations, monkeys are sold directly along the side of the road in Azrou (personal observation, 29 April 2013), but usually middlemen organize the business.

8.7 The Legal–Illegal Interface

Between poachers of wildlife and the ultimate users or traders, middlemen may be involved in the wildlife trade (Van Uhm 2012a; Nijman 2010). According to Wyatt (2013) middlemen are key individuals in smuggling operations moving wildlife along a network. They intermediate between actors in the supply chain and buy wildlife from the poacher and transfer the animals to wildlife markets (Domalain 1977; Nichol 1987; Warchol 2004). For instance, in the Barbary macaque trade middlemen arrange for a smuggler to stay in a hotel in Azrou while poachers are doing their job: "Within two days we can arrange their order and then they go back to resell the monkeys in Tangier, Oujda or Marrakesh. Usually we are prepared, because we get the orders a couple days in advance" (MF2). The monkeys are then sold to traders for about €100–150 by middlemen (MM1; MM2).[17] These agreements are often made in advance.

Generally, middlemen *semsar* (سمسار-) who are involved in the Barbary macaque business do have other businesses as well. For instance, a middleman in Fez highlighted that he was also a trader in carpets and a tourist guide by showing his business card. He traded in macaques to earn additional income and explained his mutual relationships: "Everybody wants to make some extra money, even forest

[17]Another middleman in Marrakesh complained that the profits are not high, sometimes just 250 Dirham (€25) is paid per monkey (MM2).

rangers are involved [in the Barbary macaque trade]. (…) I do business with a Moroccan man who has been living in Germany for 18 years. He is a real trader and he has contacts with clients all over Europe. We share the profits." This middleman usually arranges orders to capture monkeys alive. He was quite surprised by a recent order from an Italian lady for fur: "A couple of weeks ago I arranged an order of 'monkey fur' for an Italian lady. (…) It was her, but also my, first time in arranging for fur from a monkey. She wanted to have an exclusive coat so I ordered a dead monkey and passed it through a tailor, a friend of mine" (MM1). These middlemen are key players in the trade as they have contacts with several actors, such as traders, smugglers or even tailors (MT3; MT5).

This example highlights the blurred distinction between legality and illegality. The role of the legal businessman involved in illegal businesses has been discussed by many criminologists (e.g. Ruggiero 1996; Van Duyne et al. 2002; Passas 2002). Middlemen may be legal players who are involved in illegal businesses. They may use their legal business as a cover or use the same contacts in their legal networks to successfully arrange the illegal trade (Passas 2002). Ilahiane and Sherry (2008) underline that the informal market is much more integrated in Morocco than in the West. The *souks* (السوق-) stand in sharp contrast to the Western industrial model of doing business whereby different types of trading intertwine (Illustration 8.2). Therefore, the role of middlemen in the macaque business may be seen as ordinary middlemen who have, in this case, directed their focus towards the monkey trade.

Illustration 8.2 Macaques for sale at the souk, Marrakesh, Morocco 2013

Several informants underlined the special friendships in the trade in Barbary macaques. Besides their ordinary relationship, these friends could provide exclusive secret services, such as illegal products. According to Kleemans and Van de Bunt (1999) certain bonds of friendship are 'strong ties' that are fundamental for criminal networks. Cooperation between friends can guarantee a secure network. One of the middlemen interviewed in Fez explained that: "It is not the question whether you can arrange something, but if you have the required relationships with the right people. For example, my friend who lives just outside Fez arranges not only for living monkeys but his whole house is hanging full of skins of protected animals. He is a serious dealer. Every living or dead animal you want to obtain we can arrange" (MM1). Many informants underlined that by just one phone call these middlemen can arrange many legal and illegal services (e.g. MF1; MM1; MS4).

One of the tasks of the middleman is to arrange the transportation of the monkeys from the forests to the trade hubs in Morocco (e.g. Tangier, Marrakesh) that requires a certain degree of sophistication. The monkeys may be hidden in the trunk of a car or additional actors like bus drivers or police officers are involved. For instance, transportation between Azrou and Oujda organized by a middleman is as follows: one person gets on the bus in Azrou and registers suitcases or bags, with monkeys hidden inside, as checked-in baggage and then gets off the bus at the second or third stop, while leaving the luggage on the bus. If the bus is held for a police check and they find the macaques, the bus driver has an alibi, because he has a receipt for the suitcases or bags that have been 'forgotten' by the traveller in question. Without a police check the bus arrives in Oujda where someone else will pick up the suitcases or bags with the monkeys and the bus driver is then paid (MO4; MU3). The communication between hunters, middlemen and traders generally proceeds by mobile phone. One seller at the famous Djemaa el-Fna Square in Marrakesh underlined that the use of mobile phones is relatively safe as prepaid cards can be easily bought and changed without registration (MS3).

As highlighted in this section, middlemen play an important role in the illegal trade in Barbary macaques due to their social connections with the 'upperworld' (e.g. lorry drivers, animal shopkeepers, the police) and the 'underworld' (e.g. smugglers, poachers). These connections are necessary to transfer the monkeys from the source region to the destination.

8.8 Crossing the Ocean

The Strait of Gibraltar seems to be the natural border between Morocco and Spain. However, the presence of Spanish territory (Melilla and Ceuta) on the north Moroccan coast represents an important factor in its status as a 'smuggler's paradise'. For a long time smuggling has been a part of life in the northern Rif of Morocco. Especially since the human population almost doubled between 1960 and 1970, smuggling, of every item imaginable, was booming (McMurray 2001; Parnell and Kane 2003).[18] For example, people have become specialized in smuggling goods from Nador to Melilla (McMurray 2001). Besides the illegal trade in drugs and migration, currently the wildlife trade has become a major contraband (Cowdrey 2002; Highfield and Bayley 1996).

However, the smuggling of live animals differs substantially from the smuggling of wildlife products such as caviar, ivory or rhino horn. To hide live monkeys and to keep them alive during the smuggling process requires systematic planning and logistics (Stiles et al. 2013). Because the smugglers aim to limit the period of time in transit to ensure the survival of the monkey, the route is mostly scheduled and appointments have been made between actors in the smuggling process. "You do not want to lose time. You just have to finish the job. I smuggled monkeys from Melilla through Almeria directly to Brussels to avoid any delay. (…) As you understand, the monkey must be quiet during the trip and it must be alive in order for me to get paid" (MU2). For this reason, the smugglers prefer to transport the monkeys directly to the trader or buyer, without secondary activities (MU2; MU3).

Young Barbary macaques are usually hidden in suitcases or bags under a car seat and incidentally on the body.[19] Several dealers confirmed that in order to keep the macaque quiet and to decrease the macaque's stress levels, the monkeys are anesthetized with a sleeping aid for children, *n3as* (النعاس-), which can be bought from an ordinary pharmacy (MT1; MT4; MT6; MT7; MT10). "The syrup makes them sleep. Then you put the small monkey in a suitcase under the seat of your car and cross the border to enter Spain. That is the way to do it" (MU2). This syrup can anesthetize the monkey for up to 16 h during the border crossing (MT5). This is more than enough since the boat journey lasts for a mere 45 min. According to a trader in Tangier: "If the police stop you, you just say it is a present for a friend to show that it is not a structural business. Of course you should hide the monkey, but if they catch you and they see it is not organized business they will let you go" (MT5). This quote demonstrates how smugglers try to hide their organized business and anticipate border controls. They dodge law enforcement by pretending that they do not know about the illegality and that the monkey is an incidental gift instead of an organized smuggling line.

Generally, the macaques are transported across the country by car/van or bus and cross the Strait of Gibraltar by ferry (Table 8.2). Although most seizures in the EU-TWIX database (>85 %) include one Barbary macaque, certain cases involve large quantities. Opportunistic small-scale traffickers or tourists usually smuggle one Barbary macaque hidden in suitcases or bags in their car and cross the border by ferry to the EU. Incidentally, tourists smuggle the monkeys by aircraft hidden in hand luggage.[20] According to a Barbary macaque trader in Tangier, this happens

---

[18]For instance, in 1974 a total of 2,330 smugglers were apprehended at the Spanish–Moroccan frontier (13 per day) and, in 1996, 18,794 people were arrested for drug trafficking.

[19]Women may smuggle macaques on the body because they are not searched according to a former smuggler (MU2).

[20]For instance, during a routine check of freight at Zaventem Airport (Belgium) one Barbary macaque from Morocco was found, October 8, 2010 (EU-TWIX database).

Table 8.2 Methods for transporting Barbary macaques

Transport	Modus operandi
Transport over land by car/van	Anesthetized monkeys hidden in suitcases, bags, on the body, under a car seat or in special compartments in vehicles
Transport over land by bus	Anesthetized monkeys hidden in suitcases or bags in the luggage department of buses
Transport by sea by ferry	The car/van in which the monkeys are hidden is transported by ferry to the EU
Transport by air	Anesthetized monkeys hidden in hand luggage

only occasionally: "Generally the monkeys are smuggled by car or lorry through the Strait of Gibraltar. Then the chances of being caught are almost zero" (MT5). However, another trader in Marrakesh described in detail how an Indian woman was caught smuggling a Barbary macaque in her suitcase at the airport of Marrakesh (MS3). More organized forms of smuggling could include several anesthetized monkeys being hidden in cars or trucks. For instance, six Barbary macaques were confiscated at the border between Hungary and Serbia in 2012 (ME1) (Illustration 8.3).

A distinction can be made between three types of smugglers (Table 8.3). Firstly, tourists who buy a macaque and smuggle the monkey to keep it as a pet back home or to reduce the costs of the holiday by reselling it. Respondents explained that this

Illustration 8.3 Six seized macaques, 2012

Table 8.3 Types of Barbary macaque smugglers

Type	Method	Purpose of business
Tourist—usually family with children	Hide the monkey in their camper	To keep the monkey as a pet
Opportunistic lorry driver	Hide the monkey(s) between licit merchandise	Additional income
Border-crossing smuggler	Hide the monkey in their car or in bags	Main business
Smuggler in criminal network	Hide the monkey in special compartments in their vehicle	Major business

often involves a family with children on holiday in Morocco, usually travelling with a camper van (MM2; MT10). "The French, Belgians and Spanish are keen to bring a nice monkey pet as a companion for their children" (MM2). The second type consists of lorry drivers between Morocco and European countries who are involved in the illegal transfer of a large variety of products, including smuggling monkeys, to earn additional income. A trader in Marrakesh explained his symbiotic relationship with a lorry driver who hides monkeys between his legitimate trade: "He is my friend. He works as a truck driver between Morocco and European countries. He hides these small monkeys quite easily between the loads of his truck. He knows how to do this because of his experience in border-crossing" (MT5). The third type consists of locals in northern Morocco and southern Spain who make money by smuggling goods between the two continents. As explained at the beginning of this section, for a long time smuggling has been a part of life in the northern Rif and people specialize in smuggling contraband across the border. There are also European smugglers that specifically target the smuggling of monkeys and are part of a relatively large network. This latter type will be explained in more detail in Sect. 8.11.

The process of smuggling regularly takes place with the collaboration of legal actors, such as customs officers. A convicted drug trafficker with friends in the 'monkey business' explained that customs officers could be easily bribed for around 200–500 Dirham (€20–50) (MO1). If customs officers cannot be bribed, there is always the possibility that they do not want to confiscate monkeys, out of a lack of priority or no shelter being available (ME1). Several respondents confirmed this by pointing out the possibilities to offer bribes at the border.

8.9 Business and the Informal Economy

The illegal trade in monkeys cannot be understood without the context of the substantial part played by the informal economy in Morocco. This term represents all the activities that are not officially registered and counted, but nevertheless provide many jobs. This may be both informal jobs and small private businesses (e.g. street vending, repairs) and the illegal trade in commodities such as hashish

(Bovenkerk and Fijnaut 1995). The illegal trade in animals also takes place in the informal Moroccan economy. Generally, the traders of Barbary macaques sell their macaques, sometimes visibly, sometimes hidden, on market stalls in the *souks*. The trade is usually out of sight of the government. Regularly the sellers are registered animal shopkeepers and use their shop as cover for the illegal trade.

In the latter case, these domestic traders are pet shopkeepers involved in the legal and illegal animal trade. Local traders do sell the monkeys, similar to Russian caviar shops that sell legal and illegal caviar, in their pet shops in cities such as Tangier and Nador (MM1; MM2). Several authors highlight that this interdependence is characteristic of the illegal trade in wildlife (e.g. Cook et al. 2002; Naylor 2004; Lyons and Natusch 2011). Especially in the Moroccan informal economy the symbiotic interrelationship between the underworld and upperworld is not uncommon. While in the wildlife trade animals or animal products (e.g. caviar) are regularly laundered by companies (Lyons and Natusch 2011), so-called green-collar crimes, the majority of the traded monkeys in this business are strictly illegal. However, legal animal traders use opportunities to trade Barbary macaques under the counter to earn additional profits. The *collaboration* between animal traders, middlemen or poachers is effective due to mutual benefits (Passas 2002). Visits to several Moroccan *souks* demonstrated that Barbary macaques are for sale by pet shopkeepers or there are possibilities to arrange the provision of macaques on demand in Tangier, Oujda, Marrakech, Fez and Nador. Many pet shopkeepers showed pictures of their macaques in cages in the backyards of their houses (e.g. personal observation, March 17, 2013, Marrakesh; 24 April 2013, Tangier; 26 April 2013, Nador).

Barbary macaques are offered for sale for around €200–250 by traders in several large Moroccan cities. This takes place on a regular basis. For instance, a trader in Tangier explained during our meeting: "I just sold one monkey yesterday, but there are two more for sale. (…) Different people work for me to catch the monkeys in Azrou and then I keep the monkeys in my house in Tangier city. (…) On Monday a European guy with a lorry will pick up three ordered monkeys" (MS5). Simultaneously, another trader in Tangier sold a macaque to a European lady and later on the same day he showed pictures of a larger macaque for sale (personal observation, April 25, 2013).

A distinction can be made between different traders in Barbary macaques. First, opportunistic trade usually takes place by European tourists buying one macaque at a *souk* or along the road (e.g. Azrou or Oudja) directly from a dealer or orders a macaque from an animal broker (e.g. Casablanca and Fez). In the latter case the trader orders one or two macaques from the intermediary, who then arranges for these monkeys to be caught by a harvest group within a couple of days. The tourist smuggles the macaque in a van across the Strait of Gibraltar or incidentally by plane to Europe. While other studies (e.g. Van Lavieren 2008) refer to European Moroccans as consumers or perpetrators, this could not be confirmed by this study. Second, traders in the major outlets in Morocco order 4–10 macaques every 2–3 months. Their intermediary arranges for the ordered monkeys to be caught by a harvest group and they are then transferred from Azrou to Oujda, Tangier and Marrakesh.

Third, European organized traders driving on a structural basis every 2–3 times a month to Morocco (Marrakesh, Oujda and Tangier) to buy 2–6 macaques. They smuggle the macaques with a (company) van across the Strait of Gibraltar to Europe. Sometimes they have orders from consumers and sometimes the monkeys are sold to other traders in Europe (MT2; MT4; MT5; MT10; MU3; ME1).

Although opportunists generally trade in macaques for small-scale business purposes, it also occurs that systematic trade starts with an occasional purchase, which then develops into a more structural trade line over many years (MT5; MT10). "They ask their friends in France if they are interested in a monkey as well and come back to get more monkeys and sell them then to their friends. (…) This was the beginning of a profitable trade line" (MT10). These opportunists see the lucrative nature of the business and start to search for potential buyers over a wide area. Then they make clear agreements about the number of monkeys needed and a new trade line is established. This example demonstrates how a relatively small trade line can transform into a well-organized business.

8.10 The Monkey Route

Due to its strategic location and relatively close intercontinental border crossing, the Strait of Gibraltar traditionally operates as a gateway for the illegal wildlife trade from Africa to the EU (Cowdrey 2002; Highfield and Bayley 1996).[21] The Strait of Gibraltar, on the border of Morocco and Spain, is used for the illegal trade in Barbary macaques to Europe as well, as confirmed by seizures of Barbary macaques mainly from ports in Spain.[22]

According to multiple respondents, Azrou and its surroundings (Middle Atlas) is the main centre of the illegal trade in Barbary macaques (e.g. MT1; MT4; ME1; MS1; MS3), with structural orders (4–10 macaques every 2 months) from Tangier, Marrakesh, Oujda, Casablanca and Fez for the retail trade (MF1; MF2; MT7; MT3; MT4; MT5; MT7; MM1). According to a (former) trader around 200 macaques are currently being captured in the Azrou area for trade (MT9), which confirms the estimation based on the statistics (Fig. 8.1).[23]

Map 8.1 presents the generic trade routes of Barbary macaques. Most macaques are transported to Tangier where every 45 min a ferry departs to Tarifa and Algeciras in Spain. Several pet shops and animal traders arrange for macaques on demand, even more than 50 annually (MT5; MT10; MS5). At Djemaa el-Fna Square in the heart of Marrakesh approximately 10 Barbary macaques are present daily for

[21]Regularly spur-thighed tortoises (Znari et al. 2005; Shipp 2002), Mediterranean chameleons (Bergin and Nijman 2014) and African grey parrots are traded from Morocco, as confirmed by seizures (EU-TWIX database).

[22]CITES Belgium, France, Italy, the Netherlands and Seprona Guardia Civil, 2013.

[23]Although several respondents pointed to Azrou as the centre of the illegal trade, there are indications that it is moving to other areas in the Middle Atlas, such as Béni-Mellal (MP2; MT10).

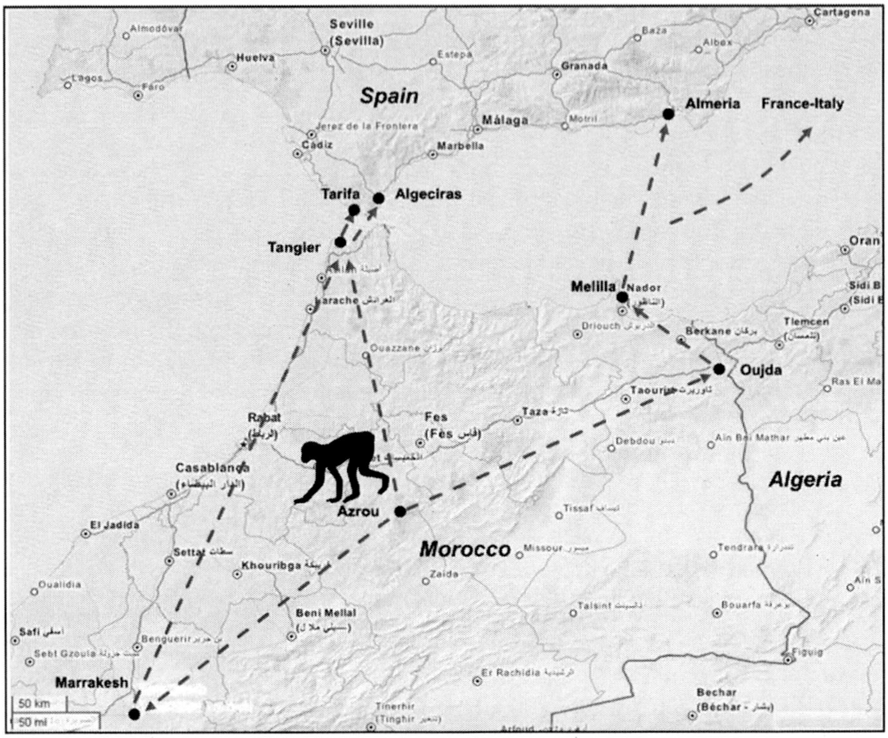

Map 8.1 Smuggling routes for Barbary macaques. *Source* Interviews and personal analyses of confiscations in the EU

entertainment and sale. According to conversations with the sellers, more than 30 macaques are sold every year in the square (MS2; MS3; MT4). To Oujda, near the Algerian border, there is a structural trade in Barbary macaques. Between 50 and 80 macaques are sold every year in Oujda. From there the monkeys are smuggled via Melilla to Spain and via Oran (Algeria) to Spain, France and probably Italy (MT7; MO4). While at the beginning of 2013 the open trade in Barbary macaques seemed to have disappeared in Casablanca and Fez, there are still possibilities to arrange for this by making an inquiry with intermediaries (MT3; MT9; MM1).

From these destinations European traders or tourists buy the macaques and smuggle them to Europe (Map 8.1). Based on data from interviews with (former) poachers of and traders in Barbary macaques, from Morocco the macaques are largely smuggled by coastal ferry to (mainly) Spain, France or Italy or incidentally by air to other (EU member) countries (MT2; MT4; MT5; MT7; MT10; MS2; MS4). A trader in Azrou underlined the major outlets in Europe: "Most of the trade in monkeys is intended for Spain, France or Italy, but we also have clients from other European countries such as the Netherlands, Germany and Belgium" (M10). The lion's share of the confiscations in the EU were in Spain. The confiscated macaques in Spain, between 2006 and 2012, were captured in the ports of Algeciras (27), Cadiz (14), Alicante (13) and Melilla (10).[24] The common smuggling route is by road and ferry through the ports of Tangier, Ceuta and Melilla to Tarifa, Cadiz, Algeciras, Almeria and Alicante in Spain (MU1; MU2; MU3; MT1; MT7; MT10; MS3; MM1). Another trade line is from Oujda to Oran in Algeria and then to Alicante and even Marseille in France (MT10; MO4). A trader and seller in Tangier explained that: "Tangier is preferred because in Ceuta you will have to pass through border controls twice. Fools will do that!" (MT5). This is in contrast to Melilla that is preferred above Nador because it would be a relatively easy to get the monkeys across the border. Both Ceuta and Melilla are Spanish enclaves in the north of Morocco.

On the other side of the Strait of Gibraltar, the Schengen treaty provides trade lines to other EU countries with very limited border controls (Cowdrey 2002). This is illustrated by seizures of Barbary macaques in Spain (102), France (28), Belgium (21), Italy (5) and the Netherlands (3) between 2006 and 2010. According to several traders, the macaques are mainly transported within the EU to France, Italy and Spain (MT1; MT2; MT3; MT4; MT5; MT7; MT10). This international operation seems to require a certain degree of criminal organization.

8.11 Colliding Criminal Networks in Morocco

Previous research (e.g. Fa 1983; Van Lavieren 2008) indicated that the trade in Barbary macaques was loosely based on the tourist industry. Principally this means that European tourists would purchase macaques during their summer holiday at local markets in Morocco. Indeed, many respondents in this research referred to opportunists, usually European tourists, who buy and smuggle one monkey to keep as a pet back home, or small-scale traders who reduce the costs of their holiday by reselling the monkey. According to a trader in Djemaa el-Fna Square in Marrakesh: "Regularly I sell them [monkeys] to European tourists who fell in love with an infant monkey. (…) They would like to keep them as pets or want to rescue them from their use in entertainment" (MT4). An animal trader in Oujda explained that European tourists go on holiday to the seaside resort of Saïdia and every time the same people bring back monkeys to sell in Europe. Therefore, monkeys are offered for sale along the road during summertime in the Rif (MO4). This is not illogical in the context of the increasing numbers of foreign visitors in Morocco, around 10 million each year, mostly from Western Europe. These tourists are probably responsible for a substantial illegal trade in live animals and their products (Esmond and Chryssee 2012).

---

[24]Confiscations by the Seprona Guardia Civil, Spain, between 2006–2012.

Nevertheless, in this case study, criminal networks with a high degree of organization have also been found to be involved in the illegal trade in Barbary macaques. Well-organized, semi-loose networks that use sophisticated methods to trade in large orders of monkeys and earn relatively high profits. The contraband is moved along a line of contacts (a chain), where key aspects (e.g. the smuggling or trading process) of the movement may be overseen by one or two central players (Morselli 2009; Elliott 2009). The organized traders have a network with several legal and illegal actors to transfer the Barbary macaques on a structural basis many times a year as a financial business. The illegal trade in Barbary macaques seems to be carried out by a chain of actors who collect, buy, transport and sell animals.

There appears to be a clear communication network with appointments and tasks in the more organized form of the illegal trade in Barbary macaques. Generally, the illegal trader contacts the middleman or poacher by mobile phone to pass on the order, before travelling to Morocco (or instructs a smuggler). When he returns to Europe, after the deal, he calls again to confirm that the mission has been accomplished (MT3; MS3). A trader in Azrou underlined the large orders and the need for professionalized business: "Sometimes they asked me to arrange 20 or even 30 monkeys. These are big operations that really need a high level of organization! In such cases, a secured network is necessary" (MT9). For many years the sale of monkeys in public was allowed in Morocco, but since the late 2000s open sales are no longer tolerated; there are examples of traffickers being arrested and imprisoned for months. According to several traders, the deterrence of imprisonment shifts the business to the dark circuit; nowadays the major deals in Azrou are made in the late evening to avoid the attention of the police (MT5; MT7; MT9).

Traders in Marrakesh draw attention to a (criminal) network that has recently been established between Moroccan and European traders. Their operations are based on a structural basis with the involvement of several people in the chain. Once every 2 months the European crime group gives an order by phone to traders in Marrakesh. In Azrou the macaques are captured by poachers and transported to Marrakesh, where couriers are ready to smuggle the anesthetized macaques hidden in suitcases with a van across the Strait of Gibraltar. When they arrive in Europe they call to indicate that the mission has been accomplished. Subsequently, the monkeys are transported to a domestic trader in the country of destination (MT4). Another trader in Azrou established a trade line to Italy: "I worked with two Italian guys who took 6 macaques to Italy every 3 months and sold them over there. The collaboration was definitively successful and we made substantial profits" (MT9). These are just single examples of illegal trade on a structural basis that is carried out by a chain of actors who poach, trade, transport and sell animals under the control of central key players (see Fig. 8.3 for other flows).

Apparently, there is a regular movement of captured macaques smuggled by road from the rural area of Azrou to urban areas, such as Tangier, Oujda and Marrakesh. From there direct lines to Europe are organized by different groups of entrepreneurs. Each actor has his own task, specialty and profit within this network. The role of a courier between countries in a semi-loose network is demonstrated by a former Spanish smuggler, who had been employed to transfer monkeys multiple

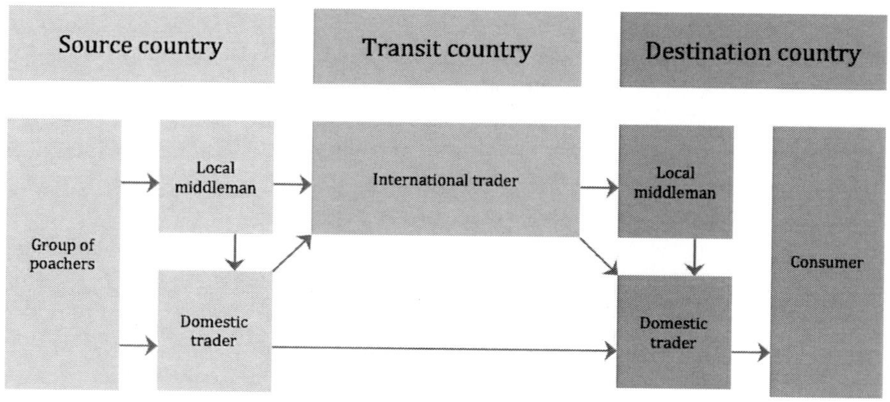

Fig. 8.3 Supply chain (simplified) of the illegal trade in Barbary macaques

times a month from a trader in Tangier (Morocco) to a trader in Algeciras (Spain). Upon arrival the animals were transferred to Northern Spain for sale. "For a period of 8 years my friend smuggled monkeys bought in Tangier to a trader in Algeciras (…) Eventually, he bought a house in Spain with the profits of €1,000 per monkey" (MU1). As mentioned in Sect. 8.8, the couriers may also be Western lorry drivers. A trader in Tangier explained that he works together with a lorry driver who regularly smuggles monkeys to Europe: "He hides the monkeys between his stuff. The border control is not able to find them. Yes, he is someone who knows what to do and what not to do" (MT5). After the smuggling operation, the monkeys are sold at the final destination: A Spanish trader near Barcelona had several monkeys under his wings in 2008. In these flourishing business times, a consumer could choose between six young macaques (ME1). The degree of organization is visible by the fact that it is even possible for the organizations to enter into a trade agreement to deliver more than 50 monkeys to Europe each year: "These monkeys can be delivered to your doorstep in the Netherlands with the help of a lorry driver I work with" (MT5).

While each actor has his own task and profit within the network, the social organization is semi-structured and flexible based on the interaction between actors (Morselli 2009). The actors react quickly to the demand and, sometimes, additional intermediaries or smugglers in the chain are needed to fuel this demand. While in the trading areas of Tangier and Melilla organized crime related to drug trafficking (e.g. the Tangiers Cartel) has been identified (e.g. UNODC 2003), the informants did not recognize the involvement of classical Moroccan crime syndicates, Moroccan *Res Kbir* (رأس كبير-), in the illegal trade in Barbary macaques. The networks are more flexible and fluid instead of hierarchical (Williams 2001). There are shared grounds in the interaction between actors and collective interests. Sometimes the trade is based on opportunistic projects, while in other situations structural trade lines are established and are coordinated by key persons (Morselli 2009).

Nevertheless, the Strait of Gibraltar is well-known, next to the illegal trade in wildlife, for both the illegal drugs trade and migration from Morocco to the EU. This kind of parallel trafficking of illegal wildlife, drugs and immigrants involves moving environmental contraband along the same smuggling routes used for other illegal commodities (Elliott 2009; UNODC 2010). Trade routes for other forms of crime, such as drugs trafficking and illegal immigration, are nowadays more often used for the illegal trade in wildlife (Europol 2011). A trader in Oujda underlined that the illegal trade in Barbary macaques is interrelated with the illicit trade in counterfeit products: "Counterfeit clothes and shoes are smuggled hidden in the car along with the monkeys. By using these touring buses from France we can cross the border without problems" (MT7). In addition, the trade may also be linked to the illegal trade in drugs. According to Van Lavieren (2004) Barbary macaques are incidentally used to smuggle drugs (cannabis) across the border to Europe and it can be expected that the monkeys are sold in Europe as a by-product. Although the interviews revealed no substantiated interdependence between the illegal trade in Barbary macaques and other forms of crime, there are several examples that highlight this interconnectedness.

The networks involved are driven by situational, rational and cultural incentives. Morocco seems to function as an important source country and transit hub of the illegal wildlife trade from Africa to the EU. The geographic location between two continents with the Strait of Gibraltar as a close border crossing underlines the opportunities provided by the infrastructure. The trading areas for monkeys in the northern Rif (Tangier, Nador, Oujda) are well-known smuggling hubs (Parnell and Kane 2003; Bovenkerk and Fijnaut 1995), where criminal entrepreneurs invest in real estate, such as luxury villas, marinas and hotels (Bovenkerk and Fijnaut 1995). Several traders highlighted this geographic advantage for other illegal wildlife trades in Morocco too (e.g. MT4; MT5). Leopard skins are bought in wildlife markets in Mali, rolled in carpets and smuggled through Morocco into the European Union (MS1) and spur-thighed tortoises are collected from the Middle Atlas and smuggled in boxes of 150–200 animals across the border (MT4). Illustration 8.4 shows various wildlife for sale at the souk in Fez.

In addition, the rational incentives based on the relatively low priority by law enforcement, relatively low sentences and rising prices on the black market are attractive to criminal networks (Zimmerman 2003; Schneider 2008; Lawson and Vines 2014). The traders, collectors and dealers are, from this point of view, intentional exploiters; they are aware of the profits of illegal hunting, trading and selling (Herbig 2010). Since the population of Barbary macaques is as few as 5,000–6,000 individuals left, the price may quickly increase in the near future due to their scarcity (Courchamp et al. 2006). Currently, the prices for other primates, such as gorillas, have already been as high as $40,000 (Van Uhm 2012a). The illegal wildlife trade is driven by high profit margins and the high prices paid for rare species, such as the Barbary macaque. While in Morocco the price for a monkey increases during the process from the poacher (€50–100), intermediaries (€120–150) to the trader (€200–250), at the end of the chain the consumer in Europe will pay 10 times its original price, €2,000 for the same Barbary macaque

Illustration 8.4 Various wildlife for sale, Fez, Morocco 2013

(MT1; MT4; MT5; MT7; MT9; MT10). Assuming that the profit from the illegal trade in 50 monkeys per year would amount to around €100,000, the potential profits to be made would be around 42 times the minimum yearly wage by Moroccan standards (United States Department of State 2012). The incentives for the illegal trade are thus obvious.

Finally, traders referred to strong family ties and connections with acquaintances (MT3; MT7; MT10). For instance, the Berber populations in the poaching area in Azrou and trading and smuggling areas in the Rif in northern Morocco may contribute to the use of existing informal cultural relationships to establish trade lines. Bovenkerk et al. (2003) described how shared ethnic or cultural components can be important factors in the formation of criminal networks. In this case, the ethnic groups of Berbers have been marginalized within Morocco and resources are scarce (Hoffman 2008). According to several respondents, informal relationships between Moroccan poachers, middlemen and traders are regularly culturally grounded. Furthermore, corruption as a social issue that attracts criminal networks in Morocco plays an important role.[25] Morocco "has been spared weapons of mass destruction, but it is being destroyed by weapons of mass corruption" is an often-heard statement in the kingdom. According to the interviewees corrupt police officers, customs officials and forest rangers are sometimes part of a criminal network in the illegal trade in Barbary macaques (MT2; MT9). The illegal trade probably started with misused certificates by officials and presently forest rangers and official guides obtain commission if they refer potential buyers and customs officers can be bribed for 200–500 Dirham (€20–50). There are even customs officials who confiscate monkeys and keep them for themselves. This culture of corruption results in a complex array of concerns and powers, which makes it more difficult to tackle this illegal trade (Siegel 2011).

However, certain Western countries point their finger at 'those' corrupt source countries in Africa (Boekhout van Solinge 2010). But blaming only the source countries ignores the other side of the market. The trade is dependent on the cultural demand for extraordinary exotic animals in Europe. In Europe the rarity of a species determines its value on the black market and subsequently the demand (Siegel and Van Uhm 2014). This progressive rarity and the parallel rising value on the black market may be an important driving force for overexploitation by illegal entrepreneurs (Courchamp et al. 2006). Factors such as scarcity (5,000–6,000 Barbary macaques remain in the wild), relatively high prices in the EU (€2,000 per monkey), no border controls within the EU (one only has to pass through one border to enter the EU), corruption and limited control in the poaching areas result in an attractive market for criminal networks.

8.12 Environmental Harms and Zoonotic Diseases

With a population of only 5,000–6,000 Barbary macaques left, the survival of this species is highly debatable. The illegally traded 200 Barbary macaques each year do have a serious impact on the remaining population, especially since the poachers

[25] According to Transparency International (2009) 58 % of households which had contact with the police in 2008 reported paying bribes.

focus on youngsters. Camperio Ciani and Mouna (2006) underline that due to the poaching of infant macaques the adult population is not adequately replaced. If this trend continues the population has little opportunities to recover (Van Lavieren 2008). In many small populations of endangered species reproduction and survival are limited due to mate shortages or a limited genetic variety. This ensures that a small population can extirpate at a higher rate than expected (Courchamp et al. 2006).

The largest population (around 70 %) of Barbary macaques lives in the Middle Atlas of Morocco (Camperio Ciani et al. 2005; Mouna et al. 1999). This cedar forest is an endangered ecosystem with several endemic and rare plant and animal species.[26] Generally, monkeys are important players in an ecosystem as disseminators of seeds (Kellert and Wilson 1993). The Barbary macaque disperses the seeds of many plants (Herrera 1995; Ménard and Vallet 1996; Drucker 1984), is the prey for golden jackals, red foxes and eagles and hosts a number of ecto- and endoparasites (Jinn 2011). According to the IUCN (2009: 1): "The loss of significant numbers of Barbary Macaques can have wide repercussions throughout the ecosystem. (…) Macaques are vital to disperse seeds in the forest. Without them the very composition of the forest would change dramatically". From this ecocentric perspective, the disappearance of the Barbary macaque may result in an unbalanced ecosystem and the extirpation of other species as well.

Furthermore, the biocentric harms to individual animals are substantial during poaching, trade and at the final destination (Sollund 2011; Nurse 2013; Wyatt 2013). Although the monkeys are drugged with syrup to smuggle them across the border, a high stress level is caused during the hunt where dogs are not incidentally used to attack the monkeys with youngsters. Consequently, the youngsters will live without their family in a human (urban) environment. These monkeys are kept as pets in cages far away from their natural environment without opportunities to exhibit natural behaviour.

Finally, anthropocentric harms include not only the risk of being bitten or aggression by the Barbary macaque towards the pet keeper, but also a potential threat to health in the context of the distribution of zoonotic diseases. Initially, most owners form emotional bonds with their infant pet macaques. This may be strengthened by physical and behavioural similarities with human babies. While for up to 2 years the macaques remain physically and emotionally dependent on their pet keepers, most macaques exhibit aggressive behaviour as they mature. Especially males tend to become aggressive, but also female macaques bite to establish dominance which plays an important role in the social hierarchy (Ostrowski et al. 1998). Several studies confirm the aggressiveness of macaques towards humans (e.g. Fuentes and Gamerl 2005; Jones-Engel et al. 2001). A study found that in 44 % of cases where macaques were kept as pets, children were bitten versus 20 %

[26]Other mixed cedar forests can only be found in small parts of Lebanon, Cyprus and in Anatolia in Turkey. The last populations of Berber lion and leopard were seen in the cedar forest ecosystem in the Middle Atlas and there are still small populations of lynx, hyena and Berber deer (Camperio Ciani and Mouna 2006).

of adults (Ostrowski et al.1998). This makes aggressive behaviour by macaques the main reason for pet owners getting rid of their macaques (Kranendonk et al. 2013; Jones-Engel et al. 2001). In addition, B virus infection is highly prevalent in adult macaques (80–90 %) and may cause a fatal meningoencephalitis, a disease of the central nervous system, in humans. Macaque bites or scratches may result in B virus disease in humans (Ostrowski 1998). These monkey bites may also threaten humans in the context of Ebola outbreaks. The Ebola outbreak in 2014 has been traced back to the trade in the meat of infected African fruit bats and monkeys. The global effect of this zoonotic disease is reflected by thousands of deaths in a short period of time (WHO 2015) and even Europeans have become infected and died as a result of the virus (EFSA 2014). While no infected Barbary macaques were recorded, the potential spread of zoonotic diseases may presumably include future concerns.

8.13 Summary

The exclusivity of monkeys as pets, their similarities to humans in the context of parental skills and anthropomorphism, but mainly their entertaining use drives the demand market. The condoned hunting of Barbary macaques in the 1990s provided opportunities for trading illegally in monkeys and, subsequently, the development of networks involved in this 'monkey business'. Although it was formally believed that the trade was loosely based on the tourist industry, a relatively high degree of (criminal) organization was found in this study on the illegal trade in Barbary macaques. Sophisticated methods combined with high profits and large numbers of Barbary macaques, coordinated by well-organized, semi-loose networks characterize this form of the illegal wildlife trade. The macaques are poached by the poor locals from Berber villages and are delivered at the doorstep of relatively wealthy European citizens. In the informal Moroccan economy social ties play a major role in the dispersion of the trade and money flows freely between pet shopkeepers and illegal entrepreneurs. This illegal trade contributes to a substantial decline in the wild population and the environmental harms are significant with a small population of as few as 5,000–6,000 Barbary macaques that remain in fragmented parts of Morocco and Algeria.

References

Akers, R. L. (2013). *Criminological theories: Introduction and evaluation*. London: Routledge.

Allela, L., Bourry, O., & Pouillot, R. (2014). *Ebola virus disease and household pets*. Geneva: WHO.

Bailey, J. F., Henneberg, M., Colson, I. B., Ciarallo, A., Hedges, R. E., & Sykes, B. (1999). Monkey business in Pompeii-unique find of a juvenile Barbary macaque skeleton in Pompeii identified using osteology and ancient DNA techniques. *Molecular Biology and Evolution, 16*, 1410–1414.

Bergin, D., & Nijman, V. (2014). Open, Unregulated Trade in Wildlife in Morocco's Markets. *Traffic Bulletin, 26* (1): 65–70.

Bierman, J., & Smith, C. (2000). *Fire in the night: Wingate of Burma, Ethiopia and Zion*. New York: Random House.

Boekhout van Solinge, T. (2010). Deforestation crimes and conflicts in the Amazon. *Critical Criminology, 18*(4), 263–277.

Bonger, W. A. (1932). *Inleiding tot de Criminologie*. Haarlem: Erven Bohn.

Bovenkerk, F., & Fijnaut, C. J. C. F. (1995). *Inzake opsporing; enquête opsporingsmethoden, Deelonderzoek VIII Georganiseerde criminaliteit in Nederland: Over allochtone en buitenlandse criminele groepen*. Den Haag: SDU.

Bovenkerk, F., Siegel, D., & Zaitch, D. (2003). Organized crime and ethnic reputation manipulation. *Crime, Law and Social Change, 39*(1), 23–38.

Bradshaw, J., & Paul, E. (2010). Could empathy for animals have been an adaptation in the evolution of Homo sapiens? *Animal Welfare, 19*(1), 107–112.

Broad, S., Luxmoore, R., & Jenkins, M. (Eds.). (1988). *Significant trade in wildlife: Mammals* (Vol. 1). Cambridge: IUCN.

Burger, J., & Hemmer, H. (2006). Urgent call for further breeding of the relic zoo population of the critically endangered Barbary lion (Panthera leo leo Linnaeus 1758). *European Journal of Wildlife Research, 52*, 54–58.

Butynski, T. M., Cortes, J., Waters, S., Fa, J., Hobbelink, M. E., Van Lavieren, E., et al. (2008). *Macaca sylvanus. IUCN Red List of Threatened Species*. Gland: IUCN.

Camperio Ciani, A. (1986). La Macaca sylvanus in Marocco: soprav- vivenza o estinzione. Osservazioni personali e dati storico-demog- rafici. *Antropologia contemporanea, 9*(2), 117–132.

Camperio Ciani, A. (2003). Antropol. *Mediterran, 1*, 57–68.

Camperio Ciani, A., & Mouna, M. (2006). *Human and environmental causes of the rapid decline of Macaca sylvanus in the Middle Atlas of Morocco. The Barbary Macaque: Biology, management and conservation*. Nottingham: Nottingham University Press.

Camperio Ciani, A., Palentini, L., Arahou, M., Martinoli, L., Capiluppi, C., & Mouna, M. (2005). Population decline of Macaca sylvanus in the middle atlas of Morocco. *Biological Conservation, 121*, 635–641.

Cato, J. C., & Brown, C. L. (2003). *Marine ornamental species: Collection, culture, and conservation*. Ames: Iowa State Press.

Chapman, F. A., Fitz-Coy, S. A., Thunberg, E. M., & Adams, C. M. (1997). United States of America trade in ornamental fish. *Journal of the World Aquaculture Society, 28*(1), 1–10.

Chomel, B. B., Belotto, A., & Meslin, F. X. (2007). Wildlife, exotic pets, and emerging zoonoses. *Emerging Infectious Diseases, 13*(1), 6.

CITES. (2011). *Selection of the long-tailed macaque (Macaca fasciculatis) for inclusion in the review of significant trade* (Resolution Conf. 12.8 [REV. COP13]).

Cook, D., Roberts, M., & Lowther, J. (2002). *The international wildlife trade and organised crime: A review of the evidence and the role of the UK*. Wolverhampton: University of Wolverhampton.

Corbey, R. H. A., & Theunissen, B. (1995). *Ape, man, apeman: Changing views since 1600*. Leiden: Department of Prehistory of Leiden University.

Courchamp, F., Angulo, E., Rivalan, P., Hall, R. J., Signoret, L., Bull, L., et al. (2006). Rarity value and species extinction: The anthropogenic allee effect. *PLoS Biology, 4*(12), e415.

Cowdrey, D. (2002). *Switching channels. Wildlife trade routes into Europe and the UK. A (Report WWF/Traffic)*. Wolverhampton: University of Wolverhampton.

Deag, J. M. (1977). Aggression and submission in monkey societies. *Animal Behaviour, 25*, 465–474.

Deag, J. M. (1984). Demography of the barbary macaque at Ain Kahla in the moroccan moyen atlas. In J. E. Fa (Ed.), *The barbary macaque* (pp. 113–133). New York: Springer.

Department for Environment, Food and Rural Affairs. (2009). *Code of practice for the welfare of privately kept non-human primates*. London: DEFRA.

Domalain, J. Y. (1977). *The animal connection. Confessions of an ex-wild animal trafficker*. London: Heinemann.
Drucker, G. R. (1984). The feeding ecology of the Barbary macaque and cedar forest conservation in the Moroccan Moyen Atlas. In J. E. Fa (Ed.), *The Barbary macaque* (pp. 135–164). New York: Springer.
Duarte-Quiroga, A., & Estrada, A. (2003). Primates as pets in Mexico City: An assessment of the species involved, source of origin, and general aspects of treatment. *American Journal of Primatology, 61*(2), 53–60.
EFSA. (2014). *An update on the risk of transmission of Ebola Virus (EBOV) via the food chain*. Parma: European Food Safety Authority.
Elliot, L. (2009). Combating transnational environmental crime: 'Joined up' thinking about transnational networks. *Eco-crime and justice: Essays on environmental crime* (pp. 55–77). Turin: UNICRI.
Endcap. (2012). *Wild pets in the European Union. An information document provided to the European Commission, the European Parliament, the European Council and the Council of Europe*. Horsham: Endcap.
Engebretson, M. (2006). The welfare and suitability of parrots as companion animals: A review. *Animal Welfare, 15*(3), 263–276.
Esmond, M., & Chryssee, P.M. (2012). Tourists underwrite Morocco's illegal trade in wildlife artefacts. *Swara*, 16–24.
Europol. (2011). *Organised crime threat assessment (OCTA)*. The Hague: Europol.
Fa, J. E. (1981). The apes on the Rock. *Oryx, 16*(1), 73–76.
Fa, J. E. (1983). The Barbary macaque—the future. *Oryx, 17*(02), 62–67.
Fa, J. E. (1984). Habitat distribution and habitat preference in Barbary Macaques (Macaca sylvanus). *International Journal of Primatology, 5*, 273–286.
Fa, J. E., Menard, N., & Steward, P. J. (1984). The distribution and current status of the Barbary Macaque in North Africa. In J. E. Fa (Ed.), *The Barbary Macaque. A case study in conservation*. New York: Plenum Press.
Ferrell, J. (2013). Tangled up in green. Cultural criminology and green criminology. In N. South & A. Brisman (Eds.), *Routledge international handbook of green criminology*. London: Routledge.
Fitzgerald, S. (1989). *International Wildlife Trade: Who's business is it?*. Washington: World Wildlife Fund.
Fox, R. (2006). Animal behaviours, post-human lives: Everyday negotiations of the animal-human divide in pet-keeping. *Social and Cultural Geography, 7*(4), 525–537.
Fuentes, A. (2007). Monkey and human interconnections: The wild, the captive, and the in-between. In R. Cassidy & M. Mullin (Eds.), *Where the wild things are now: Domestication reconsidered* (pp. 123–145). Oxford: Berg Publishers.
Fuentes, A. (2013). Pets, property, and partners: Macaques as commodities in the human-other primate interface. In Radhakrishna et al. (ed.). *The Macaque Connection: Coopertaion and conflict between humans and macaques*. New York: Springer.
Fuentes, A., & Gamerl, S. (2005). Disproportionate participation by age/sex classes in aggressive interactions between long-tailed macaques (Macaca fascicularis) and human tourists at Padangtegal monkey forest, Bali, Indonesia. *American Journal of Primatology, 66*(2), 197–204.
Gardner, M. B., & Luciw, P. A. (2008). Macaque models of human infectious disease. *ILAR Journal, 49*(2), 220–255.
Goodall, J. (2014). *Want to raise a chimp? Think again*. Retrieved from website.
Goudsmit, J., & Brandon-Jones, D. (1999). Mummies of olive baboons and Barbary macaques in the Baboon Catacomb of the Sacred Animal Necropolis at North Saqqara. *The Journal of Egyptian Archaeology, 85*, 45–53.
Green, A. (1999). *Animal underworld: Inside America's black market for rare and exotic species*. New York: PublicAffairs.
Gueguen, N., & Ciccotti, S. (2008). Domestic dogs as facilitators in social interaction: An evaluation of helping and courtship behaviors. *Anthrozoös, 21*, 339–349.

Haut Commissariat aux Eaux et Forêts et à la Lutte Contre la Désertification. (2012). *Conservation action plan for the Barbary macaque (Macaca sylvanus) in Morocco.* Rabat: Eaux et Forêts.

Herbig, J. (2010). The illegal trade as a form of conservation crime: A South Africa criminological investigation. In R. White (Ed.), *Global environmental harm. Criminological Perspectives.* Cullompton: Willan Publishing.

Herrera, C. M. (1995). Plant-vertebrate seed dispersal systems in the Mediterranean: Ecological, evolutionary, and historical determinants. *Annual Review of Ecology and Systematics, 26*, 705–727.

Herzog, H. A. (2014). Biology, culture, and the origins of pet-keeping. *Animal Behavior and Cognition, 1*(3), 296–308.

Highfield, A. C., & Bayley, J. R. (1996). The trade in tortoise-derived souvenir products in Morocco. *Traffic Bulletin, 16*(1), 33–35.

Hoffman, K. E. (2008). *We share walls: Language, land, and gender in Berber Morocco.* Hoboken: Wiley.

Hughes, J. D. (2003). Europe as consumer of exotic biodiversity: Greek and Roman times. *Landscape Research, 28*(1), 21–31.

Ilahiane, H., & Sherry, J. (2008). Joutia: street vendor entrepreneurship and the informal economy of information and communication technologies in Morocco 1. *The Journal of North African Studies, 13*(2), 243–255.

IUCN. (2009). *Deforestation spells doom for Barbary Macaque.* Gland: IUCN.

Jackson, W. G. F. (1987). *The rock of the Gibraltarians: A history of Gibraltar.* New Jersey: Fairleigh Dickinson University Press.

Janson, H. W. (1952). *Apes and Ape Lore: In the middle ages and the renaissance* (Vol. 20). London: Warburg Institute, University of London.

Jinn, J. (2011). *Ecosystem roles of the Barbary Macaque.* Ann Arbor: University of Michigan.

Jones-Engel, L., Engel, G. A., Schillaci, M. A., Babo, R., & Froehlich, J. (2001). Detection of antibodies to selected human pathogens among wild and pet macaques (Macaca tonkeana) in Sulawesi, Indonesia. *American Journal of Primatology, 54*(3), 171–178.

Kantha, S. S. (2014). Subhuman primates in Shakespeare's oeuvre. *Current Science, 106*(7), 1021.

Kellert, S. R., & Wilson, E. O. (1993). *The biophilia hypothesis.* Washington, DC: Island Press.

Kleemans, E. R., & Van de Bunt, H. G. (1999). The social embeddedness of organized crime. *Transnational Organized Crime, 5*(1), 19–36.

Kranendonk, G., van der Veen, M., & Huiskes, R. (2013). *Knock knock who's there? Analysis of AAP rescue data 2001–2012.* Almere: AAP.

Laufer, P. (2010). *Forbidden creatures. Inside the world of animals smuggling and exotic pets.* Guilford: Lyons Press.

Lawson, K., & Vines, A. (2014). *Global impacts of the illegal wildlife trade: The costs of crime, insecurity and institutional erosion.* London: Chatham House.

Lilly, A. A., & Mehlman, P. T. (1993). Conservation update on the Barbary macaque. I. Declining distribution and population size in Morocco. *American Journal of Primatology, 30*(4), 327.

Lindburg, D. G. (1980). *The Macaques: Studies in ecology, behavior, and evolution.* New York: Van Nostrand Reinhold.

Lyons, J. A., & Natusch, D. J. (2011). Wildlife laundering through breeding farms: Illegal harvest, population declines and a means of regulating the trade of green pythons (Morelia viridis) from Indonesia. *Biological Conservation, 144*(12), 3073–3081.

Mack, D., & Mittermeier, R. A. (1984). *The international primate trade.* Washington, DC: Traffic.

Majolo, B., van Lavieren, E., Maréchal, L., MacLarnon, A., Marvin, G., Qarro, M., & Semple, S. (2013). Out of Asia: The singular case of the Barbary macaque. In S. Radhakrishna, M. A. Huffman & S. Anindya (Eds.), *The macaque connection. Cooperation and conflict between humans and macaques.* New York: Springer.

McCormick, F. (1991). The dog in prehistoric and Early Christian Ireland. *Archaeology Ireland*, 7–9.

McDermott, W. C. (1936). The ape in Roman literature. *Transactions and Proceedings of the American Philological Association, 67*, 148–167.

McLennan. (2012). *Keeping of exotic animals: Welfare concerns. Import and keeping of exotic animals in the EU, 4–5 October 2012*. Brussels: Eurogroup for Animals.
McMurray, D. (2001). *In & out of Morocco. Smuggling and migration in a frontier boomtown*. London: Minneapolis.
Ménard, N., & Vallet, D. (1993). Dynamics of fission in a wild Barbary macaque group (Macaca sylvanus). *International Journal of Primatology, 14*(3), 479–500.
Ménard, N., & Vallet, D. (1996). Demography and ecology of Barbary macaques (Marara sylcanus) in two different habitats. In J. E. Fa & D. G. Lindburg (Eds.), *Evolution and ecology of macaque societies*. Cambridge: Cambridge University Press.
Modolo, L., Salzburger, W., & Martin, R. D. (2005). Phylogeography of Barbary macaques (Macaca sylvanus) and the origin of the Gibraltar colony. *Proceedings of the National Academy of Sciences, 102*, 7392–7397.
Morselli, C. (2009). *Inside criminal networks*. New York: Springer.
Mouna, M., & Camperio Ciani, A. (2006). *Distribution and demography of the Barbary Macaque (Macaca sylvanus L.) in the wild. The Barbary Macaque: Biology, management and conservation* (pp. 239–256). Nottingham: Nottingham University Press.
Mouna, M., Arahou, M., & Camperio Ciani, A. (1999). *A propos des populations du singe- magot (Macaca sylvan us L) dans le Moyen Atlas. Proceedings of the First International Conference on Biodiversity and Natural Resources Preservation*. Ifrane: Al Akawayn University Press.
Naylor, R. T. (2004). The underworld of ivory. *Crime, Law and Social Change, 42*(4–5), 261–295.
Nichol, J. (1987). *Animal smugglers*. New York: Facts on File Publications.
Nijman, V. (2010). An overview of international wildlife trade from Southeast Asia. *Biodiversity and Conservation, 19*, 1101–1114.
Nurse, A. (2013). *Animal harm: Perspectives on why people harm and kill animals*. Farnham: Ashgate.
Nyhus, P. J., Tilson, R. L., & Tomlinson, J. L. (2003). Dangerous animals in captivity: Ex situ tiger conflict and implications for private ownership of exotic animals. *Zoo Biology, 22*, 573–586.
Oates, J. F., Tutin, C. E. G., Humle, T., Wilson, M. L., Baillie, J. E. M., Balmforth, Z. et al. (2008). *Pan troglodytes: IUCN red list of threatened species (Version 2012.2.)*. Gland: IUCN.
O'Flaherty, B. A., & Shapiro, J. S. (2002). *Apes, essences, and races: What natural scientists believed about human variation, 1700–1900*. New York: Columbia University.
Ostrowski, S. R., Leslie, M. J., Parrott, T., Abelt, S., & Piercy, P. E. (1998). B-virus from pet macaque monkeys: An emerging threat in the United States? *Emerging Infectious Diseases, 4* (1), 117–121.
Parnell, P. C., & Kane, S. C. (Eds.). (2003). *Crime's power: Anthropologists and the ethnography of crime*. New York: Palgrave Macmillan.
Passas, N. (2002). Cross-border crime and the interface between legal and illegal actors. In P. C. van Duyne, K. von Lampe, & N. Passas (Eds.), *Upperworld and underworld in cross-border crime* (pp. 11–42). Nijmegen: Wolf Legal Publishers.
Perry, N. D., Hanson, B., Hobgood, W., Lopez, R. L., Okraska, C. R., Karem, K., et al. (2006). New invasive species in southern Florida: Gambian rat (Cricetomys gambianus). *Journal of Mammalogy, 87*, 262–264.
Radhakrishna, S., Huffman, M. A., & Sinha, A. (2012). *The Macaque connection: Cooperation and conflict between humans and macaque*. New York: Springer.
Reed, R. N. (2005). An ecological risk assessment of nonnative boas and pythons as potentially invasive species in the United States. *Risk Analysis, 25*, 753–766.
Ross, J.F. (2004). La forêt de l'Atlas menacée par les singes? *Courrier International No*. 712, 24–30 June, France.
Royaume du Maroc. (2012). *Conservation action plan for the Barbary macaque (Macaca sylvanus) in Morocco*. Amsterdam: MPC.
RSPCA. (2012). *Primates as pets: Is there a case for regulation?*. Horsham: RSPCA.
Ruggiero, V. (1996). *Organized and corporate crime in Europe: Offers that can't be refused*. Aldershot: Dartmouth.

Sanglim, S. (2014). *Orde Wingate: A man of genius 1903–1944*. Yorkshire: Pen and Sword Books.

Sax, B. (2001). *The mythical zoo. An encyclopedia of animals in world myth, legend and folklore*. Santa Barbara: ABC Clio.

Scheffrahn, W., Menard, N., Vallet, D., & Gaci, B. (1993). Ecology, demography, and population genetics of Barbary macaques in Algeria. *Primates, 34*(3), 381–394.

Schneider, J. L. (2008). Reducing the illicit trade in endangered wildlife: The market reduction approach. *Journal of Contemporary Criminal Justice, 24*, 274–295.

Serpell, J. (1996). *In the company of animals: A study of human-animal relationships*. Cambridge: Cambridge University Press.

Serpell, J. A. (2003). Anthropomorphism and anthropomorphic selection: Beyond the 'cute response'. *Society and Animals, 11*, 83–100.

Serpell, J. A., & Paul, E. S. (2011). Pets in the family: An evolutionary perspective. In C. A. Salmon & T. K. Shackelford (Eds.), *The Oxford Handbook of evolutionary family psychology*. New York: Oxford University Press.

Shaw, J. (2003). *Living with Michael Jackson*. Documentary, Granada Television.

Shipman, P. (2010). The animal connection and human evolution. *Current Anthropology, 51*, 519–538.

Shipp, A. (2002). Wildlife for sale in Marrakech, Morocco. *Traffic Bulletin, 19*(2), 65.

Siegel, D. (2011). Trafficking of 'conflict diamonds'. In C. Smith, S. Zhang, & R. Barberet (Eds.), *Routledge handbook of criminology*. London: Routledge.

Siegel, D., & Van Uhm, D. P. (2014). Zwarte kaviaar. Criminele netwerken, illegale handel en de bedreiging van de steur. *Justitiële verkenningen, 30*(2), 54–70.

Simmel, G. (1978). *The philosophy of money*. London: Routledge.

Smith, J. E. (2011). *Stolen world: A tale of reptiles, smugglers, and skulduggery*. New York: Crown Publishers.

Sollund, R. (2011). Expressions of speciesism: The effects of keeping companion animals on animal abuse, animal trafficking and species decline. *Crime, Law and Social Change, 55*(5), 437–451.

Soulsbury, C. D., Iossa, G., Kennell, S., & Harris, S. (2009). The welfare and suitability of primates kept as pets. *Journal of Applied Animal Welfare Science, 12*(1), 1–20.

Stiles, D., Redmond, I., Cress, D., Nellemann, C., & Formo, R. K. (Eds.). (2013). *Stolen Apes—The Illicit Trade in Chimpanzees, Gorillas, Bonobos and Orangutans. A Rapid Response Assessment. United Nations Environment Programme*. Arendal: GRID-Arendal.

Sutherland, E. H., Cressey, D. R., & Luckenbill, D. F. (1992). *Principles of criminology*. Lanham: Rowman & Littlefield.

Taub, D. M. (1975). Notes and News. *Oryx, 13*, 229.

Taub, D. M. (1977). Geographic distribution and habitat diversity of the Barbary Macaque (Macaca sylvanus L.). *Folia Primatologica, 27*, 108–133.

Taub, D. M. (1978). The Barbary macaque in North Africa. *Oryx, 14*(03), 245–253.

Thomas, K. (1984). *Man and the natural world: Changing attitudes in England 1500–1800*. London: Penguin.

Traffic. (2011). *Creative experts meeting on messaging to reduce consumer demand for tigers and other endangered wildlife species in Vietnam and China*. Hong Kong: Traffic.

United Nations Office on Drugs and Crime. (2003). *Country profile drugs and crime: MOROCCO*. Vienna: UNODC.

United Nations Office on Drugs and Crime. (2010). *The globalization of crime: A transnational organized crime threat assessment*. Vienna: UNODC.

United States Department of State. (2012). *Country reports on human rights practices*. Washington, D.C.: United States Department of State.

Van Duyne, P. C., Von Lampe, K., & Passas, N. (2002). *Upperworld and underworld in cross-border crime*. Nijmegen: Wolf Legal Publishers.

Van Lavieren, E. (2004). *The illegal trade in the Moroccan Barbary Macaque (Macaca sylvanus) and the impact on the wild population (Master's thesis)*. Oxford: Oxford Brookes University.

Van Lavieren, E. (2008). The illegal trade in Barbary macaques from Morocco and its impact on the wild population. *Traffic Bulletin, 21*, 123–130.

Van Uhm, D. P. (2009). *Illegale dierenhandel en de rol van Nederland. (Masterthesis Criminology).* Utrecht: Utrecht University.

Van Uhm, D. P. (2012a). De illegale handel in beschermde diersoorten, *Justitiële Verkenningen* 2 (themanummer Groene Criminologie), 91–100.

Van Uhm, D. P. (2016b). Monkey business: The illegal trade in Barbary macaques. *Journal.*

Vigo, J. (2010). Metaphor of hybridity: The body of Michael Jackson. *The Journal of Pan African Studies, 3*(7), 29–41.

Von Segesser, F., Ménard, N., Gaci, B., & Martin, R. D. (1999). Genetic differentiation within and between isolated Algerian subpopulations of Barbary macaques (Macaca sylvanus): Evidence from microsatellites. *Molecular Ecology, 8*(3), 433–442.

Wagner, D. A. (1993). *Literacy, culture and development: Becoming literate in Morocco.* Cambridge: Cambridge University Press.

Warchol, G. L. (2004). The transnational illegal wildlife trade. *Criminal Justice Studies, 17*(1), 57–73.

Ward, L. (2000). Salmonella perils of pet reptiles. *Communicable Disease and Public Health, 3*, 2–3.

Waters, S. (2011). Europe's other primate. *ZooQuaria, 75*, 22–23.

Westgarth, C., Heron, J., Ness, A. R., Bundred, P., Gaskell, R. M., Coyne, K. P., & Dawson, S. (2010). Family pet ownership during childhood: Findings from a UK birth cohort and implications for public health research. *International Journal of Environmental Research and Public Health, 7*, 3704–3729.

WHO. (2015). *Ebola situation report.* Washington, D.C.: WHO.

Williams, P. (2001). *Transnational criminal networks. Networks and netwars: The future of terror, crime, and militancy.* Rand Corporation Monograph.

Wright, T. F., Toft, C. A., Enkerlin-Hoeflich, E., Gonzalez-Elizondo, J., Albornoz, M., Rodríguez-Ferraro, A., et al. (2001). Nest poaching in neotropical parrots. *Conservation Biology, 15*(3), 710–720.

Wyatt, T. (2013). *Wildlife trafficking: A deconstruction of the crime, the victims, and the offenders.* Basingstoke: Palgrave Macmillan.

Zimmerman, M. E. (2003). The black market for wildlife: Combating transnational organized crime in the illegal wildlife trade. *Vanderbilt Journal of Transnational Law, 36*(5), 1657–1690.

Znari, M., Germano, D. J., & Macé, J. C. (2005). Growth and population structure of the Moorish Tortoise (Testudo graeca graeca) in Westcentral Morocco: Possible effects of over-collecting for the tourist trade. *Journal of Arid Environments, 62*(1), 55–74.

Chapter 9
Crime to Cure

The symbolic use of wildlife as a delicacy or the entertainment use as pets has been dealt with by previous case studies. Another mechanism includes not the mystique of caviar, not the rarity of pets, but the fact that simply more people can afford it. The functional use of traditional Chinese medicine (TCM) that is deeply rooted in Chinese society will be described in the last case study. Migration patterns and growing interests from the West enhanced the demand market for this form of wildlife. This final case study[1] focuses on the demand for traditional Chinese medicine (TCM) containing illegal animal products and analyses the social organization, modus operandi and trade routes of the actors involved in this illegal business. The analyses originate from fieldwork in trading areas in China in 2013. From a green criminological perspective, the harms related to the market of traditional Chinese medicine are explored at the end of this chapter.

9.1 History and Cultural Use of Traditional Chinese Medicine

An ancient Chinese legend tells of a farmer in Yunnan Province in southwest China who found a snake near his farm. The farmer tried unsuccessfully to kill the snake with a shovel but injured it nonetheless; a few days later he found the same snake with healed wounds. Again he tried to kill the snake. A few days later the farmer observed how the snake wriggled off into the weeds and ate a plant that healed it. The plant was pseudo ginseng root (*Panax notoginseng*) and is still known for its astringent properties in Chinese medicine (Mainka and Mills 1995).

According to Macioca (1989) Traditional Chinese Medicine *Zhōng Yī* (中醫) includes a broad variety of Chinese medicine practices based on culture and tradition.

[1]Parts of this chapter have been published in the article: Van Uhm, D.P. (2014). Criminaliteit en traditionele Chinese medicijnen. *Proces*, 93 (2): 130–143.

D.P. van Uhm, *The Illegal Wildlife Trade*, Studies of Organized Crime 15,
DOI 10.1007/978-3-319-42129-2_9

TCM is based on the ancient Chinese philosophy of the relationship between humans and the natural environment with its animals and plants. 'Harmony in life' is a central aspect and treatments are carried out to increase the body's natural defences (e.g. Tymieniecka 1984; Macioca 1989; Xu and Yang 2009; Tymieniecka 2012). In order to prevent or cure symptoms, medicines are used in the context of the balance between the body, the spirit and the external environment (Macioca 1989). The concepts of Qi, Yin Yang and Wu Xin are the most important in the ancient philosophy of TCM. *Qi* generally refers to metaphysical energy in terms of breath, vitality, vital energy or spiritual energy. Yin Yang expresses opposite forces that are necessary for good health. *Yin* is associated with darkness, the cold, wetness, passivity and decrease in contradiction to *Yang*, which is associated with light, heat, movement and increase. These forces occur in relation to each other and are used to stimulate conditions in TCM. Diseases with cold and lower activity refer to Yin and diseases with heat and higher activity are associated with Yang. *Wu Xin* is the relation between five human organs and five elements of the world. Wood is associated with the liver, fire with the heart, earth with the spleen, metal with the lungs and water with the kidneys. All phases are in relation with each other in an organic whole; the condition of one is always dependent on the conditions of the others (Xu and Yang 2009; Zhu and Wang 2011; Lozano 2014; Hong 2004). This is why elements from nature are important in Chinese medicine; using elements from the wild (e.g. plants or animal-derived medicine) can restore the imbalance that has given room for the disease.

TCM is estimated to have been used for more than 5,000 years and dates back to the era of the legendary Yellow Emperor of China (2698–2598 BCE). However, during the Zhou Dynasty (1122–221 BCE) important foundations of TCM were developed with the theoretical basis of Yin and Yang, the five elements 'Wu Xin' and the pathogenic factors of the external environment 'Qi' (Jia 2005). After a period of warfare among Chinese states and the defeat of the Huns, intellectuals started to record and collect information from ancient texts about Chinese medicine with the establishment of the Chinese Empire in 206 BCE (Hong 2004). The famous ancient text Huang Di Nei Jing or 'Yellow Emperor's Classic of Internal Medicine' about Chinese medicine was developed and became one of the most influential books in Chinese history. The texts were written in the form of dialogues between the Yellow Emperor and one of his ministers (Ch'I-Po) regarding interrelations between humans, the environment and the cosmos and about the treatment of symptoms in this context. This book forms the historical and philosophical foundation of TCM (Veith 2002). In 200 CE one specific disease category (infectious diseases causing fever) was extensively studied by the Chinese doctor Zhang Zhongjing. His theories and prescriptions in his book Shang Han Za Bing Lun or 'Treatise on Febrile Diseases' are, together with Huang Di Nei Jing, still used in current TCM practice. For centuries the system of Qi, Yin Yang and Wu Xin has remained intact and in almost every dynasty textbooks on medical knowledge were published. In the tenth and eleventh century CE the Chinese government developed agencies to manufacture and spread medicine and published books with 20,000 prescriptions. While in the Yuan Dynasty (1279–1368 CE) Genghis Khan controlled China, TCM developed substantially in several Chinese medicinal specializations. In the Ming Dynasty

(1386–1644 CE) one of the most popular TCM books Ben Cau Gang Mu, 'Compendium of Materia Medica', with highly informative sections (e.g. corrected errors, predecessors) was written by the physician and pharmacologist Li Shizhen.

After the Xinhai Revolution of 1911 the first Chinese Republic was founded and in 1929, under Western influence, the government proposed the abolition of TCM and measures were developed to reduce the practice and use. This happened because there was a desire to 'modernize' the country and to promote Western medicine, which was opposed to TCM. An important difference is that the primary purpose of TCM is the *prevention* of diseases, while Western medicine focuses on healing diseases (Von Moltke and Spaninks 2000; Nooren and Claridge 2001). In 1949 the Communist Party of Mao replaced the regime and started to promote the use of TCM once again, in particular to treat millions of people living in rural areas (Hong 2004; Schroeder 2002).[2] During the Great Proletarian Cultural Revolution from 1966 until 1976; in order to undermine the Maoist ideology and to preserve the Communist heritage, traditional Chinese cultural elements—such as TCM—were supressed. In other words, many TCM practitioners were jailed or killed. After Mao's death TCM was slowly re-established and TCM academics, professionals and experts re-emerged in society. Currently 40 % of health care in China is delivered by TCM practitioners (Scheid 2001) and the TCM philosophy is still deeply embedded in Chinese society (Coggins 2003; Xu and Yang 2009).

Although thousands of animal and plant species are legally used in TCM, some medications contain illegal animal elements of endangered species. About 13 % of TCM include animal parts (Still 2003) and both legal and illegal enterprises are involved in the wildlife trade for TCM (Yiming and Dianmo 1996). As a result of a sharp decrease in inflation between 1995 and 1999 in China, there is a rapidly expanding middle class that has the ability to purchase expensive TCM containing endangered species (Yiming and Dianmo 1998; Nooren and Claridge 2001: 41; Zhang et al. 2008). Moreover, consuming medicine derived from endangered species would also be a cultural symbol of status and pride (Swan and Conrad 2014). For instance, a pair of rhino horns constituted one of the Eight Precious Things or *pa pao,* represented on mandarin squares worn as badges by high-ranking military officials during the Ming and Qing Dynasties. Currently, rhino horn is still seen as a status symbol (Ayling 2013; Montesh 2013). Similar to caviar, the more endangered a species is determined to be, the higher its value (Courchamp et al. 2006; Hall et al. 2008). The more dangerous, powerful and exotic species such as tiger and rhinoceros are considered to have greater medicinal value (Nooren and Claridge 2001).

There is much Western scepticism about the effects of TCM, which are condemned as being mystical and pseudoscientific by Western doctors (Qui 2007; Swan and Conrad 2014). The function of TCM often cannot be proved, according to the Western model of an assessment of evidence-based medicines, partly because of the

[2]As a result many species used in TCM declined, including the loss of 3,000 tigers (Jackson et al. 1996).

personal and holistic approach of the use of TCM (Qui 2007). This orientalist approach results in a cultural conflict between the Western and Eastern culture with regard to the assessment and valuation of TCM. Although the Western evidence-based model might not be applicable to TCM, for a large group of people TCM is a very fundamental form of medicinal practice and has proven its value in the past. Modern Chinese state hospitals proscribe TCM all over China and the Chinese government supports the trade in TCM (Schroeder 2002). Today traditional medicine is used alongside its modern equivalent, such as antibiotics, and, from a holistic approach, much like Western homeopathy models (Xu and Yang 2009).

Chinese philosophy dictates that one should live in balanced harmony with (respect for) nature and the interconnectedness of living beings. According to ecocentric philosophy, everything on Earth is in relation to each other and nature has an inherent value (Benton 1998). Although not exceptional, (Eastern) Taoist, Buddhist and Confucian traditions are cited in support of this regulation; this is in contrast to the instrumental use and overexploitation of protected species. According to Harris (2008) since economic growth has been prioritized in China, this has contributed to an ecological nightmare. There exists a conflict between Chinese cultural and environmental values. On the one hand, environmentalists try to protect endangered species, on the other Western environmentalists are rejected, as they would impose alien values that interfere with the Chinese perspective of a balanced life. According to Swan and Conrad (2014) this 'cultural imperialism' may discount the values and commitments of local Chinese communities who believe in TCM. After the criminalization of certain TCM ingredients (e.g. tiger bone and rhino horn), TCM practitioners underlined that this has hampered their ability to reduce human suffering (Lee et al. 1998). In other words, attempts to protect endangered animals may conflict with essential Chinese values in the context of the provision of health care (Swan and Conrad 2014). Especially since the demand for wild harvested materials is higher than that for cultivated materials (Von Molte and Spaninks 2000). In this context, the last case study will describe the illegal trade in endangered species—the tiger, rhinoceros, saiga antelope and pangolin specifically—for the cultural and medicinal use of TCM.

9.2 The Implementation of CITES in Chinese National Law

In 1981 China signed CITES and implemented the legal framework in national regulations (Yiming and Dianmo 1996). The national government's protected species list generally follows the designation by CITES. All tiger species (*Panthera tigris* spp.) are on CITES Appendix I/EU Annex A. All rhino species (*Rhinocerotidae* spp.) are on CITES Appendix I/EU Annex A, with the exception of the southern square-lipped rhinoceros (*Ceratotherium simum simum*) from the population of South Africa (CITES Appendix II/EU Annex B).[3] Both saiga antelope species (*Saiga* spp.) and pangolin species (*Manis* spp.) are on CITES Appendix II/EU Annex B. The List of Wildlife under Special State Protection as designated by the Chinese State Council is laid down in Article 9 of the Law of the People's Republic of China on the Protection of Wildlife. Wildlife under special state protection consists of two classes: wildlife under first-class protection and wildlife under second-class protection.[4] It is prohibited to hunt, catch or kill species under first-class protection[5] or to sell or purchase them.[6] Except when it is necessary for scientific research, domestication and breeding, exhibition or other special purposes, a permit and approval from the relevant department under the State Council is required.[7] Tiger, rhinoceros and saiga species are included as Class I species and the pangolin as Class II species. The sale, purchase or utilization of second-class species is allowed if this is 'necessary', but the unit concerned must apply for approval at the department of wildlife administration under the government of the relevant province.[8]

Until 1993 it was allowed to sell products of captive-bred tigers and rhinos under Article 22 of the Law of the People's Republic of China on the Protection of Wildlife.[9] In 1993 the State Council of China prohibited the sale, purchase, transport, carrying and sending,[10] manufacture[11] or import and export[12] of medicines based on tiger bone and rhino horn, as well as products claiming to contain them.[13] In 2008 CITES adopted Decision 14.69 that states that tigers should not be bred for the purpose of trading their parts and derivatives thereof (CITES 2008). As a consequence, the ban on rhino horn and tiger bone added pressure on populations of other species. For instance, the ban on rhino horn has put added pressure on the population of saiga antelopes (*Saiga tatarica*) as their horns are

[3]This means that under special procedures the trade is possible, see Chap. 3.

[4]Article 9 Law of the People's Republic of China on the Protection of Wildlife.

[5]Article 16 Law of the People's Republic of China on the Protection of Wildlife.

[6]Article 22 Law of the People's Republic of China on the Protection of Wildlife.

[7]Article 22 Law of the People's Republic of China on the Protection of Wildlife.

[8]Article 22 Law of the People's Republic of China on the Protection of Wildlife.

[9]Article 22 Law of the People's Republic of China on the Protection of Wildlife: Units and individuals that domesticate and breed wildlife under special state protection may, by presenting their domestication and breeding licences, sell wildlife under special state protection or the products thereof, in accordance with the relevant regulations, to purchasing units designated by the government.

[10]Article 11.2 Circular of the State Council on Banning the Trade of Rhinoceros Horn and Tiger Bone.

[11]Article 11.3 Circular of the State Council on Banning the Trade of Rhinoceros Horn and Tiger Bone.

[12]Article 11.1 Circular of the State Council on Banning the Trade of Rhinoceros Horn and Tiger Bone.

[13]Article 11 Circular of the State Council on Banning the Trade of Rhinoceros Horn and Tiger Bone.

used as an alternative substitute in TCM (Ellis 2005). Subsequently the saiga antelope was placed on Appendix II/EU Annex B of CITES in 1995 and in China the saiga antelope was elevated to being a Class I state special protected species, which means that any sale or purchase is illegal and is classified as a 'very grievous' crime (Li et al. 2007). The use of products from pangolin species, which are commonly used in TCM, is also restricted; the pangolin is listed in China as a Class II species.

In recent decades the public use, production and sale of certain medicines, for instance those that include tiger bone (since about 500 CE) or rhino horn (since about 200 BCE), have been criminalized after more than 1,500 years (Martin and Martin 1982; Mainka and Mills 1995). While CITES and the Chinese protection lists impose a restriction on the trade in wildlife, China remains one of the largest consumer markets for illegal wildlife for TCM (e.g. UNODC 2013).

9.3 Consuming Rare Animals into Extinction

The list of endangered species around the world is growing and the impact of the wildlife trade is becoming more visible. For instance, in April 2010 the last Javan rhinoceros of the rhino population in Vietnam was the victim of illegal hunting; the animal was found with a bullet in the leg and its horn had been removed (Van Coeverden de Groot et al. 2011). Rhino horns are used in TCM and are believed to have strong healing qualities (Mainka and Mills 1995). Besides the impact of the use of well-known parts of endangered species in TCM, such as rhino horn and tiger bone, lesser-known saiga horns and pangolin scales in TCM drive wild populations to the brink of extinction.[14]

Historically tiger bone was one of the most important ingredients in TCM (Dinerstein et al. 2007; Wu and Wen 2015). Tiger bones *Hǔ Gǔ* (虎骨) in TCM are used to cure ulcers, rat-bite sores, abdominal pain, typhoid fever, malaria, hydrophobia, but especially to combat muscle cramps, migratory joint pain, pain in the bones and rheumatism (Bensky and Gamble 1993: 167; Ellis 2005). The yellow ones from males are said to be the best to strengthen the bones (Ellis 2005). The recommended daily dosage ranges from 3 to 6 g, and since the skeleton of an adult tiger weighs around 20 kg, this will only cater for 9–18 rheumatoid arthritis patients per year (Mainka and Mills 1995). Generally, tiger bones are used in medicinal wines, as powder, or in pills and toasted in oil or vinegar before use (Bensky and Gamble 1993). The growing affluence in China has provided new opportunities for more consumers to buy traditional medicine that include tiger products, making the

[14]Other endangered animal species used in TCM include musk from musk deer that is widely used in 400 patent medicines as a sedative for various ailments (Meng et al. 2011) or bear bile from bears that is used in more than 74 drugs—over 10,000 bears are kept in farms in China for bile (Sheng et al. 2012) or seahorses intended as a remedy for kidney disease, circulatory problems and impotence.

future of the tiger vulnerable (Dinerstein et al. 2007; Wu and Wen 2015).[15] At one time, the tiger (*Panthera tigris*) population was spread all over Asia, from Turkey to the Russian Far East (Nowell and Jackson 1996). During the last century, the population has disappeared from many habitats in South, East, Central and West Asia, including Java and Bali (Sanderson et al. 2006; Walston et al. 2010). Three out of the nine tiger subspecies have disappeared and this has been caused by human activities: the Caspian tiger, the Javan tiger and the Bali tiger.[16] Currently, the remaining subspecies, the Bengal tiger, the Indo-Chinese tiger, the Siberian tiger and the Malayan tiger are endangered and the South Chinese tiger and Sumatran tiger are critically endangered (Appendix XII) (Goodrich et al. 2015). The population of tigers consisted of around 100,000 in the early 1900s, while in the 1990s 5,000–7,000 specimens remained and the current population is estimated to be only 3,200 wild tigers.[17] The remaining population lives in the latter parts of the tiger's original habitat; nearly 93 % have now gone (Chundawat et al. 2011; Abbott and Van Kooten 2011). Though habitat degradation is an important cause of the declining tiger population, the illegal poaching of wild tigers for TCM is seen as the major threat (Damania et al. 2003; Ellis 2005). For instance, within a few years poachers killed all the tigers in Sariska Reserve, a national park in India (Sankar et al. 2005). The demand for the treatment of bone diseases in China is likely to drive the tiger population further towards extinction (Moyle 2009).[18]

A similar story is related to the poaching of rhinoceros driven by the demand for its highly valued horn used in TCM. Rhino horns *Xī Jiǎo* (犀角) are pulverized and processed into a medicine. It is used as a substitute to cool the blood, alleviate fever (especially children's high fever), erythema, purpura, nosebleeds, convulsion and cramp as well as heart disease (Bensky and Gamble 1993: 66–68).[19] Rhino horn is prescribed with an average dose of 1–2 g as a powder or is ground into a 'juice'

---

[15]A consumer of tiger bone wine in Guangzhou explained that it is quite popular among adolescents to order tiger bones from a dealer and to make wine from them. "We buy, with my rich friends, the tiger bones. (…) If someone wants to buy this they have to find the people in the middle. My friend has got connections and uses this network to buy the bones and we make the tiger bone wine" (CS6).

[16]During the 1930s the Bali tiger (*Panthera tigris balica*) became extinct, during the 1970s the Caspian tiger (*Panthera tigris virgate*) while the Javan tiger (*Panthera tigris sondaica*) became extinct in the 1980s (Abbott and Kooten 2011).

[17]The total population of Bengal tigers (*Panthera tigris tigris*) is estimated at <2,500 tigers (2,376), the Indo-Chinese tiger population (*Panthera tigris corbetti*) is estimated to be 352 animals (Thailand: 200, Myanmar: 85, Vietnam: 20, Cambodia: 20, Laos: 17) and the Siberian tiger population (*Panthera tigris altaica*) is estimated to be 360 tigers (Miquelle et al. 2011). The number of Malayan tigers (*Panthera tigris jacksoni*) is less than 250 animals, the South China Tiger population (*Panthera tigris amoyensis*) decreased from over 4,000 in the 1950s to perhaps now being extinct and the Sumatran tiger (*Panthera tigris sumatrae*) has an estimated population of 176–271 animals in the wild (Goodrich et al. 2015).

[18]Leopard bone is the closest substitute for tiger bone; however, more leopard bone is needed to attain the same effect (Moyle 2009).

[19]Furthermore, people would use it as a cleansing drink to combat a hangover (Montesh 2013; Sellar 2014).

(Bensky and Gamble 1993; Mainka and Mills 1995). It is believed that the horns of the Asian black rhinoceros (Yunjiou or Siam horn) are more powerful than the horns of the African rhinoceros (Guangjiao or Guangdong horn) (Nowell et al. 1992; Mainka and Mills 1995; Ellis 2005). The smaller size of Asian horns would indicate that they are more concentrated, and therefore more powerful and potent (Still 2003).[20] While in the late 1990s and early 2000s the demand for rhino horn was relatively low, this demand will probably have recently increased following the spread of unsubstantiated claims that a Vietnamese official was cured of cancer through the use of rhino horn (Ayling 2013; UNDOC 2013).[21] Consequently, more stories circulated and cancer sufferers travelled abroad for illegal treatment with rhino horn, alongside chemo and radiotherapy (Sellar 2014). Currently the horn is worth around € 30,000 per kilo (Van Uhm 2012), and as a single rhino horn may weigh up to 6–7 kg the trade is very lucrative (Ayling 2013). The horns are mainly destined for the global demand market for TCM in Southeast Asia. The rhinoceros family (*Rhinocerotidae*) already existed 35 million years ago during the late Eocene period and now the population is being pushed towards extinction (Appendix XIII) (Ayling 2013). At the beginning of the twentieth century the wild rhinoceros population was around 500,000 in Asia and Africa, the population had declined to 70,000 animals in 1970. Currently the population is estimated to be around 29,000 animals, a decline which has mainly been caused by poaching.[22] The current level of poaching is illustrated by the knowledge that the numbers of poached rhinos in South Africa had increased from 13 poached rhinos in 2007 to 1,004 in 2013 (Milliken 2014).

After the ban on the use of rhino horn, saiga horn became an alternative substitute to alleviate fever. Already in the late 1980s conservationist groups (e.g. the WWF) promoted the hunting of saiga antelopes (*Saiga tatarica*) for their horn as an alternative to rhino horn (Ellis 2005). The saiga antelope horns *Líng Yáng Jiǎo* (羚羊角) are soaked, dried and ground into a powder and used as TCM to calm the liver, as a detoxification, to assuage epilepsy and (similar to rhino horn) to alleviate

---

[20] Already in the 1970s the volume of African rhino horn was higher and its price was lower than that for Asian rhino horns (Leader-Williams 1992).

[21] There is no scientific evidence of any medicinal qualities for rhino horn. Rhino horn is composed of keratin, similar to human hair and fingernails (Ayling 2013).

[22] Although the White Rhino (*Ceratotherium simum spp.*) was on the brink of extinction with a remnant population of 20–50 left in 1895 in KwaZulu-Natal, South Africa, currently the White Rhino has the largest number of wild animals; an estimated 20,170 White Rhino in the wild in 2010 (Emslie 2012). The population of Black Rhino (*Diceros bicornis ssp.*) declined from 100,000 in 1960 to 2,410 by 1995. Since then, the population had increased to 4,880 in 2010, but this is still just a small part of the population of three generations ago (Milliken and Shaw 2012). Furthermore, the population of the Indian Rhinoceros (*Rhinoceros unicornis*) increased from 200 in the early 1900s to 2,575 in 2007 (Talukdar et al. 2008), the population of the Sumatran Rhinoceros (*Dicerorhinus sumatrensis*) declined until the 1990s with estimated losses of 50 % per decade (Foose and Van Strien 1997) and fewer than 275 individuals are estimated to remain in the wild (Van Strien et al. 2008a) and the Javan Rhinoceros (*Rhinoceros sondaicus*) population is estimated to consist of between 40–60 animals in the wild (van Strien et al. 2008b).

(infant) fevers by sedation (Bensky and Gamble 1993: 422–423; Zang 1990).[23] The dosage is 0.9–3 g in powders or pills (Bensky and Gamble 1993). While in the early nineteenth century hundreds of thousands of saiga horns were transferred from Russia to China and hunting had decapitated the population to near extinction in the first half of the twentieth century, the population recovered during the Soviet Union due to its strict control system (Bekenov, Grachevand and Milner-Gulland 1998; Li et al. 2007). This was in contrast to the saiga population in China which became extinct in the 1960s (Mallon 2008). Similar to the trade in caviar the situation changed dramatically with the collapse of the Soviet Union in the early 1990s. The dissolution has resulted in a decline in the standard of living and limited finances to control hunting and, consequently, high levels of the poaching of saiga antelopes for their horn took place in Kazakhstan, Uzbekistan and Kalmykia. The population became critically endangered (Appendix XIV), in particular because poaching is limited to (young) males with horns (Milner-Gulland et al. 2003; Zahler 2004; Kühl et al. 2009; Lam 2012). In certain saiga populations the sex ratio could be as low as only 5.7 % of the population being adult males (Von Meibom et al. 2007). Poaching for horns is believed to be the main cause of this significant decline (Milner-Gulland et al. 2003; Li et al. 2007; Von Meibom 2010). At one time the population of saiga antelopes was spread all over the Eurasian steppe from the Carpathian Mountains and the Caucasus to Dzungaria and Mongolia. The population was relatively stable between 1991 and 1994 with up to 1 million animals (mainly in Kazakhstan: 810,00–825,000 animals) (Bekenov, Grachevand and Milner-Gulland 1998). Primarily due to the demand for its horn in TCM the population has decreased by over 95 % of its total population in the last 15 years (CITES 2007; Kühl et al. 2009).[24] Currently the population of saiga antelopes is estimated to be around 56,300–61,300, compared to 1,250,000 in the mid-1970s (Von Meibom et al. 2010).

Similar to products from tigers, rhinos and saiga antelopes, parts of pangolins (*Manis ssp.)* are extensively used in TCM. The scales of pangolins *Chuān Shān Jiǎ* (穿山甲) are generally pulverized into powder and used in TCM to promote blood circulation, stimulate milk secretion and reduce skin infections or swelling (Bensky and Gamble 1993: 291; Ellis 2005). However, it is currently prescribed in particular to prevent or to cure breast cancer (e.g. CC2; CC4; CC6; CC10). The dosage is 3–9 g and the powder is the most effective (Bensky and Gamble 1993). The trade in pangolins has a long history with exports of thousands of pangolin scales from Java to China to supply the domestic market dating back to 1925. A picul (around 60 kg) would have cost 125 guilders in Batavia at that time (Herklots 1937). Currently China is the major demand market (Wu et al. 2004; Shepherd 2009; Pantel and

[23]According to TCM doctors buffalo horn would also replace rhino horn. As much as 10 times the volume is needed .

[24]The numbers of the subspecies (*Saiga tatarica tatarica*) in Kazakhstan declined from 976,000 in 1993 to 21,000 in 2003 (Milner-Gulland et al. 2001) and the subspecies (*Saiga tatarica mongolica*) in Mongolia from 5,200 in 2000 to 2,000 in 2006 (CITES 2007). Since the 1970s the saiga population in China is thought to be extinct (Zhang et al. 2006; Von Meibom et al. 2010).

Chin 2009) and the main threat to the survival of pangolins appears to be poaching for TCM (Ellis 2005). The pangolin population is found across Southeast Asia and Africa and all species of the whole population are traded for TCM at relatively high prices. Consequently all populations of pangolins are declining (Appendix XIV) (Challender 2011);[25] the global pangolin population is estimated to have reduced by up to 30 % over a 27-year period. Because the population of the Chinese pangolin has substantially reduced due to overexploitation in China, since the early 1990s pangolin scales are largely illegally exported by other range states such as Vietnam and Myanmar (SATCM 1996; Li et al. 1996; Yue 2008). The large demand for TCM is mainly fuelled by supplies of Sunda pangolins from Malaysia and Indonesia (Shepherd 2009; Challender 2011). Currently, pangolins are the most commonly seized wildlife throughout Southeast Asia (Shepherd 2009).

The dark side of the trade in raw animal products for TCM is illustrated by the significant decline of endangered species used in TCM. While habitat degradation is said to be the main reason for species decline (e.g. Zimmerman 2003), the major impact on these populations is believed to be poaching (e.g. Ellis 2005; Milliken 2014; Li et al. 2007). The tiger, rhino, saiga antelope and pangolin are all on the brink of extinction and certain subpopulations have already become extinct, such as the saiga antelope population in China. Strong cultural beliefs and the additional rumours of the healing qualities of these products, from curing cancer by using rhino horn and pangolin scales to alleviate high (infant) fever by using saiga horns and tiger bones as a remedy against rheumatism, can explain the large demand for these raw materials. In the next sections it will be clear that in order to fuel this demand China is stepping beyond its borders.

9.4 The Globalization of the Trade

In the 1960s the popularity of TCM outside Asia began to grow. According to Schroeder (2002), as an extension to the general popularity of holistic healing, TCM followed this international trend and herbal remedies became widespread.

[25]The Chinese pangolin (*Manis pentadactyla*) in China has declined by 89–94 % in comparison with the 1960s (Wu et al. 2004). Based on this substantial decline the Chinese pangolin is predicted to decline by up to 90 % over the next 21 years (Challender et al. 2014a); the Sunda pangolin (*Manis javanica*) has declined by up to 80 % in the last 21 years and this decline is expected to continue over the coming years (Challender et al. 2014b). Based on the decrease in the Chinese pangolin and Sunda pangolin over the last decade, it is expected that at least the population of the Indian pangolin (*Manis crassicaudata*) and the Philippine pangolin (*Manis culionensis*) will drop by up to 50 % in the next 21 years due to the trade in traditional medicine (Baillie et al. 2014; Lagrada et al. 2014). Furthermore, the African populations of the Black-bellied Pangolin (*Phataginus tetradactyla*), White-bellied Pangolin (*Phataginus tricuspis*), Giant Ground Pangolin (*Smutsia gigantean*) and the Temminck's Ground Pangolin (*Smutsia temminckii*) are suspected to decline by at least 30–40 % over the next 21–27 years (Waterman et al. 2014a, b, c; Pietersen et al. 2014).

This trend aroused the interests of both international and domestic businesspeople. Consequently, in the past 30 years the global trade in and the demand for TCM exploded (Schroeder 2002). While the medicinal properties of TCM are strongly doubted by Western medical practitioners, the use of elements from nature has become quite a popular approach in the US and Europe (Schroeder 2002; Henry 2004; Xu and Yang 2009). Not only has the demand for TCM increased in China in parallel with the growing prosperity and population growth (Von Moltke and Spaninks 2000), but nature-based medicines, including TCM, have also gained popularity in Europe (Patrick 1995; Schroeder 2002). Western Europeans are increasingly looking for alternative medicines (Nooren and Claridge 2001), especially for treating minor ailments, which is reflected in the popularity of homeopathy.[26] As a result of the growing supplies of TCM (often in combination with acupuncture) and the 'proto professionalization', where professional knowledge is transferred in simple 'layman's terms' (De Swaan 1989),[27] these alternative medicines have been made available to a broad public. Many high streets in Europe now have shops that sell Chinese medicines, either on request or after consultation (Williamson et al. 2013). Chinese medicines are used by more than 20 % of the world population (Schroeder 2002; Still 2003) and the worldwide demand for TCM is estimated to further increase in the coming years (WHO 2012).

The Chinese government's support since 1982, and increasing global demand markets are important aspects in the growing exports of TCM from China. Indeed, the trade in TCM has benefited from the reduction of international trade barriers with China, and the transformation to a free market economy (Nguyen and Nguyen 2008). The more open economy of China to the international market has enhanced international trade lines for the TCM market as well as improved infrastructure developments that connected previously isolated regions to the international markets (World Bank 2005). From 2007 onwards the TCM industry has increased by 20 % every year and the profits would have reached $24 billion in 2013 (IBISWorld 2014). Consequently, millions of people use TCM today, which are exported to over 160 countries (Xu and Yang 2009). This is reflected by the US that spent $7.6 billion on TCM products from China in 2010 (Cheung 2011) and exports of TCM to Europe amounted to $2 billion (Williamson et al. 2013).

Simultaneously there is a visible reduction in some forms of TCM including endangered animals. There has been a significant reduction in 162 sorts of medicine with parts from animals listed in China's Protection Lists of Wild Animals. For instance, musk (from endangered musk deer) has reduced by 70 % from the 1950s and the ban on the use of tiger bones and rhinoceros horn in TCM has substantially influenced the market supply of animal medicines (Liu et al. 2010). In the twentieth century, China (including Hong Kong) was by far the largest importer of rhino

[26]For instance, Western clients use TCM and acupuncture to stop smoking.

[27]Proto professionalization is a process whereby ordinary people start to acquire basic medicinal concepts to orient themselves under the influence of increasing medicalization.

horn, tiger bone and saiga horn (Leader-Williams 1992; Bekenov et al. 1998; Li et al. 2007).[28] Already between 1949 and 1976 East African export statistics show 56,694 kg of exported rhino horn, an equivalent of 16,500 rhinos (Mainka and Mills 1995).[29] In the late 1980s China imported around 2,000 kg rhino horn (Mills 1997)[30] and in the early 1990s, around 4 tonnes of tiger bone was used in TCM in China each year; this represents about 330–400 tigers (Moyle 2009).[31] In the early 1990s more than 200 TCM companies were manufacturing tiger bone medicine, such as tiger bone pills, plasters, gels and wine (Nowell and Ling 2007).[32] The volume of the trade in saiga horns also reached a peak of 60 tonnes in 1993 after the dissolution of the Soviet Union (Von Meibom et al. 2010). While in the early 1990s products with rhino horns and tiger bone were widely available in China (Loh and Loh 1994; Yiming and Dianmo 1996). As a result of the decline in endangered species the medicines containing these animals decreased; since 2012 no legal imports of saiga horns and pangolin scales into China were recorded by CITES.[33] Despite the high demand, the medicines containing substitutes from endangered species may become rare in the near future if the animal populations continue to decline.

9.5 The European Connection

The increasing global demand market for TCM and, simultaneously, the reduction of TCM containing endangered species provide opportunities for an illegal market for parts from endangered animals destined for this industry. Global estimates indicate that illegal wildlife trafficking and smuggling in China generate over $10 billion annually.[34] The demand for pangolins in China alone was for over 150,000 pangolins at around $1,550 per pangolin in 2007, with an estimated annual market value of more than US$176 million (Pantel and Chin 2009). The illegal trade in tiger parts globally is estimated to be around $5 million and in rhino horns $8

[28]Between 1949–1976, 42 % of East Africa's declared exports were transferred to Hong Kong (Leader-Williams 1992).

[29]Note that export statistics were widely underreported.

[30]Note the underrepresentation of declared imports (Leader-Williams 1992).

[31]In the early 1990s the tiger medicine industry in China would be 100 million CNY (USD 12.4 million). Before the ban the famous TCM company Tong Ren Tang used 2,000–3,000 kg of tiger bone each year for the production of tiger medicines. If the ban would be lifted the company would expect to use 1,000 kg of tiger bone annually (Nowell and Ling 2007).

[32]China exported over 27 million units (e.g. capsules and bottles) with tiger derivatives to 26 countries and territories between 1990 and 1992. Exports were allowed by CITES on the grounds that the tiger parts were from stocks before CITES came into force (Mills 1997).

[33]CITES Trade Database, 2015.

[34]Kathleen E. McLaughlin, "China's dangerous appetite for rare animals," Global Post, October 26, 2010.

million (UNODC 2010). According to Von Meibom (2010) the consumption of saiga horn in China is around 8,500–9,500 kg each year. This would suggest an annual market value of $4.6 million. According to these rough estimates, part of the trade in pangolins, saiga antelopes, rhinoceros and tigers is estimated to be around $195 million annually.

While there is a large demand market in China for illegal TCM, from the late 1990s onwards also large amounts of illegal TCM arrived in Europe (Sellar 2014). Each year TCM containing products from tigers, rhinos, pangolins and saiga antelopes are confiscated in Europe (Post 2013). Besides being a demand market, the EU is also a transit hub; pangolin scales and rhino horns are transferred from Africa through the EU to Southeast Asia (Challender and Hywood 2012; Milliken 2014). The EU is even used as a source for rhino horn as illustrated by more than a hundred rhino horns being stolen from museums in the EU and being destined for the Asian market (Ayling 2013; Van Uhm 2012). Based on seizures in the EU between 2001 and 2010, an image of the illegal TCM trade to the EU can be obtained. As with other forms of crime, these figures show a portion of the actual illegal trade, since only a small part of the illegal trade is intercepted; less than 10 % of all the illegal trade in wildlife is seized (Stiles et al. 2013). Therefore, 90 % remains invisible and, since not all EU Member States adequately register seizures, this analysis can only be used as an indication of the illegal trade in TCM to the EU.

An important finding is that of the 323,146 seized animal products recorded between 2001 and 2010, the largest group includes *medicines* ($N = 50{,}364$). More than 50,000 medicines containing parts of endangered animal species were intercepted in 512 seizures between 2001 and 2010 in the EU. The medicine category consists mainly of seized TCM, primarily of seahorses ($N = 30{,}458$), products from big cats—mostly tigers and leopards—($N = 7{,}198$, including >65 % tigers $N = 4{,}697$), musk from musk deer ($N = 4{,}575$), bear bile ($N = 3{,}101$), saiga antelope horns ($N = 1{,}869$), rhinoceros horns ($N = 1{,}003$) and pangolin scales ($N = 121$).[35] Besides the peak in volume in 2003 influenced by a confiscation in Great Britain of 27,000 seahorses, the incidents are relatively stable at between 23 and 109 seizures annually (Fig. 9.1).[36] According to Traffic (2014) during the last few years there has been a significant increase in the seizures of TCM in the EU. This may be caused by the popularity of TCM in the West.

The majority (>65 %) of seizures of medicines with animal products originate from the major exporter China (including Hong Kong [$N = 27$]) ($N = 284$, 66 %). Based on confiscation incidents, other (major) countries of origin for illegal TCM are Vietnam ($N = 39$, 9 %), Russia ($N = 23$, 5 %) and Ghana ($N = 21$, 5 %). The averages of the quantities being smuggled are around several dozen from the main source countries of China (including Hong Kong) ($M = 45.6$; $SD = 134$), Vietnam

[35]Seizures of plant products consist mainly of American ginseng *Panax quinquefolius*, but are not included in this study.

[36]The seizures are an underestimation because many confiscations are not recorded in the database.

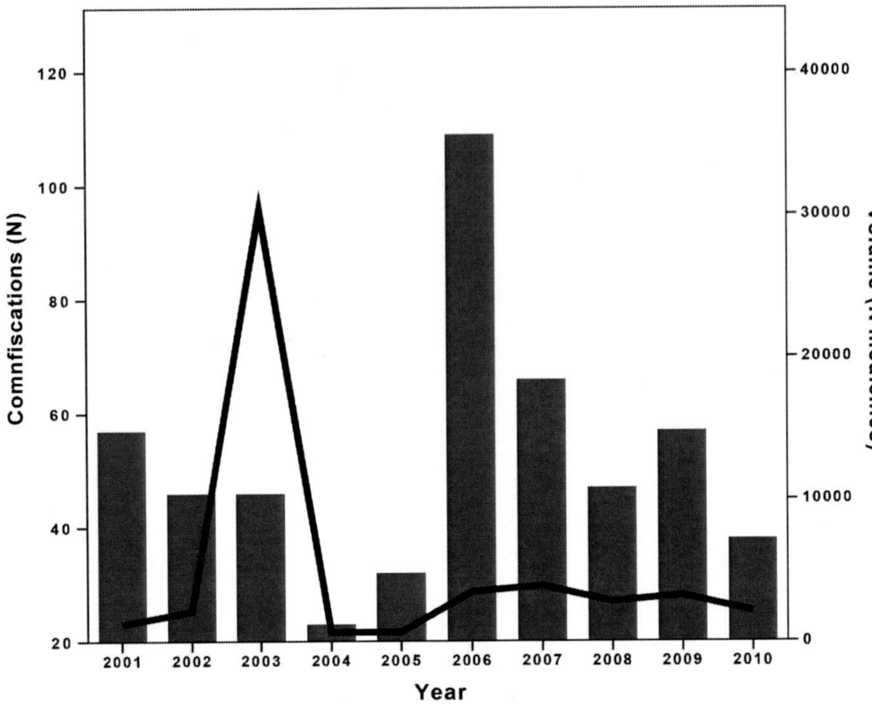

Fig. 9.1 EU confiscations of illegal animal medicine shipments. *Source* Personal analyses of the EU-TWIX database, 2001–2010

(M = 136.0; SD = 331), Russia (M = 104.9; SD = 331) and Ghana (M = 5.6; SD = 5).[37] The EU is not only a major importer of *legal* TCM, but also an important player in the importation of *illegal* TCM. Major outlets in the EU appear to be the Netherlands (N = 160, 33 %), Denmark (N = 110, 23 %), Germany (N = 54, 11 %), Belgium (N = 37, 8 %) and Hungary (N = 16, 3 %) (see Fig. 9.2). The Netherlands is well known as being a major importer of TCM. The is partly due to a large distribution centre in Amsterdam (e.g. Kemner 2010) and its large Chinese community: the Netherlands has one of the largest Chinese populations in Europe (Pieke 1999). If 10 % of the illegal trade is seized, the illegal trade in TCM to the EU could be more than 50,000 products every year.

The previous sections demonstrate that there is a growing global market for TCM and there is a substantial illegal trade in TCM in China and an illegal trade to the EU to fuel the demand for illegal ingredients. However, before the illegal shipments of TCM arrive in China and are then retransferred to the EU, several

[37]Russia and Ghana are remarkable countries regarding TCM. Based on the seizures, from Russia mainly medicines containing parts of bears and from Ghana medicines with parts of lions were confiscated.

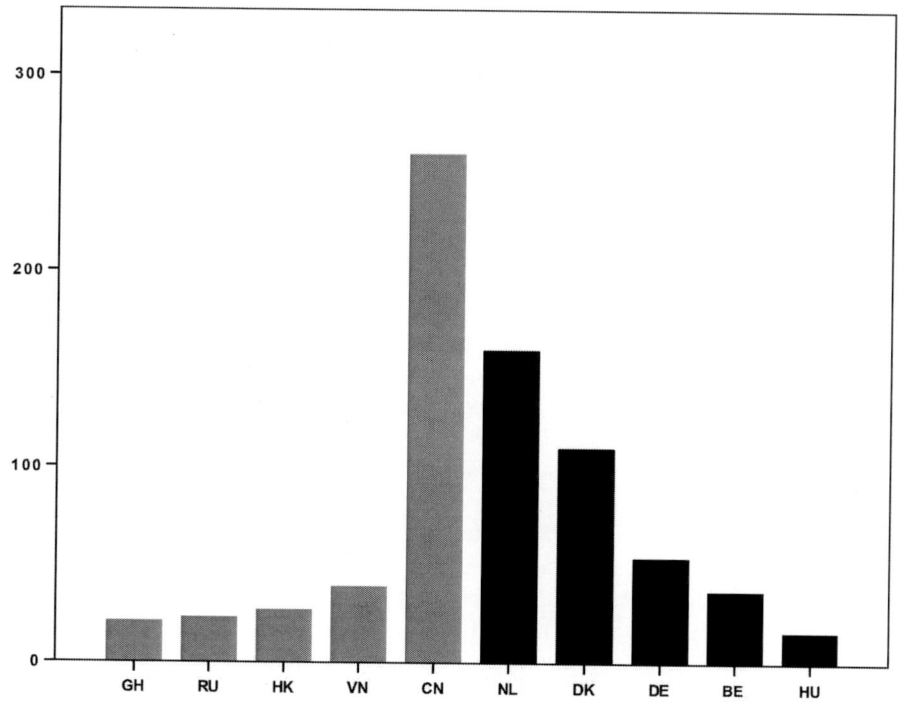

Fig. 9.2 Origin and destination countries for illegal TCM. *Export-country codes: Ghana (GH), Russia (RU), Hong Kong (HK), Vietnam (VN), China (CN). **Import-country codes: the Netherlands (NL), Denmark (DK), Germany (DE), Belgium (BE), Hungary (HU). *Source* Personal analyses of the EU-TWIX database (seizures), 2001–2010

processes will have taken place as raw materials have to be collected, trafficked and produced into TCM and then smuggled to the destination countries (Schneider 2012). Several actors in source, transit and exporting countries are involved in the network, such as poachers, smugglers, middlemen and traders. In the following sections the social organization of the illegal trade in TCM will be discussed.

9.6 Traditional and Opportunistic Hunting Abroad

From the nineteenth century until 1949 Chinese mass emigrations took place driven by wars, starvation and political corruption (McKeown 1999). The Chinese migrated to neighbouring Southeast Asian countries as well as South Africa, Europe and Australia. For centuries, the Chinese came to Vietnam and Laos to settle and to search for employment; some became workers for established Chinese businesses while others became involved in the trade in wildlife (Yongge 2000;

Nooren and Claridge 2001).[38] According to interviews held with illegal traders in TCM in China, most hunters of raw materials in TCM are local farmers *outside of* China (e.g. CT2; CT5; CT10). Since (specialist) poaching in China has resulted in a significant decline in specific endangered species used in TCM, such as the decrease in populations of tigers, saiga antelopes and pangolins (see Sect. 9.3), neighbouring countries and African areas are being targeted for animal products. Not only the demand but also the hunting for raw materials has become increasingly globalized.

Similar to the poaching of sturgeons in the Caspian Sea and the hunting of monkeys in Azrou, poverty and unemployment are push factors in the poaching of illegal wildlife for TCM. Usually the poachers live in small agricultural communities, hunt opportunistically and belong to the lower social classes (e.g. CT8; CT10; CT13). The poachers have been described as inhabitants of villages, people who live near the forests concerned or habitats where the animals are hunted (Zimmerman 2003). Sometimes these poachers are Chinese immigrants; sometimes they are national residents of the country (CT8; CT9; CT13). According to a study in 2009, 75 % of the hunters of saiga antelopes stated that unemployment was the primary factor driving the saiga antelope exploitation (Kühl et al. 2009). As the saiga antelopes are located in economically deprived regions, there seems to be a strong link between poaching and limited access to alternative livelihood options, a lack of environmental education and poverty among local communities (Milner-Gulland et al. 2001; Robinson and Milner-Gulland 2003; Von Meibom et al. 2010). In addition, poachers of pangolins in usually poor local communities make 10–50 % of their income from the trade (Pantel and Anak 2010). Especially in the early stages of the migration of Chinese abroad, an opportunistic trade in wildlife is important to establish an economic basis (Nooren and Claridge 2001).

While in the context of the migration of the Chinese poverty may explain poaching to survive, cultural explanations are applicable as well. Historically TCM is deeply rooted in Chinese culture (Coggins 2003; Xu and Yang 2009); throughout its long history the Chinese have collected animals for the use in TCM (Mainka and Mills 1995). The ancient Chinese tradition of hunting and collecting wildlife is illustrated by Vietnamese kings who paid tributes to Chinese rulers in 200 BCE, including rhinoceros horn. Hundreds of years later in 1950 after the French colonization there was still a substantial exchange between Vietnam and China in raw materials for TCM (Yiming and Dianmo 1998). Furthermore, for centuries, the Ho (from Yunnan, China) exchanged salt, metals and other goods with wildlife ingredients for TCM with the inhabitants of Laos (Nooren and Claridge 2001). The tradition of hunting and collection for medicine is embedded in the Chinese culture.

Although people have always hunted for animals for use in TCM, there are certain illegal animal products that yield more profits. In the latter case, respondents refer to endangered species to be used in TCM that are sold to collectors. According

[38] In line with this diaspora, Chinese culture has also influenced the use of TCM abroad (Swan and Conrad 2014).

to a TCM trader: "Of course there is a huge demand for highly valued products of wild animals, such as saiga horn or rhino horn. (…) The ingredients are delivered by poachers on demand to middlemen. (…) Usually this is based on informal trade agreements. (…) In the village or a city nearby, there is always someone to whom the farmers can sell these specific animal products" (CS10). Ideal candidates to recruit as poachers come from indigenous communities with strong hunting cultures, such as the Indian Bawariya and Behliya tribes for hunting tigers (Moyle 2009). Sometimes the hunters even obtain loans from middlemen to cover their daily basic expenses (Pantel and Chin 2009). Respondents mentioned several examples of local farmers from outside China being involved. For instance, farmers in Myanmar, Vietnam, Laos and Indonesia who hunt pangolins and farmers in Russia, Kazakhstan and Mongolia who hunt saiga antelopes (CT5; CT6; CT8; CT10). While these farmers originally focus on agriculture, many villagers became opportunistic hunters in addition to being traditional farmers (Pantel and Chin 2009). As one of the interviewees stated: "Farmers traditionally hunt saiga antelope because they need their meat for food, but now they sell the horns for profit. (…) The hunters of pangolins are farmers as well. They eat them in Myanmar. It is a local dish, but they sell the scales to collectors who smuggle these to Kunming. In more rural areas a lot of people make some money by hunting. They know how to find the more valuable products and get paid by a Chinese middleman" (CS8). Traditional poaching by local communities appears to have been transformed into the opportunistic poaching of endangered species. For instance, locals in Africa poach rhinos to fuel the TCM demand market in Asia (Eloff 2012).[39] While there is a potential risk of being shot by park rangers,[40] the profits appear to be limited for the poachers, but apparently still worth taking the risks (Hull 2012). Sometimes prices as low as $15 are paid for killing a tiger, while the Chinese middleman makes the real money (Ellis 2005). In many cases middlemen come from larger cities (e.g. Maputo in Mozambique) all the way to the local village to recruit poachers (Montesh 2013). If one of the poachers is killed other potential recruits are ready to replace him (Sellar 2014).

Instead of poor locals as poachers, professional groups of hunters with highly sophisticated equipment, such as night-vision goggles, heavy artillery and even helicopters to detect the animals are also involved. In the latter case, businessmen are directly involved in the organization. For instance, several (professional)

---

[39]A study on the profiles of 55 poachers in Kruger National Park (South Africa) demonstrates that the group involved 40 % Mozambican citizens and 60 % South African citizens. All were male and in 41 % of cases their ages were between 20 and 29, 41 % were between 30 and 39 while 18 % were 40 or older (Eloff 2012).

[40]Sometimes even inexperienced youths enter national parks in South Africa to shoot a rhino in the prospect of making easy money: "When you go and kill a rhino everything you want is there. Money to do anything you could want. Money for food and drink. But when you poach you can get caught and beaten up [by the police] and you can end up in jail. And in jail you can get beaten too. I don't know but I am not happy, because these people [middlemen] make big money out of this. They make a lot of money and we don't get much. We get almost nothing out of poaching" (Hull 2012).

Table 9.1 Types of poachers of animals for TCM

Type	Equipment	Method
Local villager	Guns or muskets	Poaching animals that threaten local communities and their cattle
Local farmer/poacher	Traps, tracking signs, guns	Traditional poaching using tracking signs, traps, dogs and guns
Professional groups	Helicopters, veterinary tranquilisers, night-vision goggles, guns with silencers	Professional specialist poaching with highly sophisticated equipment in order to be efficient and effective

poachers of rhinos use veterinary tranquilisers and silencers to avoid law enforcement officials or guards. Once shot, the rhino becomes weak and the poachers cut off their horns with a chainsaw (Montesh 2013). Or helicopters were used during the 1990s and 2000s to search for and shoot saiga antelopes all over Kazakhstan. A former hunter of saiga antelopes in Atyrau (Kazakhstan) mentioned: "In the past the 'saigas' were everywhere, but they were shot during the last couple of decades by professional hunters in helicopters. It was organized by the Kazakh mafia that dominates government officials. It was due to the high demand for medicines from China. By now they are all gone" (RS6). The organization of professional poachers is more sophisticated and these groups are not afraid of law enforcers or rangers (Table 9.1). At times militia or military personnel are even involved, carrying AK–47s and rocket-propelled grenades (US Senate 2014). Consequently, every year dozens of rangers are killed during confrontations with poachers (Wyler and Sheikh 2013).

As the illegal trade in raw materials consists of various types of endangered animals, the poachers use different techniques to catch specific wildlife. To catch pangolins, hunters have been reported to be using dogs, mainly during the rainy season, to follow the scent of a pangolin to its hiding place (1), using tracking signs based on experience (2), or using traps set specifically to catch pangolins near entrances or tree hollows (3) or nonselective traps for all kinds of wildlife (4) (Newton et al. 2008). As the pangolins' main defence against predators is to roll up into a ball, it is fairly easy to catch them (Pantel and Anak 2010). Tiger poaching is usually done by wire snares, steel traps and poisoned meat from buffalos and cows. The traps are prepared by blacksmiths and are used to keep the skin in good condition due to its high value on the black market (Mailley 2014). The bones are used to fuel the demand for TCM.[41] To catch saiga antelopes, poaching methods are often more professional in nature and are well organized. Certain poachers use professional traps that were formerly used by the *Kalmytzkiy* State Procurement Enterprise when commercial hunting for saiga antelopes was allowed. By using these special traps poachers may catch around 10–50 animals per day (Von Meibom et al. 2010). Furthermore, the saiga antelope poachers use cars and

[41]As discussed further in this chapter there are several opportunities to trade illegally in bones from captive-bred tigers in China.

motorbikes during organized expeditions lasting several days to ensure the necessary profit. In 2005 only nine poachers were needed to kill over 1,000 saiga antelopes each year. The poaching season is concentrated during autumn as the saiga antelopes come together (Kühl et al. 2009). While rhino poaching is incidentally done by local poor people using wire snares to trap the rhino and then kill the animal with a spear or *panga* (also known as a machete), professional poachers are regularly involved using advanced equipment. They poach in groups of 4–6 individuals to track the rhino and kill the animal with firearms by night. Poaching occurs more frequently during a more gibbous (lighter and full) moon stage (Eloff 2012; Eloff and Lemieux 2014). An even higher level of sophistication and organization is found in trained marksmen who need only one shot with a high calibre rifle (e.g. AK-47s)[42] or tranquilizer darts to immobilize the rhino and then to cut off the horn (Milliken and Shaw 2012; Montesh 2013). They shoot the rhino from a four-wheel drive vehicle or helicopter and then disappear with the horn. The poachers regularly leave the incursion site in one vehicle and change their clothes and shoes, while the rhino horns are transported by another vehicle to be collected in Johannesburg or Pretoria (Milliken and Shaw 2012). Low-flying helicopters are also used to search for rhinos to poach or transport their horns. The level of organization during professional poaching trips is demonstrated by the use of heavy-calibre rifles, dart guns, infrared sensors, helicopters and tranquilising drugs that are well beyond both the economic and technological reach of most African or Asian local people (Ayling 2013; Montesh 2013; Eloff and Lemieux 2014).

As the hunting methods differ, the motives of the hunters vary as well. The motives depend on conflict, cultural and economic incentives. Sometimes wild animals are a threat to local communities and their cattle. Due to the defragmentation and deforestation of the jungle, animals increasingly come into contact with human settlements (Michalski et al. 2006; Boekhout van Solinge 2008). In the Sundarbans mangrove forests of Bangladesh and India, locals wear masks with human faces on the back of their head so that tigers think that they are being observed (Sellar 2014).[43] At the beginning of 2014 in Northern India 10 people were killed by a tiger within 6 weeks.[44] Not exceptionally, and especially after such attacks, tigers are killed by local people and their skins, bones and teeth are sold on the black market. Furthermore, in many cultural traditions poaching is seen as a cultural activity (e.g. Manning 1993; Forsyth et al. 1998). As illustrated in this section the cultural incentives may be substantial as beliefs in the power of certain raw materials are very strong and deeply rooted in Chinese culture and philosophy. The criminalization may have resulted in a conflict and poachers could consider the regulations regarding the hunting of specific endangered animals for TCM to be Western-based prohibitions. For these reasons, several traders were quick to note

[42]For instance 0.375 and 0.458 rifles (Montesh 2013).

[43]These local communities believe that tigers have become used to the taste of human flesh due to upstream cremations of human bodies on the water (Sellar 2014).

[44]'The tiger will kill again—it has tasted human flesh', The Asian Times, February 20, 2014.

the undesirable dominant influence of the West (e.g. CT4; CT6; CT13). This would have also been the case in the collecting and poaching of animals for TCM in Chinese culture (McNeely and Wachtel 1991). Poaching driven by poverty, livelihood and profit has been well recorded (e.g. Von Meibom et al. 2010; Pantel and Anak 2010).[45] Local farmers became opportunistic poachers who hunt animals for food and profit. They keep the meat and sell certain parts of the animals to middlemen. Professional poachers who operate purely for profit by using professional equipment make the high profits. The next step in the process is the role of middlemen in the illegal trade in these raw materials.

9.7 The Emergence of Middlemen and the Culture of *Guanxi*

Since the liberation of the market in China, new opportunities for crime have been provided. China slowly developed a more open market economy, which resulted in an increase in Chinese middlemen. According to Goodman (1998) the changes in economic and social structures in the 1980s and 1990s have developed a new middle 'capital-owning' class of investors in China. The combination of decentralization, privatization and open borders has created new opportunities for both legal and illegal entrepreneurs. A local in Anguo explained the situation: "Before, you could not speak openly, China was closed such as Korea. (…) 20 years ago the Soviet Union collapsed. Communism changed and slowly a little bit more freedom came. Shenzen and Shanghai were opened for the international market. At that time the [TCM] companies did not know how to do business and how to sell their stuff. A lot of businessmen started their business at that time" (CO4). In other words, the trade in TCM came into the hands of Chinese middlemen worldwide by opening the borders. Similar to the illegal trade in caviar and Barbary macaques, middlemen became key players in the Chinese criminal networks of TCM.

Several authors mentioned the involvement of *ethnic Chinese middlemen* in the illegal trade in TCM in source or destination countries (e.g. Yongge 2000; Nooren and Clardige 2001; Xu Ling 2008; Pantel and Chin 2009; Milliken and Shaw 2012). Informants explained that the establishment of TCM networks is commonly based on family or cultural relationships with ethnic Chinese middlemen in China or abroad (CT10; CT11; CM2; CM3). Pantel and Chin (2009) highlighted that middlemen in the pangolin trade are mainly ethnic Chinese; a study in Malaysia into the illegal trade in pangolins confirmed that 7 out of 8 traders are Malaysian Chinese. Xu Ling (2008) found many ethnic Chinese in Mong La (Myanmar), 1,500 m from the

[45]Poachers of small wildlife would operate as individuals, on an ad hoc basis and sometimes based on requests from middlemen. One study indicates that the majority of poachers are adult men (women are involved in 20 % of cases and children in less than 10 %), working with small networks of family members or associates (UNODC 2013).

China-Myanmar border, trading in products from endangered species for TCM such as pangolin scales, bear bile and tiger bones. Another study on rhino poaching referred to Chinese middlemen being involved in the illegal rhino horn trade in South Africa (Milliken and Shaw 2012; Milliken 2014). As an illegal trader in Chengdu mentioned, family or ethnic relations are crucial in the illegal trade in TCM. "My uncle lives in the mountains and is the collector and my brother in law organises smuggling across the border. It is a family business, it is based on trust" (CM3). These networks rely upon family or ethnic community links to increase reliability and loyalty and to reduce the possibility of infiltration (Moyle 2009).

The role of family ties, culture, ethnicity and trust in crime has been discussed by many criminologists (e.g. Kleemans and Van de Bunt 1999; Bovenkerk et al. 2003; Von Lampe and Ole Johansen 2004; Siegel and Nelen 2007). Trust in family members would be based on the familiarity and conformity of shared norms and values (Misztal 1996). Criminal organizations follow the routes of migration and international trade. For instance, Italian Mafia migrants dominated the underworld in New York based on family ties (Bovenkerk et al. 2003). Cultural and economic globalization is assumed to have promoted the spread of ethnic criminal networks (Bovenkerk 2001). Similar trust created by familiarity and conformity would be applicable to trust based on ethnicity (Misztal 1996; Kleemans and Van de Bunt 1999).

In the source areas for wildlife for TCM ethnic Chinese middlemen usually come from larger cities near the hunting area (e.g. CT6; CT8). They pass by the small villages to collect the raw materials or, the other way around, poachers bring the products to them. These Chinese middlemen own small shops as their main business. The legal business is regularly used as a cover for their illegal business, such as a legal wildlife collection business or small businesses such as bakeries, grocery shops, and home decoration and construction suppliers (Pantel and Chin 2009). This interdependence makes it advantageous to intertwine legal and illegal products (Zhang et al. 2008). According to Passas (2002) this interconnection would be an example of how these activities are carried out within an entrepreneurial structure to earn additional profits.

The Chinese middleman in the source country is usually in direct contact with a middleman in China who recruits wildlife smugglers.[46] These middlemen are known to be investors, as certain illegal wildlife products such as rhino horn require a substantial investment. When prices increase on the black market, immediately, more investment is necessary. According to an illegal trader in Kunming: "We sell around three rhino horns a year. I buy them from a middleman who is a real investor. (…) He knows that prices for these products are on the rise and therefore he has got a lot of them in stock. Before it was cheap to buy them, but now it has become expensive. It is an investment. Prices rise rapidly from 2,000 to 3,000 to

[46]Not only ethnic Chinese middlemen involved in source countries, but also those in destination countries are of importance. According to a Dutch law enforcement agency many people involved in the illegal TCM trade were Chinese residents and TCM products have been sold by Chinese medicine stores in the destination countries. Furthermore, there are indicators that these illegal TCM products are delivered by family members (Post 2013).

Illustration 9.1 TCM market, Anguo, China 2013

150,000 yuan per kilo for rhino horn. Nowadays, we also sell rhino horn in limited quantities of 100 g, because of the high prices" (CT8) (Illustration 9.1).

Middlemen may act individually or in collaboration with others and deal with traders, on the one hand, and smugglers, on the other. They transfer the raw materials or TCM through the chain and during this process a large portion of the money is directed to them (Lin 2005). They resell the products for high profits, thus they should know the value and authenticity of their products. Another rhino horn dealer explained that: "The colour, smell, taste and softness all play a role in defining the authenticity and type of the horn" (CM4). Despite the strong cultural ties between the middlemen and other actors in the network, underhand practices also occur in the trade. The dealer continued: "A while ago I ordered two Siam horns [Asian rhino horns] from a new potential business partner. When they arrived, I looked at the horn and noticed that it was an African horn. They tried to betray me!" (CM4). This middleman involved in rhino horn trade refused to pay the high price for Asian rhino horn and made a new agreement.

Relationships based on trust are very important between criminal actors in TCM markets all over China (Van Song 2008). Especially since middlemen develop international networks with informal connections with government officials, the police and the army (Pantel and Chin 2009). The Chinese culture of *guānxì* (關係) provides opportunities to create relationships based on trust. *Guanxi* is the basic dynamic in Chinese personalized networks of influence and refers to favours gained from social connections. The Chinese rely largely on their *guanxi* or personal informal network for many aspects of their life and reciprocal benefits are necessary to maintaining one's guanxi (Myers 1995; Yeung and Tung 1996; Gold and Guthrie 2002; Zhang et al. 2009). This provides a familiar framework for illegal businesses with low penetrability as it creates an effective insider–outsider system; enforcement agents are regularly outside the *guanxi* trading relationship (Myers 1995). In such networks one could order tiger products and spread them to customers all insulated from scrutiny. The advantage is that no stock is needed as all imports are destined to go to prearranged sellers and customers would be reluctant to reveal any information (Moyle 2009: 140–141). *Guanxi* is indispensable for informal agreements underlined an illegal seller of tiger bones, rhino horn, saiga horn and pangolins in Kunming: "Middlemen do have such relations with border officials. (…) If you have money and guanxi, you can pay the border control. Nobody will make a problem since you have this special relationship" (CS11). This trader in Kunming explained that he buys seized wildlife from Chinese police officers based on *guanxi* practice. According to the coordinator of wildlife enforcement in China the sale is perfectly legal for seized saiga horns and pangolin scales, but illegal for rhino horn (CP2). Nevertheless, according to an illegal trader in all kinds of wildlife in Kunming: "If smugglers from Myanmar and Laos are caught and the Chinese police seize a rhino horn, they resell it to us illegally. If the stuff is confiscated by an international airline, they burn it. We have informal relationships with border officials" (CT8). A middleman in Anguo who explained his relationship with a friend from the army who protects the Chinese border gave another example. "My friend works as a soldier at the Guangxi border [not to be confused with 'guanxi']. Through this connection I can pass the orders across the border" (CM4). According to Sellar (2014) not incidentally militia commanders have been arrested because of their involvement in the selling of illegal wildlife products.

The upper and underworld interrelationship has been widely analysed in criminological research (e.g. Block and Chambliss 1981; Ruggiero 1996; Van Duyne et al. 2002; Passas 2002). Crucial is the long-term and trustful relationship or *guanxi* with smugglers, traders and officials. TCM shops, local clinics and even hospitals have informal connections with middlemen who can supply illegal animal parts (CM2; CM4; CT8; CT10). During the first transaction traders get in touch with the middleman, the deal will take place outside the public eye; the price, quality and quantity will be discussed. For instance, at the Anguo market a seller of rhino horns invited me to his house in a small alley to talk about the business. He explained that this is the way to do illegal businesses in raw TCM materials (CS19). A middleman at the Kunming market underlined that after a couple of deals there is more trust and *guanxi* gained and the delivery and money transfer is more of a routine. After this middleman had successfully built up his business network based on a number of small deals, he could start with the structural trade in illegal animal products. Currently, he arranges orders of tonnes of saiga horns and pangolin scales and dozens of rhino horns every year (CM2).

Chinese middlemen usually coordinate intermediation in the illegal trade in TCM. Organizing the smuggling is often the middleman's responsibility together with appointments with legal enterprises. Large-scale smuggling operations in high-value wildlife require a range of middlemen who may be involved in other forms of contraband, such as drugs (e.g. UNODC 2013). For them, the wildlife trade may not be their primary illicit activity, but rather an additional income carrying a relatively low risk.

9.8 Crossing the Chinese Borders

Smuggling is an important part of the illegal trade in TCM as raw materials have to be smuggled into China and then, after production, an amount of TCM is smuggled out of China and into the EU. A famous area for the smuggling of raw wildlife materials into China is the rich flora and fauna border region between Yunnan (Southern China) and Vietnam, Laos and Myanmar (Li and Wang 1999), that is traditionally well known for its opium cultivation (Zhang and Chin 2011). This region, notorious as the Golden triangle, is said to be dominated by drugs smuggling organizations (Chin 2009). For centuries local people would cross the borders of Yunnan and Myanmar without many problems from the law enforcement authorities. Farmers cultivate lands that straddle both countries. Successful stories of smugglers who become rich quickly spread the popularity of smuggling by the Hui minority in these regions (Zhang and Chin 2011). Since the growing restrictions on the opium trade, there is more emphasis on the illegal trade in wildlife (Nooren and Clardige 2001: 81). According to illegal traders in Yunnan province the suppression drove them into the profitable business of wildlife trafficking (CT8; CS9).

The smuggling of raw materials for TCM across the Myanmar and Laos border into Mainland China is well organized by these Chinese groups (CT8; CS9; CS11). Illegal wildlife seizures in China confirmed that 93 % of the smuggling rings were ethnic Chinese (UNODC 2013). Although Myanmar would be the primary country to smuggle illegal wildlife from South and Southeast Asia (e.g. Thailand, Malaysia, India) into China, from Cambodia and Laos the illegal trade is transferred through Vietnam and Thailand providing an important transit centre for illegal wildlife in the region (UNODC 2010). As a pangolin trader explained: "Pangolin scales are smuggled from Myanmar and Laos to Kunming on a large scale. The contraband is hidden between fruit or vegetables and, of course, it is known to be a weak border. (…) It is an organization that smuggles the scales [pangolin]. (…) The smugglers sell pangolins and musk directly to the shops. These are a few Chinese. They come along with a truck and with bags they spread it all over the market and sell it for 2,000 yuan per kilo" (CS8). These are, in particular, employees of Chinese companies in southern neighbouring countries, which are seldom controlled by customs officials (CT8; CM2; CM3). According to Yongge (2000) the company employees smuggle wildlife in their Chinese company car, jeep or truck, which is only given a rudimentary check,[47] and after crossing the border they are met by a middleman who takes the illegal wildlife products from them or they deliver the products to a prearranged destination. Transportations of ingredients such as tiger bone would be smuggled frequently by this method (Nooren and Claridge 2001). Other tricks employed by smugglers to pass through the border include grinding bones into powder form, using boxes with false bottoms or lids, using an ambulance, gas, ice, fish transportation trucks and even police prison vans and threatening influential people with weapons or attacking inspectors (Van Song 2008). Furthermore, besides the official border crossing, there are countless unofficial pathways across the border area in Yunnan that facilitate the illegal wildlife trade (Yongge 2000; Chi-yan 2005).

Another traditional smuggling area is the Hong Kong border with Mainland China (Lau et al. 1997; Lau 2014). Many illegal products from China are traded through Hong Kong that has acted as the international trade access point for the mainland for over 150 years (Nooren and Claridge 2001). The smugglers use zhongfei boats that are faster than the coast guard's cutters to traffic from Hong Kong to Shenzhen in Mainland China (UNODC 2010). Saiga horns, rhino horns and pangolins are regularly smuggled by trucks and sometimes by individuals with bags as hand luggage by train. An illegal trader in Guangzhou, a major trade hub near Hong Kong in Mainland China, explained: "Many people are involved. It is not just one person or one organization. (…) Each time the smugglers bring several kilos in bags or hide it in trucks. The same people who smuggle bird nests from Hong Kong to Guangzhou also smuggle the pangolin scales, saiga horns, bear bile and even rhino horns. (…) We pay them 400–500 yuan per kilo. (…) These smugglers deal in other illegal stuff as well" (CT6). A shopkeeper in Hong Kong proclaimed that Hong Kong is a transit hub for practical reasons: "Many illegal counterfeit products go through Hong Kong. (…) Rhino horn comes from Africa and is then smuggled through Hong Kong to Guangzhou in China. It is easier that way. (…) Of course there is more demand in Mainland China than in Hong Kong" (CS3). Several informants highlighted the Chinese perspective and social construction of Hong Kong products, including TCM; these are seen as products of greater quality and originality (CM1; CT2; CT7; CS4). This would be the reason why many Chinese come to Hong Kong to buy genuine TCM products (e.g. CS2; CS4; CS6; CT5). Furthermore, there is an open trade in saiga horns in Hong Kong, while in China it is forbidden for most TCM shops to sell them.[48] In China one has to obtain a licence from the government to sell saiga horn, which is not the case in the relatively free market of Hong Kong. However, transferring horns without CITES papers to Mainland China is strictly illegal (CP1).

According to an illegal trader and former smuggler of TCM in Guangzhou, sometimes people start by smuggling illegal raw materials to earn money in a

[47]This is because the vehicles are identified as being linked to Chinese aid projects in Laos (Yongge 2000).

[48]E.g. many shops in Wing Lok Street in Hong Kong sell saiga horns (personal observation, November 2013, Hong Kong).

relatively short period of time and then set up a legal TCM shop to cover this illegal trade. "I started with this illegal business seven years ago. (…) After I made a lot of money out of smuggling wildlife I set up my own legal TCM business, also to cover the illegal trade. Friends of mine did the same. Only if you want to take the risk can you join" (CT6). The informant referred to joining a criminal network involved in the wildlife trade that focuses on certain products. An illegal trader from the Anguo TCM market described it as follows: "The smuggling groups specialize in certain products depending on the smuggling route. Pangolins and wild tiger products are smuggled from the south of China, while saiga horns come from Northwest China and rhino horns mainly come from overseas African countries" (CT10).

Pangolins for TCM are mainly smuggled in large quantities by road (Yongping 2008). In 2010 Chinese customs officials confiscated 10,000 tonnes of pangolin parts. Gangs would be involved in this illegal activity of pangolin scale smuggling (Chakkaravarthy 2012). According to respondents, these gangs mix the pangolin scales with legal TCM materials and transport them by trucks across the border (e.g. CT6; CT8; CT10). The pangolins are typically smuggled in cargoes of 50–100 animals (Compton and Le Hai Quang 1998). An illegal seller of pangolin scales explained: "Do you know a herb we call longan. When it is fresh, it is a kind of fruit. After drying, it can be used as a medicine. Every day it can be used as soup. So its dosage is very large. (…) Longan is mainly produced in Thailand, Vietnam, and China. A lot of people from Thailand, Vietnam and other places bring it in containers and sell it in China. So someone takes advantage of this container and hides the pangolin to sneak it in with the longan" (CT6). Another trader in pangolins underlined a similar smuggling method: "Legal TCM enterprises are used to cover the illegal trade in pangolins between fruits or herbs. (…) The pangolins are packed in bags labelled with the name of another product. (…) The product name 'longan' is stated on the package while in reality pangolins or scales are hidden inside the bags (CT8)". This was confirmed by Sopyan (2009): "The pangolin traders usually use a legal business as camouflage. (…) Animals are processed and transported in packages mislabelled as products derivate from non-protected species. Local transport is done using private vehicles such as minivans painted with food or cigarette labels or public transportation such as bus." Although this method was often mentioned during the interviews, it appears—based on confiscation data—that other smuggling methods are used as well, such as Chinese fishing vessels with hidden sacks of pangolins from the Philippines to China (Pantel and Chin 2009). Large quantities of frozen pangolins are smuggled when they are declared to be frozen fish (Shepherd 2009). The hidden creatures are sometimes alive, but in most cases just the scales of the pangolin for the TCM are smuggled. To cross the borders bribery in the form of money and gifts is used to pay off the authorities and guards (Pantel and Chin 2009).

Saiga horns are smuggled in smaller quantities (dozens) in bags and hand luggage during the transfer from Hong Kong to mainland China by individuals or, more organized, (in hundreds of horns) by trucks from Kazakhstan and Russia into China. According to an illegal trader in Guangzhou: "The smugglers deliver the saiga horns from Hong Kong to Guangzhou using special bags. They are specialized in delivery" (CS7). An illegal trader in Anguo confirmed that saiga horns are mainly smuggled by trucks to cross the border between Russia (in the north) and Kazakhstan (in the west) into China: "All of the saiga horns are imported. They are from Russia and Kazakhstan. (…) Mostly it is smuggled by trucks and bus, because by train is more dangerous. They mix or hide it with fruit, but also with other items" (CS17). For instance, 719 saiga horns from Kazakhstan were smuggled along with cigarettes in 2013.[49] Additional smuggling methods consist of hidden compartments in trains, for example saiga horns under the head of a locomotive or smuggled saiga horns by shuttle bus from Kazakhstan to China (Traffic 2013). According to Hogg (2014) the poachers of saiga antelopes work together with officials in Kalmykia (Russia) who help to transport the horns to Astrakhan from where they are transferred to the final destination, China (Hogg 2014). There are also indicators that inspectors from the *Okhotzooprom* of the Kazakhstan Ministry of Agriculture, responsible for the enforcement and control of illegal hunting of saiga antelopes, are involved in the illegal trade of saiga horns to China (Von Meibom et al. 2010).

During previous years the illegality of the trade in rhino horn increased, according to several traders in TCM (e.g. CT3; CT11; CS11); smugglers of rhino horns would have been imprisoned in China (CT13). In the source countries rhino horns are regularly smuggled out of the area hidden in carpets or furniture (Milliken and Shaw 2012). Then bulk consignments with dozens of rhino horns are hidden in containers and smuggled by ship or individuals smuggle one or two rhino horns, regularly wrapped in newspapers and sealed with tape, in secret compartments in suitcases and bags by aircraft from south and east African countries (Milliken and Shaw 2012; Milliken 2014). According to a friend of a rhino smuggler who had been caught: "My friend smuggled rhino horns from Africa to the Anguo TCM market. Now he is in jail, because the police arrested him for smuggling. He smuggled it wrapped in silver foil hidden in hand luggage by airplane. He screwed it up" (CS20). Rhino horns are usually smuggled whole, because buyers prefer to purchase complete rhino horns to ensure their authenticity (Walker and Walker 2012; Montesh 2013). In contradiction to saiga horns and pangolin scales whereby smugglers deliver their contraband directly to the stores, smugglers and traders of rhino horn prefer to meet in distant areas to reduce the possibility of being seen. "It is illegal to buy and sell, that is why I meet them in my home", proclaimed an illegal rhino horn trader in Hong Kong (CS4).

"It is easier to get drugs than to get real tiger bones", mentioned an illegal TCM trader from the Anguo market. He explained that the criminalization of certain animal products for TCM has had a substantial impact on their availability: "Before it was perfectly legal, but now tiger bones are just like drugs such as heroin. Certain TCM ingredients are illegal, but everybody at TCM markets can get them through a middleman" (CS20). Similar to rhino horn, tiger smugglers receive heavy sentences; in 2003 a Tibetan faced the death penalty although it was later commuted

---

[49] '特大羚羊角走私案', China Daily, June 23, 2013.

Table 9.2 Types of smugglers of raw TCM materials

Smuggler	Medium amounts	Large amounts
Saiga antelope horn smuggler	A small amount of saiga horns is smuggled across the border in hand luggage in the back of the car or by train	Tonnes of saiga horns are smuggled in hidden compartments, a special layer or between fruits by trucks from the border with Russia and Kazakhstan
Pangolin scale smuggler	A small amount of pangolins are smuggled by individuals hidden on the body	Tonnes of pangolin scales are smuggled mixed with legal TCM materials across the border with Vietnam, Laos and Myanmar
Rhino horn smuggler	Rhino horns are smuggled in hidden compartments in suitcases or small pieces of rhino horn are smuggled on the body	Dozens of rhino horns are smuggled on a large scale from Africa to Myanmar, Vietnam and Hong Kong by containership
Tiger bones smuggler	Tiger bones are transferred in bags and smuggled across almost impassable border crossings in Tibet, Nepal and the North of China or through Myanmar	Kilos of tiger bones are smuggled by criminal groups from Nepal and India through Tibet

to a term of imprisonment (Moyle 2009). While the market for tiger bones seems to be based mainly on the illegal trade in tiger products from farms in China (see Sect. 9.9), there is a relatively small trade in parts from wild tigers from India and Myanmar (Table 9.2). Tiger products are smuggled across unguarded border crossings between India and Nepal, for example through Langtang National Park (Nowell and Ling 2007). According to an illegal trader in tiger bones in Kunming: "My middleman could arrange them from Myanmar. (…) I am not sure if the bones are from a Myanmar or Indian tiger, but he smuggles them in small packages and delivers within 2 weeks" (CT8). Another trader in Guangzhou prefers smuggling with the help of express postal services: "This company has a policy guarantee for delivering. They go through customs. They do not need to declare anything. They use a cargo company, they send it by post" (CS7). Criminal groups on the India–Myanmar border play a role in the illegal trade by avoiding the main crossings (e.g. Moreh/Tamu on the Manipur border) and use Mizoram into Myanmar's Chin State (UNODC 2010). Tiger bone smugglers have adopted two techniques to reduce the risk of detection. First, they reduce the risk by limiting the size of their shipments to China. The volumes of illegal shipments outside China would be much larger than within China. Second, the smugglers specialize in smuggling tiger products; just a small number of seizures consist of multiple species (Moyle 2009).

Subsequently, in China illegal raw materials are produced into medicine or are ground into a powder usually by legitimate registered (trading) companies. Then a part of the illegal TCM is exported to demand markets all over the world, including the EU. The illegal wildlife would be hidden in legitimate cargo (UNODC 2010). According to an international trader in Guangzhou: "We export to Chinatowns in the Netherlands and the US. The demand is growing in the EU, but in the last 5 years it has been harder to pass through customs, because the standard [for importing medicines] is different. In 2015 there will be new regulation in the EU, which makes it even harder to export to the EU. Not the raw materials but the capsules. (…) We hide illegal products between legal products or we give it another name. It is hard for EU customs officials to understand Chinese characters or to recognize powder from, for example, saiga horn" (CS7). Based on EU seizures more than 98 % of the TCM shipments to the EU are smuggled without CITES documents.

The recorded illegal entrepreneurs involved in smuggling TCM into the EU were mainly Chinese nationals ($N = 20$, 27 %). Figure 9.3 illustrates that they consist primarily of Traditional Asian Medicine suppliers (24 %), but also businessmen and public service administrative professionals were detected as being involved in the smuggling of illegal TCM. Traditional Asian medicine suppliers, businessmen and public service administrative professionals[50] together make up 43 % of the total. Smuggling into the EU takes place on a small scale by parcel post

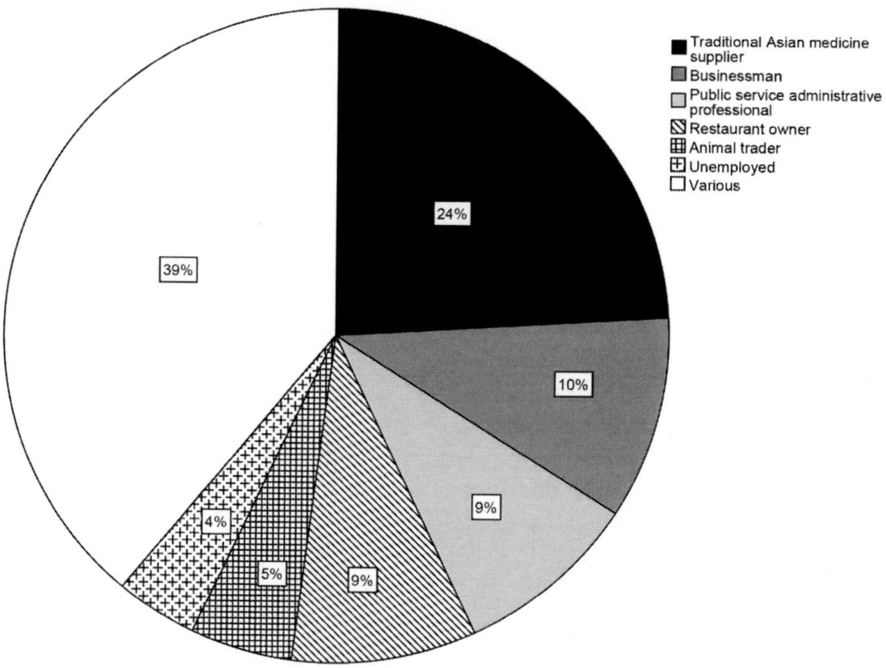

Fig. 9.3 Job of perpetrator in the illegal TCM trade. *To get a higher number of recordings, the jobs of illegal traders in endangered plants for medications are also included. *Source* Personal analyses of the EU-TWIX database, 2001–2010

[50]For instance, a Vietnamese government official was arrested when smuggling two rhino horns, diamonds and large sums of cash. However, diplomatic immunity prevented him from being prosecuted (Milliken and Shaw 2012).

or on a large scale by cargo containers through major transit hubs, such as Schiphol Airport and the Port of Rotterdam in the Netherlands (Van Uhm 2014). This is also reflected in the seizures, which range from small numbers (tens of medicines in posted parcels) to thousands of packages of medicines. In Europe increasingly large numbers of traditional Chinese medicine are seized. Especially TCM with rare ingredients are commonly seized, such as TCM including tiger or leopard parts during international flights from China. Furthermore, large amounts of pangolin scales are seized in Europe; in January 2013 alone, more than 800 kg of pangolin scales were confiscated (Post 2013: 36–37). Remarkably, forged CITES documents are rarely found; almost all cases consist of medicine without CITES documents.[51] This could mean that traders are not aware of the illegality of the medicines or that the resulting penalty or the risk of being caught is (very) low. However, the smugglers are able to anticipate the activities of law enforcers. After law enforcers found out that illegal animal ingredients were mentioned on the packing in English, suddenly the English names of the illegal animal ingredients had disappeared on the list of ingredients. Apparently Chinese characters still claimed to include these endangered species (rhino horn and tiger bone). Consequently, the Chinese characters on the medicine were also checked and now there are indicators that TCM companies send illegal raw materials to be processed in Europe (EN1; EP3). In recent years, a TCM producer in Europe was prosecuted for the production of TCM containing illegal animal ingredients (EP3).

9.9 Is Everyone Involved?

The trade in raw materials for TCM for China has already existed for centuries. Perhaps one of the earliest trade lines includes trade from Indian and Chinese merchants who had settled in the Mekong Delta and coastal areas of present-day Cambodia in the sixth century CE (Nooren and Claridge 2001: 17).[52] The Chinese merchants developed a very lucrative barter trade with locals in several neighbouring regions. For instance, Chinese minorities (Tao, Hmong, Lao Houay) started to exchange guns and other wildlife goods for TCM with ethnic groups in northern Laos. The products included highly valued raw materials, such as rhinoceros horn, animal bones and wax. Conflicts in Southeast Asia also provided opportunities for TCM traders. After the fall of the Cambodian capital in the 1970s the Chinese government had a trade agreement with the Khmer Rouge to exchange many TCM ingredients (e.g. tonnes of pangolin scales and many bones from tigers) for

[51]In 22 cases, other violations of CITES occurred, including ‘illegal use for commercial purposes’ ($N = 15$), ‘illegally selling, offering for sale, keeping or transporting’ ($N = 4$) and ‘illegal possession’ ($N = 3$).

[52]Centuries later, a flourishing wildlife trade by primarily Chinese, intermarried with locals, was noted by a French explorer (Nooren and Claridge 2001: 17).

armaments and fuel (Nooren and Claridge 2001).[53] According to Kiernan (1996) around $25 million of wildlife products were exported from Cambodia to China in only 2 years. Simultaneously in the 1970s many Chinese corporations were developed by Chinese families all over the Southeast Asia region to provide wildlife for Chinese medicines (McNeely and Wachtel 1991). In 1988 a trade agreement was signed by Laos and China to supply 'herbal medicines' by Laos in exchange for consumer goods, textiles and small agricultural equipment. The main traded items were tiger bones, bear gallbladder, sambar antlers, serow gallbladder, gaur gallbladder and pangolin scales (Nooren and Claridge 2001: 25). In the early 1990s, wildlife businesses developed by settled Chinese families in several Southeast Asian countries exploded.[54] Generally, these Chinese communities traded raw materials for TCM (e.g. tiger bone, pangolin scales) destined for China. For instance, in 1991 the Ho Chinese, involved for centuries in the wildlife trade, migrated to northern Laos in large numbers. They used their family connections to collect animal products to ship to Chinese markets. These people are still in the business and pay in advance for their ingredients based on trade agreements (ibid.: 28).

The dynamics of favours and personalized services in Chinese networks and relationships between family, friends and members of the same community plays an important role (Guthrie 1998). The strong intertwined cultural networks of the Chinese guarantee social control wherein traders work informally together based on the *guanxi* principle (e.g. CT6; CT8; CT10). The separation between private and business life is thereby limited and Chinese businessmen could take part in 'informal' activities. The social control ensures that the illegal business remains hidden (Chan et al. 2002). The structure and decision-making in ethnic Chinese trading communities are strongly influenced by family and the primacy of relationships (Ahlstrom et al. 2010). Much more than in Western societies, the borders between the formal TCM industry and informal health practices are extremely fluid and the same raw materials are offered in both the formal and informal markets. The existence of an informal TCM market alongside the official recognized structures underlines the intertwined connection between the legal and illegal trade (Von Moltke and Spaninks 2000; Nooren and Claridge 2001).

Traders in the illegal TCM trade in China are primarily TCM shopkeepers or wholesalers; some products are in stock with the shopkeeper and are sold 'under the table', while others can be supplied on demand. In every visited TCM market in China (e.g. Guangzhou, Kunming, Chengdu, Anguo) one is able to purchase illegal raw materials for TCM, such as pangolin scales, saiga horns, rhino horn and sometimes tiger bone. Generally, the illegal ingredients are not to be seen in TCM stores, but they regularly show up on request. For instance, in several cities across

[53]Between 1976 and 1978 at least 29 tonnes of deer antlers, 6 tonnes of monkey bones, 1.5 tonnes of elephant bones, 7 tonnes of pangolin scales, 2 tonnes of tortoise shell, 2.6 tonnes of snake skins, tens of thousands of dried geckos and bones and skins from more than 50 tigers, leopards and bears were imported (Nooren and Claridge 2001).

[54]For example, Lao enterprises were developed by ethnic Chinese to export several wildlife products (ibid.).

China (e.g. Guangzhou, Xi'an, Beijing, Kunming, Harbin) saiga horns are generally hidden under the counter in plastic bags and pangolins are mainly kept in glass jars. If one is interested, the TCM shopkeeper will get the illegal products or show them, sometimes initially, in a picture on his smartphone (personal observation, Hong Kong, Guangzhou, Kunming, Xi'an, Chengdu, Beijing in 2013). During fieldwork, many TCM shopkeepers presented pictures of rhino horns stored at home, while others picked them up from a middleman at the TCM market with a token from the shopkeeper.[55] According to a shopkeeper in Kunming: "We have just picked up the elephant skin from a friend. (…) The elephant skin is good for your stomach and comes from Myanmar. It costs 2,400 yuan [350 euro] per kilo and we can only sell it under the table because it is illegal. (…) There are other products such as rhino horn and tiger bones that we can arrange within a day. I will show you the picture of the rhino horn (…)" (CS9). Of course, the shopkeeper will receive commission if the sale is successful. According to Li et al. (2007), more than 50 % of the TCM pharmacies sold saiga horn and/or its derivatives and according to a study in 2008 by Xu Ling, 82 % of retail TCM shops ($N = 200$) surveyed in Kunming, Nanning, Fuzhou, Guangzhou and Haikou sold raw or processed scales of pangolins (Xu Ling 2008). In 2005–2006 less than 1 % of the surveyed TCM shops displayed medicines with tiger bone (Nowell and Ling 2007).[56] Some traders have to order the illegal ingredients in advance, while others have tonnes of illegal wildlife in stock. According to a market retailer in Anguo while discussing his business partner: "If you have big quantities of saiga [horn], this trader will buy your horns. He is a professional in this business. He has two tonnes of saiga horn from Russia in stock. The horns are bought from my friend in Harbin city. It is a transit station (…) to Anguo TCM market" (CS17). While pangolin scales and saiga antelope horns are easy to find and offered by a large variety of TCM traders at the markets (Illustration 9.2), rhino horn and tiger bones are more exclusive and expensive, and are only provided by specialists on the market. If a trader in China does not have illegal trade in stock, a middleman who has contacts with a collector in the source country will immediately order it.

The role of TCM doctors in the illegal trade is illustrated by 6 of the 11 interviewed TCM doctors in China who said that they had contacts with middlemen who can deliver illegal materials for TCM from endangered species. According to several informants, TCM doctors sell pangolin scales illegally, because of its healing quantities. The TCM doctors may advise their patients to buy it on the black market, while the consumer is not aware of the illegal background of the product (CM3; CS12; CS20). According to my interpreter in Chengdu, who used pangolin

[55]In several large cities in China (e.g. Hong Kong, Guangzhou, Beijing) fake rhino horns are also sold by minorities on the street. While real rhino horns are made of keratin (compacted hair), the fake horns are usually made of buffalo horn (Ammann 2011), or wood, plastic, fibreglass, stone or bamboo roots.

[56]A survey in China in 2008 found that 1.9 % of respondents had consumed TCM (including tonics) containing tiger products within the past 12 months. This would mean that around 25 million people in China still use the medicine (Graham-Rowe 2011).

Illustration 9.2 Saiga horns and pangolin scales for sale, China 2013

scales to ward off breast cancer: "I used some pangolins against lumps in my breasts. I know that it works. It will work. If you do not take it, it will take you a much longer time to heal. But it is very expensive. The doctor recommended me to use pangolin scales, but I could not afford it. He prescribed 5 or 10 g for 1 week. Around 50 g a month. The doctor told me that in a Western hospital they will cut a piece out of my breast, because I have a lot of lumps and perhaps it is cancer. (…) I was not informed that these scales are from an endangered animal. Now I know, but I cannot stop. Although it is not good for all those poor animals, I have to heal from cancer!" (CO3). Similar to the prescription for pangolin scales, many TCM doctors are still convinced of the strong function of rhino horn and tiger bone (CC2; CC4; CC6; CC8; CC10). According to TCM doctors in Guangzhou, Chengdu and Beijing, the demand for rhino horn has also increased in China, since people believe that it can cure cancer (CC1; CC2; CC4; CC7; CC10). Because the functionality of rhino horn is still highly valued by TCM doctors, the demand market remains. According to an illegal rhino trader in Kunming: "Rhino [horn] is good for liver cancer. A patient started treatment with rhino horn on the advice of her doctor and was cured of this disease a couple years ago. You slow down and fight the cancer with rhino horn. (…) People will usually not buy a whole rhino horn but slices" (CS11). This illustrates that the incentives and beliefs in TCM are deeply rooted in Chinese society. The Chinese may not obey laws which contradict what they believe to be 'a greater good for humanity' (Kidder 1983). However, not only the incentives to heal a patient, but also economic incentives play a role. TCM doctors prescribe expensive (illegal) ingredients so that they can earn additional money. Many informants highlighted that TCM doctors provide these additional services to feed the demand (CS10; CS14; CS17).

According to TCM traders in several cities all over China, hospitals and clinics buy their illegal raw materials through a middleman or directly at TCM markets (CT8; CT9; CT10). To buy the illegal products shopkeepers register these products under another name. For instance, pangolin scales are 'officially' bought by a TCM trader as herbs to avoid registration control. This occurs in hospitals and clinics as well, according to an experienced middleman in Anguo: "As a middleman I sell pangolins and saiga horns to hospitals, but people are afraid that they will be punished by the TCM administration office. They have a checklist. They put another name on the list of products which they buy. Once purchased, the hospitals and clinics state that they have these products in stock" (CM4). This registration fraud would be used by many shops, hospitals, manufacturers and clinics in order to buy and launder the illegal products. This fraud by legally registered TCM enterprises and hospitals could be defined as a form of corporate crime as these enterprises offer illegally obtained products to regular customers (Ruggiero and South 2010). Moreover, these companies regularly do not have a licence from the government to sell these products. For instance, all sales of saiga horn are illegal without a permit from the national-level authorities (Li et al. 2007). Furthermore, law enforcers are bribed to sell these illegal products without any legal intervention (*guanxi* plays a role here as well). According to four TCM doctors: "If you can pay enough [to local government officials] you can sell the products. No problem at all" (CC3; CC5; CC8; CC10). The legality of the sales is apparently seen as ambiguous.

Similar to the trade in caviar, laundering methods are used to legalize products obtained from illegal sources. A major laundering method is a misleading indication that products from saiga antelopes and pangolins are from existing stockpiles. According to the coordinator of wildlife enforcement in China, it is permitted for certain reputable sellers and producers to sell saiga horn and pangolin scales from stockpiles (CP2). However, the stockpiles of saiga horn and pangolins have long been calculated to have already been used. While in 1994 the total supply of saiga horn in China was estimated at 155,500 kg, in a second nationwide survey undertaken by the government (2005) the total volume was 55,000 kg (Von Meibom et al. 2010). This means that with a decrease of more than 100,000 kg in 10 years, the total amount of stockpiles will be minus 45,000 in 2015.[57] This indicates that this deficiency is solved in an alternative way; illegally obtained products are mixed with legal products. This was confirmed by many merchants on the market stalls (e.g. CS10; CS12; CS18).

Furthermore, employees of well-known TCM factories and shops, TCM doctors from state hospitals and local clinics and pharmacies claim that their saiga horn and pangolin scales are from farmed animals (CC3; CC5; CC9; CH1; CH2; CH3; CS16), which would make them legitimate. According to the coordinator of wildlife enforcement in China such farms do not exist (CP2). The necessary knowledge to breed these animals commercially is lacking (Braun 2009; Li et al. 2007; Yang et al. 2007). Both animal species, pangolins and saiga antelopes, are extremely difficult to breed in captivity (Li et al. 2007; Shepherd 2009). For instance, since 1987 efforts have been made to increase the captive-bred population of saiga antelopes in order to reintroduce them into the wild in China. Only 114 saiga antelopes have been bred after all that time (Zhao et al. 2013). According to the Chinese coordinator of Law Enforcement of CITES: "First, the population is too small for the commercial

[57]From 2007 onwards, one batch of 4,200 kg saiga horns was legally imported by China (CITES Trade Database 2015).

market, second, it is strictly prohibited to use their horns commercially" (CP2). TCM traders of raw materials all over China explained that actually hospitals, TCM doctors and large shops purchase their saiga horns and pangolin scales on the black market; these illegal products are from wild animals (e.g. CT6; CT10; CS7; CS10).

Besides claiming that the products are from existing stockpiles or from captive-bred animals, a third 'laundering' method refers to tiger farms. While in China the population of wild tigers decreased from 4,000 in 1949 to 40–50 in 2012, the tigers in China's farms increased from 8–13 in 1986 to 6,000 in 2010 (EIA 2013). In the 1980s two tiger farms were developed by the Chinese government to breed tigers for the commercial supply of bones for TCM.[58] These farms were established before the 1993 ban on tiger bones for tiger products in TCM. For instance, in the early 1990s Guilin Xiongsen Tigers and Bears Mountain Village, with 400 captive-bred tigers at that time, regularly supplied bones to the TCM industry and a factory in Harbin manufactured half a million tiger bone plasters each day with a bone-crushing machine (Nowell 2000). While the sale of products derived from captive-bred tigers has not been allowed since the ban, there are strong indications that local officials accept the trade in tiger bone products, such as tiger bone wine—a traditionally popular form of tiger medicine (Nowell and Ling 2007; EIA 2013; Nowell 2009). From my personal observations in Harbin Tiger Farm in Harbin in China with a captive-bred population of around 1,200 tigers, many bottles of tiger bone wine were for sale and this confirmed these suspicions (personal observation, December 13, 2013, Harbin) (Illustration 9.3).

Illustration 9.3 Tiger bone wine for sale, Harbin, China 2013

[58]Noteworthy is that despite the ban of tiger bone and rhino horn in TCM the Chinese government still suggested that captive breeding centres would be able to fuel the demand in the late 2000s. One proposal in 2007 was to use tiger products solely to TCM hospitals (Sellar 2014).

The differences in the prices of the tiger bone wines were based on the length of fermentation. Staff members confirmed that the tiger bones are used to make tiger bone wine. According to an employee, this is perfectly legal as they would have certificates from officials to produce and sell the wine based on tiger bones. "The government allows us to sell the wine. They gave us a certificate to sell the tiger bone wine, because we have many tigers. (…) Around 100 tigers are born and a lot of our tigers die every year. (…) Yes, all tigers that have died here are kept in ice" (CO6). The tiger farms would have been allowed to keep tiger carcasses in freezers (Nowell and Ling 2007; Nowell 2009). A seller of tiger bone wine of Harbin Tiger Park explained that all dead tigers are kept in freezers to preserve their valuable bodies and keep them 'fresh' (CS24). According to a former CITES expert this would be similar in Guilin Xiongsen Tigers and Bears Mountain Village. He observed tiger carcasses in freezers whereby the majority were cubs or juvenile tigers. Some 75–80 % of the suspicious deaths were recorded to be the result of fights between tigers (Sellar 2014). There are, however, serious concerns that tiger bones are being laundered through these farms (Nowell and Ling 2007; Nowell 2009; EIA 2013). Moreover, farm owners have a good relationship with the government and have lobbied for years for the ban on selling tiger bone wine from captive-bred tigers to be lifted (Nowell and Ling 2007; Mills 2015).[59] This laundering method was confirmed in the late 2000s when more large pieces of tiger carcasses were seized across Southeast Asia and there were indications of an increase in tiger meat in restaurants. It is believed that captive breeding tigers from farms are used for this illegal trade (Nowell 2009). For instance, a seizure of several tiger carcasses near the border with Malaysia as a range state showed, after DNA analysis, that they were carcasses of Siberian tigers (this species is bred on a large scale in farms in China) (Sellar 2014). While each year many tigers die on the farms and the employees of these farms claim that they use tiger bones in the tiger bone wine, on the ingredient list of the bottles the Latin name *Panthera leo* is mentioned. This would suggest that the bones are from lions instead of tigers. According to Nowell (2009) this may be a laundering method: the farms pretend that they are using lion bones (CITES II),[60] but in reality they use the forbidden tiger bones (CITES I). The tiger bones would be sold to medicine-producing factories and then these products are directly circulated to hospitals for treatment, such as arthritis (EIA 2013). From this perspective, parts from captive-bred tigers from Chinese tiger farms may dominate the illegal trade in tiger products.

In the early 1990s hundreds of TCM factories in China were manufacturing pills, wine, and plasters with tiger bone and exported these TCM in large quantities (Nowell 2009). When the tiger products were banned, China continued to

[59]Not only in the 'tiger farm industry', but in the 'rhino farm industry' in South Africa there is also a lobby for legalization. Moreover, it is probable that there are already farms in China that use their horns in TCM as a treatment for cancer (Cota-Larson 2013).

[60]The use of lion bones in TCM is legal with certificates from the China State Forestry Administration (SFA) (EIA 2013).

manufacture and export TCM on the premise that the content of tiger bone was not readily recognizable (Mills and Jackson 1994). Despite the significant decline in the availability of tiger bone offered by TCM traders, in the US, the EU and China large amounts of seized tiger bone or TCM containing tiger bone nevertheless indicate that the illegal trade has continued (Nowell 2009; Verheij and Engel 2010). The majority of the illegal TCM products seized in the EU, including medicine with tiger bone, are used by Asian ethnic communities in Europe (Sellar 2014). However, many of the manufactured medicines labelled as containing tiger bone are fake and tiger bone was used in even more dilute dosages as shown by several tests on tiger DNA. For instance, tiger plasters from 518 TCM stores in China were tested and showed no evidence of tiger bone (Gratwicke et al. 2008). According to a musk-tiger plaster manufacturer only 50 g of tiger bone are used for a batch of 108,000 plasters. This would mean that only 0.0023 g of tiger bone is used in a five-plaster package (Gaski and Johnson 1994). This may explain the outcome of DNA tests and the relatively low prices for products such as plasters with tiger bone. However, killing wild tigers is believed to be far cheaper than farming them (Bulte and Damania 2005) and due to the strong belief that bones from wild tigers provide a better analgesic effect than bones from farmed tigers (Ellis 2005), the illegal trade in products from wild animals will remain.

9.10 Follow the Medicines

As China is the largest consumer of TCM in East and Southeast Asia (World Bank 2005), it comes as no surprize that, based on seizures, the illegal TCM in the EU are mainly from China. Some animals are being bred for the (illegal) production of medicines in China, such as bears and tigers, while other animal products are smuggled in by truck or aircraft. For instance, saiga horns from Russia and Kazakhstan or pangolins from Vietnam, Laos, Thailand and Myanmar arrive by truck, whereas rhino horn in particular arrives by plane from South Africa (e.g. CT2; CT5; CT8; CS13; CM2). Especially the Vietnam border would have largely influenced the illegal wildlife trade in the provinces of China. Many illegally imported raw materials for TCM have been found in markets in Guangzhou, Shenzhen, Hong Kong and Macao and they originated from Vietnam from where they have been smuggled through the Guangxi border (Li et al. 1996; Lau et al. 1997). Vietnam would be a 'crossing point' for the trade in wildlife from Indochina (Vietnam, Laos and Cambodia) to China (Van Song 2008; Van and Tap 2008). Generally, the products travel along existing trade routes which were already in existence long before the bans were introduced. The substitutes are distributed or produced in China and then exported, for instance, to the EU. This illegal trade is often conveyed through legal trade structures by land, air or sea, but the routes change according to an illegal TCM trader in Kunming: "The trade lines are changing all the time, it is like selling drugs. If people know about it, it is going to be changed. The black market in TCM is like this. Therefore, I cannot tell you the trade lines" (CT8). While some of the illegal traders were reluctant to speak about the trade lines, others were willing to provide more details about specific smuggling lines.

Since the early 1990s the Chinese pangolin population has significantly declined and pangolin scales for TCM originate largely from other range countries, such as Myanmar, Thailand, Indonesia, Laos, Vietnam and Malaysia (Li et al. 1996; Duckworth et al. 1999; Pantel and 2009; Yue 2008; Pantel and Anak 2010). According to an illegal trader in Guangzhou: "The pangolin is no longer found in China, so the majority of scales originate from Southeast Asian countries, Laos and Myanmar in particular" (CT6). Especially large numbers of pangolins are smuggled into China through the Guangxi and Yunnan Province. From there the scales are transferred to the provinces of Guangdong, Hainan and Fujian to be sold (Yue 2008). Chinese border cities, such as Hekou and Daluo in Yunnan, and transit hubs, such as Kunming, play an important role in the illegal wildlife trade (Yongge 2000; UNODC 2013). The pangolins are smuggled by road from Myanmar and Laos to Kunming or from Vietnam to Nanning in Guangdong. These two cities are not the only destinations, but function as transit hubs in China. The scales are then transported to other large TCM markets in Guangzhou, Chengdu, Xian, Beijing, Anguo and even Harbin in the upper north. Pangolins from Myanmar are mainly from Shan State with border crossings from Mong La and Muse/Ruili, from Boten in Laos and Bien and Hanoi in Vietnam.[61] Mong La and Mong Mit are important wildlife trade hubs in Myanmar (Oswell 2010). According to illegal pangolin traders in Guangzhou, Kunming and Chengdu, pangolins are being smuggled on a large scale by road from Southeast Asian countries, with Myanmar, Laos and Vietnam as source and transit countries from Malaysia, Indonesia and Thailand (CT6; CM2; CT9). In exceptional cases, containerships are used to transfer the scales to the harbour in Shenzhen. Since 2003 the illegal cross-border wildlife trade from Laos to China has mainly focused on pangolins with China as the major demand market (World Bank 2005).

China is also the largest importer of saiga horns originating primarily from Russia and Kazakhstan (Von Meibom et al. 2007, 2010). One important illegal route which is used to smuggle hundreds of kilograms of saiga horns per year flows from Kazakhstan to Urumchi, an important transit city in Xinjiang in the western part of China (Li et al. 2007; Von Meibom et al. 2010). Saiga antelopes in Russia are mainly poached around the villages of Utta, Khulkhuta, Chilgir, Molodezhnyi and Artezian in the Yashkulskiy and Chernozemelskiy districts of the Republic of Kalmykiya. The saiga horns are then transported through Elista to Moscow and, from there, further on to the eastern part of Russia and then into China (Von Meibom et al. 2010). Saiga horns from Uzbekistan are mainly smuggled through Kazakhstan into China.[62] Although in previous years saiga horns from Kazakhstan and Russia were generally transported to Beijing through Moscow, horns are

[61]In the 1990s, at least 400 pangolins were smuggled from Vietnam into China each week (Compton and Le Hai Quang 1998).

[62]Networks of poachers are located in Nukus, Kungrad, Khojeili and Tashkent in Uzbekistan (Von Meibom et al. 2010).

nowadays illegally exported directly into China. According to illegal traders of saiga horns in Kunming, Chengdu and Harbin, saiga horns come from Kazakhstan and Uzbekistan and enter China through Xinjiang and are then transported through Tibet to different cities (CT8; CT9; CT13). Chengdu appears to be a transit hub for saiga horns for western China. In the north, the saiga horns originate from Heilongjiang (Li et al. 2007) with Harbin as a transit hub in China. The smugglers cross the border at Heihe which, according to respondents, is 'a smugglers' town in the upper north'. "The horns are bought from my friend in Harbin city. It is a transit station. From Russia he sends them through Heihe at the China–Russia border to Harbin and from Harbin to Anguo TCM market" (CS17). The saiga horns from Hong Kong originate from Russia, but are most likely illegally transferred through Singapore (Von Meibom et al. 2010). This was confirmed by several saiga horn traders in Hong Kong (CT3; CT4).

While in the past rhino horn for TCM originated from Asian countries, this slowly changed as Asian rhinos are now almost extinct in the wild (Milliken and Shaw 2012). Consequently, the illegal trade in rhino horn has largely moved to African countries (Milliken 2014; Milliken and Shaw 2012). Already in the 1960s and 1970s Hong Kong was the world's main importer of rhino horn (Leader-Williams 1992). After the government banned imports of rhino horn in 1979, it was subsequently smuggled from Macao, Burma, Indonesia, Malaysia, India, Taiwan and South Africa (Ellis 2005). According to illegal rhino horn traders, Hong Kong is still a major hub for rhino horn for two reasons. First, Hong Kong is well connected with African source countries (with the transit cities being Johannesburg and Maputo) and destinations such as China and Taiwan (Leader-Williams 1992; Milliken and Shaw 2012). Second, the Chinese come to buy original and quality products in Hong Kong. According to a rhino horn dealer: "While there are many fake rhino horns sold on the street in several big cities in China, the Chinese buy the 'real deal' in Hong Kong" (CT2). The market in Hong Kong is seen as genuine in the trade in wildlife. It even occurs that rhino horns are smuggled from Mainland China to Hong Kong to be sold for a higher price to the Chinese who then smuggle the horns back to Mainland China. According to an interview with a rhino horn middleman in Kunming, the rhino horns originate incidentally from India, but in general they are coming from South African countries (CM2). The rhino horns are transferred by container ships from Africa to Myanmar or Vietnam (CS11; CS19). While the former rhino range state Vietnam is well known as a destination market for rhino horn (Milliken and Shaw 2012), according to illegal traders in China, Vietnam functions primarily as a transit country instead of the final destination; rhino horns are smuggled from Vietnam through Yunnan and Guangxi into China (CS11; CT8).

The main trade in TCM that contain tiger bones, like tiger bone wine, originates from tiger farms in China underlined several traders. The two biggest farms are Harbin Siberian Tiger Park in the upper north and Guilin Tiger Farm in the south.

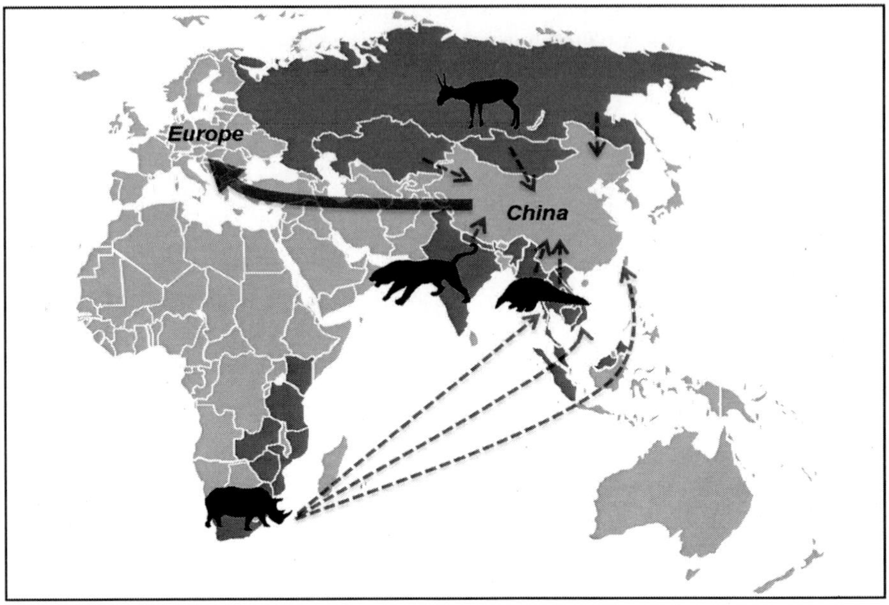

Map. 9.1 Smuggling routes for TCM. *Source* Interviews and personal analyses of confiscations in the EU

According to several TCM traders, these farms sell raw tiger materials on the black market, sometimes even with certificates from governmental institutions (see also Nowell 2009; EIA 2013). Based on interviews with traders in Chengdu and Kunming, there exists a relatively small trade line for wild tigers from India and Myanmar (Map. 9.1). The smugglers cross the border in Nepal–Tibet or from Myanmar into Yunnan province in China (e.g. CS13; CT8; CM2). According to a tiger bone dealer: "The tiger bones are hidden in small packages. My friends use unofficial routes to enter China and bring the bones to me in Kunming" (CT8). Another smuggling route consists of wild tiger products being smuggled from Russia through Heilongjiang Province in China. It is noteworthy that most arrests regarding wild Bengali or Indo-Chinese subspecies of tigers have taken place in Yunnan (in the south), while most arrests for smuggling wild Siberian tiger products were in Heilongjiang (in the north) (Moyle 2009).

In China the illegal raw materials are generally turned into medicines, which are then exported to demand markets all over the world. Large harbours and airports are used to smuggle the illegal TCM into the EU. According to a geographical analysis of data from illegal exporters in China to the EU, the main trade comes from three large 'business' cities: Guangzhou, Hong Kong and Beijing. Hong Kong is well known as the 'import and export window' of China. Less than 0.1 % of the sea freight which contains 90 % of the total movement of freight in Hong Kong is inspected (Lau 2014). Guangzhou and Beijing are important transit hubs in China with a high level of connectivity by airports and seaports. Some 80 % of all interceptions of wildlife occurred in Beijing and Guangzhou in 2010 (UNODC 2013). Moreover, the two biggest TCM markets in China, Qingping market in Guangzhou and Anguo market near Beijing, could be of explanatory relevance as well. While the major (illegal) exports of TCM from China go to other Asian countries, such as Malaysia, Thailand and Indonesia, within the EU the Netherlands, Denmark and Germany seem to be major demand markets. According to the coordinator of wildlife enforcement in China, the exporters are sometimes unaware of the EU regulation; they export illegal TCM to the EU by accident (CP2). On the other hand, illegal wholesalers in Guangzhou and Beijing may be well aware of this illegality, but prefer to pay the fine if they are caught (CM1; CT12).

9.11 Chinese Triads or Crime that is Organized?

Criminal networks in China have been traditionally described as banned underworld organizations, mysteriously branded as secret societies *Mìmì shèhuì* (幫會). While these organizations were believed to have been almost eradicated during the Communist period from 1949 onwards, in the post-Mao area these secret societies returned due to less political control, the market being reformed and more socioeconomic freedoms for Chinese citizens. The emergence of these secret societies or triads would be closely related to massive criminal unemployment, economic inequality, relative deprivation, criminal subcultures, political corruption and globalization (Chen 2005; Zhang and Chin 2009). Based on United Nations studies on the illegal trade in wildlife, wildlife experts assume that the Chinese triads, such as the Wo Shing Wo and 14K, are involved in the smuggling of wildlife, including rhino horn (ECOSOC 2002, 2003). The Chinese criminal organizations trade in parts of endangered species on a regular basis to fuel the demand for TCM products derived from those species (ECOSOC 2002). Recent studies confirm the involvement of the Chinese triads in the illegal trade in rhino horns for TCM from South Africa to China. They are directly involved in organizing and financing the illegal rhino horn trade and have connections with deeper trade channels in Asia. These triads are also believed to trade in arms, drugs and ivory (Gastrow 2001; Milliken and Shaw 2012; Montesh 2013). Although, according to previous studies, it seems that organized crime is involved in the TCM trade in Southeast Asia and South Africa, there are also indicators of the involvement of (Chinese) criminal organizations in the EU. According to several police investigations criminal organizations in the EU are closely involved in the illegal trade in (raw materials of) TCM.

For instance, in the 1990s the British police dismantled a Chinese triad group in England which sold medicinal substances derived from endangered animals to customers in Asia (Berry et al. 2003) and an Irish criminal syndicate, the Rathkeale Rovers, stole dozens of rhino horns from museums between mid-2011 and 2012; 100 rhino horns were (probably) traded to China or Vietnam for the TCM industry (Van Uhm 2012; Milliken and Shaw 2012; Europol 2012). Asian criminals may be

Illustration 9.4 Seized rhino horns, the Netherlands 2013

travelling throughout Europe, Canada and the US in search of rhino horns (Illustration 9.4). The level of organization is illustrated by smugglers who have been caught with up to eight horns worth 30,000 euro per kilo (Sellar 2014). Furthermore, Chinese criminal organizations, mainly based in Hong Kong, specialize in trading TCM containing derivatives of endangered species to several companies in the EU, especially in northwestern Europe (Europol 2011). Large seizures in the EU of TCM with derivatives of saiga antelopes, pangolins, tigers, sea horses, musk and bear bile prove at least a substantial capital investment and a high level of coordination and organization (see Sect. 9.4).

The sophisticated smuggling methods also indicate a high level of organization. Already in the 1980s rhino horn smuggling was highly organized and in the hands of powerful organizations of a military nature, such as the South African Defence Force (SADF) (Van Vuuren 2006; Montesh 2013). Simultaneously, Chinese criminal groups in South Africa, with connections to the Chinese triads 14 K and the Wo Shing Wo in Hong Kong, became—besides the shark fin and abalone trade—active in the rhino horn trade (Gastrow 2001). Currently, organized forms of rhino horn smuggling are still present. An important method that has been used is based upon permits in South Africa for hunting a rhino that allow people to poach one white rhino each year (CITES 2010). According to Rademeyer (2012) an international wildlife trafficking syndicate hired Thai prostitutes and strippers from clubs in Pretoria and Midrand to pose as 'hunters' in sham rhino trophy hunts. 'The women, whom had never fired a shot in their lives, would be paid R5,000 each for their participation in a hunt. (…) Once the permits were issued, Chunchom would fetch the women and drive them to a farm where the hunt was due to take place. (…) The girls would pose with the kill, holding a rifle.'[63] This 'pseudo-hunting' of white rhinos seems to be linked to sex workers who would have been trafficked to South Africa, where they work illegally to pay off their debts (Milliken and Shaw 2012). In addition, many hunters in South Africa (48 % of the total number of foreign hunters between 2009–2012) came from Vietnam without any experience of hunting (Milliken and Shaw 2012; Sellar 2014). While after restrictions on Vietnamese hunters the amount dropped, an increase in rhino hunters from the Czech Republic could be an indicator of Czech proxy hunters on behalf of Asian crime syndicates (Milliken and Shaw 2012).[64] The rhino crime syndicates would be typically multinational operations that include other criminal activities like the trade in drugs, diamonds, humans and other wildlife products such as elephant ivory and abalone (Hübschle 2010; Rademeyer 2012; Montesh 2013).[65] Generally the more wildlife products are criminalized, such as tiger bone and rhino horn, the more covert, organized and insidious the trade may become.

Several authors underlined the connection between organized crime and government officials in China (e.g. Wang 2013). Chinese organized crime would use its 'protective umbrella' *Bbǎohùsǎn* (保護傘): officials take bribes and provide protection to continue illegal activities (Zhang and Chin 2008; Wang 2013). Wang (2013) notes that it would be difficult to have a long-term illegal trade line without connections to government officials (Wang 2013). In the illegal trade in raw materials for TCM officials are regularly involved in this illegal trade by taking bribes or arranging border crossings. The high level of organization in the illegal trade in pangolin scales is discussed by Yongping (2008: 78): "The head of the group cleverly stays away from the goods and only makes transactions by phone using a tea business for protection. He bribed some of the post office clerks in the

[63]'Sex workers used to 'hunt' rhino', News 24, July 22, 2011.

[64]In addition, the sale of two rhino horns by a trader to a federal agent for $55,000 in a hotel in Las Vegas on March 19, 2014, indicates a connection with the Medellin drug cartel, as the same trader was involved in the illegal trade in cocaine from the Medellin drug cartel to the United States. "Operation Crash has documented how individuals involved in other non wildlife-related crimes have branched out into wildlife crimes", says US Fish and Wildlife's officer (Christy 2014).

[65]Another example is the involvement of the Groenewald syndicate in the illegal rhino horn business. For over 4 years the Groenewald syndicate is alleged to have kept rhinos for conservation purposes, while actually the real purpose was the dehorning and killing of rhinos to make profits from the sale of their horns. The case is one of the most serious cases regarding rhinos with 1,872 charges of racketeering, illegal hunting, dealing in rhino horns, and fraud and money laundering (Rademeyer 2012; Ayling 2013). Due to the involvement of professional hunters and game farmers predominantly with an Afrikaans membership, these groups have been referred to 'Boere mafia' or 'khaki-collar criminals' (Milliken and Shaw 2012).

Menlian County, and sent pangolin scales to producers of traditional medicine in places such as Anguo, Hebei, Bozhou Anhui, Sichuan and Hunan. Members of the group are specifically trained to be responsible for transport, communication, purchase, packaging and storing". In the absence of governmental authority large numbers of government officials tend to specialize in abusing power and stimulating profitable illegal trade flows (Wang 2013).

The process of bribing officials starts with the *guanxi* practice of gifts. When the official accepts the gift, there is a strong possibility that the official is willing to repay the debt and the bribe process can be developed within the *guanxi* practice (Li 2011). The officials can make use of their position in several ways. According to a number of TCM traders, customs officials arrange for the illegal trade to cross the border, but these officials also sell seized rhino horns and tiger bone (CT3; CT8; CT10). In addition, TCM clinics pay government officials to sell certain materials, such as pangolins or saiga horn. The government officials do not specifically protect these TCM traders, but arrange that other officials do not hinder them. Indeed, diplomatic immunity prevents the officials from being prosecuted (CC5; CC8).

Based on information from a TCM trader in Chengdu one highly organized trade line operates as follows: saiga antelope horns are poached in Kazakhstan under the protection of local Kazakh organized crime groups and are then smuggled across the border into West China by trucks. The customs officials are bribed in advance and the trucks carrying the horns can cross the border at Dostyk in Kazakhstan without any border controls. Within a couple of days, the horns are delivered in Chengdu at the TCM market. The trader then retransfers several horns hidden between other materials being transported by his TCM company to a Western European trader (CT9). Four important players operate in the process: a representative of the crime group in Kazakhstan, the Chinese middleman who bribed the border officials at the Russia–Kazakhstan border, the TCM trader in Chengdu and the TCM trader in Europe (see Fig. 9.4 for other flows).

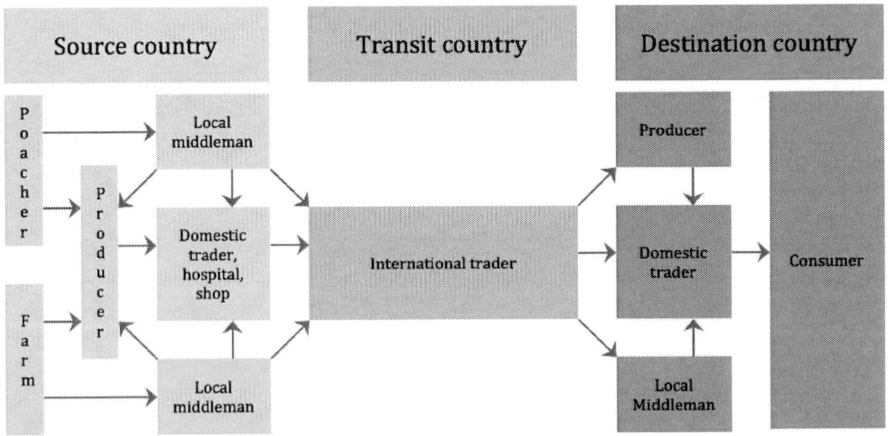

Fig. 9.4 Supply chain (simplified) of the illegal trade in TCM

Table 9.3 Prices of illegal TCM ingredients on the market

	Price/kg (range states)	Price/kg (China)
Pangolin	€ 30–40	€ 197–580 (1,700–5,000 CNY)
Saiga horns	€ 130	€ 1,622–2,086 (14,000–18,000 CNY)
Rhino horn	€ 3,500–4,000	€ 15,065–23,176 (130,000–200,000 CNY)
Tiger bone	€ 500–800	€ 2,318–3,476 (20,000–30,000 CNY)

Besides the social organization and the modus operandi, the profits may be very attractive for organized crime networks. The profits increase with every step in the model from hunters, collectors, and smugglers to middlemen, traders and consumers, and attract criminal groups along the way. The value of animals and wildlife products typically increases by 25–50 % as they pass through consecutive links in the supply chain. This is particularly true in the case of rare medicinal and luxury items (tiger parts and rhino horn) (UNODC 2013). Whereas pangolins are purchased for around € 30–40 a kilo from the hunter, the market price for consumers in China or Europe would be between 1,700 and 5,000 CNY (€ 197–580) per kilo. According to Liddick (2011), from the sources in Myanmar to the final market in China, the price of pangolin increases 40–50-fold. Saiga horns can be purchased for € 130 for one kilo from the hunters and the market price would be around 14,000–18,000 CNY (€ 1,622–2,086), thus easily tenfold the price. A kilo of rhino horn on the black market in South Africa is sold for around R65,000 (€ 3,500–4,000) and is sold in China for around 130,000–200,000 CNY (€ 15,065–23,176), while tiger bones are bought in range states for around € 500–800 and sold for around 20,000–30,000 CNY (€ 2,318–3,476) (Table 9.3). Thus the profits can reach highly attractive levels.

Furthermore, the criminal organizations may present a high level of connectedness to other illegal products. According to the CITES coordinator of Law Enforcement in China, confiscated materials are sometimes found to have been combined with other counterfeit products, for instance weapons and drugs: “When we recently arrested a wildlife smuggler, we found some other illegal items together with endangered species, such as guns and drugs. (…) The smugglers are involved in other forms of crime” (CP2). According to UNODC (2013), especially long-distance transfers of high-value wildlife, such as rhino horns from Africa, require the involvement of a wide range of brokers, middlemen and shippers who are not necessarily wildlife traders, but are rather experts in the smuggling of illegal goods, including drugs (UNODC 2013). This has been confirmed in China by recent confiscations of saiga horns combined with cigarettes,[66] rhino horns with arms, drugs, abalone and ivory, tiger bones with arms and pangolin scales with imitation products.[67] While some informants indicated that there is no interconnection, other informants highlighted this interconnectedness. According to two illegal rhino horn traders in Hong Kong, the trade in rhino horns has connections

[66]‘特大羚羊角走私案’, China Daily, June 23, 2013.

[67]E.g. ‘一根犀牛角 五走私网 跨越两大洲的 犀牛角上的中国魅影’, Infzm, October 10, 2013; ‘物 消失 伙内榕破特大犀牛角走私案’, Fznews, November 20, 2013.

with the trade in abalone: "Chinese from Africa smuggle and deliver abalone and rhino horn. They bring it in plastic bags and I meet them at my home. You have to be careful" (CS4). He stated that he was cautious so as to avoid being caught or spotted by government officials. The connection between the trade in rhino horn and that in abalone has been confirmed by previous research (e.g. Milliken and Shaw 2012; Montesh 2013) and it is suggested that 90 % of abalone and rhino horn smugglers are associated with each other. According to illegal traders in Kunming wildlife smugglers in the Myanmar-China border town, Daluo, are also involved in drugs trafficking (CT8; CS9). Moreover, based on confiscations in China, rhino horn is (frequently) smuggled together with abalone, ivory and lion bone and is often combined with other drugs and guns in the operation.[68] Domestic and international specialists in storage, handling, transport, processing, packaging, exporting, marketing, security and retailing may all be involved. They provide the official expenditure (e.g. purchasing permits and paying fines) as well as the unofficial expenditure (e.g. bribes and loans against future deliveries of wildlife) (UNODC 2013).[69]

However, not all the respondents were convinced of the involvement of organized crime. On the one hand, several informants were totally aware of highly organized groups being deeply involved in the illegal trade in TCM. Some illegal traders referred to their 'mafia-structured' organizations. "We have already been active for 20 years and it has become highly organized, you know, just like a mafia business. (…) We work with the upper and underworld and it is based on strong friend and family relations. Many people are involved in one illegal shipment and our relations with officials work to our advantage" (CT8). Another trader proclaimed: "It is a long-term relationship based on trust. The price is determined by this relationship when large amounts of products and the involvement of border officials are concerned. It is similar to the drug business. You have a relationship with the black business and the white business. It is like a mafia business. (…) They smuggle tonnes of hidden pangolins and saiga horns with big trucks" (CS17).

On the other hand, some respondents mentioned the fact that, based on their personal knowledge, no organized crime is involved because the profits are somewhat higher than in a normal business or they referred to the involvement of legally registered TCM corporations instead of organized crime (e.g. CT1; CT9; CS22). From this point of view, the illegal trade in TCM would be characterized as a form of corporate crime as several TCM companies, TCM producers and TCM clinics are involved in several illegal practices. Ruggiero and South (2010) described how powerful legally registered companies conduct illegal activities in the waste and oil industry. Similar to these industries, in the illegal TCM trade, legally registered TCM companies, producers and clinics as well as TCM shops are

---

[68]'一根犀牛角 五走私网 跨越两大洲的 犀牛角上的中国魅影', Infzm, October 10, 2013.

[69]The overlap is illustrated by an arrested trader of two rhino horns in Las Vegas in 2014 who was allegedly also involved in the smuggling of cocaine from the Medellin drug cartel to the United States (Christy 2014).

involved in the illegal production or sale of TCM with illegal ingredients. One illegal seller at the TCM market in Chengdu described it as shared interests in the illegal TCM trade. "The smuggling gangs make money in cooperation with customs officials in the south, we sell the stuff under the counter to large TCM shops, clinics, hospitals and Chinese citizens, while they [corporations] profit from their branch names" (CT9). These legal corporations conceal their illegal practices by using their legal infrastructure.

In conclusion, elements of organized crime such as continuity and resilience, its long-standing nature, protection to continue illegal activities and the high degree of rationality were present in the illegal trade in TCM. Illegal traders and middlemen are aware of the risks and the illegality involved and their family ties or long-term relationships protect their activities. However, the use of violence to maintain power seems to be less connected with the illegal trade in TCM. Having said this, the illegal trade is nevertheless well organized and many actors do have a share in the profits deriving from the illegal trade in TCM.

9.12 The Impact of Poaching

The tiger and the rhinoceros are already on the brink of extinction and pangolins and saiga antelopes may become extremely rare in the near future with the current high level of illegal trading. The disappearance of these species will result in incalculable harm that is often not legally defined as crime; harm to animals, ecosystems and humans (e.g. White 2008, 2011).

From a biocentric perspective the harms caused to animals during poaching are unnecessarily excessive. During the poaching process several activities are extremely harmful, such as rhino horn being hacked off while the rhino is still alive (Samuel 2013) or the transporting of live pangolins in stressful and anxious situations (Pantel and Chin 2009). Furthermore, the populations are sometimes genetically very small; some tiger populations consist of less than 20 animals (Goodrich et al. 2015). These species' chances of survival are extremely slim in the context of inbreeding and the lack of mature animals. For instance, only one male is left of the Northern White Rhinoceros (*Ceratotherium simum cottoni)*, a subspecies of the White Rhino, and that male is old and may no longer be able to mate with the other three remaining females on Earth.[70] This rhino population has been decimated during the last couple of decades and will probably become extinct in the very near future (Emslie 2011). In addition, the focus on a specific sex can dramatically reduce the population. Since the sex ratio of saiga antelopes is as low as 5.7 % of the population being adult males, this clearly influences the species' chances of survival (Von Meibom et al. 2007).

Similar to monkeys and sturgeon, from an ecocentric perspective several large mammals being used in TCM are considered to be keystone species. According to

[70]The last 40-year-old male, 'Sudan', is under 24-h protection by armed guards at Ol Pejeta Conservancy in Central Kenya.

Power et al. (1996) keystone species do have a disproportional large effect on the function and composition of an ecosystem, such as the predator-prey dynamic. According to Seidensticker et al. (1999) the tiger is a keystone species in its ecosystem and plays an important role as a top predator of several species in order to retain a proper balance in the ecosystem. Mega herbivores, such as rhinos, could be defined as keystone herbivores due to the fact that the population is likely to be food rather than predator-limited and due to their large food requirements per individual (Owen-Smith 1988). Waldram (2005) argued that the White Rhino is an example of a keystone species due to its role in mesic savannahs as it has a controlling influence on the height of grass. Other species of 'short-grass grazers' have disappeared from areas where the White Rhinos have disappeared, while the appearance of White Rhinos in arid savannahs resulted in the arrival of species of grazers that were able to control grass height. The disappearance of rhinos on a large scale may lead to a trophic cascade (Waldram 2005). Another herbivore that could be regarded as a keystone species is the saiga antelope in the wider steppe ecosystem (Bykova and Milner-Gulland 2010; Offord 2011). The saiga antelope is the only migratory ungulate within its range and grazing results, for instance, in maintaining floral diversity. The saiga antelope is an important prey of the caracal, the grey wolf and the jackal (Milner-Gulland et al. 2001). And because pangolins feed on insects they may play an important role within their ecosystems as a form of 'pest control'. One adult pangolin can consume more than 70 million insects each year (Chao 2002). This demonstrates the role and importance of certain species for an ecosystem and the environmental harm caused by the disappearance of a species due to overexploitation.

Furthermore, humans who rely on natural resources for their livelihoods will be affected as well. In the context of the interrelation between animals and humans in their ecosystem, these local communities may lose their natural resources. Moreover, several authors have highlighted the duty to preserve species for future generations. In this context large admired mammal species are mentioned, such as the tiger and rhinoceros. The disappearance of these animals would leave a poorer emotional planet behind if children will only be able to see these iconic animals stuffed in museums or in pictures in books (Still 2003).

9.13 Summary

The use of TCM has existed for thousands of years and is deeply rooted in Chinese society. In the context of Chinese migration and growing markets from the West, the TCM market has developed into a lucrative drug industry. However, not all medicines are legal, some illegal medicines contain sinister components, such as tiger bone, rhino horn, pangolin scales or saiga antelope horn. Large numbers of TCM seizures in Europe confirm its presence on the black market in Europe. The actors involved range from poor local hunters to legally registered medicinal companies and criminal organizations dominating all stages of the trade. In the criminal networks social ties, such as family and culture, play a fundamental role in trade, in particularly as the *guanxi* practice provides an effective insider–outsider system to protect entrepreneurs in the illegal business. Relationships with migrant Chinese abroad are important for a secure and familiar business and established trade routes. Both organized crime and corporate crime appear in the illegal TCM trade where TCM companies provide illegally obtained elements for TCM and special relationships with officials make large-scale smuggling operations possible. Unlike other forms of illegal demands, the demand for illegal TCM is primarily aimed at curing diseases. Therefore, the demand is based on the functional value of criminalized ingredients such as tiger bone and rhino horn. Consequently, environmental harms can be widely seen with several species on the brink of extinction; some species have already disappeared and others may soon be about to.

References

Abbott, B., & Van Kooten, G. C. (2011). Can domestication of wildlife lead to conservation? The economics of tiger farming in China. *Ecological Economics, 70*(4), 721–728.

Ahlstrom, D., Chen, S. J., & Yeh, K. S. (2010). Managing in ethnic Chinese communities: Culture, institutions, and context. *Asia Pacific Journal of Management, 27*(3), 341–354.

Ammann, K. (2011). The Vietnamese and Rhino horn—A dealer speaks. *Swara,* 10–11.

Ayling, J. (2013). What sustains wildlife crime? Rhino horn trading and the resilience of criminal networks. *Journal of International Wildlife Law & Policy, 16*(1), 57–80.

Baillie, J., Challender, D., Kaspal, P., Khatiwada, A., Mohapatra, R., & Nash, H. (2014). *Manis crassicaudata. The IUCN Red List of Threatened Species*. Gland: IUCN

Bekenov, A. B., Grachevand, A., & Milner-Gulland, E. J. (1998). The ecology and management of the Saiga antelope in Kazakhstan. *Mammal Review, 28*(1), 1–52.

Bensky, D., Gamble, A., & Kaptchuk, T. J. (1993). *Chinese herbal medicine: Materia medica*. Vista: Eastland Press.

Benton, T. (1998). Rights and justice on a shared planet: More rights or new relations? *Theoretical Criminology, 2*(2), 149–175.

Berry, L. B., Curtis, G. E., Elan, S. L., Hudson, R. A., & Kollars, N. A. (2003). *Transnational activities of chinese crime organisations (A report prepared by the federal research division, library of congress under an interagency agreement with the crime and narcotics center, directorate of central intelligence)*. Federal Research Division Library of Congress: Washington D.C.

Block, A. A., & Chambliss, W. J. (1981). *Organizing crime*. New York: Elsevier.

Boekhout van Solinge, T. (2008). The land of the orangutan and the bird of paradise under threat. In Sollund, R. (Ed.), *Global Harms: Ecological crime and speciesism* (pp. 51–70). New York: Nova Science Publishing.

Bovenkerk, F. (2001). Organized crime and ethnic minorities: Is there a link? In P. Williams, & D. Vlassis (Eds.), *Combating transnational crime. concepts, activities and responses* (pp. 109–126). ISPAC, Frank Cass Journal.

Bovenkerk, F., Siegel, D., & Zaitch, D. (2003). Organized crime and ethnic reputation manipulation. *Crime, Law and Social Change, 39*(1), 23–38.

Braun, D. M. (2009). *Asian Pangolins being consumed to extinction*. Washington, DC: National Geographic.

Bulte, E. H., & Damania, R. (2005). An economic assessment of wildlife farming and conservation. *Conservation Biology*, 19(4): 1222-1233.

Bykova, E., & Milner-Gulland, E. J. (2010). *Year-Start Work Plan Report for 2011*. Internal Report, Saiga Conservation Alliance.

Chakkaravarthy, Q. A. (2012). Research and conservation needs of the Indian pangolin (*Manis crassicaudata*). In H. B. Katuwal & S. Koirala (Eds.), *Proceedings of third seminar on small mammals issues*. Small Mammals Conservation and Research Foundation: Kathmandu.

Challender, D. W. S. (2011). Asian pangolins: Increasing affluence driving hunting pressure. *Traffic Bulletin, 23*(3), 92–93.

Challender, D. W. S., & Hywood, L. (2012). African pangolins under increased pressure from poaching and intercontinental trade. *Traffic Bulletin, 24*(2), 53–55.

Challender, D., Baillie, J., Ades, G., Kaspal, P., Chan, B., Khatiwada, A., et al. (2014a). *Manis pentadactyla. The IUCN Red List of Threatened Species.* Version 2014.3. Gland: IUCN.

Challender, D., Nguyen Van, T., Shepherd, C., Krishnasamy, K., Wang, A., Lee, B., et al. (2014b). *Manis javanica. The IUCN Red List of Threatened Species.* Version 2014.3. Gland: IUCN.

Chan, R. Y., Cheng, L. T., & Szeto, R. W. (2002). The dynamics of guanxi and ethics for Chinese executives. *Journal of Business Ethics, 41*(4), 327–336.

Chao, J. (2002). *General status offormosan pangolin Manis pentadactyla*. Taipei, Taiwan: Taiwan Forestry Research Institute.

Chen, A. (2005). Secret societies and organized crime in contemporary China. *Modern Asian Studies, 39*(01), 77–107.

Cheung, F. (2011). TCM made in China. *Nature, 480*, S82–S83.

Chin, K. L. (2009). *The golden triangle: Inside Southeast Asia's drug trade*. Ithaca: Cornell University Press.

Chi-yan, S. (2005). *A comparative study of the wildlife trade in Southern China and the Bushmeat Trade in Africa (Doctoral dissertation)*. Hong Kong: The University of Hong Kong.

Christy, B. (2014). *Convicted drug dealer indicted for selling Rhino Horns. Undercover investigation nets alleged wildlife trafficker with ties to former medellín drug cartel.* Washington: National Geographic, April 17, 2014.

Chundawat, R. S., Habib, B., Karanth, U., Kawanishi, K., Ahmad Khan, J., Lynam, T., et al. (2011). *Panthera tigris. The IUCN red list of threatened species.* Version 2014.3. Gland: IUCN.

CITES (2007). *Trade in Saiga antelope horns and other parts: An overview of recent global trade trends and conservation aspects with a focus on market demand in South-east Asia,* CITES 2007, CoP14 Inf. 18.

CITES. (2008). Asian big cats. *Decision, 14*, 69.

CITES (2010). *Illegal killing of rhinoceros in South Africa, CoP15 Inf. 32, Annex I, 2.5, Fifteenth Meeting of the Conference of the Parties*, Doha, 13–25 March 2010.

Coeverden, Van, de Groot, P., Mahood, S., & Long, B. (2011). *Extinction of the Javan Rhinoceros (Rhinoceros sondaicus) from Vietnam.* Ha Noi: WWF Vietnam.

Coggins, C. (2003). *The Tiger and the Pangolin: Nature, culture, and conservation in China.* Hawaii: University of Hawaii Press.

Compton, J., & Le Hai Quang. (1998). *Borderline: an assessment of wildlife trade in Vietnam.* Hanoi: WWF Indochina Programme.

Cota-Larson, R. (2013). *Rhinos from South Africa to China. A troubling timeline*. Petaluma: Annamiticus.

Courchamp, F., Angulo, E., Rivalan, P., Hall, R. J., Signoret, L., Bull, L., et al. (2006). Rarity value and species extinction: The anthropogenic allee effect. *PLoS Biology, 4*(12), e415.

Damania, R., Stringer, R., Ullas Karanth, K., & Stith, B. (2003). The economics of protecting tiger populations: Linking household behavior to poaching and prey depletion. *Land Economics, 79* (2), 198–216.

De Swaan, A. (1989). *Zorg en de staat. Welzijn, onderwijs en gezondheidszorg in Europa en de Verenigde Staten in de nieuwe tijd.* Amsterdam: Bert Bakker.

Dinerstein, E., Loucks, C., Wikramanayake, E., Ginsberg, J., Sanderson, E., Seidensticker, J., et al. (2007). The fate of wild tigers. *BioScience, 57*(6), 508–514.

Duckworth, J. W., Salter, R. E., & Khounboline, K. (1999). *Wildlife in Laos PDR: 1999 status report*. Vientiane: IUCN.

Economic and Social Council United Nations. (2002). Progress Made in the Implementation of Economic and Social Council Resolution 2001/12 on Illicit Trafficking in Protected Species of Wild Flora and Fauna. Report of the Secretary-General.

Economic and Social Council United Nations. (2003). Illicit Trafficking in Protected Species of Wild Flora and Fauna and Illicit Access to Genetic Resources (E/CN.15/2003/8).

EIA. (2013). *Hidden in plain sight: China's clandestine tiger trade*. London: EIA.

Ellis, R. (2005). *Tiger Bone & Rhino Horn: The destruction of wildlife for traditional Chinese medicine*. Washington: Island Press.

Eloff, C. (2012). Rhino poaching in South Africa-is it a losing battle. *Position IT*, 57–62.

Eloff, C., & Lemieux, A. M. (2014). Rhino poaching in Kruger National Park, South Africa. In A. M. Lemieux (Ed.), *Situational prevention of poaching* (pp. 18–43). Oxford: Routledge.

Emslie, R. (2011). *Ceratotherium simum ssp. cottoni. The IUCN Red List of Threatened Species*. Version 2015.2. Gland: IUCN.

Emslie, R. (2012) *Ceratotherium simum. The IUCN Red List of Threatened Species. Version 2014.3*. Gland: IUCN.

Europol (2011). *Organised crime threat assessment (OCTA)*. The Hague: Europol.

Europol (2012). *OC-scan policy brief. involvement of an irish mobile OCG in the illegal trade in Rhino Horn* (pp. 2521–2586). The Hague: Europol, June 2012. File nr.

Foose, T. J., & Van Strien, N. (Eds.). (1997). *Asian Rhinos. Status Survey and Conservation Action Plan*. Gland: IUCN/SSC Asian Rhino Specialist Group.

Forsyth, C. J., Gramling, R., & Wooddell, G. (1998). The game of poaching: Folk crimes in southwest Louisiana. *Society & Natural Resources, 11*(1), 25–38.

Gaski, A. L., & Johnson, K. A. (1994). *Prescription for extinction: Endangered species and patented Oriental medicines in trade*. Washington, DC: Traffic USA.

Gastrow, P. (2001). Triad societies and Chinese organised crime in South Africa. *Institute for Security Studies Papers*, (48).

Gold, T., & Guthrie, D. (2002). *Social connections in China: Institutions, culture, and the changing nature of guanxi (No. 21)*. Cambridge: Cambridge University Press.

Goodman, D. S. (1998). In search of China's new middle classes: The creation of wealth and diversity in Shanxi during the 1990s. *Asian Studies Review, 22*(1), 39–62.

Goodrich, J., Lynam, A., Miquelle, D., Wibisono, H., Kawanishi, K., Pattanavibool, A., et al. (2015). *Panthera tigris. The IUCN red list of threatened species*. Gland: IUCN.

Graham-Rowe, D. (2011). Biodiversity: Endangered and in demand. *Nature, 480*(7378), S101–S103.

Gratwicke, B., Mills, J., Dutton, A., Gabriel, G., Long, B., Seidensticker, J., et al. (2008). Attitudes toward consumption and conservation of tigers in China. *PLoS One, 3*(7), e2544.

Guthrie, D. (1998). The declining significance of guanxi in China's economic transition. *The China Quarterly, 154*, 254–282.

Hall, R. J., Milner-Gulland, E. J., & Courchamp, F. (2008). Endangering the endangered: The effects of perceived rarity on species exploitation. *Conservation Letters, 1*(2), 75–81.

Harris, R. B. (2008). *Wildlife conservation in China, Armonk*. New York: M.E. Sharpe.

Henry, L. A. (2004). *A tale of two cities: A comparative study of traditional chinese medicine markets in San Francisco and New York city*. Washington, DC: TRAFFIC North America.

Herklots, G. A. C. (1937). The pangolin or scaly ant-eater. *The Hong Kong Naturalist, 8*(2), 79–83.

Hogg, F. (2014). *Consumption and conservation: Assessing the prevalence and nature of the illegal (Doctoral dissertation, Imperial College London)*. London: Imperial College London.

Hong, F. F. (2004). History of medicine in China: When medicine took an alternative path. *McGill Journal of Medicine, 8*(1), 74–84.

Hübschle, A. (2010). *Organised crime in Southern Africa: First annual review*. Pretoria: Institute for Security Studies.

Hull, J. (2012). *The Last Rhino*. Al Jazeera Documentary.

IBISWorld. (2014). *Traditional Chinese medicine manufacturing in China*. IBISWorld: Market Research Report. Santa Monica.

Jackson, P., Kemf, E., Bhalla, P., Fernhout, A., Dillon, T., & Egli, K. L. (1996). *Wanted Alive. Tigers in the wild*. Gland: WWF.

Jia, Q. (2005). *Traditional Chinese Medicine Could Make "Health for One" True*. Ministry of Science and Technology China.

Kemner, J. (2010). *Illegale handel in exotische diersoorten uitgestorven?*. Amsterdam: Bureau Milieu Criminaliteit.

Kidder, R. L. (1983). *Connecting law and society*. Englewood: Prentice Hall Inc.

Kiernan, B. (1996). *The pol pot regime: Race, power, and genocide in Cambodia under the Khmer Rouge, 1975–79*. New Haven: Yale University Press.

Kleemans, E. R., & Van de Bunt, H. G. (1999). The social embeddedness of organized crime. *Transnational Organized Crime, 5*(1), 19–36.

Kühl, A., Balinova, N., Bykova, E., Arylov, Y. N., Esipov, A., Lushchekina, A. A., et al. (2009). The role of saiga poaching in rural communities: Linkages between attitudes, socio-economic circumstances and behaviour. *Biological Conservation, 142*(7), 1442–1449.

Lagrada, L., Schoppe, S., & Challender, D. (2014). *Manis culionensis. The IUCN red list of threatened species. Version 2014.3*. Gland: IUCN.

Lam, Y. K. J. (2012). *Estimating the extent of illegal traditional Chinese medicine trade in Guangzhou, China Using occupancy modelling* (Doctoral dissertation). Imperial College London). London: Imperial College London.

Lau, W. (2014). *Taking from the Wild: Moving towards sustainability in Hong Kong's Wildlife trade*. Hong Kong: Civic Exchange.

Lau, M. W. N., Ades, G., Goodyer, N., & Zou, F. S. (1997). Wildlife trade in southern China including Hong Kong and Macao. *Conserving China's Biodiversity*, 141–159.

Leader-Williams, N. (1992). *The world trade in Rhino Horn: A review*. Cambridge: Traffic International.

Lee, S., Hoover, C., Gaski, A., & Mills, J. (1998). *A world apart?: Attitudes toward traditional Chinese medicine and endangered species in Hong Kong and the United States*. Washington: Traffic.

Li, L. (2011). Performing bribery in China: Guanxi practice, corruption with a human face. *Journal of Contemporary China, 20*(68), 1–20.

Li, W., Fuller, T. K., & Sung, W. (1996). A survey of wildlife trade in Guangxi and Guangdong, China. *Traffic Bulletin, 16*(1), 9–16.

Li, W., & Wang, H. (1999). Wildlife trade in Yunnan Province, China, at the border with Vietnam. *Traffic Bulletin, 18*(1), 21–30.

Li, L., Zhao, Y., & Bennett, E. L. (2007). *Report of a survey on Saiga Horn in markets in China*. CoP14 Inf, 14.

Liddick, D. R. (2011). *Crimes against nature. Illegal industries and the global environment*. Oxford: Praeger Publishers.

Lin, J. (2005). Tackling Southeast Asia's illegal wildlife trade. *Sybil, 9*, 191–208.

Ling, X. (2008). *Wildlife trade on the China-Myanmar Border in the State of Wildlife in China*. Beijing: Traffic China.

Liu, Y., Zhang, Y., & Xu, C. (2010). Analysis of the international competitiveness of Chinese medicine.

Loh, J., & Loh, K. (1994). A spot check on the availability of rhino products in Guangzhou and Shanghai. *China. Traffic Bulletin, 14*(2), 79–80.

Lozano, F. (2014). Basic theories of traditional Chinese medicine. In Y. C. Lin & E. Shen (Eds.), *Acupuncture for Pain Management*. New York: Springer.

Maciocia, G. (1989). *The foundations of Chinese medicine*. Edinburgh: Churchill Livingstone.

Mailley, J. (2014). Can the Problem Analysis Module (PAM) help us imagine new preventative solutions to a specific tiger poaching issue? In A. Lemieux (Ed.), *Situational Prevention of Poaching*. London: Routledge.

Mainka, S. A., & Mills, J. A. (1995). Wildlife and traditional Chinese medicine: Supply and demand for wildlife species. *Journal of Zoo and Wildlife Medicine*, 193–200.

Mallon, D. P. (2008). *Saiga Tatarica. The IUCN Red List of Threatened Species. Version 2015.2*. Gland: IUCN.

Manning, R. B. (1993). *Hunters and poachers: A social and cultural history of unlawful hunting in England, 1485–1640*. Oxford: Oxford University Press.

Martin, E. B., & Martin, C. (1982). *Run, Rhino, Run*. London: Hodder & Stoughton.

McKeown, A. (1999). Conceptualizing Chinese diasporas, 1842 to 1949. *The Journal of Asian Studies, 58*(02), 306–337.

McNeely, J. A., & Wachtel, P. S. (1991). *Soul of the tiger: Searching for nature's answers in Southeast Asia*. Hawaii: University of Hawaii Press.

Meng, X., Gong, B., Ma, G., & Xiang, L. (2011). Quantified analyses of musk deer farming in China: A tool for sustainable musk production and ex situ conservation. *Asian-Australasian Journal of Animal Sciences, 24*(10), 1473–1482.

Michalski, F., Boulhosa, R. L. P., Faria, A., & Peres, C. A. (2006). Human-wildlife conflicts in a fragmented Amazonian forest landscape: Determinants of large felid depredation on livestock. *Animal Conservation, 9*(2), 179–188.

Milliken, T. (2014). *Illegal trade in Ivory and Rhino Horn: An assessment report to improve law enforcement under the wildlife TRAPS project*. Cambridge: Traffic.

Milliken, T., & Shaw, J. (2012). *The South Africa-Viet Nam Rhino Horn Trade nexus: A deadly combination of institutional lapses, corrupt wildlife industry professionals, and asian crime syndicates*. Cambridge: Traffic.

Mills, J. A. (Ed.). (1997). *Rhinoceros horn and tiger bone in China: An investigation of trade since the 1993 Ban*. Cambridge: Traffic International.

Mills, J. A. (2015). *Blood of the tiger. A story of conspiracy, greed, and the battle to save a magnificent species*. Boston: Beacon Press.

Mills, J. A., & Jackson, P. (1994). *Killed for a cure: A review of the worldwide trade in tiger bone*. Cambridge: Traffic International.

Milner-Gulland, E. J., Kholodova, M. V., Bekenov, A., Bukreeva, O. M., Grachev, I. A., Amgalan, L., et al. (2001). Dramatic declines in saiga antelope populations. *Oryx, 35*(4), 340–345.

Milner-Gulland, E. J., Bukreeva, O. M., Coulson, T., Lushchekina, A. A., Kholodova, M. V., Bekenov, A. B., et al. (2003). Conservation: Reproductive collapse in saiga antelope harems. *Nature, 422*(6928), 135.

Miquelle, D., Darman, Y., & Seryodkin, I. (2011). *Panthera Tigris ssp. Altaica. The IUCN Red List of Threatened Species 2011*. Gland: IUCN.

Misztal, B. (1996). *Trust in modern societies: The search for the bases of social order*. Cambridge: Polity Press.

Montesh, M. (2013). *Rhino peaching: A new form of organised crime*. Pretoria: College of Law Research and Innovation Committee of the University of South Africa.

Moyle, B. (2009). The black market in China for tiger products. *Global Crime, 10*(1–2), 124–143.

Myers, W. H. (1995). Orb weavers—the global webs: The structure and activities of transnational ethnic chinese criminal groups. *Transnational Organized Crime, 1*(4), 1–36.

Newton, P., Thai, N. V., Robertson, S., & Bell, D. (2008). Pangolins in peril: Using local hunters' knowledge to conserve elusive species in Vietnam. *Endangered Species Research, 6*(1), 41–53.

Nguyen, D. N. V., & Nguyen, T. (2008). *An overview of the use of plants and animals in traditional medicine systems in Viet Nam*. Ha Noi: Traffic Southeast Asia.

Nooren, H., & Claridge, G. (2001). *Wildlife Trade in Laos: The End of the Game*. Gland: IUCN-The World Conservation Union.

Nowell, K. (2000). *Far from a cure: The tiger trade revisited*. Cambridge: Traffic International.

Nowell, K. (2009). Tiger farms and pharmacies: The central importance of China's trade policy for tiger conservation. In R. Tilson & P. J. Nyhus (Eds.), *Tigers of the world: The science, politics, and conservation of panthera tigris* (pp. 463–475). Amsterdam: Elsevier.

Nowell, K., & Jackson, P. (1996). *Wild Cats*. Status Survey and Conservation Action Plan. IUCN/SSC Cat Specialist Group: Gland, IUCN.

Nowell, K., & Ling, X. (2007). *Taming the tiger trade. China's markets for wild and captive tiger products since the 1993 Domestic Trade Ban.* Hong Kong: Traffic East Asia.

Nowell, K., Chyi, W. L., & Pei, C. J. (1992). *The horns of a Dilemma: The market for rhino horn in Taiwan: Final Report for WWF Project II3637. 03.* Cambridge: Traffic International.

Offord, S. (2011). *An evaluation of potential monitoring strategies for saiga antelopes on the Ustyurt Plateau (thesis).* London: Imperial College London.

Oswell, A. H. (2010). *The big cat trade in Myanmar and Thailand.* Petaling Jaya: Traffic Southeast Asia.

Owen-Smith, R. N. (1988). *Megaherbivores.* Cambridge: Cambridge University Press.

Pantel, S., & Anak, N. W. (2010). *A preliminary assessment of sunda pangolin trade in Sabah.* Petaling Jaya: Traffic South East Asia.

Pantel, E. B. S., & Chin, S. (2009). *Proceedings of the workshop on trade and conservation of pangolins native to South and Southeast Asia.* Singapore: Traffic.

Passas, N. (2002). Cross-border crime and the interface between legal and illegal actors. In P. C. van Duyne, K. von Lampe, & N. Passas (Eds.), *Upperworld and underworld in cross-border crime* (pp. 11–42). Nijmegen: Wolf Legal Publishers.

Patrick, H. (1995). Traditional Chinese medicine and public health: The Yin and the Yang. *Journal of the Royal Society of Medicine, 88*(9), 485–486.

Pieke, F. N. (1999), The Netherlands. In L. Pan (Ed.), *The encyclopedia of the Chinese overseas* (pp. 322–327). Harvard: Harvard University Press.

Pietersen, D., Waterman, C., Hywood, L., Rankin, P., & Soewu, D. (2014). *Smutsia Temminckii. The IUCN red list of threatened species. Version 2014.3.* Gland: IUCN.

Post, S. (2013). *Strategische analyse traditionele medicijnen & voedingsupplementen.* Utrecht: NVWA.

Power, M. E., Tilman, D., Estes, J. A., Menge, B. A., Bond, W. J., Mills, L. S., et al. (1996). Challenges in the quest for keystones. *BioScience,* 609–620.

Qiu, J. (2007). Traditional medicine: A culture in the balance. *Nature, 448*(7150), 126–128.

Rademeyer, J. (2012). *Killing for profit: Exposing the Illegal Rhino Horn Trade.* Cape Town: Random House Struik.

Robinson, S., & Milner-Gulland, E. J. (2003). Political change and factors limiting numbers of wild and domestic ungulates in Kazakhstan. *Human Ecology, 31*(1), 87–110.

Ruggiero, V. (1996). *Organized and corporate crime in Europe: Offers that can't be refused.* Aldershot: Dartmouth.

Ruggiero, V., & South, N. (2010). Green criminology and dirty collar crime. *Critical Criminology, 18*(4), 251–262.

Samuel, G. (2013). *Assessing the risks of rhino horn trade.* South Africa: International Rhino coalition.

Sanderson, E., Forrest, J., Loucks, C., Ginsberg, J., Dinerstein, E., Seidensticker, J., et al. (2006). *Setting priorities for the conservation and recovery of wild tigers: 2005–2015.* New York and Washington, DC: WCS, WWF, Smithsonian, and NFWF-STF.

Sankar, K., Goyal, S. P., & Qureshi, Q. (2005). *Assessment of status of tiger in sariska tiger reserve Rajasthan. A report submitted to the project tiger, ministry of environment and forests.* New Delhi: Government of India.

SATCM (1996). Prices for pangolin scales in the Guangxi cross-border trade increase even more. *Journal of Chinese Medicinal Materials, 19*(4).

Scheid, V. (2001). Shaping Chinese medicine: Two case studies from contemporary China. In E. Hsu (Ed.), *Innovation in Chinese medicine* (pp. 370–404). Cambridge: Cambridge University Press.

Schneider, J. (2012). *Sold into extinction: The global trade in endangered species.* Santa Barbara: Praeger.

Schroeder, T. (2002). Chinese regulation of traditional Chinese medicine in the modern world: Can the Chinese effectively profit from one of their most valuable cultural resources. *Pac. Rim L. & Pol'y J., 11,* 687–716.

Seidensticker, J., Jackson, P., & Christie, S. (Eds.). (1999). *Riding the tiger: Tiger conservation in human-dominated landscapes*. Cambridge: Cambridge University Press.

Sellar, J. M. (2014). *The UN'S lone ranger: Combating international wildlife crime*. Dunbeath: Whittles.

Sheng, X., Zhang, H., & Weng, Q. (2012). Traditional Chinese medicine: China's bear farms prompt public outcry. *Nature, 484*(7395), 455.

Shepherd, C. R. (2009). Overview of pangolin trade in Southeast Asia. In *Proceedings of the workshop on trade and conservation of pangolins native to South and Southeast Asia*. Singapore: Traffic.

Siegel, D., & Nelen, H. (2007). *Organized crime: Culture, markets and policies*. New York: Springer.

Sopyan, E. (2009). Malayan Pangolin Manis javanica trade in Sumatra, Indonesia. In *Workshop on trade and conservation of pangolins native to South and Southeast Asia*. Singapore: Traffic.

Stiles, D., Redmond, I., Cress, D., Nellemann, C., & Formo, R. K. (Eds.). (2013). *Stolen apes—the illicit trade in Chimpanzees, Gorillas, Bonobos and Orangutans. A rapid response assessment. United Nations Environment Programme*. Arendal: GRID-Arendal.

Still, J. (2003). Use of animal products in traditional Chinese medicine: Environmental impact and health hazards. *Complementary Therapies in Medicine, 11*(2), 118–122.

Swan, K., & Conrad, K. (2014). The conflict between Chinese cultural and environmental values in wildlife consumption. In *Routledge handbook of environment and society in Asia*. London: Routledge.

Talukdar, B.K., Emslie, R., Bist, S.S., Choudhury, A., Ellis, S., Bonal, B.S., Malakar, M. C., Talukdar, B.N. & Barua, M. (2008). *Rhinoceros Unicornis. The IUCN Red List of Threatened Species*. Version 2014.3. Gland: IUCN.

Traffic (2013). *China's wildlife enforcement news digest* (September 2013). Beijing: Traffic.

Traffic. (2014). *Wildlife trade in the European Union*. Brussels: Traffic Europe.

Tymieniecka, A. T. (Ed.). (1984). *Phenomenology of life in a dialogue between Chinese and occidental philosophy (Vol. 17)*. New York: Springer Science & Business Media.

Tymieniecka, A. T. (Ed.). (2012). *Heaven, earth, and in-between in the harmony of life (Vol. 47)*. New York: Springer Science & Business Media.

United Nations Office on Drugs and Crime. (2010). *The globalization of crime: A transnational organized crime threat assessment*. Vienna: UNODC.

United Nations Office on Drugs and Crime. (2013). *Transnational organized crime threat assessment—East Asia and the pacific*. Vienna: UNODC.

Van Duyne, P. C., Von Lampe, K., & Passas, N. (2002). *Upperworld and underworld in cross-border crime*. Nijmegen: Wolf Legal Publishers.

Van Song, N. (2008). Wildlife trading in Vietnam situation, causes, and solutions. *The Journal of Environment & Development, 17*(2), 145–165.

Van Strien, N. J., Manullang, B., Sectionov, Isnan, W., Khan, M. K. M, Sumardja, E., Ellis, S., et al. (2008a). *Dicerorhinus Sumatrensis. The IUCN Red List of Threatened Species. Version 2014.3*. Gland: IUCN.

Van Strien, N. J., Steinmetz, R., Manullang, B., Sectionov, Han, K. H., Isnan, W., et al. (2008b). *Rhinoceros Sondaicus. The IUCN Red List of Threatened Species. Version 2014.3*. Gland: IUCN.

Van, N. D. N., & Tap, N. (2008). *An overview of the use of plants and animals in traditional medicine systems in Viet Nam*. Ha Noi: Traffic Southeast Asia.

Van Uhm, D. P. (2012). Organised crime in the wildlife trade. *Centre for Information and Research on Organised Crime (CIROC) Newsletter, 10*(2): 2–4.

Van Uhm, D. P. (2014). *Criminaliteit en traditionele Chinese medicijnen. Proces, 93*(2), 130–143.

Van Vuuren, H. (2006). *Apartheid grand corruption. Assessing the scale of crimes of profit from 1976 to 1994: A Report prepared by civil society in terms of a resolution of the second national anti-corruption summit for presentation at the national anti-corruption forum, May 2006*. Pretoria: Institute for Security Studies.

Veith, I. (2002). *The yellow emperor's classic of internal medicine*. Berkeley: University of California Press.
Verheij, P. M., Foley, K. E., & Engel, K. (2010). *Reduced to skin and bones. An analysis of tiger seizures from 11 tiger range countries (2000–2010)*. Cambridge: Traffic International.
Von Lampe, K., & Ole Johansen, P. (2004). Organized crime and trust: On the conceptualization and empirical relevance of trust in the context of criminal networks. *Global Crime, 6*(2), 159–184.
Von Meibom, S., Vaisman, A., Leong, S. H., Ng, J. L., & Xu, H. F. (2007). *Trade in saiga antelope horns and other parts: An overview of recent global trade trends and conservation aspects with a focus on market demand in Southeast Asia*. CoP14 Inf. 18. The Hague: CITES.
Von Meibom, S., Vaisman, A., Neo Liang, S. H., Ng, J., & Xu, H. (2010). *Saiga antelope trade: Global Trends with a focus on South-East Asia*. Traffic Europe: TRAFFIC Project Report to the CITES Secretariat. Brussels.
Von Moltke, K., & Spaninks, F. (2000). *Traditional Chinese medicine and species endangerment: An economic research Agenda,* London: International Institute for Environment and Development/Amsterdam: Institute for Environmental Studies.
Waldram, M. (2005). *The ecological effects of grazing by the white Rhino (Ceratotherium Simum Simum) at a Landscape Scale*. Rondebosch: University of Cape Town.
Walker, C., & Walker, A. (2012). *The Rhino keepers*. Auckland Park: Jacana Media.
Walston, J., Robinson, J. G., Bennett, E. L., Breitenmoser, U., da Fonseca, G. A. B., Goodrich, J., et al. (2010). Bringing the tiger back from the brink—The 6 % solution. *PLoS Biology, 8*(9), e1000485.
Wang, P. (2013). The rise of the Red Mafia in China: A case study of organised crime and corruption in Chongqing. *Trends in Organized Crime, 16*(1), 49–73.
Waterman, C., Pietersen, D., Hywood, L., Rankin, P., & Soewu, D. (2014a). *Smutsia gigantea. The IUCN Red List of Threatened Species. Version 2014.3*. Gland: IUCN.
Waterman, C., Pietersen, D., Soewu, D., Hywood, L., & Rankin, P. (2014b). *Phataginus tetradactyla. The IUCN Red List of Threatened Species. Version 2014*. Gland: IUCN.
Waterman, C., Pietersen, D., Soewu, D., Hywood, L., & Rankin, P. (2014c). *Phataginus tricuspis. The IUCN Red List of Threatened Species. Version 2014.3*. Gland: IUCN.
White, R. (2008). *Crimes against nature: Environmental criminology and ecological justice*. Devon: Willan Publishing.
White, R. (2011). *Transnational environmental crime. Toward an eco-global criminology*. London: Routledge.
WHO. (2012). *Traditional Chinese medicine could make "Health for One" True*. Washington, D.C.: WHO.
Williamson, E. M., Lorenc, A., Booker, A., & Robinson, N. (2013). The rise of traditional Chinese medicine and its materia medica: A comparison of the frequency and safety of materials and species used in Europe and China. *Journal of Ethnopharmacology, 149*(2), 453–462.
World Bank (2005). *Going, going, gone ...the illegal trade in wildlife in East and Southeast Asia*. Washington, DC: The World Bank.
Wu, F., & Wen, B. (2015). Nongovernmental organizations and environmental protests. *Routledge Handbook of Environment and Society in Asia.*
Wu, S., Liu, N., Zhang, Y., & Ma, G. (2004). Assessment of threatened status of Chinese Pangolin (Manis Pentadactyla). *Chinese Journal of Applied Environmental Biology,* 10(4), 456–461.
Wyler, L. S., & Sheikh, P. A. (2013). *International illegal trade in wildlife: Threats and US policy*. Washington, D.C.: Congressional Research Service report for Congress.
Xu, J., & Yang, Y. (2009). Traditional Chinese medicine in the Chinese health care system. *Health Policy, 90*(2), 133–139.
Yang, C. W., Chen, S., Chang, C.-Y., Lin, M. F., Block, E., Lorentsen, R., et al. (2007). History and dietary husbandry of pangolins in captivity. *Zoo Biol, 26*, 223–230.
Yeung, I. Y., & Tung, R. L. (1996). Achieving business success in confucian societies: The importance of guanxi (connections). *Organizational Dynamics, 25*(2), 54–65.
Yiming, L., & Dianmo, L. (1996). A preliminary investigation on the status of the wildlife trade in Guangxi. *China, 4*, 57–63.

Yiming, L., & Dianmo, L. (1998). The dynamics of trade in live wildlife across the Guangxi border between China and Vietnam during 1993-1996 and its control strategies. *Biodiversity and Conservation, 7*(7), 895–914.

Yongge, S. (2000). *Ecology without borders. where china meets southeast asia: Social and cultural change in the border regions*. Singapore: Institute of Southeast Asian Studies.

Yongping, G. (2008). Pangolin trafficking-related crimes in China. In *Workshop on trade and conservation of pangolins native to South and Southeast Asia.* Singapore: Traffic.

Yue, Z. (2008). Conservation and trade control of pangolins in China. In *Workshop on trade and conservation of pangolins Native to South and Southeast Asia.* Singapore: Traffic.

Zahler, P. (2004). Recent management and conservation initiatives for mongolian gazelle, mongolian saiga antelope, and gobi bear. *Mongolian Journal of Biological Sciences, 2*(2), 47–49.

Zang, Z. (1990). A textual research on the history of lingyang. *Nanjing Chinese Medical College Magazine, 6*(1), 57–59.

Zhang, S. X., & Chin, K. (2008). Snakeheads, mules, and protective umbrellas: A review of current research on Chinese organized crime. *Crime, Law and Social Change, 50*(3), 177–195.

Zhang, S., & Chin, K. (2011). Ants moving houses. Cross-border drug trafficking in the Golden Triangle. In *Routledge handbook of international criminology.* London: Routledge.

Zhang, X. L., Bai, S. Y., & Xu, Y. C. (2006). Molecular biological identification of 140 saiga. *J Northeast Forestry Univ, 34*, 106–108.

Zhang, L., Hua, N., & Sun, S. (2008). Wildlife trade, consumption and conservation awareness in Southwest China. *Biodiversity and Conservation*, 1493–1516.

Zhang, L., Messner, S. F., Liu, J., & Zhuo, Y. A. (2009). Guanxi and fear of crime in contemporary urban China. *British Journal of Criminology, 49*(4), 472–490.

Zhao, S., Xu, C., Liu, G., Liu, S., Zhao, C., Cui, Y., et al. (2013). Microsatellite and mitochondrial DNA assessment of the genetic diversity of captive Saiga antelopes (Saiga tatarica) in China. *Chinese Science Bulletin, 58*(18), 2163–2167.

Zhu, B., & Wang, H. (Eds.). (2011). *Basic theories of traditional chinese medicine.* Beijing: Singing Dragon.

Zimmerman, M. E. (2003). The black market for wildlife: Combating transnational organized crime in the illegal wildlife trade. *Vanderbilt Journal of Transnational Law, 36*(5), 1657–1690.

Chapter 10
Overarching Views and the Future

The previous case studies provide background insights into the illegal trade in caviar, Barbary macaques and TCM based on fieldwork in source countries: Russia, Kazakhstan, Azerbaijan, Morocco and China. In the three case studies, dynamic alliances developed in order to transfer the illegal wildlife from the source to the destination countries. The chain of the illegal wildlife trade consists of different stages, actors and networks. The wildlife moves along a line of contacts from the source areas to the final destinations. These functions as a combination of chain and hub networks where the illegal trade persists and flourishes (Arquilla and Ronfeldt 2001; Vander Beken et al. 2004). Generally, in the first stage, there is a demand for wildlife and to answer this demand local people poach animals in the source area. Then a middleman or trader from outside the local village collects the goods. He arranges, by the use of his network, that the wildlife is smuggled across the border to a wildlife trader abroad. In the final stage the trade is transferred to the transit or destination area. In this chapter, the three case studies are analysed as to their similarities and differences in the context of the social construction of the value, global anomie and criminogenic asymmetries, the social embeddedness and the organization of wildlife crime, and finally, the (environmental) harms. During these comprehensive analyses the following research questions are answered:

- Why is there a demand market for wildlife? (Sects. 10.1 and 10.2)
- Which actors are involved in the illegal wildlife trade? (Sect. 10.3)
- How is the illegal wildlife business organized? (Sect. 10.4)
- What are the harmful consequences of the wildlife trade? (Sect. 10.5)

This exploratory study provides a general picture of the illegal trade in wildlife that enables one to understand the nature of the harmful wildlife trade. The last section (Sect. 10.6) discusses how the perspectives of wildlife crimes have changed in their social context and what can be expected in the near future.

D.P. van Uhm, *The Illegal Wildlife Trade*, Studies of Organized Crime 15,
DOI 10.1007/978-3-319-42129-2_10

10.1 Social Construction of Value

The value of an object is not an established fact, but is dependent on the scarcity and judgement of an object. For instance, iron would have a limited economic value if its acquisition would have been similar to the acquisition of air for breathing (Simmel 1978). While the functional use of wildlife was present in many ancient societies that used wildlife as 'basic needs'; food to survive, fur to stay warm or as medicine to fight diseases, the exclusivity of certain animals or animal products formed the foundation of their value. The rarer an animal or animal product the higher its value (Courchamp et al. 2006). This is illustrated by examples from the pharaohs collecting extraordinary animal species for their private menageries to the demand for rare objects for curiosity cabinets from the elite during the Renaissance. The value of these objects was determined by exclusivity and scarcity (Kisling 2001; Baratay and Hardouin-Fugier 2003). That the current economic value of rhino horn on the black market exceeds the price of gold and cocaine confirms this assumption. This is especially true since the 'originality' of wildlife products also plays a role in the determination of their value. The idea has taken hold that wildlife products from wild animals are more 'pure and natural' than products from captive-bred species. Therefore the value of rhino horn, tiger bones and caviar from species from the wild is higher due to the belief that the taste would be more exquisite or the healing qualities more profound. Consequently, tiger bones from Chinese farms are of a lower value than the tiger bones of real wild tigers, rhino horns from farmed rhinos are believed to have lower medicinal values and caviar from cultivated caviar is being sold as 'illegal' wild caviar to increase its monetary value.

However, simply attributing value to only the degree of 'scarcity' or 'originality' would detract from the social meaning of things. In fact, the vast majority of almost extinct animals are humble insects (Dunn 2005) and, generally, the assigned (economic) value of these insects is extremely low compared to their vulnerable status. According to Appadurai (1986) the social meaning of things is dependent on human transactions, attributions and motivations. He explains that value is a property that is attributed to an object in its social context instead of a property which is inherent in an object. According to Saffron (2002: 152) 'stripped of its shroud of legend and tradition, caviar would just be fish eggs'. Due to the social construction of the value of caviar, it developed from food for the poor to a status symbol of the Tsars and upper-class society. Fish eggs have even become a national symbol of Russia. According to Mintz (1985) the value will increase as the meaning of the object in a certain social context increases. The same construction is viable to the downward transition. He argued that tea, originally considered as a luxury product for the wealthy elite, transformed into a daily necessity adopted by the lower classes. Veblen (1912) underlined that increasing wealth in the leisure class provided opportunities to display products symbolizing wealth. Imitation would be a form of social equalization as the masses imitate to reduce the external distinctions of class (Simmel 1957). During various historical periods this transformation process of copying fashions from the upper classes has happened with, for instance, sugar, tea and wildlife. The symbolic use of wildlife was already noticeable during the era of the ancient Egyptians and later the Greeks and Romans; these ancient societies kept exotic animals or products thereof as symbols of status, spirituality and power (e.g. Jennison 1937; Kalof 2007). While menageries were restricted to aristocrats and the royalty, in the Renaissance some were made available to the public; keeping exotic animals had been adopted by the middle and lower classes, thereby emulating the fashions of the upper classes (Kalof 2007; Herzog 2014). Consequently, the social meaning and thus the value of things are subject to change.

Since the social construction of the value of wildlife is explainable by the social meaning attributed to an object, the influence of culture is considerable. For instance, keeping birds is deeply ingrained in Indonesian culture (Nijman et al. 2009) and the cultural demand for bush meat plays an important role in several African tribes (Pailler 2007). The clarification of cultural meanings and the values of consuming wildlife is reflected in the case study on TCM. The cultural incentives to use certain raw materials from endangered species in TCM are deeply rooted in the Chinese philosophy (Coggins 2003; Xu and Yang 2009). This is illustrated by laws and regulations that provide insufficient guidance in the context of their cultural demand for TCM; these laws prohibit what is culturally believed to be 'a greater good for humanity' (Kidder 1983). It is obvious that the implementation of rules that are not socially founded is poor (e.g. Locke 1689; Rousseau 1762). From this perspective the cultural context is necessary to understand the social meaning and value of TCM in Chinese culture.

Finally, states or powerful companies also construct the value in the wildlife business. These stakeholders have an interest in maintaining a high price. Comparable to the value of diamonds, controlling supply and creating and stimulating demand are used as economic strategies by the caviar industry to maintain the high value. Moreover, the Soviet authorities guarded the caviar production by a highly efficient state monopoly. In addition, the international trade in and the branding of Chinese medicines has been sponsored by the Chinese government for decades in order to emphasize its value. This is in stark contrast to the monkeys smuggled into the EU without (international) companies or state influences being involved.

The social judgement of wildlife can historically be approached in the context of three initiated major purposes of wildlife; the functional, symbolic and entertainment use. While these major purposes may be applicable to all three case studies, a distinction can be drawn based upon the *main* purpose of each of the three forms of the wildlife trade. First, caviar is primarily a food; however, the symbolic function seems to be of higher importance: "You do not eat caviar, but you enjoy caviar!" is a commonly used saying in the context of luxury and delicacy. The social construction of caviar as a luxury product exceeds its original use as food (Saffron 2002). Second, keeping monkeys as pets would be biologically explainable from an instinctive tendency to develop parental skills in the context of the anthropomorphization of monkeys (Serpell 2003; Bradshaw and Paul 2010). Historically, keeping monkeys as pets was driven by their attributed symbolic value as a status symbol (e.g. Janson 1952), while currently most people would argue that monkeys are kept as pets for entertainment (e.g. Laufer 2010; Green 1999). Finally, similar to the symbolic status of caviar and exotic pets, certain expensive raw ingredients for TCM function as status symbols (Ayling 2013; Montesh 2013). For example, badges with rhino horns were worn by high-ranking military officials in the Ming and Qing dynasties (Ayling 2013). Nevertheless, the cultural incentives and beliefs of the function of using TCM to prevent or heal diseases are of higher importance (Coggins 2003; Xu and Yang 2009). This is illustrated by the increased demand for rhino horn after claims that it can cure cancer. Concluding, the social construction of the value of the three forms of wildlife differs in their cultural-historical contexts as well as in the social construction of their function. The symbolic use of caviar is illustrated by its luxury status, the demand for monkeys is mainly based on entertainment purposes and the functional use of TCM is fundamental in Chinese culture. While the value of wildlife is socially constructed by scarcity and social meanings, the market dynamics for these products depend on global anomies and criminogenic asymmetries.

10.2 Global Anomie and Criminogenic Asymmetries

In recent decades the wildlife trade has developed into a professional globalized industry in the context of improved technology and modern transportation. Large flows of the illegal trade in wildlife traditionally originate from developing countries driven by the demand from wealthy European countries (Roe 2002; Duffy 2010; see also the quantitative analyses in Chap. 6). According to Passas (2000) in a globalized world new international inequalities or global anomies are created primarily between the poor developing countries and the powerful Western industrialized world. In the context of global communication and improved trade lines, illegal entrepreneurs abuse economic and power inequalities. Wealthy consumer countries overexploit natural resources in developing countries and leave the damage behind (Lynch and Stretesky 2003, 2014; Passas and Goodwin 2005). This is reflected in the case studies as Barbary macaques are smuggled to fuel the exotic pet market in Europe, tigers, rhinos, saiga antelopes and pangolins are poached for their valuable parts as TCM consumed by wealthy Chinese in both China and Europe, while caviar is destined for upper class society in the West. The socioeconomic discrepancy between relatively poor poachers and wealthy consumers is perhaps best illustrated by the illegal trade in caviar. While poor fishermen in the Caspian basin poach sturgeon and risk their lives to feed their families, upper-class society nevertheless consume the illegally obtained black caviar without limit.

Criminogenic asymmetries between the source and destination countries provide opportunities for crime (Passas 1999). In the context of economic asymmetries, poverty, unemployment and poor social conditions appear to be important incentives for poaching (Martin and Martin 2006; Duffy 2010). According to Mainka and Trivedi (2002), on a global basis rural poverty and the exploitation of resources are often closely connected. Research by wildlife experts who examined the economic and social driving forces of the trade in wildlife have concluded that most poachers originate from the poorest one third of all households.[1] In just a few cases were middle-income groups or the wealthiest involved in the harvesting of wildlife (World Bank 2008). The criminogenic potential would be activated through the awareness of economic asymmetries and, subsequently, frustration and strain experienced by suffering local communities (Bonger 1932; Passas 1999). While mainly local people are said to be involved in harvesting illegal wildlife, they usually work for 'outsiders' (e.g. Raymakers 2002; Nooren and Clardige 2001; Pantel and Chin 2009; Milliken and Shaw 2012). The poor conditions (e.g. unemployment, poverty) in the source countries are abused to recruit potential poachers by criminal organizations to fuel the demand of wealthy consumers. The case studies have confirmed that middlemen exploit poverty and inequality to allure people; from poor farmers in Southeast Asia who opportunistically poach endangered species for TCM to Berber communities in Morocco who catch monkeys for the pet industry. The poachers are supplied with loans, expensive equipment and weapons, while the criminal organizations remain unaffected, make the real profits and operate on a high level in the upperworld along with government officials and legally registered companies. The global anomies between wealthy and relatively poor countries provide opportunities for these criminal organizations to exploit both the natural resources and the local communities.

In addition, political reasons, such as the dissolution of the USSR, have provided several opportunities for organized crime in the context of political asymmetries (Shelly 1995; Passas 1999). The existing regulatory systems collapsed and informal criminal systems were developed to replace the formal state services (Dinerstein et al. 1994). According to Varese (1997: 580) the end of socialism resulted in a high amount of corruption and 'Mafia-style crime'. Illegal activities such as racketeering, the drugs trade, but also the wildlife trade emerged. Consequently, in a short period of time sturgeon and saiga populations significantly reduced due to overexploitation by criminal networks. High levels of corruption in combination with the emergence of organized crime groups caused the lucrative illegal trade in products, such as caviar and saiga horns, to fuel the global demand markets (e.g. Kühl et al. 2009; Birstein et al. 1997). Another example is the 'liberation' of the Chinese market that provides new opportunities for legal *and* illegal entrepreneurs. The Chinese economy slowly changed into a more open market and, therefore, an increase in Chinese middlemen in legal and illegal businesses emerged (Goodman 1998). Because the trade connections with European countries improved, these can be used for both legal and illegal trade. These two examples illustrate how political asymmetries can provide a breeding ground for wildlife crime.

Furthermore, power asymmetries are illustrated by the historically dominant position of the West in conservation issues. CITES was initiated by Western

---

[1]Poor households are much more dependent upon income (for their livelihood) generated from the wildlife trade than wealthier households.

countries without much attention to the underlying problems in poor source countries in the context of maintaining their natural resources (Dickson 2003). Several authors see the development of CITES and the trade bans in the context of species protection as a post-colonial approach of the conservation of the rich Western societies (e.g. Van Spaandonk 2000; Dickson 2003). Based on fieldwork this Western attitude of superiority over other countries was frequently mentioned in the previous chapters. Especially in China, TCM traders underlined the undesirable Western interference in the Chinese political and economic system regarding species conservation. The Western focus is considered to be too much on African and Southeast Asian source countries, without a critical reflection on their own market. According to Duffy (2010) instead of focusing on the creation and continuation of wildlife demand markets by the wealthy world, the focus is on coercion and enforcement in the world's poorest communities. Conservation and enforcement efforts are largely embedded in identifying problems in the source countries and, consequently, this produces marginalization, exclusion and violence towards the local communities. Accordingly, local people do not believe in the Western measures or enforcement efforts. Moreover, problematizing the issues regarding poaching in the local communities neglects the actual problem: the demand for wildlife (Duffy 2010). This is definitively an important issue as the EU is a major demand market of both legal and illegal wildlife worldwide. From this perspective, the traditional power asymmetries between wealthy developed countries and poor developing countries are used to distract attention from and the responsibility for the illegal market for wildlife. By understanding the social construction of the value and the provided opportunities for crime due to global anomie, the question remains how are these criminal wildlife networks socially embedded in society.

10.3 The Social Embeddedness of Crime

Criminal networks operate in relatively hostile and uncertain environments due to shifting illegal markets and changing law enforcement activities. Especially in the criminal environment of a lack of rules and mechanisms, which make formal trade and transactions possible, other connections and mechanisms appear. Criminal networks have a habit of interacting with their social environment, instead of performing in a social vacuum (Van de Bunt et al. 2014). Therefore, social ties, such as family, friends, ethnicity and culture are crucial to and embedded in criminal networks (e.g. Bruinsma and Bernasco 2004; Kleemans and Van de Bunt 2003; Van de Bunt et al. 2014). In the three case studies, the social ties indeed appeared to be fundamental in the establishment of criminal wildlife networks. Social relations are not only important to get in touch with criminal networks and to benefit from resources from other actors (e.g. knowledge, money), but also to cooperate within an unregulated hostile environment (Kleemans and Van de Bunt 1999).

Family ties regularly become a foundation for criminal networks; "family members can be trusted" (Kleemans and Van de Bunt 1999: 6). Family ties ensure the smooth running of criminal operations (Van de Bunt et al. 2014). Several informants in the caviar trade underlined the use of family members to transfer illegal caviar across the Russian border. A crucial middleman in the caviar trade in Baku explained how he financed the apartments of his two sons in Russia and thus how the family business expanded across the borders. The commitment from generation to generation in the illegal trade in caviar was illustrated by two family generations involved in this trade in Lagan, whereby the third generation was on the rise. According to Misztal (1996) trust in family members is a foundation of shared norms and values. He explains that within the family the greatest secrets can be kept and therefore this shields attention from the outside world.

The same holds true for the closeness of Chinese networks in which family and cultural aspects play fundamental roles. The cultural or family connection between the Chinese was regularly emphasized; this made it possible to smoothly coordinate illegal trade from collectors and smugglers to middlemen and wholesale traders. The Chinese practice of *guanxi* is important in creating an effective culturally based insider–outsider system (Myers 1995; Zhang et al. 2009). Informal relations provide opportunities for a familiar framework for illegal businesses. The cultural relationships between Berber populations in the poaching areas for monkeys in Morocco and the smuggling regions in the northern Rif provide similar advantages for the establishment of criminal wildlife networks. Informants underlined that relationships between Moroccan poachers, middlemen and traders are regularly culturally grounded.

In addition, bonds of friendship include 'strong ties' that influence criminal networks (Kleemans and Van de Bunt 1999). Informants involved in the illegal trade regularly emphasized the substantial importance of friends. Several Barbary macaque traders in Morocco referred to their ties with 'special friends' in their (criminal) network. By 'special' they meant that in addition to ordinary friendship, a secret relationship exists based on illegal activities, such as the trade in monkeys. This dual relationship is also frequently seen in Chinese networks where the *guanxi* practice intertwines the strict distinction between formality and informality.

Differences between the case studies are well presented as the fieldwork took place in different parts of the world; the social ties were often distributed differently. For instance, the importance of family, culture and ethnicity turned out to be especially important in Chinese criminal networks. Business partners preferably belong to the same ethnic Chinese group from the same region and it is notable that in the destination countries Chinese who distributed the illegal trade are established. According to Bovenkerk (2001) criminal networks are constituted based on migration flows. He explains how, after immigration, ethnic underworlds are connected to their country of origin. Chinese migration has ensured that in the source countries for wildlife, Chinese communities are established with potential business partners. On the other side, the Russians involved in the illegal wildlife trade were more open to social ties with other ethnicities, such as Polish or German traders. However, similar to the Chinese networks, the European caviar outlets regularly included Russian traders or shopkeepers. While several relationships between Moroccan involved actors were based on a cultural foundation, informants in Morocco highlighted cooperation with non-Moroccan European traders too. These traders had different nationalities, such as French and Italian traders.

The informal social ties between the upper and underworld are in particular noteworthy. Wildlife crime networks are not only based on social ties in the underworld, these also cooperate with legally registered wholesalers or shops and law enforcers.[2] The interconnection between the under and upperworld in the illegal wildlife trade is very visible (e.g. Lyons and Natusch 2011; Wyatt 2013). Crimes committed by business entities or individuals within the company are defined, respectively, as corporate crime and white-collar crime (Sutherland 1949; Braithwaite 1984; Hoefnagels 1981).[3] The term dirty-collar crimes or green-collar crimes has been introduced to underline the role of legally registered companies in the illegal activities of environmental crime (Ruggiero and South 2010; Barrett 1997; O'Hear 2004; Wolf 2011). Legally registered wildlife companies use their legal infrastructures to trade in illegal wildlife. In the illegal trade in caviar, saiga horns and pangolin scales the same species are offered on the formal *and* informal markets (e.g. Nooren and Claridge 2001; Knapp et al. 2006; Li et al. 2007; Pantel and Chin 2009). Although breeding centres or caviar farms are often praised for conservation purposes, they provide a perfect cover to hide illegal activities. The motivation may be, first, based on an antithetical relationship, in which the legal actors sell illegally obtained products, such as caviar, in the context of competition (antagonistic) or want to harm other players by sabotage (injurious). For instance, a 'parasitical' relationship takes place when armed protection is sold to the poachers of sturgeons or a 'predatory' relationship develops by efforts to destroy another company. Second, a symbiotic relationship exists when interests are shared and enhance mutual benefits. For example, police officers work together with illegal TCM traders at the China–Myanmar border in passing illegal trade and selling seized rhino horns (collaboration) or legal TCM traders who work together with illegal traders due to mutual benefits (reciprocity) (Passas 2002). In the previous case studies we have seen the existence of numerous social ties between criminal networks and legally registered enterprises in the illegal wildlife trade. In the illegal caviar trade sturgeon farms, caviar dealers, restaurants and caviar shops are all involved, the illegal selling of Barbary macaques regularly takes place in legally registered pet shops, while TCM producers, shops, wholesalers, tiger farms all have a share in the illegal TCM trade.

[2]Furthermore, wildlife products provided by illegal entrepreneurs are in demand by legal actors too.

[3]Criminal activities by corporations would often be unrecognized as those who hold economic power would be the same persons who make the law (Coleman 1997; Friedrichs 1996).

10.4 Mafia, Triads and (Semi-)Organized Criminal Networks

During the 1990s, organized crime was linked to the traditional hierarchical mafia, such as the Italian mafia, that gained control over economic sectors and regions as an alternative to civil society (Fijnaut and Paoli 2004; Kleemans 2007). Since then, many criminologists have discussed what is defined as organized crime and whether criminal networks are considered to be organized or disorganized. While organized crime remains an unclear and ambiguous concept (Siegel 2008), indications of organized crime could involve the degree of organization and structure (Passas 1995). Continuity and resilience are important aspects as well as a high level of rationality and the use of violence and counterstrategies (Fijnaut et al. 1996). Traditionally, organized crime has been portrayed as pyramidal structured organizations with a strict hierarchy and clear divisions of tasks and internal rules and sanction systems (c.f. Block and Chambliss 1981). The current perspective on organized crime has changed into more fluid and flexible organized networks anticipating opportunities for illegal markets (e.g. Paoli 2002; Fijnaut and Paoli 2004; Morselli 2009). According to Van Duyne (1995) the majority of the organized crime trade involves the illegal transfer of goods and services across borders.

Based on the three case studies the degree of organization and structure varies considerably. Next to several opportunistic poachers or traders who are involved in the illegal wildlife trade, there are also highly organized poaching and trade networks. Several groups involved in the illegal trade in caviar, Barbary macaques and TCM appear to have longer-term arrangements that stem from before the criminalization of these wildlife products. These criminal entrepreneurs were able to become unperturbed professional criminals due to long-term priorities in other areas of crime and new players became involved in the black market for wildlife. However, certain traders considered themselves to be part of a criminal organization, while others claimed to be working in flexible semi-structured networks that anticipate market changes. Whether organized crime is involved or not may differ: The high degree of organization, continuity and the use of violence was most visible in the criminal networks involved in the illegal caviar trade. Several respondents addressed the involvement of a 'caviar mafia' that controls the entire caviar sector, dominates the police and maintains power by violence (e.g. Dagestan, Atyrau oblast). However, the actors involved did not consider themselves to be a mafia organization, but rather a network of entrepreneurs. These informants explained their agreements with local government officials to command many aspects of the illegal trade and possibilities to obtain higher positions over time. An important illegal trader in caviar in Baku once started as a poacher on the Caspian Sea and due to his long engagement in the network he was promoted to a middleman. The caviar networks regularly maintain their position by the use of excessive violence illustrated by military attacks, bombings and kidnappings. Counterstrategies take place in both the Caspian countries and Europe. In the illegal trade in rhino horn criminal networks with a high degree of organization have also been highlighted. According to several traders the rhino horn trade has become a highly organized business in recent years. The deployment of prostitutes in pseudo hunts in South Africa to pay off their debts illustrates the level of sophistication behind the organization. In addition, the involvement of real professionally equipped rhino poachers in South Africa with high-calibre rifles, dart guns, infrared sensors, tranquilising drugs and even helicopters demonstrates that the criminal networks finance the equipment, as most African locals cannot afford such items. Less violent networks were found in the illegal trade in Barbary macaques where opportunistic animal traders work together with European entrepreneurs on a regular basis; every three months the European tradesmen arrive in Morocco and smuggle the monkeys to the EU. Even this latter group of illegal entrepreneurs may be considered as an organized crime group in the definition of organized crime set out in the United Nations Convention against Transnational Organized Crime.[4]

Another indicator of the involvement of organized wildlife crime groups is that organized crime usually operates in illegal markets in economically vulnerable and underdeveloped areas worldwide. Especially organized crime thrives well in weak states and in regions in which the government fails to effectively use the monopoly of violence (e.g. Bovenkerk 2003). Poaching and trade in wildlife usually takes place in such areas (see Sects. 6.1 and 10.2) and is therefore an attractive business for criminal organizations. During my fieldwork many such remote areas were visited to uncover the illegal markets for wildlife. The distant fishing areas with high levels of unemployment in Dagestan (in the Caucasus) provide perfect conditions for poaching sturgeons, the remote Rif Mountains in the upper north of Morocco represent a traditional 'smuggler's paradise' in the context of poverty, while the Golden Triangle in Southeast Asia is known to be one of the most undeveloped places in the region. In such areas other forms of crime regularly take place and an overlap between contraband products occurs. The Caucasus is an important region for weapons, drugs and human trafficking (e.g. Arasli 2007), the Rif Mountains region is well known as a window to Europe in relation to smuggling hashish and humans (e.g. Lehtinen 2008; Soddu 2006), while the Golden Triangle is notorious for the flourishing opium trade (e.g. Zhang and Chin 2011). The socioeconomic background of these regions provides a fertile breeding ground for criminal networks.

While the interrelation between the wildlife trade and other forms of crime becomes increasingly visible (Elliott 2009), several historical cases of intertwined networks have been seen (e.g. Christy 2008; Toufexis 1993)[5] and combined

[4]The Convention defined organized crime as 'a structured group of three or more persons, existing for a period of time and acting in concert with the aim of committing one or more serious crimes or offences established in accordance with this Convention, in order to obtain, directly or indirectly, a financial or other material benefit'.

[5]One of the first big wildlife cases in history is 'Operation Cobra' which took place in Miami. The wildlife trader Tabraue was 'chairman of the board' of the Tabraue syndicate, a 79 million dollar drug-smuggling operation and one of Florida's most violent organizations. He 'owned' Miami police officers and politicians, dealt in cocaine from Colombia and was involved in a murder case.

seizures underline the overlaps (e.g. Wyler and Sheikh 2013), most involved traders have been operating in specific illegal wildlife. For instance, while caviar and weapons are confiscated together, according to people involved in the caviar business weapons are only used for protection. On the other hand, traders also referred to smugglers involved in other illegal businesses, such as counterfeit products in combination with monkeys in Morocco and illegal caviar along with cigarettes. Several investigations have indicated that those who trade illegally in wildlife were once involved in other illegal activities as well, such as the drugs trade. When penalties and enforcement increased, they looked for safer criminal enterprises (e.g. South and Wyatt 2011). While these claims were not completely confirmed by this research, it has been noticed that more priority on drugs, for instance in the Golden Triangle, resulted in a shift to the wildlife trade. This may also explain the sudden rise of Irish criminal groups targeting museums for their rhino horns (Europol 2011) and former Medellin drug cartel members who have become rhino horn traders (Christy 2014). The wildlife trade has become attractive for organized crime due to the high profits, low sentences and a low risk of being caught.

Another overlap is the embeddedness of organized crime in the upperworld. The embeddedness of organized crime in legal sectors of the economy was largely discussed in the 1990s and 2000s (e.g. Van Duyne 1995; Ruggiero 1996; Passas 2002). The line between legal and criminal is regularly blurred, especially when legal and illegal actors interact with each other, such as the Italian mafia and the corruption of officials or cooperation between the Yakuza and Japanese politicians (Passas 2002). Both white-collar crime and corporate crime may have connections with organized crime due to encounters between legal and illegal economies (Ruggiero 1996). In the presented case studies the embeddedness of criminal organizations in legal sectors of the wildlife trade became particularly obvious in the caviar trade and rhino horn trade. Legally registered caviar companies in Kazakhstan, Russia and Azerbaijan were involved in the illegal catching of

(Footnote 5 continued)

He was sentenced to 100 years imprisonment by a federal judge in 1989 for trafficking in cocaine, marijuana and murder. Tabraue worked together with Van Nostrand, sentenced to a lenient five years because he had betrayed Tabraue (his son became well known as the 'Lizard King' years later when he was convicted in an international investigation into a large-scale illegal trade in animals), and they used codes such as "I need three cockatoos", meaning three kilos of cocaine or 'three lesser-crested cockatoos' which meant three ounces (Christy 2008: 36–40; Scott 1992). Another example is the secret passion for collecting wildlife by the drug lord Pablo Escobar. From the late 1970s he started to fly illegally endangered species from all over the world to *Hacienda Napoles* as he called his 530 ha of jungle and grassland along the Magdalena River. He hired expert advice on which species could survive in this place and bribed customs officials to import illegal species. This collection of 1900 animals from more than 100 species became one the most valuable collections on the continent and Escobar even opened it to the public. Besides the illegal importation of animals, according to the police camel and elephant droppings for his zoo were used in the wrapping of cocaine in order to confuse the law enforcers' drug-sniffing dogs (Toufexis 1993).

sturgeons in the Caspian Sea (sometimes under the guise of scientific quotas), while sturgeon farms were used as laundering operations. In the rhino horn trade a syndicate was active for over four years keeping rhinos for conservation purposes, while the rhinos were actually dehorned and killed to make profits of their illegal sale (Rademeyer 2012; Ayling 2013). This is not expected to be an isolated incident, but rather a practice that takes place on a large scale (Department Environmental Affairs South Africa 2011). Finally, the mutual benefits from cooperation with law enforcers were broadly highlighted by illegal traders in all three forms of the wildlife trade. The traders in caviar underlined the deep involvement of officials whereby bribery and protection takes place on a huge scale. Chinese TCM traders explained the role of local government and border officials to make the trade possible. Moroccan traders highlighted the 'ordinary' process of bribing border officials. Corruption appears to be a crucial element in the organized illegal wildlife trade that connects the upper and underworld.

To conclude, criminal networks in the wildlife trade vary from opportunistic flexible trade networks to long-term, highly organized criminal groups with a high degree of rationality and the use of violence. The embeddedness of the criminal networks in legally registered wildlife companies, the symbiotic or antithetical relationships with (corrupt) officials and legal companies, the use of violence and counterstrategies and the overlap with other forms of crime illustrate the sophisticated level of the criminal organizations involved. Especially the rational incentives that lie behind the wildlife crimes, such as high profits in the context of low priorities and low sentences, are very attractive for organized crime (Schneider 2008; Bennett 2011; Lawson and Vines 2014). However, the short-term gain of the well-organized criminal organizations and corrupt officials does not outweigh the irreparable harm to humans and nature.

10.5 Ecological Interaction and Harms

Traditionally the question of what is crime has challenged many criminologists. "Would there be any crime tomorrow if the criminal law was repealed today?" (Jeffery 1956: 658). The answer is ambiguous as the social construction of crime is dependent on the legal definitions of criminal behaviour defined by lawmakers and politicians (Hulsman 1986). Definitions of crime may change over the course of time in the context of changing norms and morals (Becker 1963). Consequently, there are harmful human activities that are not registered by law as being criminal in nature, while certain registered crimes are disputed (Brants 2013). In the trade in wildlife many harmful activities, such as the global destruction of the environment and violent activities regarding animals, are not criminalized. Generally, natural resources are exploited without any regulation (Wyatt 2013; Sollund 2015). With the emergence of green criminology the focus has transcended the borders of orthodox criminology and its definition of crime (White 2008; Lynch and Stretesky 2014). From a green criminological perspective, the harm principle is extended with species and ecosystems as victims of (human) actions in general and the symbiosis between man and nature in particular (South 1998; White 2008, 2011). As crime has no ontological reality, studying harmful activities is important to uncover potential future crimes by studying inequalities among people, ecosystems and wildlife.

Due to the 'artificial boundaries' of criminal law, scholars started to study social harms (e.g. Hillyard et al. 2004; Hillyard and Tombs 2004, 2007). From an anthropocentric perspective the organized wildlife trade can be extremely harmful for local communities. The poaching takes place in underdeveloped regions where poor local people live from the natural resources in the forests (e.g. Martin and Martin 2006; Duffy 2010). They are regularly indirect victims of a decline in economic security and a threat to their well-being (Wyatt 2013). Poachers of sturgeons in Dagestan complained that mafia groups use grenades to blast sturgeons to the surface quickly. Therefore, the entire ecosystem will be destroyed whereby local communities are no longer able to benefit from the natural resources. Another example is poaching in tourist areas in the case of the Barbary macaque. A guide in the cedar forests explained that besides local poachers, which, they agreed, poach outside tourist areas, sometimes they encounter unfamiliar poachers who catch the monkeys. The removal of these monkeys from tourist areas can reduce local incomes from (eco-)tourism. Direct anthropocentric harms include rangers who are killed during attacks by rhino poachers in South Africa or violent conflicts between sturgeon poachers and the police in Dagestan whereby people are regularly injured or face death. However, the harms started in the source countries are moving increasingly towards Western society. According to Beck (1999) the negative effects of the overexploitation in relatively poor countries create new risks in the modern world. For example, outbreaks of zoonotic diseases, that can be spread through the illegal trade in monkeys or by transmission from TCM animal preparations, illustrate how dangerous side-effects emerge in the Western world (Still 2003; EFSA 2014; Ostrowski et al.1998).

Although humans are part of ecosystems, these ecosystems are rarely conceptualized or considered as victims of human activities (White 2008, 2011). However, from an ecocentric perspective the disappearance of specific (keystone) species could have a disastrous impact on perennial species and their ecosystem due to the complex symbiotic interaction between plants and animals (Kellert and Wilson 1993; Mills et al. 1993; Power et al. 1996). Both predator and prey keystone species have a disproportionately large impact on the function and composition of an ecosystem (Power et al. 1996). The complex role of these species in unique ecosystems, such as the Caspian Sea or the cedar forests in Morocco, with many endemic species, is difficult to estimate. Sturgeons have already been swimming for millions of years in the ecosystem of the Caspian Sea and monkeys are traditionally well-known seed dispersers. What would happen if these species disappear? With the local removal of White Rhinos, short-grass grazers also disappeared (Waldram 2005) or with the decline of Barbary Macaques the forest may change dramatically (IUCN 2009). Especially the poaching of specific sexes of species can have disastrous effects. The ratio of saiga antelopes due to poaching for the horns of male antelopes is in certain populations as low as 5.7 % males. The poaching of female sturgeons with eggs for caviar results in female sturgeons making up only 15–17 % of the total population in Russia. Small populations are particularly vulnerable due to a mate shortage or a limited genetic variety (Courchamp et al. 2006). While many sub-populations of rhinos and tigers are believed to be on the brink of extinction, small populations of Barbary macaques (5,000–6,000) or saiga antelopes (56,300–61,300) are also extremely vulnerable in the context of poaching. The additional anthropogenic component of the overexploitation of highly valued endangered species may ensure that a small population can extirpate at a higher rate than expected (Lindsey et al. 2012; Myers et al. 2007). Consequently, direct and indirect ecocentric harms can result in trophic cascades by the reduction or removal of the top predators, such as tigers, or large herbivores, such as rhinos and saiga antelopes; the entire ecosystem with its ecosystem functions may collapse due to the decline in important keystone species (Lindsey et al. 2012; Myers et al. 2007).

Finally, animals are generally seen as human property by law, which can be bred, killed, and tortured by their owners (White 2011). According to Sollund (2008) the underlying harms resulting from this social anthropocentric legitimation of abusive or exploitative acts towards non-human animals should be studied. From a biocentric perspective, harm reduction towards animals is preferred above human interests (Halsey and White 1998). Several green criminologists emphasize the harmful human activities towards individual animals in the wildlife trade (Sollund 2008; Wyatt 2013). Wyatt (2013) noticed that non-human animals in the wildlife trade are moved out from their natural environment by methods that can cause injury and stress to the animal. Indeed, poachers of Barbary macaques use dogs and sticks to separate baby monkeys from their mothers. In the other two case studies animals are usually killed for their products; sturgeon for caviar, saiga antelopes for horn, pangolins for scales and tigers for bones. During poaching certain activities may also be harmful; traps can cause injury and the saiga antelopes and rhinos are sometimes alive during when their horns are removed (Samuel 2013). In addition, practices in the farming of exotic animals are comparable to those in the livestock industry: close quarters regularly affect animal welfare (Wyatt 2013). The tiger farms in China, where many tigers are kept close together in small cages, illustrate the disruption to animals' natural behaviour and a degrading animal welfare. The transportation of animals can be stressful and traumatic as they are packed in containers which are too small; Barbary macaques are usually smuggled across the border in relatively small suitcases without food or water. According to Sollund (2013) at the final destination the animals often suffer in captivity (e.g. Agnew 1998).[6] Another harmful activity at the final destination is illustrated by pangolins being boiled alive to be made into soup (Pantel and Anak 2010). From this biocentric perspective, at all stages harm to individual animals occurs; victimization within the illegal wildlife trade is illustrated starting with the poaching process and ending up with the final destination.

[6]Sollund (2013) exemplified this statement by wild-caught parrots that regularly die after only a few years in captivity.

As demonstrated in this section many harmful activities occur in the wildlife trade, from harm to local communities, ecosystems and individual animals. Compared to high priority offences such as property crimes (theft or burglary), in which products such as mobile phones or computers change ownership, the harm caused by wildlife trafficking is certainly more global and comprehensive. In other words, the priority being given to property crimes that threaten replaceable people's ownership is disproportional in the context of environmental crimes that are destructive for the entire planet.

10.6 The Future

To understand the approach to wildlife crimes in the near future, it is useful to analyse current processes of criminalization. The criminalization of the wildlife trade can be explained by the three major waves that have changed Western perspectives on biodiversity, security threats to society and animal welfare. Moral entrepreneurs who advocate criminalizing these activities have influenced the perspectives. First, international efforts to stop the biodiversity decline began around 1900, motivated by Western hunters, fishermen and a small group of the social elite as described in Chap. 3. For a long time the process to criminalize the trade in wildlife was obstructed by strong economic and industrial interests, but in the second half of the twentieth century the situation changed (Nadelmann 1990). Public awareness increased significantly from the 1960s onwards in the context of international waves of environmental protests enhanced by authoritative groups that underlined the reduction of species. The media increasingly focussed on environmental and ecological concerns, such as the harmful effects of whaling and the ivory trade on remaining populations (Benton 1998; Nadelmann 1990; Jenkins 2000) and species extinction in our lifetime, such as the Javan tiger (Seidensticker 1987). Consequently, CITES came into force to regulate the trade in endangered species (Van Male 2003). In the 1980s the term 'biodiversity' (biological diversity), introduced by Wilson, gained widespread recognition and serious concerns arose with regard to global defaunation and the effects on biodiversity (Wilson 1988). In the 1990s reports on the decline in biodiversity highlighted the impact of human activities on the environment and strengthened concerns with warnings of the beginning of the sixth mass extinction (e.g. Leakey and Lewin 1995; May et al. 1995; Pimm et al. 1995). Knowledge about the significant function of ecosystems for the world, including humans, animals and plants, simultaneously increased. The reduction in biodiversity was linked to human health as it would contribute to the disappearance of potential medicines (Balick et al. 1996) and species decline would immediately affect people who rely most directly on ecosystem services, for instance farmers, the rural poor and traditional societies (Díaz et al. 2006). Species protection has become a global concern in the context of the environment *and* human interests. The process of criminalization is illustrated by the growth in the CITES lists since 1975; in the last five years alone around 1,000 species have been added to the CITES lists; an overall growth of 200 each year. Simultaneously there is a trend for species to be moved up on the CITES' gradation scale (Hutton and Dickson 2000).

Second, security threats to society caused by the wildlife trade have been given a prominent place in the last few decades. Already in the early 1990s journalists referred to the involvement of organized crime in the wildlife trade. The Los Angeles Times referred to the involvement of 'Chinese, Japanese, Sicilian and Russian gangsters', while the Cali drug cartel would use regional fishing fleets to smuggle both drugs and animals across the Caribbean into the US and Europe.[7] Time magazine underlined that 'traditional organized-crime operations have finally awakened to the huge profit potential of wildlife smuggling'. The article referred to the Russian mafia targeting animal markets, South American drug cartels that combine the cocaine trade with the wildlife trade and the involvement of the Yakuza in the whale-meat trade.[8] Galster supported these claims by undercover investigations undertaken by the Endangered Species Project (Søyland 2000; Fröhlich 2003). He underlined the involvement of organized crime such as the Russian mafia and the Yakuza, and the combined smuggling operations of drugs and animals (Søyland 2000). Until that time it was commonly believed that only opportunists and tourists were driving the illegal trade in wildlife without much organization. From the 2000s onwards UN reports started to underline the involvement of organized crime partly based on previous claims by researchers and journalists; organized crime would be 'strongly present' and 'significant and growing' (e.g. ECOSOC 2002, 2003, 2005). A team from the CITES secretariat partially confirmed the claims: 'Intelligence (…) appeared to more than justify suspicions that organized criminal gangs, including the Russian Mafia and Chinese Triads, may well be involved in wildlife crime' (ECOSOC 2003: 11). NGOs strengthened the claims with several private investigations (e.g. Cook et al. 2002). Furthermore, reporters and journalists also found new drugs-wildlife overlaps, such as 'elephant tusks stuffed with hashish' and 'exotic parrots smuggled with methamphetamine pills' (Wyler and Sheikh 2013).

During the 2010s not only the involvement of organized crime in the wildlife trade poses a threat to state security, also the involvement of terrorism has emerged. Various reports have pointed to the possible involvement of 'terrorist' groups, such as the Sudanese janjaweed, the Lord's Resistance Army (LRA), and the Somali Al Shabaab. These groups rely on selling ivory for their financing or exchange ivory for military equipment (Wyler and Sheikh 2013). A recent report by the UN also indicated the involvement of groups such as Harkat-ul-Jihad-al-Islami and Jama'atul Mujahideen Bangladesh that poach tigers, elephants and rhinos to raise funds (Nellemann et al. 2014). Several investigations by NGOs and journalists have referred or tried to confirm these suspicions (e.g. IFAW 2013). "The UN links elephant poaching to crime and terrorism (…) [O]rganized crime, militias, and

[7]Los Angeles Times 'Animal Subtraction' by Steven Ambrus, July 25, 1995.

[8]Time 'Animal Genocide, Mob Style' by Michael Lemonick, November 14, 1994.

terrorist entities have become more involved in the illegal trade of wildlife" (IFAW 2013: 5–13). Simultaneously, the wildlife trade became increasingly connected to public health security issues. According to several reports zoonotic diseases such as SARS, Avian influenza and Ebola could be transferred through the illegal wildlife trade (e.g. Brooks-Moizer et al. 2008; Bell et al. 2004). The wildlife trade has become a risk for public health security in the context of these zoonotic diseases. Consequently the wildlife trade has become increasingly criminalized due to the security threats from organized crime, terrorist organizations and the potential spread of zoonotic diseases.

Third, non-human animals are increasingly approached as individuals with an intrinsic value and therefore attributed rights. Traditional Western perspectives of animals whereby animals are mere automata without souls, minds, or reason (Descartes 1637) were subject to change in the context of the increased scientific knowledge about animals in the eighteenth and nineteenth century (e.g. Darwin 1871). Several authors argued that if an animal has the ability to suffer it should be treated properly (e.g. Bentham 1789). Based on the idea that animals can suffer, the question of to what extent it is morally acceptable to treat animals as inferior to humans naturally arose. The distinction between humans and non-human animals would be completely arbitrary based upon an anthropocentric attitude rather than a priori differences (Singer 1975; Regan 1997). From the early 1970s onwards NGOs and the media increasingly focussed on non-human victims and environmental problems that became intertwined with a growing awareness of the suffering non-human animals (Benton 1998). Consequently, under pressure from several moral entrepreneurs, animal rights were slowly extended and the keeping of certain exotic animals became more restricted during the 1990s and 2000s. A growing opposition to animals used in experiments emerged and the protection of animals from human exploitation moved to the legal arena (Granfield and Colomy 2005). In the last few decades *positive lists* have been developed in several EU countries that present exotic animals that are legal to keep as pets partly based on animal welfare aspects (e.g. Koene et al. 2013).[9] Simultaneously, NGOs have focussed on the 'poor conditions' regarding the welfare of animals in the wildlife trade (e.g. RSPCA 2004). The question arose whether the exhibition of non-human animals in circuses or zoos is still morally acceptable. In several countries in the EU it became forbidden to exhibit wild animals in circuses (e.g. Austria, Croatia, Greece) (Department for the Environment and Rural Affairs, House of Commons 2013), while other countries introduced the idea of closing their zoos. Costa Rica proposed a ban on the use of animals in circuses and hunting as a sport and has recently decided to close the country's only two public zoos.[10] Moreover, a court in Argentina extended the

[9]Several criteria have been developed to identify exotic species which are suitable to be kept as pets. One of the most important criteria is related to the intrinsic value of an animal: can the animal be kept under normal and realistic conditions in relation to its environment (e.g. natural behaviour, natural environment) and is it free from chronic negative stress (e.g. social behaviour, biorhythm) (Koene et al. 2013).

[10]National Geographic, 'Costa Rica closes zoos', August 5, 2013.

human right to freedom to an orangutan in Buenos Aires Zoo: "She was in a situation of illegal deprivation of freedom as a non-human person".[11] The perspective of animals changed from being mere objects into sentient beings. Just as Elias (1939) underlined how standards regarding violence gradually transformed, violence regarding exotic animals may become outlawed in the 'civilising process'. Kuhn (1962) explains in his controversial book 'The Structure of Scientific Revolutions' that by breaking down existing beliefs space for new insights, a new conceptual framework, will be created. This paradigm shift or scientific revolution can be seen in the context of humans' changing relationship with animals.

These three major waves have significantly influenced views on the wildlife trade. An awareness of the reduction in biodiversity through human activities and the complex symbiosis between humans, animals and plants has been created. In addition, the illegal wildlife trade is no longer considered to be an industry driven by opportunists and tourists, but rather as an industry that threatens international security due to the involvement of organized crime and terrorist organizations. Furthermore, the potential spread of zoonotic diseases through the wildlife trade makes the industry vulnerable to public health issues. Finally, the perspectives of animals changed from animals as 'automata' into animals as sentient beings with an intrinsic value and, consequently, a growing awareness of the suffering of non-human animals emerged. In the near future it can be expected that the mass extinction of species will continue and that concerns regarding biodiversity will increase. This study has confirmed that sophisticated criminal networks are involved in the wildlife crime business, in which species may become extinct more quickly than expected. By criminalizing the wildlife trade it should not be expected that these criminal networks will disappear. Although the trade will become less attractive for criminal networks because the punishments may increase and the possibility of being caught might increase, prices on the black market may also rise and that is just as appealing for criminal networks. Most likely, in line with the current developments in animal welfare, non-human animals will be given more rights in the near future. From this perspective, it is plausible to say that the entire wildlife business will become a more serious form of crime in the near future.

References

Agnew, R. (1998). The causes of animal abuse: A social-psychological analysis. *Theoretical Criminology, 2*(2), 177–209.

Appadurai, A. (Ed.). (1986). *The social life of things: Commodities in cultural perspective*. Cambridge: Cambridge University Press.

Arasli, J. (2007). The rising wind: Is the caucasus emerging as a hub for terrorism, smuggling, and trafficking? *The Quarterly Journal, 6*, 5–26.

[11]BBC "Court in Argentina grants basic rights to orangutan", December 21, 2014.

Arquilla, J., & Ronfeldt, D. (2001). The advent of netwar. In J. Arquilla & D. Ronfeldt (Eds.), *Networks and netwars: The future of terror, crime and militancy*. RAND: Santa Monica.

Ayling, J. (2013). What sustains wildlife crime? Rhino horn trading and the resilience of criminal networks. *Journal of International Wildlife Law & Policy, 16*(1), 57–80.

Balick, M. J., Elisabetsky, E., & Laird, S. A. (1996). *Medicinal resources of the tropical forest: Biodiversity and its importance to human health*. New York: Columbia University Press.

Baratay, E., & Hardouin-Fugier, E. (2003). *Zoo: A history of zoological gardens in the west*. London: Reaktion books.

Barrett, J. F. (1997). Green collar criminals: Why should they receive special treatment. *Maryland Journal of Contemporary Legal Issues, 8*, 107–117.

Beck, U. (1999). *World risk society*. Cambridge: Polity Press.

Becker, H. S. (1963). *Outsiders: Studies in the sociology of deviance*. New York: The Free Press.

Bell, D., Robertson, S., & Hunter, P. R. (2004). Animal origins of SARS coronavirus: Possible links with the international trade in small carnivores. *Philosophical Transactions of the Royal Society B: Biological Sciences, 359*, 1107–1114.

Bennett, E. L. (2011). Another inconvenient truth: The failure of enforcement systems to save charismatic species. *Oryx, 45*(4), 476–479.

Bentham, J. (1789). *An introduction to the principles of morals and legislation*. Oxford: Clarendon Press.

Benton, T. (1998). Rights and justice on a shared planet: More rights or new relations? *Theoretical Criminology, 2*(2), 149–175.

Birstein, V. J., Bemis, W. E., & Waldman, J. R. (1997). The threatened status of acipenseriform species: A summary. In V. J. Birstein, W. E. Bemis, & J. R. Waldman (Eds.), *Sturgeon biodiversity and conservation* (pp. 427–435). Netherlands: Springer.

Block, A. A., & Chambliss, W. J. (1981). *Organizing crime*. New York: Elsevier.

Bonger, W. A. (1932). *Inleiding tot de Criminologie*. Haarlem: Erven Bohn.

Bovenkerk, F. (2001). Organized crime and ethnic minorities: Is there a link? In P. Williams, & D. Vlassis (Eds.), *Combating transnational crime. Concepts, activities and responses. ISPAC, Frank Cass Journal*, 109–126.

Bovenkerk, F. (2003). *Misdaadprofielen*. Amsterdam: Meulenhoff.

Bradshaw, J., & Paul, E. (2010). Could empathy for animals have been an adaptation in the evolution of Homo sapiens? *Animal Welfare, 19*(1), 107–112.

Braithwaite, J. (1984). *Corporate crime in the pharmaceutical industry (Routledge Revivals)*. London: Routledge.

Brants, C. (2013). De sociale constructive van criminaliteit. In M. Boone, & C. Brants (Eds.), *Criminologie en strafrecht*. The Hague: Boom Lemma uitgevers.

Brooks-Moizer, F., Roberton, S. I., Edmunds, K., & Bell, D. (2008). Avian influenza H5N1 and the wild bird trade in Hanoi, Vietnam. *Ecology and Society, 14*(1), 28.

Bruinsma, G., & Bernasco, W. (2004). Criminal groups and transnational illegal markets. *Crime, Law and Social Change, 41*(1), 79–94.

Christy, B. (2008). *The Lizard King: The true crimes and passions of the world's greatest reptile smugglers*. New York: Twelve.

Christy, B. (2014). *Convicted drug dealer indicted for selling rhino horns. Undercover investigation nets alleged wildlife trafficker with ties to former Medellín Drug Cartel*. Washington. *National Geographic, 17*, 2014.

Coggins, C. (2003). *The tiger and the pangolin: Nature, culture, and conservation in China*. Hawaii: University of Hawaii Press.

Coleman, J. W. (1997). *The criminal elite: Understanding white-collar crime*. New York: MacMillan.

Cook, D., Roberts, M., & Lowther, J. (2002). *The international wildlife trade and organised crime: A review of the evidence and the role of the UK*. Wolverhampton: University of Wolverhampton.

Courchamp, F., Angulo, E., Rivalan, P., Hall, R. J., Signoret, L., Bull, L., et al. (2006). Rarity value and species extinction: The anthropogenic allee effect. *PLoS Biology, 4*(12), e415.

Darwin, C. R. (1871). *The descent of man, and selection in relation to sex*. London: John Murray.
Department Environmental Affairs South Africa. (2011). *A study on the dehorning of African rhinoceroses*. Pretoria: Department Environmental Affairs South Africa.
Descartes, R. (1637). *Discours de la Méthode*. Philosophie Publishers.
Díaz, S., Fargione, J., Chapin, F. S., & Tilman, D. (2006). Biodiversity loss threatens human well-being. *PLoS Biology, 4*(8), 1300–1305.
Dickson, B. (2003). What is the goal of regulating wildlife trade? Is regulation a good way to achieve this goal? In: S. Oldfiels (Ed.), *The trade in wildlife. Regulation for conservation*. London: Earthscan Publications.
Dinerstein, E., Krever, V., Olson, D. M., & Williams, L. (1994). An emergency strategy to rescue Russia's biological diversity. *Conservation Biology, 8*(4), 934–939.
Duffy, R. (2010). *Nature crime: How we're getting conservation wrong*. New Haven: Yale University Press.
Dunn, R. R. (2005). Modern insect extinctions, the neglected majority. *Conservation Biology, 19*(4), 1030–1036.
Economic and Social Council United Nations. (2002). *Progress Made in the Implementation of Economic and Social Council Resolution 2001/12 on Illicit Trafficking in Protected Species of Wild Flora and Fauna*. Report of the Secretary-General.
Economic and Social Council United Nations. (2003). *Illicit Trafficking in Protected Species of Wild Flora and Fauna and Illicit Access to Genetic Resources* (E/CN.15/2003/8).
Economic and Social Council United Nations. (2005). *Illicit Trafficking in Protected Species of Wild Flora and Fauna*. Report of the Secretary-General, 17 March 2005 (E/CN.15/2005/1).
EFSA. (2014). *An update on the risk of transmission of Ebola Virus (EBOV) via the food chain*. Parma: European Food Safety Authority.
Elias, N. (1939). *The civilizing process*. Oxford: Basil Blackwell.
Elliot, L. (2009). Combating transnational environmental crime: 'Joined up' thinking about transnational networks. *Eco-Crime and Justice: Essays on Environmental Crime* (pp. 55–77). Turin: UNICRI.
Europol. (2011). *Organised crime threat assessment (OCTA)*. The Hague: Europol.
Fijnaut, C., & Paoli, L. (2004). *Organised crime in Europe: Concepts, patterns, and control policies in the European Union and beyond*. Dordrecht: Springer.
Fijnaut, C., Bovenkerk, F., Bruinsma, G., & van de Bunt, H. (1996). *Eindrapport onderzoeksgroep Fijnaut. App. 7 in Inzake opsporing: Enquête opsporingsmethoden*. The Hague: Sdu Uitgevers.
Friedrichs, D. (1996). *Trusted criminals: White collar crime in contemporary society*. Belmont: Wadsworth, Cengage Learning.
Fröhlich, T. (2003). *Organised environmental crime in the EU Member States*. Freiburg: Max Planck Institute for Foreign and International Criminal Law.
Goodman, D. S. (1998). In search of China's new middle classes: The creation of wealth and diversity in Shanxi during the 1990s. *Asian Studies Review, 22*(1), 39–62.
Granfield, R., & Colomy, P. (2005). Paradise lost: The transformation of wildlife law in the vanishing wilderness. *Mad about wildlife*, 147–169.
Green, A. (1999). *Animal underworld: Inside America's black market for rare and exotic species*. New York: PublicAffairs.
Halsey, M., & White, R. (1998). Crime, ecophilosophy and environmental harm. *Theoretical Criminology, 2*(3), 345–371.
Herzog, H. A. (2014). Biology, culture, and the origins of pet-keeping. *Animal Behavior and Cognition, 1*(3), 296–308.
Hillyard, P., & Tombs, S. (2004). Beyond criminology? In P. Hillyard, C. Pantazis, S. Tombs, & D. Gordon (Eds.), *Beyond criminology. Taking harm seriously*. London: Pluto Press.
Hillyard, P., & Tombs, S. (2007). From 'crime' to social harm? *Crime, Law and Social Change, 48*(1–2), 9–25.
Hillyard, P., Pantazis, C., Tombs, S., & Gordon, D. (Eds.). (2004). *Beyond criminology. Taking harm seriously*. London: Pluto Press.

Hoefnagels, G. P. (1981). *Witte boordencriminaliteit: opstellen over misdaad en macht*. Assen: Van Gorcum.

Hulsman, L. H. (1986). Critical criminology and the concept of crime. *Crime, Law and Social Change, 10*(1), 63–80.

Hutton, J., & Dickson, B. (Eds.). (2000). *Endangered species, threatened convention: The past, present, and future of CITES, the convention on international trade in endangered species of Wild Fauna and Flora*. London: Earthscan.

IFAW. (2013). *Criminal nature: The global security implications of the illegal wildlife trade*. Yarmouth Port: International Fund for Animal Welfare, Report.

IUCN. (2009). *Deforestation Spells Doom for Barbary Macaque*. Gland: IUCN.

Janson, H. W. (1952). *Apes and ape lore: In the middle ages and the renaissance* (Vol. 20). London: Warburg Institute, University of London.

Jeffery, C. R. (1956). The structure of American criminological thinking. *The Journal of Criminal Law, Criminology, and Police Science*, 658–672.

Jenkins, R. W. (2000). The significant trade process: Making Appendix II work. In Endangered Species (Ed.), *Threatened convention: The past, present and future of CITES, the convention on international trade in endangered species of Wild Fauna and Flora*. London: Earthscan.

Jennison, G. (1937). *Animals for show and pleasure in Ancient Rome*. Manchester: Manchester University.

Kalof, L. (2007). *Looking at animals in human history*. London: Reaktion Books.

Kellert, S. R., & Wilson, E. O. (1993). *The Biophilia hypothesis*. Washington, DC: Island Press.

Kidder, R. L. (1983). *Connecting law and society*. Englewood: Prentice Hall Inc.

Kisling, V. N. (Ed.). (2001). *Zoo and aquarium history: Ancient animal collections to zoological gardens*. Boca Raton, Fla: CRC Press.

Knapp. A., Kitschke, C. & von Meibom, S. (Eds.). (2006). *Proceedings of the International Sturgeon Enforcement Workshop to Combat Illegal Trade in Caviar. Prepared by TRAFFIC Europe for the European Commission*. Brussels: Traffic.

Kleemans, E., & van de Bunt, H. G. (2003). The social organisation of human trafficking. In H. Van de Bunt, D. Siegel, & D. Zaitch (Eds.), *Global organized crime. Trends and developments* (pp. 97–104). Dordrecht: Kluwer Law International.

Kleemans, E. R. (2007). Organized crime, transit crime, and racketeering. *Crime and Justice, 35*(1), 163–215.

Kleemans, E. R., & Van de Bunt, H. G. (1999). The social embeddedness of organized crime. *Transnational Organized Crime, 5*(1), 19–36.

Koene, P., Ipema, B. & de Mol, R. M. (2013). *Zoogdiersoorten die geschikt zijn als Gezelschapsdier*. Wageningen: UR Livestock Research.

Kühl, A., Balinova, N., Bykova, E., Arylov, Y. N., Esipov, A., Lushchekina, A. A., et al. (2009). The role of saiga poaching in rural communities: Linkages between attitudes, socio-economic circumstances and behaviour. *Biological Conservation, 142*(7), 1442–1449.

Kuhn, T. S. (1962). *The structure of scientific revolutions*. Chicago: University of Chicago Press.

Laufer, P. (2010). *Forbidden creatures. Inside the world of animals smuggling and exotic pets*. Guilford: Lyons Press.

Lawson, K., & Vines, A. (2014). *Global impacts of the illegal wildlife trade: The costs of crime, insecurity and institutional erosion*. London: Chatham House.

Leakey, R., & Lewin, R. (1995). *The sixth extinction*. London: Weidenfeld and Nicolson.

Lehtinen, T. (2008). At the gates of El Dorado. In F. Söderbaum (Ed.), *Afro-regions: The dynamics of cross-border micro-regionalism in Africa*. The Nordic Africa Institute: Villavägen.

Li, L., Zhao, Y., & Bennett, E. L. (2007). *Report of a survey on saiga horn in markets in China*. CoP14 Inf, 14.

Lindsey, P. A., Masterson, C. L., Beck, A. L., & Romañach, S. (2012). Ecological, social and financial issues related to fencing as a conservation tool in Africa. In M. J. Somers & M. Hayward (Eds.), *Fencing for conservation* (pp. 215–234). New York: Springer.

Locke, J. (1689). *Two treatises of government*. London: University Press.

Lynch, M. J., & Stretesky, P. B. (2014). *Exploring green criminology: Toward a green criminological revolution*. Farnham: Ashgate Publishing.
Lynch, J. M., & Stretsky, B. P. (2003). The meaning of green: Contrasting criminological perspectives. *Theoretical Criminology, 7*(2), 217–238.
Lyons, J. A., & Natusch, D. J. (2011). Wildlife laundering through breeding farms: Illegal harvest, population declines and a means of regulating the trade of green pythons (Morelia viridis) from Indonesia. *Biological Conservation, 144*(12), 3073–3081.
Mainka, S., & Trivedi, M. (2002). *Links between biodiversity conservation, livelihoods and food security: The sustainable use of wild species for meat (No. 24)*. Gland: IUCN.
Martin, E. B., & Martin, C. (2006). Insurgency and poverty: Recipe for rhino poaching in Nepal. *Pachyderm, 41*, 61–73.
May, R. M., Lawton, J. H., & Stork, N. E. (1995). *Assessing extinction rates. Extinction rates*. Oxford: Oxford University Press.
Milliken, T., & Shaw, J. (2012). *The South Africa-Viet Nam Rhino Horn Trade Nexus: A deadly combination of institutional lapses, corrupt wildlife industry professionals, and Asian Crime Syndicates*. Cambridge: Traffic.
Mills, L. S., Soulé, M.E., & Doak, D. F. (1993). The keystone-species concept in ecology and conservation. *BioScience*, 219–224.
Mintz, S. W. (1985). *Sweetness and power*. New York: Viking.
Misztal, B. (1996). *Trust in modern societies: The search for the bases of social order*. Cambridge: Polity Press.
Montesh, M. (2013). *Rhino peaching: A new form of organised crime*. Pretoria: College of Law Research and Innovation Committee of the University of South Africa.
Morselli, C. (2009). *Inside criminal networks*. New York: Springer.
Myers, W. H. (1995). Orb weavers—the global webs: The structure and activities of transnational ethnic Chinese criminal groups. *Transnational Organized Crime, 1*(4), 1–36.
Myers, R. A., Baum, J. K., Shepherd, T. D., Powers, S. P., & Peterson, C. H. (2007). Cascading effects of the loss of apex predatory sharks from a coastal ocean. *Science, 315*(5820), 1846–1850.
Nadelmann, E. A. (1990). Global prohibition regimes: The evolution of norms in international society. *International Organization, 44*(04), 479–526.
Nellemann, C., Henriksen, R., Raxter, P., Ash, N., & Mrema, E. (Eds.). (2014). *The environmental crime crisis—Threats to sustainable development from illegal exploitation and trade in wildlife and forest resources. A UNEP rapid response assessment*. Nairobi and Arendal: United Nations Environment Programme and GRID-Arendal.
Nijman, V., Shepherd, C. R., & van Balen, S. (2009). Declaration of the Javan hawk eagle Spizaetus bartelsi as Indonesia's National Rare Animal impedes conservation of the species. *Oryx, 43*(01), 122–128.
Nooren, H., & Claridge, G. (2001). *Wildlife Trade in Laos: The End of the Game*. Gland: IUCN-The World Conservation Union.
O'Hear, M. M. (2004). Sentencing the green-collar offender: Punishment, culpability, and environmental crime. *Journal of Criminal Law and Criminology*, 133–276.
Ostrowski, S. R., Leslie, M. J., Parrott, T., Abelt, S., & Piercy, P. E. (1998). B-virus from pet macaque monkeys: An emerging threat in the United States? *Emerging Infectious Diseases, 4*(1), 117–121.
Pailler, S. (2007). *Bushmeat hunting among the Malinke tribe of Guinea, West Africa*. New York: State University of New York College of Environmental Science & Forestry.
Pantel, S., & Anak, N. W. (2010). *A preliminary assessment of Sunda Pangolin Trade in Sabah*. Petaling Jaya: Traffic South East Asia.
Pantel, E. B. S., & Chin, S. (2009). *Proceedings of the Workshop on Trade and Conservation of Pangolins Native to South and Southeast Asia*. Singapore: Traffic.
Paoli, L. (2002). The paradoxes of organized crime. *Crime, Law and Social Change, 37*(1), 51–97.
Passas, N. (1995). *Organized crime*. Brookfield: Dartmouth.

Passas, N. (1999). Globalization, criminogenic asymmetries and economic crime. *European Journal of Law Reform, 1*, 399–424.

Passas, N. (2000). Global anomie, dysnomie, and economic crime: Hidden consequences of neoliberalism and globalization in Russia and around the world. *Social Justice, 27*(2), 16–44.

Passas, N. (2002). Cross-border crime and the interface between legal and illegal actors. In P. C. van Duyne, K. von Lampe, & N. Passas (Eds.), *Upperworld and underworld in cross-border crime* (pp. 11–42). Nijmegen: Wolf Legal Publishers.

Passas, N., & Goodwin, N. (2005). *It's legal but it ain't right: Harmful social consequences of legal industries*. Ann Arbor: University of Michigan Press.

Pimm, S. L., Russell, G. J., Gittleman, J. L., & Brooks, T. M. (1995). The future of biodiversity. *Science, 269*(5222), 347–349.

Power, M. E., Tilman, D., Estes, J. A., Menge, B. A., Bond, W. J., Mills, L. S., et al. (1996). Challenges in the quest for keystones. *BioScience*, 609–620.

Rademeyer, J. (2012). *Killing for profit: Exposing the illegal rhino horn trade*. Cape Town: Random House Struik.

Raymakers, C. (2002). *Study on the social and economic aspects of illegal fishing in the Caspian Sea*. Brussels: Traffic Europe.

Regan, T. (1997). The rights of humans and other animals'. *Ethics and Behavior, 7*(2), 103–111.

Roe, D., Mulliken, T., Milledge, S., Mremi, J., Mosha, S., & Grieg-Gran, M. (2002). *Making a killing or making a living. wildlife trade, trade controls and rural livelihoods*. London: IIED, and Cambridge: Traffic.

Rousseau, J. J. (1762). *The social contract*. London: Penguin Books.

RSPCA. (2004). *Handle with care. A look at the exotic animal pet trade*. RSPCA: Horsham.

Ruggiero, V. (1996). *Organized and corporate crime in Europe: Offers that can't be refused*. Aldershot: Dartmouth.

Ruggiero, V., & South, N. (2010). Green criminology and dirty collar crime. *Critical Criminology, 18*(4), 251–262.

Saffron, I. (2002). *Caviar. The strange history and uncertain future of the world's most coveted delicacy*. New York: Broadway Books.

Samuel, G. (2013). *Assessing the risks of rhino horn trade*. South Africa: International Rhino coalition.

Schneider, J. L. (2008). Reducing the illicit trade in endangered wildlife: The market reduction approach. *Journal of Contemporary Criminal Justice, 24*, 274–295.

Scott, P. D. (1992). *Cocaine politics: Drugs, armies, and the CIA in Central America*. Los Angeles: University of California.

Seidensticker, J. (1987). Bearing witness: Observations on the extinction of Panthera tigris balica and Panthera tigris sondaica. In R. L. Tilson and U. S. Seal (Eds.), *Tigers of the World: The biology, biopolitics, management and conservation of an endangered species*. New York: Noyes Park Ridge.

Serpell, J. A. (2003). Anthropomorphism and anthropomorphic selection: Beyond the 'cute response'. *Society and Animals, 11*, 83–100.

Shelley, L. I. (1995). Post-Soviet organized crime. *European Journal on Criminal Policy and Research, 3*(4), 7–25.

Siegel, D. (2008). Diamonds and organized crime: The case of Antwerp. In D. Siegel, & H. Nelen (Eds.), *Organized crime. Culture, markets and policies*. New York: Springer.

Simmel, G. (1957). Fashion. *American Journal of Sociology*, 541–558.

Simmel, G. (1978). *The philosophy of money*. London: Routledge.

Singer, P. (1975). *Animal liberation: A new ethics for our treatment of animals*. New York: Random House.

Soddu, P. (2006). *Ceuta and Melilla: Security, human rights and frontier control. Institut Europeu de la Mediterrània (eds) IEMED Mediterranean Yearbook Med*, 212–214.

Sollund, R. A. (Ed.). (2008). *Global harms; ecological crime and speciesism*. New York: Nova Science Publishers.

Sollund, R. (2013). Animal trafficking and trade: Abuse and species injustice. In D. S. Westerhuis, R. Walters, & T. Wyatt (Eds.), *Emerging issues in green criminology: Exploring power, justice and harm*. Basingstoke: Palgrave Macmillan.

Sollund, R., & Maher, J. (2015) *The illegal wildlife trade. A case study report on the illegal wildlife trade in the United Kingdom, Norway, Colombia and Brazil.* Oslo & Wales: University of Oslo and University of South Wales.

South, N. (1998). A green field for criminology: A proposal for a perspective. *Theoretical Criminology, 2*(2), 211–233.

South, N., & Wyatt, T. (2011). Comparing illicit trades in wildlife and drugs: An exploratory study. *Deviant Behavior, 32*(6), 538–561.

Søyland, S. (2000). *Criminal organisations and crimes against the environment—A desktop study.* Turin: United Nations Interregional Crime and Justice Research Institute.

Still, J. (2003). Use of animal products in traditional Chinese medicine: Environmental impact and health hazards. *Complementary Therapies in Medicine, 11*(2), 118–122.

Sutherland, E. (1949). *White collar crime*. New York: Dryden Press.

Toufexis, A. (1993). The animal trade. *Time magazine*, no. 29.

Van de Bunt, H., Siegel, D., & Zaitch, D. (2014). The social embeddedness of organized crime. In L. Paoli (Ed.), *The Oxford Handbook of Organized Crime*. Oxford: Oxford University Press.

Van Duyne, P. C. (1995). The phantom and threat of organized crime. *Crime, Law and Social Change, 24*(4), 341–377.

Van Male, B. (2003). *Wild feest: de bestrijding van de handel in bedreigde dier- en plantsoorten is al dertig jaar succesvol dankzij het CITES verdrag., 25*(4), 24–27.

Van Spaandonk, J. A. M. (2000). *Katern CITES. Toelichting op de Overeenkomst inzake de internationale handel in bedreigde in het wild levende dier- en plantensoorten.* Lelystad: Koninklijke Vermande.

Vander Beken, T., Hansens, J., Black, C., Defruytier, M., De Ruyver, B., & Cuyvers, L. (2004). *Kwetsbaarheid voor georganiseerde criminaliteit.* Een gevalstudie van de diamantsector. Gent: Academia Press.

Varese, F. (1997). The transition to the market and corruption in post-socialist Russia. *Political Studies, 45*(3), 579–596.

Veblen, T. (1912). *The theory of the leisure class.* Oxford: Oxford University Press.

Waldram, M. (2005). *The ecological effects of grazing by the white rhino (Ceratotherium Simum Simum) at a landscape scale.* Rondebosch: University of Cape Town.

White, R. (2008). *Crimes against nature: Environmental criminology and ecological justice.* Devon: Willan Publishing.

White, R. (2011). *Transnational environmental crime. Toward an eco-global criminology.* London: Routledge.

Wilson, E. O. (1988). The current state of biological diversity. *Biodiversity, 521*(1), 3–18.

Wolf, B. (2011). 'Green-collar crime': Environmental crime and justice in the dociological perspective. *Sociology Compass, 5*(7), 499–511.

World Bank. (2008). *What's driving the wildlife trade? A review of expert opinion on economic and social drivers of the wildlife trade and trade control efforts in Cambodia, Indonesia, Lao PDR, and Vietnam.* Washington, DC: The World Bank.

Wyatt, T. (2013). *Wildlife trafficking: A deconstruction of the crime, the victims, and the offenders.* Basingstoke: Palgrave Macmillan.

Wyler, L. S., & Sheikh, P. A. (2013). *International illegal trade in wildlife: Threats and US policy.* Washington, D.C.: Congressional Research Service report for Congress.

Xu, J., & Yang, Y. (2009). Traditional Chinese medicine in the Chinese health care system. *Health Policy, 90*(2), 133–139.

Zhang, S., & Chin, K. (2011). Ants moving houses. Cross-border drug trafficking in the Golden Triangle. In *Routledge handbook of international criminology.* London: Routledge.

Zhang, L., Messner, S. F., Liu, J., & Zhuo, Y. A. (2009). Guanxi and fear of crime in contemporary urban China. *British Journal of Criminology, 49*(4), 472–490.

Conclusion

The trade in wildlife is as old as the hills. Wildlife has been traded since the earliest civilizations: from the pharaohs and rulers of ancient Egypt to the aristocrats and elites in the Middle Ages and Early Modernity. Initially, wildlife was functionally used to provide protection against the cold, for work and warfare and as medicine. Later on, luxury wildlife products also gained a symbolic status and animal products served as fashion and religious purposes, while nowadays live animals are widely displayed for entertainment in circuses and zoos or kept as pets. The criminalization of the wildlife trade emerged from the 1900s influenced by social dominant groups in society with a passion for natural history and hunting. Although initiatives for the protection of endangered species got regularly stagnated by the economic and personal interests of powerful stakeholders, in the second half of the twentieth century public concerns regarding the environment increased significantly due to declining animal populations. Norms and values were subject to change by a conservation ethic that began to take shape. While as early as Roman and Greek times the decrease in species had been noticed with a reduction in elephants, lions and hippos, at present the overexploitation is more widespread and at a more alarming pace than ever before. Scientists warn that we are on the brink of the sixth mass extinction, marked by the disappearance of thousands of species from our planet each year. The wildlife trade is one of the major driving forces behind this process.

This process accelerated in times of globalization, whereby the transport and communication opportunities for the wildlife trade improved. Direct flights from faraway source countries, crossings without border controls-e.g. within the Schengen area-and the use of the internet provide incentives for the illegal wildlife trade. The world is becoming smaller and, therefore, local political alterations can directly affect worldwide trade flows, as shown with the dissolution of the Soviet Union and the 'liberation' of the Chinese economy. In a globalized world, criminal entrepreneurs benefit from these practical advantages, especially in the context of socioeconomic asymmetries between origin and destination countries. This is illustrated by the expansion of the illegal trade from relatively poor countries by actors from powerful industrialized countries that leave the damage behind. Usually countries with rich biodiversity density experience lower development levels and higher levels of corruption. Organized crime usually operates in such economically

D.P. van Uhm, *The Illegal Wildlife Trade*, Studies of Organized Crime 15,
DOI 10.1007/978-3-319-42129-2

vulnerable and underdeveloped areas like the Caucasus, the Rif Mountains and the Golden Triangle. Both natural resources and local communities are exploited to fuel the demand in the West. However, destination countries are also affected through wildlife trafficking with dangerous side effects, such as ecological instability and outbreaks of zoonotic diseases. The wildlife trade has become a social problem and thus needs anticipation in social and scientific thinking.

This exploratory study outlined the nature of the illegal wildlife trade to fill the gap of empirical knowledge about incentives, criminal actors and harms. Both quantitative and qualitative research methods have been used to uncover the mechanisms behind the illegal flows of wildlife together with extensive literature research. These data triangulation and methodological triangulation made it possible to compare the information from the different sources with each other for verification and to increase internal validity and reliability. The EU wildlife confiscations over a 10-year period were statistically analyzed to identify patterns of the illegal wildlife trade. To gain more in-depth information on the actors and how the trade is organized, qualitative research based on semi-structured interviews with people who are directly involved in the illegal wildlife business was conducted in major source countries, such as China, Morocco and Russia. The three following case studies were selected:

- The illegal trade in caviar
- The illegal trade in Barbary macaques
- The illegal trade in traditional Chinese medicine.

The case studies illustrate that the value of an object is not an established fact, but is dependent on the meaning and judgement of an object by humans. Wildlife is often socially and culturally constructed into high value, renowned and attractive products. For example, traditional medicine containing animal parts is deeply rooted in Chinese culture, the widespread popularity of exotic pets for entertainment is influenced by fashion trends and role models, while caviar as a luxury product became associated with the upper classes. Increasing prosperity made it possible to obtain expensive wildlife products by the leisurely classes. Generally, the rarer an animal or animal product the higher its value in the black market. Nowadays, the current economic value of rhino horn on the black market exceeds the price of gold and cocaine and caviar is exchanged for stolen cars. At the top of the list are wildlife products from wild animals, that are allegedly more 'pure and natural' than products from captive-bred species.

The demand from middle and upper-class society for scarce highly valued wildlife from abroad is enthusiastically answered by a diversity of criminal actors. The wildlife market has been able to develop into a professional criminal business on the fertile ground of low priority, weak punishments by law enforcement and high profits in the last few decades. The business has been unperturbed due to long-term priorities in other areas of crime and, subsequently, new players emerged in the market, some of them with other criminal backgrounds, such as involvement in trading drugs. For a long time it was commonly believed that only tourists and opportunists were involved in the illegal trade in wildlife. This exploratory study uncovered semi-structured dynamic networks where the degree of organization is higher. Not only small-scale businesses but also sophisticated criminal organizations that do not shun the use of violence and counterstrategies have been exposed here. These criminal networks manifest themselves at all levels of the trade: from the poaching areas where organized criminal groups cooperate with law enforcers and possess top-notch equipment, such as GPS, heavy-calibre rifles and helicopters, to major smuggling operations in the hands of sophisticated criminal networks that cooperate with local officials.

The interrelationship between the underworld and upperworld highlights the dual nature of the illegal wildlife business. The criminal organizations do not operate outside the legal world, but are regularly operating as legally registered companies that use their legal structures to hide and facilitate their businesses. Farms that are praised for conservation purposes and established, well-respected companies function as laundering machines for the illegally obtained wildlife. The formal and informal markets offer usually legal and illegal species. A perfect harmony between what is legal and that which is illegal is visible with the involvement of government officials in illegal enterprises driven by mutual benefits. Instead of performing in a social vacuum, the criminal organizations are embedded in the upperworld. The criminal organizations are socially embedded as illustrated by the role of social ties, such as family and friends. The use of informal relations that were regularly kinship or culturally grounded, appeared to be fundamental in the wildlife crime networks.

The incentives and efforts from international law enforcement are, and have been, disproportionally low in comparison to conventional and prioritized forms of crime. This is incomprehensible from the perspective of the broad spectrum of harms derived from the illegal wildlife trade. Besides the predominant anthropocentric harms whereby the habitat of local communities is being exploited, potential life-saving drugs disappear and zoonotic diseases create a field of incalculable harm to the world, an extended harm level has been introduced: environmental harms. Species disappear at an extremely high rate, animals as primary victims are approached without taking their intrinsic value into account and ecosystems become unbalanced and may collapse. Especially the disappearance of keystone species may result in the extirpation of endemic species and affect ecosystem functions due to complex symbiotic interactions in these compounds. In other words, the priority being given to property crimes that threaten replaceable people's ownership is disproportional in comparison to these environmental crimes that are scathing for the entire world.

Criminology has neglected these global environmental crimes and harms for a long period of time. This study answers the call for empirical research on these crimes by exploring the illegal trade in wildlife. In this green criminological study I have provided background information that can assist in understanding wildlife crimes in a changing world in which people become more aware of environmental issues and where ecosystems and species are declining at a high rate. In order to turn the tide, a cultural shift is needed in which society and its policymakers recognize and assess environmental harms in a more objective non-anthropocentric manner with attention being given to the future of all life on Earth. I therefore encourage criminologists to intervene in the discussions surrounding global issues and to uncover environmental crimes that threaten the entire planet.

Appendix I
Status Category by Major Taxonomic Animal Groupings

D.P. van Uhm, *The Illegal Wildlife Trade*, Studies of Organized Crime 15,
DOI 10.1007/978-3-319-42129-2

Class*	EX	EW	SE	CR	EN	VU	ST	NT	LR	DD	LC	Total
Mammalia	78	2	**80**	209	481	507	**1197**	324	0	790	3111	**5502**
Aves	140	5	**145**	218	416	741	**1375**	971	0	61	7872	**10,424**
Reptilia	21	1	**22**	180	361	403	**944**	316	2	867	2518	**4669**
Amphibia	33	2	**35**	528	810	656	**1994**	400	0	1604	2427	**6460**
Cephalaspidomorphi	1	0	**1**	2	1	3	**6**	3	0	4	21	**35**
Myxini	0	0	**0**	1	2	6	**9**	2	0	30	35	**76**
Chondrichthyes	0	0	**0**	20	45	116	**181**	124	0	480	303	**1088**
Actinopterygii	65	6	**71**	422	566	1085	**2073**	377	9	2435	8293	**13,258**
Sarcopterygii	0	0	**0**	1	0	1	**2**	0	0	0	3	**5**
Holothuroidea	0	0	**0**	0	7	9	**16**	0	0	244	111	**371**
Echinoidea	0	0	**0**	0	0	0	**0**	1	0	0	0	**1**
Arachnida	9	0	**9**	47	70	47	**164**	6	0	10	21	**210**
Chilopoda	0	0	**0**	3	5	1	**9**	0	0	0	1	**10**
Diplopoda	3	0	**3**	7	16	10	**33**	0	0	7	10	**53**
Branchiopoda	0	0	**0**	6	10	22	**38**	1	1	1	1	**42**
Malacostraca	7	1	**8**	125	170	306	**601**	71	0	1130	1193	**3003**
Maxillopoda	2	0	**2**	7	0	71	**78**	0	8	22	0	**110**
Ostracoda	2	0	**2**	2	0	9	**11**	0	0	0	0	**13**
Insecta	58	1	**59**	176	305	565	**1046**	274	3	1560	2631	**5573**
Merostomata	0	0	**0**	0	0	0	**0**	1	0	3	0	**4**
Onychophora	0	0	**0**	3	2	4	**9**	1	0	1	0	**11**
Clitellata	1	0	**1**	0	2	1	**3**	2	0	2	0	**8**
Polychaeta	0	0	**0**	1	0	0	**1**	0	0	1	0	**2**
Bivalvia	29	0	**29**	68	57	48	**173**	52	5	172	291	**722**

(continued)

(continued)

Class*	EX	EW	SE	CR	EN	VU	ST	NT	LR	DD	LC	Total
Gastropoda	281	14	**295**	507	444	821	**1772**	475	1	1516	1941	**6000**
Cephalopoda	0	0	**0**	1	2	2	**5**	1	0	291	197	**494**
Enopla	1	0	**1**	1	1	1	**3**	0	0	1	1	**6**
Turbellaria	1	0	**1**	0	0	0	**0**	0	0	0	0	**1**
Anthozoa	0	0	**0**	6	26	202	**234**	175	0	164	293	**866**
Hydrozoa	0	0	**0**	1	2	2	**5**	1	0	2	8	**16**
Total	**732**	**32**	**764**	**2542**	**3801**	**5639**	**11,982**	**3578**	**29**	**11,398**	**31,282**	**59,033**

Source IUCN 2015

IUCN Red List Categories EX—Extinct, EW—Extinct in the Wild, CR—Critically Endangered, EN—Endangered, VU—Vulnerable, NT—Near Threatened, LR—Lower Risk/conservation dependent, DD—Data Deficient, LC—Least Concern

Subtotals SE—Subtotal EX + EW, ST—Subtotal CR + EN + VU

**Animals* Mammalia (mammals), Aves (birds), Reptilia (reptiles), Amphibia (amphibians), Cephalaspidomorphi (lampreys and hag fish), Chondrichthyes (sharks, skates, rays and chimaeras), Actinopterygii (bony fishes), Sarcopterygii (coelacanth), Holothuroidea (sea cucumbers), Echinoidea (sea urchins, starfish, etc), Arachnida (spiders and scorpions), Chilopoda (centipedes), Diplopoda (millipedes), Branchiopoda (fairy shrimp, clam shrimp, tadpole shrimp and water fleas), Malacostraca (crabs, lobsters, shrimp, krill, woodlice, amphipods, mantis shrimp, etc.), Maxillopoda (barnacles, copepods, etc.), Ostracoda (seed shrimp), Insecta (insects), Merostomata (horshoe crabs), Onychopora (velvet worms), Clitellata (leeches and earthworms), Polychaeta (marine bristle worms), Bivalvia (mussels and clams), Gastropoda (snails, etc), Enopla (nemertine worms), Turbellaria (flatworms), Anthozoa (sea anemones and corals), Hydrozoa (corals)

Appendix II
The World Country List by Continents

Country	Continent
Bermuda	North America
Canada	North America
Clipperton Island	North America
Greenland	North America
Mexico	North America
Saint Pierre and Miquelon	North America
United States	North America
Anguilla	Central America
Antigua and Barbuda	Central America
Aruba	Central America
Bahamas, The	Central America
Barbados	Central America
Belize	Central America
British Virgin Islands	Central America
Cayman Islands	Central America
Costa Rica	Central America
Cuba	Central America
Curacao	Central America
Dominica	Central America
Dominican Republic	Central America
El Salvador	Central America
Grenada	Central America
Guatemala	Central America
Haiti	Central America
Honduras	Central America
Jamaica	Central America
Montserrat	Central America
Navassa Island	Central America

(continued)

D.P. van Uhm, *The Illegal Wildlife Trade*, Studies of Organized Crime 15,
DOI 10.1007/978-3-319-42129-2

(continued)

Country	Continent
Nicaragua	Central America
Panama	Central America
Puerto Rico	Central America
Saint Barthelemy	Central America
Saint Kitts and Nevis	Central America
Saint Lucia	Central America
Saint Vincent and the Grenadines	Central America
Sint Maarten	Central America
Trinidad and Tobago	Central America
Turks and Caicos Islands	Central America
Virgin Islands	Central America
Argentina	South America
Bolivia	South America
Brazil	South America
Chile	South America
Colombia	South America
Ecuador	South America
Falkland Islands (Islas Malvinas)	South America
French Guiana	South America
Guyana	South America
Paraguay	South America
Peru	South America
South Georgia and the South Sandwich Islands	South America
Suriname	South America
Uruguay	South America
Venezuela	South America
Algeria	Africa
Angola	Africa
Benin	Africa
Botswana	Africa
Burkina Faso	Africa
Burundi	Africa
Cameroon	Africa
Cape Verde	Africa
Central African Republic	Africa
Chad	Africa
Comoros	Africa
Congo, Democratic Republic of the	Africa
Congo, Republic of the	Africa
Cote d'Ivoire	Africa

(continued)

(continued)

Country	Continent
Djibouti	Africa
Egypt	Africa
Equatorial Guinea	Africa
Eritrea	Africa
Ethiopia	Africa
Gabon	Africa
Gambia, The	Africa
Ghana	Africa
Guinea	Africa
Guinea-Bissau	Africa
Kenya	Africa
Lesotho	Africa
Liberia	Africa
Libya	Africa
Madagascar	Africa
Malawi	Africa
Mali	Africa
Mauritania	Africa
Mauritius	Africa
Mayotte	Africa
Morocco	Africa
Mozambique	Africa
Namibia	Africa
Niger	Africa
Nigeria	Africa
Rwanda	Africa
Saint Helena	Africa
Sao Tome and Principe	Africa
Senegal	Africa
Seychelles	Africa
Sierra Leone	Africa
Somalia	Africa
South Africa	Africa
Sudan	Africa
Swaziland	Africa
Tanzania	Africa
Togo	Africa
Tunisia	Africa
Uganda	Africa
Western Sahara	Africa

(continued)

(continued)

Country	Continent
Zambia	Africa
Zimbabwe	Africa
Akrotiri	Europe
Albania	Europe
Andorra	Europe
Austria	Europe
Belarus	Europe
Belgium	Europe
Bosnia and Herzegovina	Europe
Bulgaria	Europe
Croatia	Europe
Cyprus	Europe
Czech Republic	Europe
Denmark	Europe
Dhekelia	Europe
Estonia	Europe
Faroe Islands	Europe
Finland	Europe
France	Europe
Germany	Europe
Gibraltar	Europe
Greece	Europe
Guernsey	Europe
Hungary	Europe
Iceland	Europe
Ireland	Europe
Isle of Man	Europe
Italy	Europe
Jan Mayen	Europe
Jersey	Europe
Kosovo	Europe
Latvia	Europe
Liechtenstein	Europe
Lithuania	Europe
Luxembourg	Europe
Macedonia	Europe
Malta	Europe
Moldova	Europe
Monaco	Europe
Montenegro	Europe

(continued)

(continued)

Country	Continent
Netherlands	Europe
Norway	Europe
Poland	Europe
Portugal	Europe
Romania	Europe
San Marino	Europe
Serbia	Europe
Slovakia	Europe
Slovenia	Europe
Spain	Europe
Svalbard	Europe
Sweden	Europe
Switzerland	Europe
Ukraine	Europe
United Kingdom	Europe
Kazakhstan	Central Asia
Kyrgyzstan	Central Asia
Russia	Central Asia
Tajikistan	Central Asia
Turkmenistan	Central Asia
Uzbekistan	Central Asia
Afghanistan	South Asia
Bangladesh	South Asia
Bhutan	South Asia
British Indian Ocean Territory	South Asia
India	South Asia
Maldives	South Asia
Nepal	South Asia
Pakistan	South Asia
Sri Lanka	South Asia
Brunei	East and Southeast Asia
Burma	East and Southeast Asia
Cambodia	East and Southeast Asia
China	East and Southeast Asia
Hong Kong	East and Southeast Asia
Indonesia	East and Southeast Asia
Japan	East and Southeast Asia
Korea, North	East and Southeast Asia
Korea, South	East and Southeast Asia
Laos	East and Southeast Asia

(continued)

(continued)

Country	Continent
Macau	East and Southeast Asia
Malaysia	East and Southeast Asia
Mongolia	East and Southeast Asia
Paracel Islands	East and Southeast Asia
Philippines	East and Southeast Asia
Singapore	East and Southeast Asia
Spratly Islands	East and Southeast Asia
Taiwan	East and Southeast Asia
Thailand	East and Southeast Asia
Timor-Leste	East and Southeast Asia
Vietnam	East and Southeast Asia
Armenia	Middle East
Azerbaijan	Middle East
Bahrain	Middle East
Gaza Strip	Middle East
Georgia	Middle East
Iran	Middle East
Iraq	Middle East
Israel	Middle East
Jordan	Middle East
Kuwait	Middle East
Lebanon	Middle East
Oman	Middle East
Qatar	Middle East
Saudi Arabia	Middle East
Syria	Middle East
Turkey	Middle East
United Arab Emirates	Middle East
West Bank	Middle East
Yemen	Middle East
American Samoa	Australia/Oceania
Ashmore and Cartier Islands	Australia/Oceania
Australia	Australia/Oceania
Baker Island	Australia/Oceania
Christmas Island	Australia/Oceania
Cocos (Keeling) Islands	Australia/Oceania
Cook Islands	Australia/Oceania
Coral Sea Islands	Australia/Oceania
Fiji	Australia/Oceania
French Polynesia	Australia/Oceania

(continued)

(continued)

Country	Continent
Guam	Australia/Oceania
Howland Island	Australia/Oceania
Jarvis Island	Australia/Oceania
Johnston Atoll	Australia/Oceania
Kingman Reef	Australia/Oceania
Kiribati	Australia/Oceania
Marshall Islands	Australia/Oceania
Micronesia, Federated States of	Australia/Oceania
Midway Islands	Australia/Oceania
Nauru	Australia/Oceania
New Caledonia	Australia/Oceania
New Zealand	Australia/Oceania
Niue	Australia/Oceania
Norfolk Island	Australia/Oceania
Northern Mariana Islands	Australia/Oceania
Palau	Australia/Oceania
Palmyra Atoll	Australia/Oceania
Papua New Guinea	Australia/Oceania
Pitcairn Islands	Australia/Oceania
Samoa	Australia/Oceania
Solomon Islands	Australia/Oceania
Tokelau	Australia/Oceania
Tonga	Australia/Oceania
Tuvalu	Australia/Oceania
United States Pacific Island Wildlife Refuges	Australia/Oceania
Vanuatu	Australia/Oceania
Wake Island	Australia/Oceania
Wallis and Futuna	Australia/Oceania
Antarctica	Antarctica
Bouvet Island	Antarctica
French Southern and Antarctic Lands	Antarctica
Heard Island and McDonald Is	Antarctica

Appendix III
Species in EU Wildlife Seizures

Wildlife groupings	Live species	%	Dead species	%	Description
Mammals	*Macaca sylvanus*	24.9	*Loxodonta africana*	45.1	Ivory and medicine
	Chlorocebus aethiops	7.7	*Panthera pardus*	6.0	
	Panthera tigris	5.9	*Equus africanus*	5.1	
	Callithrix jacchus	2.4	*Elephas maximus*	4.8	
	Canis lupus	2.4	*Panthera tigris*	3.3	
	Hystrix cristata	2.4	Ursus arctos	3.3	
	Macaca mulatta	2.4	*Hippopotamus amphibius*	2.7	
	Panthera pardus	2.4	*Saiga tatarica*	2.2	
	Saimiri oerstedii	2.4	*Canis lupus*	2.1	
	Ursus americanus	1.8	*Odobenus rosmarus*	1.6	
Birds	*Psittacus erithacus*	14.7	*Buteo buteo*	14.4	Bodies and feathers
	Platycercus eximius	4.4	*Struthio camelus*	6.8	
	Psittacula krameri	2.8	*Accipiter gentilis*	5.4	
	Platycercus elegans	2.6	*Asio otus*	3.5	
	Falco tinnunculus	2.5	*Pernis apivorus*	3.1	
	Polytelis anthopeplus	2.2	*Anas crecca*	2.8	
	Amazona leucocephala	1.9	*Accipiter nisus*	2.4	
	Poicephalus senegalus	1.9	*Ara macao*	1.9	
	Cacatua moluccensis	1.7	*Nyctea scandiaca*	1.9	
	Falco peregrinus	1.7	*Strix aluco*	1.9	
Reptiles	*Testudo graeca*	49.5	*Naja naja*	26.0	Small and large leather products
	Trachemys scripta elegans	11.4	*Python sebae*	9.3	
	Testudo hermanni	5.5	*Python reticulatus*	6.7	
	Testudo horsfieldii	3.5	*Alligator mississippiensis*	6.2	
	Chamaeleo chamaeleon	2.3	*Python molurus molurus*	6.0	
	Testudo kleinmanni	2.0	*Crocodylus niloticus*	4.4	
	Iguana iguana	1.8	*Python molurus*	2.7	
	Python molurus molurus	1.3	*Boa constrictor occidentalis*	2.5	
	Boa constrictor	1.0	*Ptyas mucosus*	2.2	
	Chamaeleo calyptratus	0.8	*Xenochrophis piscator*	1.9	

(continued)

D.P. van Uhm, *The Illegal Wildlife Trade*, Studies of Organized Crime 15,
DOI 10.1007/978-3-319-42129-2

(continued)

Wildlife groupings	Live species	%	Dead species	%	Description
Fish	*Hippocampus kuda*	27.3	*Acipenser sturio*	44.4	Caviar and bodies
	Hippocampus comes	13.6	*Huso huso*	10.5	
	Acipenser baerii	4.5	*Acipenser gueldenstaedtii*	8.5	
	Acipenser ruthenus	4.5	*Carcharodon carcharias*	7.2	
	Caecobarbus geertsi	4.5	*Acipenser stellatus*	5.2	
	Hippocampus barbouri	4.5	*Arapaima gigas*	3.9	
	Hippocampus erectus	4.5	*Acipenser baerii*	3.3	
	Hippocampus fuscus	4.5	*Acipenser persicus*	2.6	
	Scleropages formosus	4.5	*Hippocampus kuda*	2.6	
			Acipenser brevirostrum	2.0	
Coral	N/A	N/A	*Tubipora musica*	21.9	Coral
			Heliopora coerulea	17.2	
			Pocillopora verrucosa	6.6	
			Acropora humilis	2.6	
			Dendrophyllia ramea	2.0	
			Merulina ampliata	2.0	
			Pocillopora damicornis	2.0	
			Stylophora pistillata	1.3	
			Acropora elseyi	1.3	
			Acropora horrida	0.7	
Molluscs	*Strombus gigas*	66.7	*Strombus gigas*	93.3	Shells and bodies
	Tridacna crocea	11.1	*Tridacna maxima*	2.5	
	Tridacna gigas	11.1	*Hippopus hippopus*	1.8	
	Tridacna squamosa	11.1	*Tridacna squamosa*	1.1	
			Tridacna gigas	0.5	
			Tridacna derasa	0.3	
			Tridacna crocea	0.3	
			Papustyla pulcherrima	0.2	
			Hippopus porcellanus	0.1	

Source Personal analyses of the EU-TWIX database, 2001–2010

Appendix IV
Source Countries of EU Wildlife Seizures

Seizures with live animals (%) of total *N*	Wildlife groupings					
	Mammals	Birds	Reptiles	Amphibians	Fish	Molluscs
Algeria	2.8	3.1	**17.8**			
Angola		1.5				
Austria					4.5	
Azerbaijan					4.5	
Belgium	1.1	3.6				
Brazil		1.2				
Cameroon	1.7					
China			1.3			
Congo	2.2	1.1				
Costa Rica				3.1		
Czech Republic		8.5	2.1	**21.9**		
Dominican Republic						**25.0**
Egypt						5.0
France	6.8					
Germany		1.6		3.1		
Guinea	2.3					
Guinea-Bissau		1.1				
Guyana		1.3				
Indonesia			1.1			**30.0**
Iran		1.2				
Kenya						5.0
Libyan Arab Jamahiriya	2.8					
Malaysia						**20.0**
Marshall Islands						5.0
Mauritius						5.0

(continued)

D.P. van Uhm, *The Illegal Wildlife Trade*, Studies of Organized Crime 15,
DOI 10.1007/978-3-319-42129-2

(continued)

Seizures with live animals (%) of total *N*	Wildlife groupings					
	Mammals	Birds	Reptiles	Amphibians	Fish	Molluscs
Morocco	**20.3**	4.7	**22.3**			
Netherlands					4.5	
Nigeria		1.2			4.5	
Panama				**28.1**		
Peru				3.1		
Poland			3.2			
Russian Federation	1.1					
Sao Tome and Principe	2.8	1.3				
Senegal	1.1	1.2				
Slovakia		1.8		6.3		
South Africa				3.1		
Sri Lanka					9.1	
Suriname		1.7				
Switzerland		1.8				
Syria	1.1	2.3				
Tanzania			2.4			
Thailand					9.1	
Tunisia			6.5			
Uganda			1.3			
Ukraine			2.2			
United States of America		1.2	2.1	**28.1**	4.5	5.0
Vietnam			1.0		**18.4**	
Nihil	15.8	8.7	1.8		4.5	
Unknown	26.0	33.1	13.8	3.1	36.4	
Total *N*[*]	178	877	2171	32	22	20

Source Personal analyses of the EU-TWIX database, 2001–2010
[*]Empty cells were removed

Seizures with animal products (%) of total N	Wildlife groupings					
	Mammals	Birds	Reptiles	Fish	Coral	Molluscs
Algeria			1.0			
Angola	4.6					
Aruba					1.7	
Australia			2.9		2.7	1.5
Azerbaijan				**10.9**		
Bahamas						4.6
Belarus				1.9		
Belgium	1.2					
Bolivia		1.1				
Brazil	1.0	**10.0**	1.3			
Bulgaria					1.6	
Burundi	1.3					
Cameroon	2.5		1.9			
Canada	2.1					
China	**14.4**		2.8	2.0	1.5	
Congo	4.8		1.3			
Croatia					2.3	
Cuba					**5.8**	**7.0**
Czech Republic		3.1				
Dominican Republic					3.9	**12.6**
Egypt		4.7	1.0		**7.3**	3.5
French Polynesia						1.0
Ghana	1.1		1.0			
Guinea	1.2		1.0			
Hong Kong	2.3		1.0			
India		1.1				
Indonesia			1.3		4.4	2.6
Iran				3.3		
Ivory Coast	1.8					
Jamaica						2.3
Kazakhstan		1.4		4.0		
Malaysia					1.1	
Maldives					1.3	
Mauritius					2.6	1.4
Mexico		1.3			2.4	4.9
Morocco		1.1				
Mozambique	2.9					
Namibia	1.8					
Netherlands Antilles					**7.9**	1.7
Nigeria	2.2		3.9			

(continued)

(continued)

Seizures with animal products (%) of total N	Wildlife groupings					
	Mammals	Birds	Reptiles	Fish	Coral	Molluscs
Peru		3.1				
Philippines					1.9	2.4
Poland		3.4		4.5		
Romania		1.4				
Russian Federation	2.8	2.5		**33.6**		
Senegal			2.3			
Seychelles					2.8	1.4
South Africa	4.1	1.8	1.8			
Sudan			1.3			
Suriname		1.4				
Switzerland		2.7	2.9	1.0		
Syria		**6.5**				
Tanzania		1.6				1.1
Thailand	2.1		**12.5**		**7.2**	**5.2**
Trinidad and Tobago						1.0
Ukraine		1.3		**11.5**	1.3	
United Arab Emirates				2.8	1.9	
United States of America	**5.3**	2.7	**15.6**	1.4	3.9	**7.5**
Venezuela					1.1	1.5
Vietnam	1.8		**7.8**	**5.2**	2.0	
Yugoslavia		2.0				
Zimbabwe	1.1					
Nihil		5.4				
Unknown	11.6	19.9	11.2	5.5	9.9	13.9
Total N^*	3327	559	4883	1835	4385	2762

Source Personal analyses of the EU-TWIX database, 2001–2010
*Empty cells were removed

Appendix V
Import Countries of EU Wildlife Seizures

Seizures with live animals (%) of total N	Wildlife groupings					
	Mammals	Birds	Reptiles	Amphibians	Fish	Molluscs
Austria	1.7	2.2	3.5	5.9		
Belgium	**12.9**	6.8	4.1	**26.5**	9.1	**40.0**
Czech Republic		3.6	1.2			
Denmark		1.4	1.0	**17.6**	9.1	
France	**21.3**	7.4	**15.1**		9.1	5.0
Germany	3.9	**14.1**	**18.3**	**32.4**	**13.6**	10.0
Great Britain		5.2	6.6	2.9	**36.4**	10.0
Hungary		1.9	1.7			**15.0**
Italy	6.7	2.9	5.0			**20.0**
Malta	2.8					
Netherlands	6.2	**10.5**	3.0	2.9	4.5	
Poland	1.1	**16.1**	4.7	5.9	9.1	
Portugal	3.9	5.0		2.9		
Slovakia	7.9	**12.7**	2.2	2.9	9.1	
Spain	**29.2**	8.6	**31.3**			
Total N^*	178	877	2171	32	22	20

Source Personal analyses of the EU-TWIX database, 2001–2010
*Empty cells were removed

D.P. van Uhm, *The Illegal Wildlife Trade*, Studies of Organized Crime 15,
DOI 10.1007/978-3-319-42129-2

Seizures with animal products (%) of total *N*	Wildlife groupings					
	Mammals	Birds	Reptiles	Fish	Coral	Molluscs
Austria			2.1	3.8	1.6	2.8
Belgium	**12.5**		5.2	2.8		
Czech Republic		1.4				
Denmark	6.8	3.6	5.2	1.2	4.1	3.4
France	8.5	8.1	3.4	**16.1**	2.3	1.2
Germany	**20.5**	**36.5**	**48.7**	**53.7**	**49.1**	**45.3**
Great Britain	1.9	1.1	2.1	2.8		1.0
Hungary	3.0	1.8	1.2		1.0	
Italy	2.5	7.3	4.2	4.4	4.3	7.5
Lithuania	1.1	2.9				
Malta		5.9				
Netherlands	**17.9**	**10.9**	8.1	4.7	**19.0**	**13.1**
Poland	5.1	5.0	5.6	6.0	**11.0**	**19.5**
Portugal	8.7		3.4			
Slovakia		3.2				
Slovenia		1.1				
Spain	6.2	2.9	5.6	1.5	4.4	4.4
Sweden		5.4	1.1			
Total *N*[*]	3327	559	4883	1835	4385	2762

Source Personal analyses of the EU-TWIX database, 2001–2010

[*]Empty cells were removed

Appendix VI
Overview of Informants in Russia, Kazakhstan and Azerbaijan

Respondent	Organization, function	Place of interview	Date	Country
Poachers				
RF1	Local poacher	Kirovskiy	March 2014	RU
RF2	Local poacher	Kirovskiy	March 2014	RU
RF3	Local poacher	Kirovskiy	March 2014	RU
RF4	Local poacher	Gandurino	March 2014	RU
RF5	Local poacher	Poldnevoye	March 2014	RU
RF6	Local poacher	Atyrau	March 2014	KZ
RF7	Local poacher	Pakywa	March 2014	KZ
RF8	Local poacher	Lagan (Kalmykia)	March 2014	RU
RF9	Local poacher	Lagan (Kalmykia)	March 2014	RU
RF10	Local poacher	Babayurt region (Dagestan)	September 2014	RU
RF11	Local poacher	Sulak (Dagestan)	September 2014	RU
RF12	Local poacher	Salyan	September 2014	AZ
RF13	Local poacher	Neftçala	September 2014	AZ
Traders				
RT1	Director fish and caviar company	Astrakhan	March 2014	RU
RT2	Spokesman caviar company and farm	Astrakhan	March 2014	RU
RT3	Sales caviar company and farm	Astrakhan	March 2014	RU
RT4	Director caviar company and farm	Astrakhan	March 2014	RU
RT5	Spokesman caviar company and farm	Astrakhan	March 2014	RU

(continued)

D.P. van Uhm, *The Illegal Wildlife Trade*, Studies of Organized Crime 15,
DOI 10.1007/978-3-319-42129-2

(continued)

Respondent	Organization, function	Place of interview	Date	Country
RT6	Manager caviar company and farm	Astrakhan	March 2014	RU
RT7	Director caviar farm	Ikryanoye	March 2014	RU
RT8	Employee caviar farm	Ikryanoye	March 2014	RU
RT9	Employee fish trade centre	Atyrau	March 2014	KZ
RT10	Head of fish company (from Dagestan)	Lagan (Kalmykia)	March 2014	RU
RT11	Former boss fish company	Lagan (Kalmykia)	March 2014	RU
RT12	Manager sturgeon farm	Babayurt region (Dagestan)	September 2014	RU
RT13	Spokesman caviar company	Baku	September 2014	AZ
RT14	Manager caviar company	Merdekan	September 2014	AZ
RT15	Manager caviar farm	Neftçala	September 2014	AZ
Middlemen				
RM1	Middleman	Astrakhan	March 2014	RU
RM2	Middleman	Astrakhan	March 2014	RU
RM3	Middleman	Astrakhan	March 2014	RU
RM4	Middleman	Atyrau	March 2014	KZ
RM5	Middleman	Moscow	March 2014	RU
RM6	Middleman	Izberbash (Dagestan)	September 2014	RU
RM7	Middleman	Baku	September 2014	AZ
Sellers				
RS1	Local salesman	Astrakhan	March 2014	RU
RS2	Local salesman	Astrakhan	March 2014	RU
RS3	Local salesman	Pakywa	March 2014	KZ
RS4	Local salesman	Atyrau	March 2014	KZ
RS5	Local salesman	Atyrau	March 2014	KZ
RS6	Local salesman	Atyrau	March 2014	KZ
RS7	Local salesman	Atyrau	March 2014	KZ
RS8	Local salesman	Atyrau	March 2014	KZ
RS9	Local salesman	Astrakhan	March 2014	RU
RS10	Local salesman	Astrakhan	March 2014	RU
RS11	Local salesman	Astrakhan	March 2014	RU
RS12	Local salesman	Moscow	March 2014	RU
RS13	Local salesman	Moscow	March 2014	RU
RS14	Local salesman	Moscow	March 2014	RU

(continued)

(continued)

Respondent	Organization, function	Place of interview	Date	Country
RS15	Local salesman	Makhachkala (Dagestan)	September 2014	RU
RS16	Local salesman	Kaspiysk (Dagestan)	September 2014	RU
RS17	Local salesman	Baku	September 2014	AZ
Smugglers				
RU1	Smuggler	Poldnevoye	March 2014	RU
RU2	Smuggler	Moscow	March 2014	RU
RU3	Smuggler	Makhachkala (Dagestan)	September 2014	RU
Police				
RP1	Police officer Astrakhan	Astrakhan	March 2014	RU
RP2	Police officer Atyrau	Atyrau	March 2014	KZ
RP3	Police officer Makhachkala	Makhachkala (Dagestan)	September 2014	RU
RP4	Frontier guard	Neftçala	September 2014	AZ
RP5	Inspector	Baku	September 2014	AZ
Experts				
RE1	Head of scientific and educational centre sturgeon breeding/ex-director farm	Astrakhan	March 2014	RU
RE2	Marine coordinator WWF Russia	Moscow	March 2014	RU
RE3	Director of quota issues ministry of environment	Baku	September 2014	AZ
RE4	Enforcement manager ministry of environment	Baku	September 2014	AZ
Other				
RO1	Local taxi driver	Kirovskiy	March 2014	RU
RO2	Local bus driver	Poldnevoye	March 2014	RU
RO3	Local son of fisherman	Atyrau	March 2014	KZ

Appendix VII
Overview of Informants in Morocco

Respondent	Organization, function	Place of interview	Date	Country
Poachers				
MF1	Ex-poacher	Azrou	March 2013	MO
MF2	Poacher	Azrou	April 2013	MO
Traders				
MT1	Animal trader	Casablanca	March 2013	MO
MT2	Ex-trader	Azrou	March 2013	MO
MT3	Trader	Azrou	March 2013	MO
MT4	Trader	Marrakesh	March 2013	MO
MT5	Trader	Tangier	April 2013	MO
MT6	Animal trader	Nador	April 2013	MO
MT7	Trader	Oujda	April 2013	MO
MT8	Animal trader	Oujda	April 2013	MO
MT9	Trader	Azrou	April 2013	MO
MT10	Trader	Azrou	April 2013	MO
MT11	Animal trader	Fez	March 2013	MO
Middlemen				
MM1	Middleman	Fez	March 2013	MO
MM2	Middleman	Marrakesh	March 2013	MO
Seller				
MS1	Local salesman	Marrakesh	March 2013	MO
MS2	Salesman at el-Fna Square	Marrakesh	March 2013	MO
MS3	Salesman at el-Fna Square	Marrakesh	March 2013	MO
MS4	Roadside seller	Azrou	March 2013	MO
MS5	Seller in animal shop	Tangier	April 2013	MO
Smuggler				
MU1	Friend of smuggler	Tétouan	April 2013	MO
MU2	Ex-smuggler	Nador	April 2013	MO

(continued)

D.P. van Uhm, *The Illegal Wildlife Trade*, Studies of Organized Crime 15,
DOI 10.1007/978-3-319-42129-2

(continued)

Respondent	Organization, function	Place of interview	Date	Country
MU3	Ex-smuggler	Azrou	April 2013	MO
Police				
MP1	Police officer Tangier	Tangier	April 2013	MO
MP2	Forest ranger	Nador	April 2013	
Experts				
ME1	Director of Barbary Macaque Conservation in the Rif (BMC)	Tétouan	April 2013	MO
Other				
MO1	Local	Marrakesh	March 2013	MO
MO2	Local guide	Ouzoud	March 2013	MO
MO3	Local guide	Ouzoud	March 2013	MO
MO4	Bus ticket seller and convicted drug trader	Oujda	April 2013	MO
MO5	Politician	Nador	April 2013	MO
MO6	Local taxi driver	Fez	March 2013	MO

Appendix VIII
Overview of Informants in China

Respondent	Organization, function	Place of interview	Date	Country
Poachers				
CF1	Ex-poacher	Kunming	November 2013	CN
Traders				
CT1	TCM trader	Hong Kong	November 2013	CN
CT2	Rhino horn trader	Hong Kong	November 2013	CN
CT3	Trader saiga horn and pangolin scales	Hong Kong	November 2013	CN
CT4	Wholesaler of saiga horn, bear bile, pangolin scales	Hong Kong	November 2013	CN
CT5	TCM seller	Guangzhou	November 2013	CN
CT6	Trader of pangolins, saiga horn, musk	Guangzhou	November 2013	CN
CT7	Trader bird nests	Guangzhou	November 2013	CN
CT8	Trader and seller of tiger bones, rhino horn, saiga horns, pangolin scales	Kunming	November 2013	CN
CT9	Wholesaler in pangolins scales and saiga horn	Chengdu	November 2013	CN
CT10	Trader pangolin and saiga horn	Anguo	December 2013	CN
CT11	Ex-rhino horn trader	Anguo	December 2013	CN
CT12	Trader TCM	Beijing	December 2013	CN
CT13	Trader saiga horn	Harbin	December 2013	CN
Middlemen				
CM1	Middleman	Guangzhou	November 2013	CN
CM2	Middleman in rhino horn, tiger bone, pangolin scales, saiga horn	Kunming	November 2013	CN
CM3	Middleman pangolin scales, rhino horn	Chengdu	November 2013	CN
CM4	Middleman tiger bones, rhino horn	Anguo	December 2013	CN

(continued)

D.P. van Uhm, *The Illegal Wildlife Trade*, Studies of Organized Crime 15,
DOI 10.1007/978-3-319-42129-2

(continued)

Respondent	Organization, function	Place of interview	Date	Country
Seller				
CS1	Local salesman TCM	Hong Kong	November 2013	CN
CS2	Local salesman saiga horn	Hong Kong	November 2013	CN
CS3	Local seller rhino horn	Hong Kong	November 2013	CN
CS4	Rhino horn seller	Hong Kong	November 2013	CN
CS5	Fake rhino horn, tiger bone, saiga horn seller	Guangzhou	November 2013	CN
CS6	Seller pangolin scales	Guangzhou	November 2013	CN
CS7	Seller pangolin scales and saiga horn	Guangzhou	November 2013	CN
CS8	Seller saiga horn and pangolin scales	Kunming	November 2013	CN
CS9	Seller elephant skin	Kunming	November 2013	CN
CS10	Seller pangolin scales, saiga horn	Kunming	November 2013	CN
CS11	Seller rhino horn, tiger bone, pangolin scales and saiga antelope horn	Kunming	November 2013	CN
CS12	Seller saiga horn and pangolin scales	Chengdu	November 2013	CN
CS13	Seller saiga horn and pangolins scales	Chengdu	November 2013	CN
CS14	Pangolin seller	Chengdu	November 2013	CN
CS15	Fake rhino horn and saiga horn seller	Beijing	December 2013	CN
CS16	Seller pangolin scales, saiga horn	Beijing	December 2013	CN
CS17	Seller saiga horn	Anguo	December 2013	CN
CS18	Seller pangolins	Anguo	December 2013	CN
CS19	Seller rhino horn	Anguo	December 2013	CN
CS20	TCM shopkeeper	Anguo	December 2013	CN
CS21	Pharmacy pangolin and saiga horn	Xian	December 2013	CN
CS22	Seller saiga horn	Xian	December 2013	CN
CS23	Pharmacist saiga horn	Harbin	December 2013	CN
CS24	Seller tiger bone wine	Harbin	December 2013	CN
TCM doctors				
CC1	TCM doctor	Hong Kong	November 2013	CN
CC2	TCM doctor	Hong Kong	November 2013	CN
CC3	TCM doctor	Guangzhou	November 2013	CN
CC4	TCM doctor	Kunming	November 2013	CN
CC5	TCM doctor	Kunming	November 2013	CN
CC6	TCM doctor	Kunming	November 2013	CN
CC7	TCM doctor	Chengdu	November 2013	CN
CC8	TCM doctor	Chengdu	November 2013	CN
CC9	TCM doctor	Anguo	December 2013	CN

(continued)

(continued)

Respondent	Organization, function	Place of interview	Date	Country
CC10	TCM doctor Beijing University	Beijing	December 2013	CN
CC11	TCM doctor Beijing University	Beijing	December 2013	CN
TCM doctors (hospitals)				
CH1	Hospital Guangzhou	Guangzhou	November 2013	CN
CH2	Hospital Chengdu	Chengdu	November 2013	CN
CH3	Hospital Beijing	Beijing	December 2013	CN
Smuggler				
CU1	Former smuggler illegal TCM	Guangzhou	November 2013	CN
Police				
CP1	Endangered species protection officer (Agriculture, Fisheries and Conservation Department)	Hong Kong	November 2013	CN
CP2	Head of enforcement wildlife crime	Beijing	December 2013	CN
Experts				
CE1	Professor at CUHK	Hong Kong	November 2013	CN
CE2	Doctor at HKU	Hong Kong	November 2013	CN
CE3	Employee Civic Exchange	Hong Kong	November 2013	CN
Other				
CO1	PhD candidate criminology (University of HK)	Hong Kong	November 2013	CN
CO2	PhD candidate	Guangzhou	November 2013	CN
CO3	Local	Chengdu	November 2013	CN
CO4	Local consumer	Anguo	December 2013	CN
CO5	Breeding centre	Xian	December 2013	CN
CO6	Employer Harbin tiger park	Harbin	December 2013	CN

Appendix IX
Overview of Informants in Europe

Respondent	Organization, function	Place of interview	Date	Country
Traders				
ET1	Opportunistic caviar trader	Utrecht	May 2015	NL
ET2	International caviar trader	The Hague	April 2014	NL
ET3	Caviar trader	Near Venlo and the German border	August 2014	NL
ET4	Caviar trader	Hamburg	May 2015	DE
ET5	Bird trader	Woerden	March 2013	NL
ET6	TCM trader	Utrecht	September 2013	NL
ET7	Caviar trader	The Hague	February 2014	NL
ET8	Caviar trader	Hamburg	May 2015	DE
ET9	TCM trader	The Hague	October 2013	NL
Seller				
ES1	Russian shopkeeper	Utrecht	January 2014	NL
ES2	Russian shopkeeper	The Hague	January 2014	NL
ES3	Russian shopkeeper	Amsterdam	February 2014	NL
ES4	TCM shopkeeper	The Hague	October 2013	NL
ES5	TCM shopkeeper	The Hague	October 2013	NL
Police				
EP1	Environmental police officer IMT	The Hague	February 2014	NL
EP2	Anonymous	X	April 2013	NL
EP3	Europol	The Hague	September 2013	NL
EP4	National police/IPOL	The Hague	November 2012	NL
EP5	Environmental police officer IMT	Ridderkerk	February 2013	NL

(continued)

D.P. van Uhm, *The Illegal Wildlife Trade*, Studies of Organized Crime 15,
DOI 10.1007/978-3-319-42129-2

(continued)

Respondent	Organization, function	Place of interview	Date	Country
Experts				
EE1	Director of AAP	Almere	December 2013	NL
EE2	Coordinator seizures AAP	Almere	February 2013	NL
EE3	Animal behaviourist	Almere	February 2013	NL
EE4	EU-TWIX officer	Utrecht	June 2012	NL
EE5	Wildlife crime expert WWF	Zeist	March 2012	NL
EE6	CITES expert	The Hague	August 2012	NL
EE7	Traffic expert	The Hague	July 2013	NL
EE8	CITES authority NL	Utrecht	February 2014	NL
EE9	Former chief of enforcement of CITES	Utrecht	January 2015	NL
EE10	Wildlife expert IFAW	The Hague	May 2013	NL
EE11	Wildlife expert EIA		February 2014	NL
Law enforcement				
EN1	Law enforcer food and consumer product safety authority	Utrecht	September 2013	NL
EN2	Border customs	Schiphol	February 2013	NL
EN3	Law enforcer food and consumer product safety authority	Utrecht	January 2013	NL
EN4	Public prosecutor	The Hague	February 2013	NL
EN5	Former CITES Permit Officer	The Hague	June 2015	NL
Other				
EO1	Chef	Utrecht	October 2014	NL
EO2	Former owner of Yab Yum brothel	Amsterdam	October 2014	NL

Appendix X
IUCN-CITES Status of Sturgeons

Critically endangered	Endangered	Vulnerable	Near threatened	Least concern
Acipenser dabryanus (Yangtze Sturgeon) APPENDIX II	*Acipenser baerii* (Siberian Sturgeon) APPENDIX II	*Acipenser brevirostrum* (Shortnose Sturgeon) APPENDIX I	*Acipenser medirostris* (Green Sturgeon) APPENDIX II	*Acipenser fulvescens* (Lake Sturgeon) APPENDIX II
Acipenser gueldenstaedtii (Russian Sturgeon) APPENDIX II	*Scaphirhynchus albus* (Pallid Sturgeon) APPENDIX II	*Acipenser ruthenus* (Sterlet Sturgeon) APPENDIX II	*Acipenser oxyrinchus* (Gulf Sturgeon) APPENDIX II	*Acipenser transmontanus* (White Sturgeon) APPENDIX II
Acipenser mikadoi (Sakhalin Sturgeon) APPENDIX II		*Polyodon spathula* (Paddlefish) APPENDIX II		
Acipenser naccarii (Adriatic Sturgeon) APPENDIX II		*Scaphirhynchus platorynchus* (Shovelnose Sturgeon) APPENDIX II		
Acipenser nudiventris (Ship Sturgeon) APPENDIX II				
Acipenser persicus (Persian Sturgeon) APPENDIX II				
Acipenser schrenckii (Amur Sturgeon) APPENDIX II				

(continued)

D.P. van Uhm, *The Illegal Wildlife Trade*, Studies of Organized Crime 15,
DOI 10.1007/978-3-319-42129-2

(continued)

Critically endangered	Endangered	Vulnerable	Near threatened	Least concern
Acipenser sinensis (Chinese Sturgeon) APPENDIX II				
Acipenser stellatus (Stellate Sturgeon) APPENDIX II				
Acipenser sturio (Atlantic Sturgeon) APPENDIX I				
Huso dauricus (Kaluga) APPENDIX II				
Huso huso (Beluga) APPENDIX II				
Psephurus gladius (Chinese Paddlefish) APPENDIX II				
Pseudoscaphirhynchus fedtschenkoi (Shovelnose Sturgeon) APPENDIX II				
Pseudoscaphirhynchus hermanni (Dwarf Sturgeon) APPENDIX II				
Pseudoscaphirhynchus kaufmanni (False Shovelnose Sturgeon) APPENDIX II				
Scarphirhychus sittkusi (Alabama Sturgeon) APPENDIX II				

Appendix XI
IUCN-CITES Status of Macaques

Critically endangered	Endangered	Vulnerable	Near threatened	Least concern
Macaca nigra (Celebes Crested Macaque) APPENDIX II	*Macaca maura* (Moor Macaque) APPENDIX II	*Macaca arctoides* (Stump-tailed Macaque) APPENDIX I	*Macaca assamensis* (Assam Macaque) APPENDIX II	*Macaca cyclopis* (Taiwan Macaque) APPENDIX II
Macaca pagensis (Pagai Island Macaque) APPENDIX II	*Macaca munzala* (Arunachal macaque) APPENDIX II	*Macaca hecki* (Heck's macaque) APPENDIX II	*Macaca thibetana* (Milne-edwards' Macaque) APPENDIX II	*Macaca fascicularis* (Crab-eating Macaque) APPENDIX II
	Macaca silenus (Lion-tailed Macaque) APPENDIX I	*Macaca leonina* (Northern Pig-tailed Macaque) APPENDIX II		*Macaca fuscata* (Japanese Macaque) APPENDIX II
	Macaca sinica (Toque Macaque) APPENDIX II	*Macaca nemestrina* (Southern Pig-tailed Macaque) APPENDIX II		*Macaca mulatta* (Rhesus Macaque) APPENDIX II
	Macaca sylvanus (Barbary macaque) APPENDIX II	*Macaca nigrescens* (Gorontalo Macaque) APPENDIX II		*Macaca radiata* (Bonnet Macaque) APPENDIX II

(continued)

D.P. van Uhm, *The Illegal Wildlife Trade*, Studies of Organized Crime 15,
DOI 10.1007/978-3-319-42129-2

(continued)

Critically endangered	Endangered	Vulnerable	Near threatened	Least concern
		Macaca ochreata (Booted Macaque) APPENDIX II		
		Macaca siberu (Siberut macaque) APPENDIX II		
		Macaca tonkeana (Tonkean Macaque) APPENDIX II		

Appendix XII
IUCN-CITES Status of Tigers

Extinct	Critically endangered	Endangered	Vulnerable	Near threatened
Panthera tigris balica (Bali Tiger) †	*Panthera tigris amoyensis* (South China Tiger) APPENDIX I	*Panthera tigris altaica* (Amur Tiger) APPENDIX I	N/A	N/A
Panthera tigris sondaica (Javan Tiger) †	*Panthera tigris jacksoni* (Malayan Tiger) APPENDIX I	*Panthera tigris corbetti* (Indochinese Tiger) APPENDIX I		
Panthera tigris virgata (Caspian Tiger) †	*Panthera tigris sumatrae* (Sumatran Tiger) APPENDIX I	*Panthera tigris tigris* (Bengal Tiger) APPENDIX I		

D.P. van Uhm, *The Illegal Wildlife Trade*, Studies of Organized Crime 15,
DOI 10.1007/978-3-319-42129-2

Appendix XIII
IUCN-CITES Status of Rhinoceros

Critically endangered	Endangered	Vulnerable	Near threatened	Least concern
Dicerorhinus sumatrensis (Sumatran Rhinoceros) APPENDIX I	N/A	*Rhinoceros unicornis* (Indian Rhinoceros) APPENDIX I	*Ceratotherium simum* (White Rhinoceros) APPENDIX I*	N/A
Diceros bicornis (Black Rhinoceros) APPENDIX I				
Rhinoceros sondaicus (Javan Rhinoceros) APPENDIX I				

*Except the Southern White Rhino Ceratotherium simum which is on Appendix II

D.P. van Uhm, *The Illegal Wildlife Trade*, Studies of Organized Crime 15,
DOI 10.1007/978-3-319-42129-2

Appendix XIV
IUCN-CITES Status of Saiga Antelopes and Pangolins

Critically endangered	Endangered	Vulnerable	Near threatened	Least concern
Saiga tatarica (Saiga Antelope) APPENDIX II	*Manis crassicaudata* (Indian Pangolin) APPENDIX II	*Phataginus tetradactyla* (Black-bellied Pangolin) APPENDIX II	N/A	N/A
Manis javanica (Sunda Pangolin) APPENDIX II	*Manis culionensis* (Philippine Pangolin) APPENDIX II	*Phataginus tricuspis* (White-bellied Pangolin) APPENDIX II		
Manis pentadactyla (Chinese Pangolin) APPENDIX II		*Smutsia gigantea* (Giant Ground Pangolin) APPENDIX II		
		Smutsia temminckii (Temminck's Ground Pangolin) APPENDIX II		

D.P. van Uhm, *The Illegal Wildlife Trade*, Studies of Organized Crime 15,
DOI 10.1007/978-3-319-42129-2

Index

D.P. van Uhm, *The Illegal Wildlife Trade*, Studies of Organized Crime 15,
DOI 10.1007/978-3-319-42129-2